'HANG ONTO THESE WORDS'
Johnny David's *Delgamuukw* Evidence

Edited by Antonia Mills

In 1985 and 1986, ninety-year-old Witsuwit'en Chief Maxlaxlex – or Johnny David as he is better known – was the first Witsuwit'en to give commission evidence in the *Delgamuukw* land claims case, in which the Witsuwit'en and Gitxsan of Northern British Columbia were battling for title to their traditional territories.

'Hang Onto These Words' presents the actual transcripts of the questions and answers between lawyers working on both sides and this knowledgeable and outspoken Native elder, who spoke in his own language and whose words were then translated by an interpreter into English. The evidence was given in a makeshift courtroom set up in David's own home. Anthropologist Antonia Mills was present during these proceedings, and, in this book, she introduces and contextualizes the evidence in the *Delgamuukw* case.

In the commission evidence, David provides a rich description of the Witsuwit'en way of life as well as the injustices his people suffered at the hands of Indian agents and settlers. In providing access to Johnny David's eloquent testimony, this book offers unique insight into one of the most historically significant examples of Aboriginal peoples' ongoing struggle for self-determination.

ANTONIA MILLS is an associate professor in the First Nations Studies Program at the University of Northern British Columbia.

'Hang Onto These Words'

Johnny David's
Delgamuukw Evidence

Edited by Antonia Mills

UNIVERSITY OF TORONTO PRESS
Toronto Buffalo London

© University of Toronto Press Incorporated 2005
Toronto Buffalo London
Printed in Canada

ISBN 0-8020-3746-1 (cloth)
ISBN 0-8020-8534-2 (paper)

Printed on acid-free paper

Library and Archives Canada Cataloguing in Publication

Hang onto these words : Johnny David's Delgamuukw evidence /
edited by Antonia Mills.

Includes bibliographical references and index.
ISBN 0-8020-3746-1 (bound).   ISBN 0-8020-8534-2 (pbk.)

1. David, Johnny – Trials, litigation, etc.   2. Wet'suwet'en Indians –
History.   3. Wet'suwet'en Indians – Claims.   4. Wet'suwet'en Indians –
Land tenure.   5. Trial transcripts – British Columbia.   I. Mills,
Antonia Curtze.   II. Title.

E99.W56M45 2005   346.71104'32'089972   C2005-901530-6

This book has been published with the help of a grant from the Canadian
Federation for the Humanities and Social Sciences, through the Aid to
Scholarly Publications Programme, using funds provided by the Social
Sciences and Humanities Research Council of Canada.

University of Toronto Press acknowledges the financial assistance to its
publishing program of the Canada Council and the Ontario Arts Council.

University of Toronto Press acknowledges the financial support for its
publishing activities of the Government of Canada through the Book
Publishing Industry Development Program (BPIDP).

This book is dedicated to Johnny David's grandchildren and the next seven generations as well as to my grandchildren and the next seven generations.

Contents

Foreword

Hagwilneghl / Ronald A. Mitchell

I grew up with the late Karl David, who was one of the grandchildren raised by Johnny and his wife, Marion. Witsuwit'en is our first language. I remember one day when Karl was sitting on a fence as my brother John and I were going home from our grandparents'. Karl would always ask in a caring way, 'Are you not scared walking all the way back to *Lhc'etiy* [the highway crossing]?' When I think about it now, Karl was a lot like Johnny in the way he treated people around him.

Johnny referred to me as *Ye'* (meaning son or young man) in a caring way. To the day he passed away, I was always *Ye'*. One time I sat with him by the window talking. We were facing outside – I remember this very clearly because we noticed birds flying about. He then proclaimed that we were going to have a very good fishing season with warmer weather that coming summer. This is one of the ways he passed on his knowledge. He always knew what to say to make me feel good about myself, as a child and into my adulthood.

When I was being prepared for the name Hagwilneghl, he was one of the elders and chiefs who supported and guided me. As Jennifer, another grandchild of Johnny and Marion's, said when we were feeling down, 'we can rise above' – that is what he and others taught me. He never told me what to do or not to do, he always asked me. In the last eight to ten years of his life, he would call me into his room and say, *'Ye' janet so'c'io be ghun le.'* This translates more or less as 'Son, look after my responsibilities.'

When I get discouraged I think about him and I can still hear him tell me 'You are a good and strong leader.' This was the way he spoke to me over the years. He always spoke to me of encouragement, and I am still thriving on it today. I remember this encouraging way when I speak to my children and nieces and nephews. No educational institution in the world can teach a person what he taught me about who we are, our social structure, our language and our land (territories), and about life in general.

HAGWILNEGHL / RONALD A. MITCHELL
KYA WIGET, WITSUWIT'EN TERRITORY / MORICETOWN, BC

Foreword

Misalos / Victor Jim

I tell many people in my travels that I received my PhD in Witsuwit'en culture and language from my esteemed mentor Tsits Mots, as he was known in Witsuwit'en country. Tsits Mots means 'Small Grandfather,' and the term was applied to Mikhikhlekh (Maxlaxlex) / Johnny David because he was not tall. He was an exceptional elder. I worked with the gentleman for many months along with one of our lawyers, Peter Grant, and our Witsuwit'en researcher, Dr Antonia Mills.

Due to his advanced age, Mikhikhlekh was one of our Witsuwit'en chiefs who gave commission evidence in the *Delgamuukw* [*Gisdaywa*] v. *the Queen* land claims court case. The evidence was given at his home with a lawyer present from the province and of course our own lawyer. All the evidence was videotaped to be seen later by the judge in the privacy of his own chambers. I was Johnny David's official translator from Witsuwit'en to English and vice versa. During and before the time we worked with Tsits Mots, I figured I knew my Witsuwit'en language fluently. Then he began to use words that stumped me. Yet, between myself and one of Tsits's relatives – Kela, known in English as Mabel Critch – who fortunately was present then, we figured out what he was saying. This was such an educational experience for me, and I felt so honoured to be working with a man I thought of as an icon. Whenever he gave evidence, he spoke truthfully with conviction, honesty, and integrity. He said things that were controversial, but I know he was speaking with his heart. He stated over and over again that the evidence he was giving was for our Witsuwit'en children born and yet to be born.

After Tsits Mots had been giving evidence for many months, the province's lawyer asked him if he had any closing comments. He must have been waiting for this for a long time, because he straightened up and began pounding the floor and table with his cane. I still remember this like it happened yesterday. What he said was related with such forceful conviction that I am sure the premier of that day, if he were present, would have been squirming in this seat.

The decision by Chief Justice McEachern came down on Johnny David's birthday. He was sitting with the Witsuwit'en in his button blanket to hear the decision. Once it was translated into Witsuwit'en from English, Tsits Mots was devastated. He could not believe what he was hearing. He vowed never to give up, and he didn't.

The evidence Mikhlikhlekh / Johnny David gave was so powerful that I consider myself very fortunate to have been a part of this moving testimony of our proud Witsuwit'en history. I will cherish the very fond memories I have of this expérience. I could not have received the education I did from this man from any university in the world. I will always cherish the knowledge and wisdom Tsits Mots shared with me and the world. Yet this is only one of the many memories I will cherish of working along with our Witsuwit'en chiefs. They all handled themselves with the utmost respect for the white man's court, but the white man's court did not reciprocate with the respect our chiefs deserved. Many of the chiefs we worked with are no longer with us, but their memories are kept in books written by various academics, and in the transcripts of this important court case.

The experience I had with this fine gentleman will be etched in my memory for as long as I live. Tsits Mots, I hope your journey to the next world was safe and joyous, and we shall all rejoice and celebrate sometime in the future.

MISALOS / VICTOR JIM
KYA WIGET, WITSUWIT'EN TERRITORY / MORICETOWN, BC

Foreword

Michael Jackson

The land claims case initiated by the hereditary chiefs of the Witsu wit'en and Gitxsan in 1987 culminated in the landmark judgment of the Supreme Court of Canada a decade later in what is now known as the *Delgamuukw* judgment. The Supreme Court judgment is arguably one of the court's most significant decisions in the twentieth century. I hope it will provide a secure legal foundation for the negotiation in the twenty-first century of just and honourable treaties in British Columbia and elsewhere, treaties that honour First Nations histories, laws, and culture and secure the economic and institutional framework for self-determination. The tomes of Johnny David's commissioned evidence in the *Delgamuukw* case, the subject of Tonia Mills's 'Hang Onto These Words,' might appear far removed from the pronouncements of the Supreme Court of Canada and a realizable vision of a Canadian federation that includes First Nations as equal partners. However, as a careful reading of this book will reveal, Johnny David's evidence in his own home in Kya Wiget, or Moricetown, one of the two main Witsuwit'en villages, lies not at the periphery but at the heart of the struggle of First Nations for recognition and respect. Through this evidence, complemented by the excellent introduction by Dr Mills, we are taken on a remarkable journey that brings to life the ancient histories of the Witsuwit'en, the physical and ecological geography of the Nation's territories, the rich complexity of its social and ceremonial fabric, the articulation of its laws for ensuring an orderly succession and transfer of legal rights to lands and resources, and the record of the injustices and the wounds that colonialism has inflicted on the Witsuwit'en. Johnny David's description of the dispossession of the Witsuwit'en from the Bulkley Valley in the early part of the twentieth century by settlers armed with documents of land title issued by non-Aboriginal governments in the wake of the Boer War, and the resultant burning of Witsuwit'en homes, cabins, and smoke houses, demonstrates how the process and legacy of colonialism torches the spirit of a people as well as its possessions.

'*Hang Onto These Words*' is an important book because it brings into a broad forum evidence that would otherwise remain invisible to the public. The reason for this is that although Johnny David's evidence was placed before Chief Justice McEachern in the *Delgamuukw* trial, like much of the evidence of the hereditary chiefs, it was given little weight. This was in part because of the cross-cultural barriers that the chief justice was unable to navigate and in part because of his legal rulings on the law governing Aboriginal title and the rules of evidence. The judgment of the Supreme Court of Canada overturned much of the trial judgment on the law governing Aboriginal title and significantly broadened the rules of evidence to ensure that greater weight is given to oral history. However, the fact remains that Johnny David's evidence, until now, has been confined within the transcripts of the court proceedings. '*Hang Onto These Words*' brings these transcripts into the light of day. Through her introduction, Dr Mills explains the cross-cultural problems inherent in bringing into a courtroom, even a 'court within a home,' the 'evidence' necessary to prove a legal claim to Aboriginal title. Dr Mills's exposition of the difficulties of linguistic translation, compounded by the larger problems of cultural translation, raises important questions about the limitations of litigation in achieving justice founded on recognition and respect.

MICHAEL JACKSON, Q.C.
FACULTY OF LAW, UNIVERSITY OF BRITISH COLUMBIA

Acknowledgments

There are many people to whom I am grateful. Certainly Mikhlikhlekh (Maxlaxlex) / Johnny David is the first person I want to acknowledge. His niece Kela / Mabel Sam Crich, his granddaughter Jennifer David, and Hagwilneghl / Ron Mitchell have also been most helpful and supportive through the long process of preparing this material for publication. The head chiefs of all the Witsuwit'en houses have guided me throughout this work, from the beginning of my work towards preparing a report for the *Delgamuukw* court case, through the editing of Johnny David's commission evidence. I thank each and every one of them. I am grateful to Smogelgem / Leonard George for his support. I thank Gisdaywa / Alfred Joseph in particular for his encouragement, and his foreword. Misalos / Victor Jim I thank especially for his involvement in this project and his foreword. Again, I thank Hagwilneghl for his foreword.

I am grateful to all the people at the Office of the Witsuwit'en, particularly Gyologyet / Darlene Glaim for her enthusiasm and her assistance with carrying out this project, and to all the staff who always welcomed and assisted me splendidly. I thank Donna Vermette for her continued assistance with the Witsuwit'en genealogies, and all the students who also worked on them, particularly Priscilla LePine, Gary George, and Ellen Huse. I thank Chris Thomas for his assistance with the genealogy programs, Michael Mahoney for supplying the Latter Day Saints genealogy program, and Dr Jim McDonald for supplying us with the Family Tree Maker program.

I am most grateful to Lisa Krebs, Travis Holyk, and Ellen Huse – students or former students at the University of Northern British Columbia – for their assistance in converting the original court transcript into its present form. My thanks also go to UNBC graduate student Rheanna Caden for her assistance in editing this manuscript, and to graduate student Galksagaban / Andrew Robinson for checking the edited version against the original. My thanks to both Rheanna and Andy for gathering the Babine Barricade War material and to the Tache Band for sharing it with us. Thanks, Andy, for all your work to convert the video recordings of Johnny David's testimony to DVDs. My gratitude also to Norm Skelton for his assistance as I neared the home stretch of this long project and to Catherine Siermacheski, Dimple Joshi, Yuka Izu, Judy Tobin, and Shari Wallace for their help. I hope I have not forgotten any of the students who have assisted me.

Thanks to the Canadian Museum of Civilization, the B.C. Provincial Museum / Royal B.C. Museum, the National Museum of Canada, the Provincial Archives of British Columbia, and the National Archives of Canada for providing photographs entered as exhibits in the evidence.

I also want to thank Dr Sharon Hargus, Professor of Linguistics at the University of Washington, for her assistance with the proper spellings and the translations of Witsuwit'en words, which have been added to the glossary, and to Lillian Morris for reading through the whole text to check on the spelling of further Witsuwit'en names. I am most grateful to Dr Bruce Rigsby, Professor Emeritus of the University of Queensland, for his assistance with the spellings and meanings of the words of Gitxsan origin in the glossary.

I am grateful to the Social Sciences and Humanities Research Council of Canada for awarding me a grant to fund the project 'Giving Voice to Johnny David.' I thank Dr Max Blouw, dean of research at UNBC, for his assistance with the administration of the SSHRC grant with the help of Catherine Foster and Sean Kinsley. I gratefully acknowledge the grant from the Aid to Scholarly Publications Programme and the extension they provided to make it possible to incorporate the changes suggested by the conscientious copy editor, Barbara Tessman. Her careful work has helped me clarify my intentions and present the Johnny David evidence. I am also grateful to Janine Luggi, my son, Lucian Mills, and especially Will Lawson for their assistance checking the typeset book and to Jim Matlock for preparing the index. Thanks also to Jean Wilson at UBC Press and Virgil Duff at the University of Toronto Press. Each of them has been indispensable. I alone am responsible for any errors that remain. There are many more people who have assisted with this project; know that I am grateful to you even if your name does not appear in these acknowledgments.

'HANG ONTO THESE WORDS'
Johnny David's *Delgamuukw* Evidence

Introduction

If you know the territory well, it is like your own skin. Sometimes you can even feel the animals moving on your body as they are on the land, the fish swimming in your bloodstream ... If you know the territory well enough, you can feel the animals.

Johnny David quoted in Monet and Skanu'u 1992

Eagle down is our law ... It is blown in the direction of the people and it is similar to white man's way now where they sign their name, eagle down is our law ... Once the eagle down is blown the revenge or murder is stopped and once that is done you are not allowed to break that law. The same is done with the passing of a mountain or territory.

Johnny David, Commission Evidence, vol. 5

If you hang onto these words that I have told you, everything will be fine.

Johnny David, Commission Evidence, vol. 8

This book makes available the commission evidence that Witsuwit'en elder Johnny David provided before the British Columbia Supreme Court in the ground-breaking land claims case *Delgamuukw v. the Queen*. The intent in publishing Johnny David's commission evidence, and this introduction to it, is to come closer to a time when eagle down can be distributed between the Witsuwit'en and the provincial and federal governments regarding First Nations rights to their traditional territories. That was the intent of Johnny David in giving his commission evidence, as it was the intent of the Witsuwit'en and Gitxsan in the *Delgamuukw* court case.

Maxlaxlex (Mikhlikhlekh) / Johnny David was the first Witsuwit'en chief to give commission evidence for the epic *Delgamuukw* case. Four other Witsuwit'en chiefs and four Gitxsan chiefs also gave such evidence, and seven more Witsuwit'en and many Gitxsan chiefs gave testimony once the *Delgamuukw* case officially opened in court. Apprehensive that they might not live long enough to give testimony during the hearing of the case, the court decided to take the commission evidence of some of the more elderly Gitxsan and Witsuwit'en chiefs.

In many ways Johnny David's commission evidence set the tone for the monumental *Delgamuukw* case. His evidence itself was epic, lasting from 20 September 1985 to 29 April 1986.[1] It fills some eight volumes, five of direct evidence led by Peter Grant, one of the lawyers retained by the Witsuwit'en and Gitxsan, plus two and a half volumes of cross-examination led by John Milne, the lawyer representing the province of British Columbia and the government of Canada; the final half volume is redirect evidence led by Grant. In their original form as court transcripts, the first five volumes of Johnny David's evidence comprise 200 pages. The two volumes of cross-examination and redirect examination comprise another 147 pages. Johnny David's testimony was also recorded on video by Mike McDonald, a professional photographer. Unlike the court transcripts, which are only in English, that record, consisting of twenty-six two-hour videotapes, contains the questions as they were translated into Witsuwit'en by the interpreter Misalos / Victor Jim, and the answers Johnny David gave in Witsuwit'en. The length and complexity of Johnny David's evidence foreshadowed the testimony in court for *Delgamuukw*, which took 369 days over the span of three and a half years, from 1987 to 1991.

I was present during the recording of Johnny David's testimony because – having been commissioned to write an 'expert opinion report' on Witsuwit'en feasts and laws in support of their case – I was asked to provide the court reporters with the spellings of Witsuwit'en words. Representation of foreign words and their meanings is one part of the complex task of cross-cultural communication. The glossary at the end of this book explains that the spellings I rendered are not those the trained linguists hired by the Witsuwit'en and Gitxsan provided later.[2] The glossary provides the spellings as given in Johnny David's commission evidence and the corrected forms and, where available, the literal meaning of the words.

After summarizing the history behind the legal situation of the Gitxsan and Witsuwit'en at the beginning of the case, this introduction briefly describes how the initial decision Chief Justice McEachern rendered in *Delgamuukw* repeated the injustice and preserved the impasse that had led the Witsuwit'en and Gitxsan to launch the case in the first place. The Witsuwit'en and Gitxsan responded by immediately taking the case to the British Columbia Court of Appeal, and finally to the Supreme Court of Canada. The introduction summarizes those decisions and then describes the agonizingly slow progress, since the Supreme Court of Canada *Delgamuukw* decision, in addressing land and treaty issues for the Witsuwit'en and the Gitxsan.

The introduction then explains why Johnny David was chosen to be the first Witsuwit'en to give commission evidence. I explicate Johnny David's evidence, using it as a primer on the problems of unmasking colonization and of creating cross-cultural communication and mutual accord on a series of levels. Some of the problems of cross-cultural understanding exemplified by Johnny David's testimony are due to the difficulties in communication across language and culture, even in the presentation of Johnny David's evidence by the lawyer seeking to assist this process. I then examine causes of cross-cultural conflict that result from the cultures using different parameters and definitions – problems that are at the core of the difficulty of resolving who has what rights to land and resources. The Witsuwit'en believe the rights are theirs, but the government of British Columbia held that First Nations do not have the right to make treaties, let alone the right of ownership of their communally held territories. Johnny David's commission evidence portrays some of the major injustices the Witsuwit'en people experienced as a consequence of the government's position: he portrays how they were moved off their land with no recourse, given no rights and no voice, and jailed for protesting their removal from their lands. The obstacles experienced by Aboriginal peoples, in having their concerns heard is a symptom of what Little Bear (2000) calls 'jagged worldviews colliding.' Problems in cross-cultural mutual appreciation and understanding and their impact on rights to land and resource allocation remain the biggest challenges humans face all over the globe.[3] It is time that Johnny David's voice be heard.

The final section of the introduction discusses questions that arose in editing the commission evidence, several of which are relevant to the issue of cross-cultural communication. After addressing the pros and cons of various ways of rendering Johnny David's evidence, I explain how and why the format in this volume was arrived at. I provide a guide to the presentation of the evidence and to the type of changes I have made.

The Background of *Delgamuukw*

The Witsuwit'en and Gitxsan launched their epic land claims court case, *Delgamuukw v. The Queen*, in 1984 because they had been stymied in their attempts to convince the provincial government of British Columbia or the federal government of Canada to discuss their rights to their traditional territories. The Witsuwit'en and the Gitxsan system of goverance of their territories is based on their matrilineal house and clan system, head chiefs act as the overseers or stewards of the use of their well-specified territories and house fishing sites. Fifty-one Witsuwit'en and Gitxsan head chiefs (twelve Witsuwit'en and thirty-nine Gitxsan) collectively launched this court case on behalf of their house members, who constitute all of the Witsuwit'en and Gitxsan.[4] The *Delgamuukw* case was groundbreaking: the Gitxsan and Witsuwit'en First Nations were seeking to establish that they had the rights to ownership and jurisdiction over their traditional territories, some 55,000 square kilometres (22,000 square miles) of north-central British Columbia.[5] The Witsuwit'en and Gitxsan were laying claim to this land (an area about the size of Nova Scotia) on the basis that they (as almost all other First Nations of mainland British Columbia) had never made a treaty with the government or otherwise relinquished their rights to their territory.

The situation in 1984 was the result of the failure of British Columbia to address First Nations' rights to their land.[6] Sir James Douglas, as the Hudson's Bay Company chief factor and governor of the Crown colony of Vancouver Island, had forged fourteen treaties with the First Nations on Vancouver Island in 1850–4, when the First Nations outnumbered the settlers by 158 to 1.[7] Later, when Joseph Trutch became British Columbia's commissioner of lands and works, he attacked Aboriginal land rights. In 1865, despite the fact that the First Nations were playing a significant role in the fur trade economy (Fisher 1992a), he reduced the size of existing and future First Nations reserves and prohibited First Nations people from buying or preempting land (Drucker 1958: 80). After British Columbia joined the Canadian confederation in 1871, and as the population balance shifted to a settler majority, only one further treaty was forged. Treaty 8 was made with the First Nations in north-

Map 1. The Gitxsan and Witsuwit'en Territories

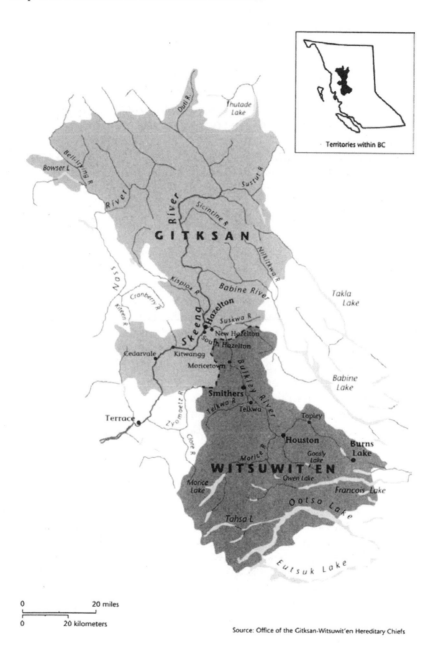

Source: Office of the Gitksan-Witsuwit'en Hereditary Chiefs

eastern British Columbia in 1899, as Tennant (1990) notes, because of the obstacles the Beaver and Slavey were posing to the Klondike gold rush. At the time the *Delgamuukw* case began, Treaty 8 was the only other exception, besides the Douglas treaties, to the absence of treaty settlements in the province of British Columbia. Indeed, under Trutch, British Columbia had stopped making treaties with its dwindling First Nations population, quibbling over whether the provincial or federal government should shoulder the cost (Tennant 1990). Tacitly expecting extermination or assimilation of its First Nations population, the government dealt with the land question only through the establishment of reserves.[8] In 1884 the federal Indian Act banned the potlatch, the ceremony through which Northwest Coast First Nations passed on rights to specific territories and resources; the Canadian government never acknowledged the potlatch as being a form of governance for passing on rights to traditional territories and settling disputes. The official ban was not lifted until 1951.[9]

When the McKenna-McBride Commission (1912–16) travelled through Gitxsan and Witsuwit'en territory, establishing reserves at places of Native settlement, the Witsuwit'en and Gitxsan, particularly the Gitxsan from Kitwancool, were explicit that the small reserves allocated in the areas of population density did not address their concern that the land question remained unsolved.[10] Nonetheless, the commission often downsized reserves, the excised parts becoming known as 'cut-off lands,' which were taken over by settlers.

The provincial government refused to recognize that they were infringing on Witsuwit'en land and the feast process when, in 1901, the British Columbia legislature 'enacted a law providing that volunteers from this Province who served in the Boer War were eligible to receive scrip entitling them to a free homestead of 160 acres of "unoccupied, unclaimed and unreserved land" anywhere in the Province' (Lane 1987: 1). The land referred to, as Johnny David explains in his commission evidence, was anything but unclaimed and unoccupied: it was land on which Witsuwit'en head chiefs, such as Round Lake Tommy and others, had built cabins and barns, had fenced fields to keep in their horses and cattle, and were raising crops. Yet these lands were given away to white war veterans.[11] Often these takeovers occurred when the Witsuwit'en owners were participating in their annual round of fishing for salmon at Kya Wiget / Moricetown or Tse Kya / Hagwilget, or were further afield in their vast territories, hunting, trapping, and fishing, or were working elsewhere for wages, as was the case with Johnny David.[12] When they protested about their land being taken over, they were ignored or put in jail. As Johnny David eloquently testifies, the Indian agent, R.E. Loring, who was also the local justice of the peace, prosecuted the Witsuwit'en who protested.

The *Delgamuukw* case was launched not only because land was taken from the Gitxsan and Witsuwit'en but because they were denied the right to run businesses as well as access to the resources on their land and were left without recourse to redress these injustices. In 1889, once fishing had become a commercial enterprise, Natives were prohibited from selling fish. Further, in 1927, the federal government adopted section 141 of the Indian Act, which made it illegal for Natives to hire lawyers to bring land claims before the government. Native people in British Columbia were not allowed to vote in provincial elections until 1949 or in federal elections until 1960. Indians (Witsuwit'en, Gitxsan, or other) who graduated from high school, automatically lost their Indian status and were consequently prohibited from spending even a night on an Indian reserve.

Some of these injustices have been addressed, but others remain. Only in 1951 was the law rescinded that had made it illegal for First Nations to hire lawyers to address their land claims. This change was partly a reflection of a rebounding First Nations population but also the result of the participation of Aboriginal people in the Second World War and of the formation of the United Nations after the war. The UN began to address, among other things, interference with human rights, which extends to issues of sovereignty, colonization, and domination.[13] Yet land claims remained unsettled. To try to force recalcitrant governments to act, the Nisga'a in 1969 launched the pivotal case *Calder v. British Columbia (A.G.)*, stating that Aboriginal title to lands still exists. On appeal, a split decision in the Supreme Court of Canada (1973) marked a sea change, forcing the state to recognize that Aboriginal rights were legal rights that had to be settled. Section 35 of the Constitution Act, 1982, affirmed Aboriginal and treaty rights, although the meaning of these rights remains unresolved. Because the federal and provincial governments refused to negotiate with other British Columbia First Nations, in 1984 the Witsuwit'en and Gitxsan nations filed the *Delgamuukw* land claims case, based on their traditional law and culture in which head chiefs represent the house members. In the *Calder* case, no Nisga'a spoke in court: lawyers and the anthropologist Wilson Duff spoke for them. *Delgamuukw* was to be a different sort of case, as Johnny David's commission evidence shows. *Delgamuukw* was designed to address the failure of earlier settlers and the Canadian government to listen to First Nations peoples and settle Aboriginal land rights. Through it the Witsuwit'en and Gitxsan were able to tell their side of the story and to assert the legally recognized right of indigenous peoples to be treated as nations whose land belongs to them until they make a just treaty with the federal government.

I had had the privilege of being hired by the Gitskan-Carrier Tribal Council (as it was then named) to write an expert opinion report for the *Delgamuukw* case on the subject of Witsuwit'en laws and feasts. To be able do this, I lived three years in the Witsuwit'en territory (1985–8).[14] I was one of the many people – including, first, Gitxsan and Witsuwit'en chiefs, and then other experts ranging from geologists to anthropologists – who testified in court on behalf of the plaintiffs.

The *Delgamuukw* Decision

On 8 March 1991, Johnny David and the other Witsuwit'en chiefs dressed in their button blankets and assembled to hear Chief Justice McEachern's decision. They were profoundly disappointed to learn that, after listening to three years of evidence, most of it given by eloquent chiefs, the judge had decided that the Witsuwit'en and Gitxsan did not have title to their traditional territories. Chief Justice McEachern's decision reiterated the notion that land not privately owned is Crown land burdened only by limited Aboriginal rights and belongs to the state rather than to the indigenous people who occupied it at the time of contact. He ruled that the Royal Proclamation of 1763, which had acknowledged Aboriginal title to all lands that First Nations had not sold or ceded, did not apply to British Columbia because it was not yet a British colony in 1763. He cited a legal precedent about colonized African indigenous peoples being too low on a scale of civilization to have property rights (*Delgamuukw* 1991: 226). Further, he stated that '[I]t would not be accurate to assume that even pre-contact existence in the territory was in the least bit idyllic. The plaintiffs' ancestors had no written language, no horses or wheeled vehicles, slavery and starvation was not uncommon, wars with neighbouring peoples were common and there is no doubt, to quote Hobbes, that aboriginal life in the territory was, at best, "nasty, brutish and short"' (*Delgamuukw* 1991: 13). He refused to give weight to oral history evidence to establish rights and title to territory. His reasons reflected his perception that the powerful, competent indigenous societies that had thrived on these territories for a vast period of time were 'so low' on a scale of civilization that they had

no system of governance that warranted recognition: 'The pre-Confed-
eration colonial enactments ... exhibit a clear and plain intention to
extinguish aboriginal interests in order to give an unburdened title to
settlers ... It is the law that Aboriginal rights exist at the "pleasure of the
Crown," and they may be extinguished whenever the intention of the
Crown to do so is clear and plain ... The plaintiffs' claims for aboriginal
rights are accordingly dismissed' (ibid.: ix).

The Gitxsan and Witsuwit'en were not about to be dismissed. From
their perspective (and mine), the first *Delgamuukw* decision reverber-
ated with the dismissive colonial Eurocentric ethic manifested before
Trutch, by Trutch, and since Trutch that the plaintiffs were seeking to
change.[15] It was as if they had not been heard. The Witsuwit'en and
Gitxsan immediately appealed the decision, first to the BC Court of
Appeal (*Delgamuukw II*), and then to the Supreme Court of Canada (*Delgamuukw III*).[16] In making these appeals, the Witsuwit'en and Gitxsan
opted to pursue their rights as separate First Nations rather than as a
conjoined tribal council or association. They also responded by lobbying the provincial Ministry of Forests and Ministry of Environment to
make investigations of First Nations interest in 'Crown land' manda-
tory. They pointed out that First Nations cannot pursue the meager
Aboriginal rights Chief Justice McEachern acknowledged – to hunt,
fish, trap, and gather plants – on lands that have been clear-cut or otherwise damaged environmentally. This lobbying resulted in new regulations requiring an archaeological assessment to be made of areas
designated for timber licences.[17]

The appeals of *Delgamuukw* were decided in the political climate following the Oka crisis of 1990, which heightened awareness that questions of Aboriginal title were not simply going to go away. The
pressure from First Nations in British Columbia, where land claims
had yet to be addressed, made industry and the government in the
province want to establish some assurance or 'certainty' about who
had rights to use and control the resources on 'Crown land.' Therefore
the British Columbia Treaty Commission (BCTC) was formed in 1993.
That same year the British Columbia Court of Appeal rendered its
decision in *Delgamuukw II*. While the court was divided on the nature
and scope of Aboriginal title, the judges unanimously rejected Chief
Justice McEachern's judgment that there had been a de facto blanket
extinguishment of all Aboriginal rights and acknowledged the need to
define constitutional rights for Aboriginal peoples.

Some of the Witsuwit'en and Gitxsan chiefs had gone to Vancouver to hear the *Delgamuukw II* decision. Although they knew that the Supreme Court of Canada would ultimately decide the case, they were discouraged by the need to appeal again. However, the day after the announcement of the decision by the appellate court, 26 June 1993, their spirits were shored up when a number of the Gitxsan and Witsuwit'en chiefs met with his holiness the Dalai Lama, who was in Vancouver at the time.[18] The meeting was profound. The Dalai Lama held the hands of each chief, looking deeply into his or her eyes. Communication was both with and without words: they spoke to each other from the heart. The Dalai Lama spoke of the parallels between his own displacement from his homeland and the situation of the Witsuwit'en and Gitxsan First Nations. They noted the difficulties of establishing cross-cultural appreciation and understanding, and of the impact of such difficulties on land rights issues. He observed that such challenges confronted people across the globe.[19] The Dalai Llama spoke of the need to continue to look after the spiritual aspect of the homeland. They acknowledged their shared belief in reincarnation as affording a link between the spiritual past, present, and future. The chiefs left the meeting feeling blessed and aglow. They knew their concerns about their land had been heard, shared, and appreciated on a profound level. The meeting expressed the Gitxsan and Witsuwit'en hope that they would be listened to in the final appeal.

Before proceeding to the appeal to the Supreme Court of Canada, in 1994 the Gitxsan and Witsuwit'en independently entered into treaty negotiations to see if the British Columbia Treaty Commission's admission of the need to negotiate treaties could address their land claims goals. However, the province forced the appeal of *Delgamuukw II* to the Supreme Court of Canada by taking the position that, because the Witsuwit'en and Gitksan wanted the government to recognize their rights to all of their traditional territories, the First Nations were being 'too hard line' in the treaty negotiations.

It would be another three years before the Supreme Court of Canada rendered its decision. In the meantime, long before the Supreme Court Decision was rendered, I had decided to bring out my 'expert' opinion report and then to bring out the commission evidence of Witsuwit'en Chief Maxlaxlex, Johnny David.[20] While the *Delgamuukw III* appeal process was underway, the Nisga'a, a neighbor of the Gitxsan and Witsuwit'en, continued to forge a post-*Calder* treaty. The province would allow no more than 8 per cent of traditional Nisga'a territory to be granted to them. On 7 August 1996, before the Nisga'a treaty was finalized and before the Supreme Court decision in *Delgamuukw* was rendered, Johnny David passed away. As he said in his commission evidence, he was taking this action on behalf of his descendants. He was ready to go.

A little over a year later, on 11 December 1997, the Supreme Court of Canada reversed much of the judgment of Chief Justice McEachern. The court held, first of all, that Aboriginal title does exist as an inherent right and that it is an exclusive right to land, including subsurface resources such as minerals. It also clearly stated that Aboriginal title allows indigenous peoples to use their land in ways that were not part of the Aboriginal tradition at the time of contact.

Moreover, *Delgamuukw III* set out the test for establishing Aboriginal title: a First Nation must prove exclusive possession at the time of assertion of Crown sovereignty – which the court established as being 1846 in British Columbia – with continuity in the occupation to the present. The court also recognized that questions of overlapping claims by different First Nations do not preclude establishing title.

As well as defining Aboriginal title, *Delgamuukw III* articulated that such title cannot extend to an Aboriginal group using their land in an environmentally degrading way, such as paving over traditional hunting or berry-picking grounds. The court puts it this way: 'First, aboriginal title encompasses the right to exclusive use and occupation of the land; second aboriginal title encompasses the right to choose to what uses land can be put, subject to the ultimate limit that those uses cannot destroy the ability of the land to sustain future generations of aboriginal peoples; and third the lands held pursuant to aboriginal title have an inescapable economic component' (*Delgamuukw v. British Columbia*: para. 166).

The court held that, under some circumstances, governments could infringe Aboriginal title, and it established a standard by which to measure whether the infringement is lawful. When interests in their land are granted, Aboriginal people's interest must be given priority, and they must be consulted and compensated. Despite these conditions, some First Nations scholars have found the right to make infringements troubling (see, e.g., Alfred 1998).

Significantly, the Supreme Court of Canada reversed that part of *Delgamuukw I* regarding the inadmissibility of oral traditions, concluding that Chief Justice McEachern had made an error in not considering these traditions. Because *Delgamuukw I* did not give appropriate weight to the Gitxsan and Witsuwit'en oral traditions, the Supreme Court of Canada declared that the Witsuwit'en and Gitxsan could go back to court or, preferably, negotiate a treaty outside of court. The court noted that the oral histories were used 'in an attempt to establish their occupation and use of the disputed territory, an essential requirement for aboriginal title. The trial judge, after refusing to admit, or giving no independent weight to these oral histories, reached the conclusion that the appellants had not demonstrated the requisite degree of occupancy for "ownership." Had the trial judge assessed the oral histories correctly, his conclusions on these issues of fact might have been very different' (para. 107). Of course, such pronouncements do not eliminate the difficulty, for judges raised in the Western concept of what is valid evidence, of interpreting and understanding oral traditions as histories.[21] However *Delgamuukw III* opens the possibility of truly listening to First Nations world views. In addition, for First Nations who can establish Aboriginal title, *Delgamuukw III* promises a significant land base and permits the modern usage of this land. This was a decision that the Witsuwit'en and Gitxsan could celebrate – and they did, with celebratory potlatches. Yet, once the celebrating was over, the hard question remained: How will *Delgamuukw III* be implemented? Because court cases are costly, the Witsuwit'en and Gitxsan have continued to engage in separate treaty negotiations, with no final settlement in sight. The terms the province has offered did not change after *Delgamuukw III*.

In some arenas there has been little impact, while in others the *Delgamuukw III* decision is honoured. Before the Supreme Court of Canada decision of December 1997, the Nisga'a signed an Agreement in Principle with the province of British Columbia in 1996, accepting the 8 per cent allotment and opting for democratic rather than hereditary chief–based government. Despite the clear and broad definition of Aboriginal title rendered in *Delgamuukw III*, the Nisga'a did not renegotiate the conditions of their treaty. The Nisga'a treaty was passed in the provincial legislature on 4 August 1998 amidst vocal opposition by the provincial Liberal Party and in the federal Parliament on 10 May 2000 amidst vocal opposition from the Canadian Alliance. Opposition to treaties and land claims was mounted on right-wing Eurocentric grounds as a sure way to attract voter support. Before the 2001 provincial election in British Columbia, Liberal leader Gordon Campbell initiated, and lost, a court case claiming the Nisga'a treaty was unconstitutional. Indeed, part of Campbell's election campaign in 2001 was the promise to hold a referendum on the conduct of treaty making in the province. Once elected, the Liberals proceeded with a costly referendum, the results of which were announced in July 2002. The provincial government claimed the results are binding, despite voter turnout of only 37 per cent, significantly less than the average of 71 per cent for provincial elections (Leeder 2002: A1). As Nettie Wild (1993) says in the National Film Board video *Blockade*, the question is really about 'the land and who controls it' – First Nations or the government. The Campbell referendum attempted to imply that public opinion over-ruled the Canadian Constitution and the *Delgamuukw III* decision.

Delgamuukw III has been cited in a number of cases, including the Marshall decisions (1999a, 1999b), which stated that the Mi'kmaq of eastern Canada have a right to make a modest living from the fishery, arising from a treaty right. Despite this decision, the federal Ministry of Fisheries and Oceans saw fit to intercept Mi'kmaq lobster boats in the summer and fall of 2002 for carrying out such fishing. This action was supposedly in the interest of gaining votes from maritime fishers, whose livelihoods have been decimated by the disappearance of the cod off the east coast, an ecological disaster that Fisheries Canada was unable to prevent.[22]

Despite *Delgamuukw III*, much remains to be resolved. In April 2002 the Haida First Nation filed suit to establish their Aboriginal title, as defined by *Delgamuukw III*, to Haida Gwaii, also known as the Queen Charlotte Islands. It will be some time before that case is heard and a decision is rendered and appealed. In the meantime, about two-thirds of the 150 British Columbia First Nations are engaged in treaty negotiations, while a third refrain from entering into such negotiations on the basis that they are about the extinguishment of Aboriginal title. To the consternation of the Ministry of Forests, one of these First Nations has used the *Delgamuukw III* decision to take logs from their traditional territory for building houses on reserve without applying for timber licences. Implementation of *Delgamuukw III* will take time and good will on the part of both First Nations and government negotiators. The Witsuwit'en are at present still attempting to make a treaty but at the same time negotiate interim measures regarding timber licences on their traditional territories with the province of British Columbia. The Gitxsan are similarly attempting to forge meaningful negotiations in the post–treaty referendum climate, although the Gitxsan and the provincial government do not agree on the percentage of traditional territory to be alotted.

The government of British Columbia, like that of other provinces, and the federal government have yet to learn that it is in their own interest to listen to First Nations' ecological concerns about the impact of logging, mining, and fishing practices in order to better manage natural resources and wildlife. When timber, oil, gas, and mining interests are held responsible for the long-term impact of exploitation, they will have to carry out their practices in more environmentally responsible ways. This is one of the issues at stake in land claims, expressed in Gisday Wa and Delgam Uuk (1989) as well as in Suzuki and Knudtson (1992). Johnny David was eloquent in expressing his position:

> You can see throughout our territory all the stumps and the white people have pocketed millions and millions of dollars. All the money that has been taken off our territory, we want that back and we want our territory back to the way they were. Once we get back the money we would like to go back to our old Indian laws, to make life better for our people. The other Hereditary Chiefs as well as the other leaders are thinking about some way and it is with their words and my words that I am giving you today. It's the generation that will follow me that will use these resources. I will not be able to use it. I am ready to go. That's all. (7: 373)

Johnny David and the Witsuwit'en

Johnny David's testimony portrays his concern for the Witsuwit'en's legal, political, and social struggle to have their rights to their land recognized. His testimony effectively describes the injustices that the Witsuwit'en have suffered, without recourse, and how and why they acted when finally it was legal for them to bring their issues to court. Yet Johnny David's side of the story has never been told to the wider public. It is my hope that bringing out his voice will encourage a wider audience to listen to why First Nations people are seeking to establish a nation-to-nation relationship with and within the Canadian state.

There were good reasons for the selection of Maxlaxlex / Johnny David as the first Witsuwit'en chief to give commission evidence in *Delgamuukw I*.[23] His mother, Suwitsbaine, was a member of the Ginehklaiya (House of Many Eyes) of the Laksilyu (Small Frog) Clan. Her father was head chief of the Gitxsan house of Spookx. Johnny David's father was Smogelgem, the head chief of the Witsuwit'en Laksamshu (Fireweed) Clan. Johnny's wife, her mother, and her mother's brother were successive head chiefs of the Yatsadkus (Dark House) of the Gilseehyu (Frog) Clan. Johnny David spent much of his life – which began around 1894 and spanned more than one hundred years – out on the territories of his father, Smogelgem, on his own territory (which in this

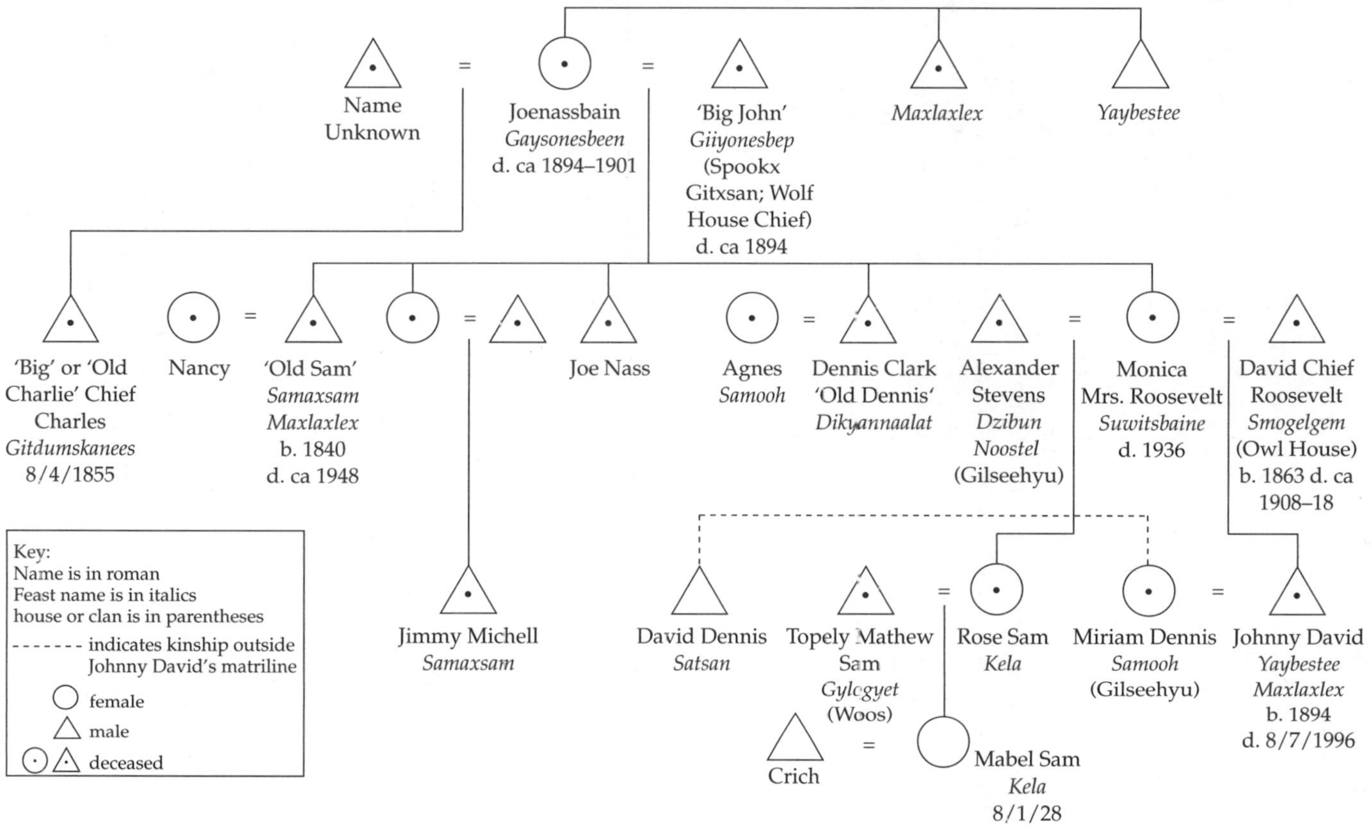

Figure 1 Partial Matriline of Johnny David of Ginehklaiya House (House of Many Eyes) and Laksilyu (Small Frog) Clan

matrilineal society meant his mother's and maternal uncles' territory), and on that of his wife, who was necessarily from a different clan than Johnny's. As John Milne, the lawyer for the province and the Crown noted, Johnny had trapped or travelled on almost all of the Witsuwit'en territories, with the permission of their head chief. He knew the lands well; his knowledge was vast. Indeed, as Johnny David's testimony went on and on, the set of questions he answered laid out much of the content of the *Delgamuukw* case.

Most of the chiefs who gave testimony were the head chiefs of their respective matrilineal houses. Maxlaxlex / Johnny David was not the head chief of his house, the House of Ginehklaiya of the Laksilyu (Small Frog) Clan. At that time, the head chief of the house, Hagwilnegh, was Sylvester Williams; the next high chief of the house, Gitdumskanees, was Willie Simms. Johnny's chiefly title, Maxlaxlex (Mikhlikhelkh), ranks about third in the system of chiefly names for his house.[24] He was selected by these chiefs to be their spokesman because their advanced age and ill health rendered them unable to give testimony. He was chosen by all concerned to be the first Witsuwit'en to give commission evidence because he was a very articulate and spirited chief and healer, a member of the Witsuwit'en healing or shamanic society, who had lived an active life in the feast hall at Tse Kya / Hagwilget and Kya Wiget / Moricetown and out on the territories.

In order to understand Johnny's testimony, it is helpful to have a grasp of the clan and house structure of Witsuwit'en society. Because that information appears only near the end of the commission evidence, it is summarized here. Figure 4 shows that the Witsuwit'en First Nation comprises five matrilineal clans that each have two or three houses. The head chiefs' and the next highest or wing chiefs' titles are passed on in perpetuity. There are usually two wing chiefs in each house. Along with the head chief, they are the three most important chiefs of the house. Sometimes Johnny refers to these chiefs as the head chiefs of the house.

Johnny David was highly knowledgeable not only about the structure of his society and its government but also about the territories, including the landmarks that demarcate Witsuwit'en land. Indeed, in preparation for the case, Gisdaywa / Alfred Joseph had made audio casettes of Johnny David out on the territories identifing the mountains, streams, and rivers that serve as the boundaries.[25] The context of the commission evidence proved an even more impressive arena for Johnny David: in no way was he going to allow the Crown lawyer to

Figure 2 Partial Matriline of Chief David Roosevelt, Johnny David's father of Owl House of Laksamshu (Fireweed) Clan

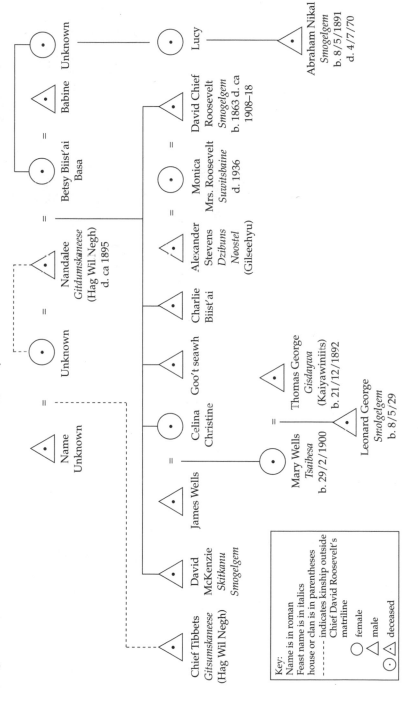

Figure 3   Partial Matriline for Miriam Dennis, wife of Johnny David of Yatsalkas (Dark) House of Gilseehyu (Frog) Clan

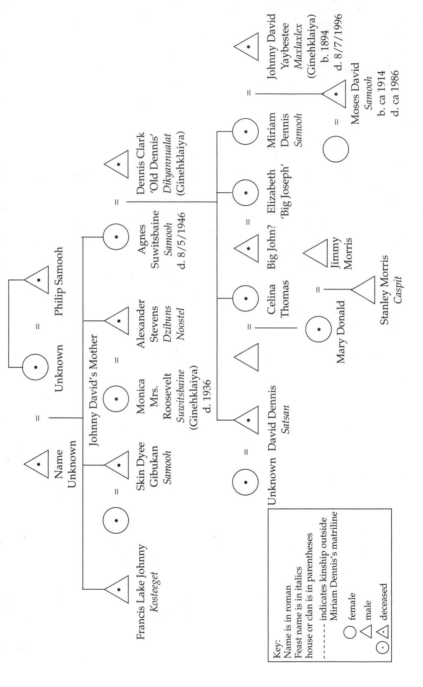

Figure 4   Witsuwit'en Clans and Houses

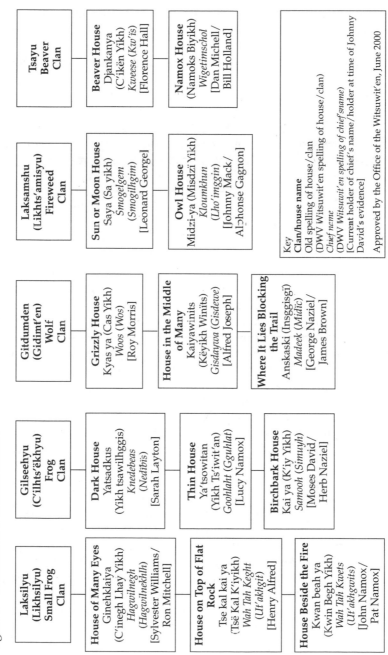

Laksilyu (Likhsilyu) Small Frog Clan

House of Many Eyes
Ginehklaiya
(C'inegh Lhay Yikh)
Hagwilnegh
(*Hagwilnekhlh*)
[Sylvester Williams / Ron Mitchell]

House on Top of Flat Rock
Tse kal kai ya
('Tsë Kal K'iyikh)
Wah Tah Keght
(*Ut'akhgit*)
[Henry Alfred]

House Beside the Fire
Kwan beah ya
(Kwin Begh Yikh)
Wah Tah Kwets
(*Ut'akhgwits*)
[John Namox / Pat Namox]

Gilseehyu (C'ilhts'ëkhyu) Frog Clan

Dark House
Yatsadkus
(Yikh tsawilhggis)
Knedebeas
(*Nedibïs*)
[Sarah Layton]

Thin House
Ya'tsowitan
(Yikh Ts'iwit'an)
Goohlaht (*Gguhlat*)
[Lucy Namox]

Birchbark House
Kai ya (K'iy Yikh)
Samooh (*Simuyh*)
[Moses David / Herb Naziel]

Gitdumden (Gidimt'en) Wolf Clan

Grizzly House
Kyas ya (Cas Yikh)
Woos (*Wos*)
[Roy Morris]

House in the Middle of Many
Kaiyawinits
(Këyikh Winïts)
Gisdaywa (*Gisdewe*)
[Alfred Joseph]

Where It Lies Blocking the Trail
Anskaski (Insggisgi)
Madeek (*Midic*)
[George Naziel / James Brown]

Laksamshu (Likhts'amisyu) Fireweed Clan

Sun or Moon House
Saya (Sa yikh)
Smogelgem
(*Smogilhgim*)
[Leonard George]

Owl House
Midzi-ya (Misdzi Yïkh)
Kloumkhun
(*Lho'imggin*)
[Johnny Mack / Alphonse Gagnon]

Tsayu Beaver Clan

Beaver House
Djankanya
(C'ikën Yïkh)
Kweese (*Kw'is*)
[Florence Hall]

Namox House
(Namoks Biyikh)
Wigetimschol
[Dan Michell / Bill Holland]

Key
Clan/house name
Old spelling of house/clan
(DWV Witsuwit'en spelling of house/clan)
Chief name
(*DWV Witsuwit'en spelling of chief'sname*)
[Current holder of chief's name/holder at time of Johnny David's evidence]

Approved by the Office of the Witsuwit'en, June 2000

belittle what he had to say. Johnny, correctly, saw John Milne as the opposition and minced no words in response to his questions.

The Setting for Johnny David's Evidence: A Court within a Home

It is important to appreciate that Johnny David's commission evidence was given in the environment of his own home in Kya Wiget / Moricetown, one of the two main Witsuwit'en villages. Kya Wiget / Moricetown, a village of 500 people, is situated on the edge of the Moricetown Canyon, where the Bulkley River dramatically plummets 200 feet, providing one of the most important sites for catching salmon as they migrate upstream to spawn. Some fifty miles upstream of Kya Wiget / Moricetown is Smithers, a town of 6,000. About the same distance downstream lie the clustered towns of Hazelton, the Witsuwit'en and Gitxsan village of Tse Kya / Hagwilget, and the Gitxsan village of Gitanmaax. Originally the Witsuwit'en lived at Kya Wiget in matrilineal longhouses, or 'smokehouses,' as Johnny David referred to them in his evidence. Exhibits 1, 6, 7, and 8 show photographs of these houses. Today the residents of Kya Wiget / Moricetown live in modern single-family dwellings on roads mostly parallel to the river's edge. Johnny David's home is at the southern crest of the hill above the canyon, facing the road rather than the river. His totem pole, and that of his niece Kela / Mabel Crich, stands in front of his house. His smokehouse is to the right and behind his house, towards the canyon.

The living room of Johnny's home became an official place of court during the days of testimony. Sitting at the tables that had been set up were Johnny David, the plaintiff; Victor Jim, the translator; Peter Grant, a lawyer working on behalf of the Gitxsan and Witsuwit'en; John Milne, a lawyer working on behalf of the provincial government; a court stenographer; myself, as the speller of Witsuwit'en words; and Mike McDonald, a professional photographer who was hired by the Gitxsan-Witsuwit'en to record all the commission evidence on video. Three court reporters (Veronica Harper, Linda Malinowski, and Beverly Ferguson) served over the course of the long proceedings.[26]

Questions were put to Johnny David, first by Peter Grant on the direct examination, and then by John Milne in cross-examination. Each question was translated into Witsuwit'en by Misalos / Victor Jim who was well qualified for the job. As a native of Kya Wiget / Moricetown, Victor Jim is fluent in his native language and very articulate in English. A graduate of the University of British Columbia, he was at the time a teacher at the Kya Wiget / Moricetown school. He has since become principal of that school, and he has completed a master's degree in education at UBC. Two generations younger than Johnny, he is grounded and active in his culture, requirements for translating Johnny's words from Witsuwit'en to English.

Once the lawyer had asked a question, and Victor had translated it into Witsuwit'en, Johnny would answer in Witsuwit'en and Victor would translate what Johnny said into English. My job was to provide the court reporters with a spelling of the Witsuwit'en words, such as names and place names, that were part of the translated answer, so that the use of unfamiliar Witsuwit'en words would not impede the process of stenographically recording the testimony.

The court stenographer recorded the English segments – that is, the original question and the translation of the answer (with my spelling of the Witsuwit'en words). This transcript became the official court proceeding. Only twenty-three two-hour video recordings, made by Mike McDonald, preserve the translation of the questions and the testimony spoken in the native language. These preserve the actual words so that future generations can hear and see what took place. How important that record is!

There were both anomalies and advantages of the 'court within a home' scenario. Johnny David would sometimes leave his seat at the table and go to his bedroom to get a sample of something he was talking about. He did this, for example, to provide a sample of abalone, the material from which the hairpieces of the two girls in the *Tas Dleese* story were made (see volume 5). He also disappeared to get his Indian status card, which gives an incorrect birth date (see volume 6). In the commission evidence, John Milne says, 'Maybe we can go off the record for a moment, the Witness has walked away!' (6: 280). The next line is 'Back on the record. The witness has now sat down again' (ibid.). Peter Grant then adds, 'He just stepped out into his bedroom for a couple of moments.' Such behaviour was tantamount to leaving the witness box when giving evidence. If this had been explained to Johnny, he would have understood the matter very well: chiefs at a potlatch do not leave their seats for many hours. Yet, these irregularities were minor.

Johnny's home became an effective court addressing the many issues of Aboriginal title that have plagued the relationship between the Witsuwit'en and both the Canadian government and settler society. This court within a home preserved the formal aspect of both Western court proceedings and Witsuwit'en feasts or potlatches, where opposition is formally expressed. There was a strong sense that those unfamiliar with Johnny David – the stenographers and the crown attorney – grew to respect this vibrant, eloquent elder. However, Johnny David made it clear that he saw Milne as a representative of the forces that have thwarted, opposed, and oppressed the Witsuwit'en. He testified that 'the people, the white people, had no respect for the Indian people. The Indian people would chase them off their land, they would go and get their law and they would throw our people in jail.' The translator explained further to Milne: 'Right now, pointing at you he is saying that "It is just like you, you don't care about Indian people"' (7: 370). These were strong words. There was no doubt in Johnny David's mind that he was in a legal battle and that the lawyer representing the province and the federal government was the opposition.[27] Yet after Johnny made this statement the commission evidence continued as before. Milne showed no sign of being affected by the words.

There were some major advantages of the court within a home: to see the totem poles of Johnny David and Kela, the parties had only to go outside. This setting provided an appropriate place for Johnny to wear his button blanket and headdress and to play his drum and sing his song. There he sang and danced his Maxlaxlex song and sang, with permission, Kela's song (1: 88). Later (2: 95) he sang the song of Samaxsam. Johnny's singing these songs was an important part of his expressing and demonstrating what it means to be a Witsuwit'en chief. The songs were poignant parts of what he wanted to record.[28] The written record cannot capture those songs; all it says is that they were sung. Only the video recordings preserve these moments. Johnny David was giving evidence in the Witsuwit'en way: the songs are evidence of rights to titles and territories and are used in the feast hall as demonstrations of this. He tried to make the Witsuwit'en court vibrant with the testimony he gave; unfortunately, the Western court system has difficulty hearing such culturally embedded messages. Again, it is fortunate that these moments are preserved in the video.

The Adversaries: What Each Side Was Trying to Establish

In *Delgamuukw* and in the court within Johnny David's home, Johnny David and his lawyer, Peter Grant, were seeking to establish that the Witsuwit'en, and the Gitxsan, had maintained their matrilineal system of governance of their territories 'since time immemorial' and that the honour of the Crown required that their rights to their territory be recognized. This latter argument was based on the Royal Proclamation of 1763, which stated that the Crown had an obligation to make treaties with the indigenous peoples because they were the first inhabitants of the land. The Gitxsan and Witsuwit'en argued that the governance of the head chiefs of the territories was the means of administering their jurisdiction and that this system had been maintained into the present and needed to be legally recognized as establishing Aboriginal title to the land.

The province of British Columbia and the federal government took the position that the Gitxsan and Witsuwit'en were living on Crown land, and that the small reserves that had been established in the nineteenth century and adjusted by the McKenna-McBride Commission were all that they needed or were entitled to. In essence, the two levels of government represented the position that the Department of Indian Affairs had taken since its inception – that Indians were wards of the state and have been well provided for by that state. An undercurrent in Johnny David's testimony is the common belief that Native people should be grateful for the provision of the roads, railways, schools, and electricity that came their way after trappers, gold-rush adventurers, and settlers came to live in the same geographical space. Also reflected is the assumption that because Johnny David had preempted some land, he had no rights to his Witsuwit'en traditional territory, as if his preemption of land extinguished the traditional system.

Topics and Issues Covered in Johnny David's Testimony

Johnny David gave testimony about the vast array of Witsuwit'en culture. As his lawyer, Peter Grant, asked question after question, the Witsuwit'en tradition began to make itself manifest. Johnny David described the Witsuwit'en feast system and the relation of the territories to the chiefly titles (volumes 1–3). He performed the dance and song that go with his hereditary chief's name (volume 1), and he sang the songs of Kela and Samaxsam (volumes 1 and 2). He related how the tree was secured for his totem pole and how it was carved and erected (volume 2). Describing how peace was made after a Witsuwit'en was killed by the Nisga'a for inadvertently overturning what proved to be a grave marker, he recounted how this incident brought a Nisga'a feast name, Samaxsam, into the Witsuwit'en potlatch (volume 2). In volume 4 he decribed fishing sites and smokehouses at Tse Kya / Hagwilget and Kya Wiget / Moricetown, and how disputes over who had rights

Map 2. The territories of the Witsuwit'en houses as presented in the *Delgamuukw* case

Source: Office of the Gitksan-Witsuwit'en Hereditary Chiefs

to use particular territory were resolved. He related how the Carrier /
Witsuwit'en at Cheslatta were flooded off their lands (volume 5).[29] In
the same volume, he told one of the numerous Witsuwit'en oral traditions or *Kungax*, that of Tas Dleese. Throughout the last four volumes,
he related how the Witsuwit'en lived through and dealt with the vast
changes that occurred as white prospectors, settlers, and government
agents arrived and established mines, farms, towns, and policies without reference to, understanding, or honouring the Witsuwit'en and
Gitxsan traditions. With strength and tenacity he described the out-
rages his people suffered, relating how their homes, cabins, and
smokehouses in the territories were often burned, their cleared and
fenced land was taken over, and the Witsuwit'en were left with no
redress. In particular, he described the strong stand Head Chief Jean
Baptiste took when a party including Indian Agent Loring tried to evict
him from his land (volume 5), and he described how Lame Arthur
Michell and Nazel were evicted from their land at Barrett Lake and
jailed (volume 7). Johnny David related how Looseeya, grandfather of
Hagwilnegh /Sylvester Williams was fined and jailed for protesting
eviction from his home and land at Kya Wiget / Moricetown by Pete
Van Happy (volume 7). He further related how Van Happy chased
Witsuwit'en Peter Michell from the land where he was reaping hay he
had planted at Glentana (volume 7). Johnny describes in volume 4 how
the fishing sites at Kya Wiget / Moricetown were destroyed by the
Department of Fisheries without Witsuwit'en permission, and underscores his assumption that someone had to have given permission for
this to take place. Johnny David described, through cross-examination,
how he integrated the new society into his life, working for wages and
taking a preemption on farmland; he also described a traditional life
lived on the territories.

Johnny David's commission evidence is an impressive account of the
life of a Witsuwit'en who lived for over one hundred years, who never
went to school or learned to read or write, but who worked, voted,
served as a chief for his house, and generally led the active life of a First
Nations man. Johnny David continues to live and grow in the imagina-
tion of all those who had the good fortune to know him. By publishing
his commission evidence, I hope that more people will begin to know
him a little, too, and learn why the Witsuwit'en and Gitxsan feel
strongly about their rights to their way of life and to their territories.
Only then can there be meaningful dialogue and negotiation.

Problems in Cross-Cultural Communication:
From Misunderstanding to 'Jagged Worldviews Colliding'

Johnny David's commission evidence, like the whole *Delgamuukw* case, is an exercise in exposing the injustices that took place after Native – white contact and through the process of colonization. The testimony is a sampler of the many challenges in settling land rights and resolving the major areas of conflict. It presents the monumental, age-old, and ongoing difficulty in resolving conflicts between indigenous people and those colonizing forces that assume they alone have rights and law and deserve respect. Johnny David gave his voluminous testimony to counter those assumptions.

The various levels of cross-cultural misunderstandings and conflicts present in Johnny David's evidence provide a primer on the difficulties in establishing mutually beneficial discourse – difficulties that parallel to a large extent the historical problems of First Nations–settler society interaction. In the following sections, I discuss various ways in which cross-cultural misunderstandings and colliding world views provide challenges in establishing meaningful discourse and interaction.

Communication Problems between Johnny David and His Lawyer
Even in the direct examination, where Peter Grant and Johnny David were trying to establish the same thing, there were sometimes difficulties in communication. Translation across languages and cultures poses unexpected challenges, even when both parties are working cooperatively to achieve the same goals. Sometimes, through quirks of phrasing and the inevitable challenge of translation across cultures and languages, Peter Grant's question was unclear to Johnny. The attempt by Grant to cue Johnny David to relate the story of a Witsuwit'en woman named Hakasbaine provides an example of this kind of misunderstanding. Prior to the commission evidence, Johnny David had told Grant about an incident when people came to his father, Smogelgem, to settle a disagreement about who had rights to a particular territory. During the testimony Grant tried to lead to this situation by asking, 'Are there some cases where ... a Wet'suwet'en Chief may transfer a territory to another Chief or to another person when that person has helped for example at a feast?' Johnny responded by giving the generic rule, 'After a person spends a lot of money at the feast he is sometimes given a territory forever, it never goes back' (4: 167). Grant tried again to lead him to the Hakasbaine story, but the lawyer's failure to use the woman's cor-

rect name led Johnny to relate a different aspect of her family's story. In fact, Peter Grant's queries led to Johnny's relating a different story: how Tom Alex's wife found gold and how Tom set up a line for working the gold.[30] It was only later, after moving to a different set of questions, that Johnny David returned to Hakasbaine and recounted this interesting example of how rights can get confused:

> Hakasbaine's father had given Klayslahtl a box of berries which had some oolican grease mixed with it. He had given it to him because there was star-vation ... Klayslahtl told Hakasbaine ['lyou can use my territory for one year for giving me the berries and the grease.['] ... Hakasbaine's sister Jean-nies Kyo – means big Jenny – came they made big trouble with each other, and Klayslahtl came into the House of Smogelgem ... and then they talked about the land in question and Smogelgem helped Klayslahtl get his terri-tory back ... After Klayslahtl died Jeannies Kyo had registered the line in her name ... I wanted to talk about it and I've told you now. (4: 172–3)

Peter Grant wanted Johnny David to tell this story because it illustrates several points, including the way the hereditary chiefs settled disputes and the way Aboriginal rights can be confused since the introduction of the trapline registry and the Western patriarchal expectation that a man's children are his heirs. Hakasbaine's father had been given the rights to use Klayslahtl's territory for only a year. In Witsuwit'en law this right would not go beyond one year or extend to his children, Hakasbaine included, after that year. However, Hakasbaine's sister, Jeannies Kyo, registered the trapline as if the right could go from a man to his children, rather than to his sister's children, and as if the right to use a territory for a year, given as a gesture of thanks, could be interpreted as rights in perpetuity. Klayslahtl came to Smogelgem to resolve the dispute and get back his land. Smogelgem's decision tem-porarily achieved this correct resolution, but, according to Johnny, 'after Klayslahtl died Jeannies Kyo had registered the line in her name.' In other words, Jeannies Kyo had not accepted the Witsuwit'en settlement made by Smogelgem and had misrepresented her rights to the commissioner of traplines. In 1926 the government began to regis-ter traplines but did so without understanding the Witsuwit'en matri-lineal system or which chiefs had rights over which territories. That Jeannies Kyo could get the trapline registered in her name by the white agent is an example of how much confusion was created by those mis-representing their rights. Two competing systems came up against each other: the traditional matrilineal system of the Witsuwit'en and the government patriarchal system of registering traplines.

Issues of Cultural Vision
Another manifestation of the problem of cross-cultural communication is exemplified in the great difficulty Johnny David had in seeing the photographs shown to him by his lawyer. I think Peter Grant assumed that Johnny would be able to identify the people and sites in the photographs with no difficulty, but that was not so. In Volume 4 it is clear that Johnny had a hard time making out what was in the photographs. Was his eyesight impaired? Perhaps. He was aged, and both lawyers were frequently concerned about whether he was too tired to continue. A magnifying glass was provided but did not help Johnny discern what was in the pictures. Before these photos had been put to him, no one had been aware that the exercise would pose a problem – he was not known to suffer from poor eyesight. Was he perhaps not used to the two-dimensional representation of photographs – of not knowing how to 'read' photographs like he did not know how to read a text? I remember being impressed to see an elder from another British Columbia First Nation sitting at a table putting together a complex 500-piece jigsaw puzzle, even though the image was upside down. Cultural assumptions about how to look at images pose puzzles in themselves.

'The Only Thing I Will Tell You Is about the Things I Know Of':
Contrasting Paradigms of Knowledge and Hearsay
Under Witsuwit'en law, there are customs regulating what one can and cannot say in formal settings. In response to a number of questions raised by lawyers, Johnny David explained that he *could not*, according to Witsuwit'en law or protocol, talk about other clan histories or disputes that were finished. For example, Johnny declined to tell the story of the Kweese War on the Kitimat (5: 257). It is not appropriate in a formal context for one chief to tell the oral traditions or histories of another clan. Johnny knew the story well, as he had a grandfather from the Kweese clan.[31] In an informal context he had told it repeatedly to his grandchildren as part of their education. But he knew it was inappropriate for him to tell the story in the feast hall or in his commission evidence: Kweese / Florence Hall (Mrs Dennis Hall, as Johnny refers to her) later vividly told that kungax (history) in her own commission evidence.[32]

Johnny recounted two stories of battles with the Nutseni, or Carrier, in which the Witsuwit'en had been the victors (7: 366–7). Nonetheless he also explained that there were issues about talking about past wars. When asked whether he had heard about them, he said he had but could not talk about them because he was not sure which versions were correct (7: 365–9) and because once a conflict has been resolved and eagle down has been distributed, one does not raise the issue again.

Johnny's words about eagle down deserve to be highlighted here. The following is part of an exchange between Peter Grant and Johnny David about how peace is made in Witsuwit'en society:

MR GRANT: I would like to just ask you about how Wet'suwet'en people settled murders or killings I should say. Is there Wet'suwet'en laws for settlement as to when a person has been killed by somebody else?

MR DAVID: There is a way this is settled when someone is murdered, for example, when Mooseskin Johnny killed someone two of his relatives were given to people who were killed. That is how it was done ...

...

[E]agle down is used. Eagle down is our law ... once the eagle down is blown the revenge or murder is stopped and once that is done you are not allowed to break that law. The same is done with the passing of a mountain or territory.

MR GRANT: You referred to when white people sign papers, so the analogy you're making is to a peace treaty between [combatants], for example, after a war?

MR DAVID: Yes, they quit.

MR GRANT: Now, in the case you referred to of Mooseskin Johnny was his nephew or his nieces given as compensation?

MR DAVID: Mooseskin Johnny's sister's kids were given as compensation.

...

MR GRANT: Was a woman given to Satsan as compensation in this incident?

MR DAVID: It was Satsan's brother, Kuminyay, who received the girl for compensation.

...

MR GRANT: Did Mr. Loring, the Indian Agent, and Father Morice try to stop this practice of settlement?

MR DAVID: Yes, they tried to stop this practice. That is all I'm going to tell. (5: 265–7)

In the Witsuwit'en tradition, instead of taking a life – doing a revenge killing or executing a murderer – peace may be restored by giving one or two lives to the victim's family in marriage. In the example Johnny David provides, Kwees / Mooseskin Johnny, head chief of the Tsayu Clan, gave his sister's son, his own heir, in marriage to a woman in Satsan's family and his sister's daughter to the brother of the victim. Satsan's brother and his family would have usage rights to Mooseskin Johnny's territory through marriage, and Mooseskin Johnny and his heir would have usage rights to Satsan's territory; Mooseskin Johnny would henceforth have to care for Satsan's family as one closely related by marriage, and vice versa.[33] This kind of arrangement of marriages and transfer of people as compensation is an effective way of making peace in a kin-based society. So is transference of chiefly names, as in the story of the Nisga'a gifting the name Samaxsan as a part of the peace settlement after the Nisga'a killing of Gitdumskanees, a Witsuwit'en from Johnny David's house (see 2: 95–7). Johnny David's maternal uncle, Old Dennis, described to anthropologist Diamond Jenness the use of eagle down in this incident, which he had witnessed, saying 'the principal Chief of the [Nisga'a] village sent round word to all the Houses that the fighting should cease and that our people should move over to his house along a path strewn with the white eagle down that symbolizes peace' (Jenness 1943: 479).

Eagle down is an effective law, as Johnny states, for once it is distributed over the contesting or estranged parties, the settlement is final.[34] Significantly, one does not thereafter talk about the incident, lest it stir up hard feelings.

Another example of what one cannot talk about is described in the following exchange:

MR MILNE: Have you ever heard of the territory not being transferred on [or within] the mother's side?[35]
MR DAVID: No, I haven't. I have heard of some instances before my time, and it's very difficult for me to speak about.

MR MILNE: Is it difficult to speak about because it's before your time?
MR DAVID: Yes, and the reason I'm reluctant to talk about this is because it was before my time and I don't know whether I will be telling the correct

version, a different version. And I don't want to talk about anything that
I'm unsure of. (8: 389–90)

Johnny David and his fellow Witsuwit'en follow strict regulations
about not speaking beyond their knowledge. Johnny says: 'It happened before my time, and I didn't see' (ibid.). In answer to the question from John Milne, 'Do you know from what House it happened?'
Johnny answered, 'No, I don't know. The only thing I will tell you is
about the things that I know of' (ibid.).

Different Concepts of Hearsay
The Witsuwit'en understanding of what one is empowered to talk
about is not the same as the concept of hearsay in Western jurisprudence. A thorny issue in *Delgamuukw* was the willingness and ability of
the lawyers for the Crown and the judge to listen to and understand
the import of Witsuwit'en (and Gitxsan) oral traditions and to accept
as valid evidence testimony about events that were not observed by
the witness, but that he or she had the authority, under Witsuwit'en
tradition, to talk about.

John Milne began his cross-examination by spelling out the terms of
what, in Western and Canadian jurisprudence, is hearsay:

MR MILNE: When I ask you questions during the cross-examination I'm
going to refer to 'you' and when I say 'you' I mean you personally, and
when I say 'your people' or in some other context I mean the Wet'suwet'en
people. When I ask you questions would you confine your answers to
whether or not you're talking personally or whether you're talking on
behalf of the Wet'suwet'en. What I want to do then, when you give your
answer, if you have not personally seen what you're giving your evidence
about, I would like you to tell me if you have not personally seen it but
somebody else may perhaps have told you about it. Is that all right?
A Yes.
THE INTERPRETER: He said: If we don't know about it we don't tell about
it.

Q What I am concerned about, that you know about it personally and
that you have seen these things and if you have not seen them, it's fine to
say that somebody else told you, but I want to know when that circumstance arises, do you understand that?
A Yes. (6: 271–2)

In Western jurisprudence, one can talk about something one has witnessed, but if one has only heard about something, it is hearsay. In such instances, other witnesses or written accounts or documents must be produced to validate a particular event. The understanding and criteria in Witsuwit'en culture is quite different. Because it is a culture with a deep oral tradition, oral traditions and accounts are important means of knowing about the past. From their early years, children are trained to listen to sacred oral traditions and contemporary accounts and to learn them well enough to be able to tell them accurately. The rebuke 'You have no ears' means a child (or adult) has not listened carefully, attentively. Many of the events Johnny talked about were ones he had heard about but not seen. In Witsuwit'en culture he was generally authorized to talk about these events. Thus his cross-examination ends with the same refrain as it began, underscoring the different cultural perceptions of what is valid evidence:

> MR MILNE: All I want to know is on some of those places you said that white people burned down the houses or the smokehouses. Did you see that happen, or is it from what people have told you?
> MR DAVID: People told me about it.
>
> MR MILNE: Those are all of my questions, Mr David. Thank you very much. (8: 414)

This closing statement minimalized what Johnny David had said about what he had seen as well as heard:

> MR DAVID: At Kooty Creek (phonetic), where our main settlement was, there were two cabins there. At Midzi-ya, there was one. Kuskabay-wonnee there was one. And white people really made us suffer by burning down our buildings.
>
> MR MILNE: Did you see the white people burn down buildings on Smogel-gem's territory?
> MR DAVID: I have seen them, I knew them, but I didn't say anything.
>
> MR MILNE: Why didn't you say anything?
> MR DAVID: I was afraid of the law. As soon as we talk about something, they put us in court and jail us.
>
> MR MILNE: Which cabin did you see burned down by white people?

MR DAVID: Kooty Creek, which is Neloo kwah in our language, that is where I saw white people burn a cabin down. (8: 381)

Johnny had not only been told about these events, he had seen the charred remains of the smokehouses, cabins, and houses, as is clear in his commission evidence. 'I have not made this up' becomes a refrain in Johnny's evidence.

Even more problematic in *Delgamuukw* was the status of oral tradition. Johnny related the Witsuwit'en oral tradition of Tas Dleese, the story of the monster at Dzikins Lake (5: 254–5). Johnny takes this story seriously, as accurate and valid, not myth. Yet, the judge's response to such testimony was quite different, highlighting the different cultural premises about what is accurate and what is sacred. Oral traditions that the judge considered unreliable 'myth' are to First Nations valid and sacroscant validation of rights to land. Although McEachern allowed such oral traditions to be given by the plaintiffs – that is, the Witsuwit'en and Gitxsan chiefs – and thereby entered into the court record, in his reasons for judgment he deemed them inappropriate as the basis for establishing rights to territory.

Misunderstanding between the Crown Lawyer and Johnny David
There were inevitable areas of cultural misunderstanding between the Crown lawyer and Johnny David. Again the misunderstanding operates on many levels. After establishing that he wanted Johnny to distinguish between what he had seen and what he had heard about, John Milne asked who the Wit'suwit'en are:

MR MILNE: What does the name Wet'suwet'en mean?
MR DAVID: It's the name given to people from this area.

MR MILNE: Is it true that the people from this area used to be called Gitksan-Carrier? ... Did the Wet'suwet'en people used to be called Gitksan-Carrier?
...
MR DAVID: The Gitneys are called Gitksan.

MR MILNE: Has he ever heard the term 'Gitksan-Carrier' before?
MR DAVID: Can't recall. (6: 277)

Milne was asking about terminology because the original statement of claim (filed in 1984) was made by the Gitksan-Carrier, who at that time had a combined tribal council. This title was later amended to the Gitksan-Wet'suwet'en, the Carrier being a much larger group than just the Witsuwit'en. The Witsuwit'en are the Bulkley River or Western Carrier, and their claim did not represent either the Lake Babine Carrier to their north, the Carrier of Stuart Lake, or the more easterly and southerly Fraser River drainage Carrier. The word *Witsuwit'en*, I had been told, means 'people of the lower drainage.' Sharon Hargus, a linguist, says, 'Witsuwit'en appears to be a loan from Carrier, with a literal meaning something like "people downhill in general area."' (See glossary.) The terminology and systems of naming and categorizing peoples, chiefs, and houses are not easy to translate back and forth across the linguistic and cultural chasm between Aboriginal and Western thought. There is no one people called the Gitksan-Carrier. The Gitksan-Carrier Tribal Council was renamed the Gitksan-Witsuwit'en Tribal Council after the initial *Delgamuukw* court case was filed. Apparently Milne was unaware of this change and the relationship between the Gitksan and the Witsuwit'en.

Confusion also ensued from Milne's attempt to understand who the head chiefs of the Witsuwit'en were and that they were the plaintiffs (6: 279–81). All of the Witsuwit'en head chiefs backed *Delgamuukw* completely, but Milne was concerned about whether they represented all Witsuwit'en. The simple answer is yes, but the issue engendered complex questioning during cross-examination.

There was also confusion over the relation of the head chiefs to the houses, as evidenced by the following exchange in the cross-examination in volume 6:

MR MILNE: Are there hereditary Chiefs who currently have names and who are not heirs that are not mentioned in the Statement of Claim?
MR DAVID: There are others and the Chief's name doesn't go to just anyone.

MR MILNE: Are there other Houses other than those listed in the Statement of Claim for the Wet'suwet'en?
MR DAVID: Yes. There's Chiefs that have names, they all come from a House.
...
From each House there are usually three *main* Chiefs, from each of the clans. Also three *main* Chiefs at the table when the feast is on.

MR MILNE: So the number of Houses is, what?

MR DAVID: There were four potlatch Houses.

...

MR MILNE: Well, I'm getting quite confused about this whole issue of who the plaintiffs are and who else might be out there that is not a plaintiff but are still in the same position as the plaintiffs, namely they are hereditary Chiefs of certain Houses.

MR GRANT: Before you go on – could you translate that to Wet'suwet'en?

THE INTERPRETER: He was just talking about just three *main* Chiefs from each clan who get up to speak on behalf of all the Chiefs from their clans.

MR MILNE: Do you know if some of these people in the Statement of Claim which we've just gone through are those three main Chiefs?

MR DAVID: Yes, they are. Yes, the names we just went over are some of the leading Chiefs of those Clans.

MR MILNE: Do you know if they are all of the leading Chiefs of those Clans?

MR DAVID: Yes. (6: 282–3)

Some of the confusion was over the term 'hereditary chiefs.' There are more hereditary chiefs than head chiefs of the houses. As Johnny notes, there are three main, or head chiefs for each clan. They are the plaintiffs for the Witsuwit'en. When Johnny says 'There were four potlatch Houses,' he is referring, presumably, to the fact that at Hagwilget / Tse Kya, where much of the potlatching was done during his lifetime, there were four potlatch houses or smokehouses – one for each clan, rather than one for each house. These were built during a time when the Wit-suwit'en population had been decimated by smallpox. Indeed, Diamond Jenness wrote, on the basis of his visit in 1922, that the Bulkley River Carrier were on their way to extinction.[36] When their numbers were so seriously depleted, the *Tsayu* (Beaver) and the *Laksamshu* (Fireweed) Clans amalgamated, so there were potlatch houses for the Wolf Clan, the Frog Clan, the Small Frog Clan, and the combined Beaver-Fireweed Clan at Tse Kya / Hagwilget. At Kya Wiget, literally 'Old Village,' there came to be twelve houses again as the population increased, as shown in figure 4, where the houses listed are the houses of the head chiefs who are the plaintiffs.

Going from clans to houses, it is useful to know that the Witsuwit'en have a different set of names for their houses than for their head chiefs. This contrasts somewhat with the Gitxsan system, where the head chief's name is usually the same as that of the matrilineal house; thus, for example, the Gitxsan House of Delgamuukw has Chief Delgamuukw as its head chief. The Witsuwit'en not only have different names for their houses and their head chiefs, they sometimes have two or three sets of names for their houses, depending on whether the house is in Kya Wiget / Moricetown, Tse Kya / Hagwilget, or the outlying territories. In his testimony, Johnny refers to the Kilwoneetz House – the house that had existed on the Kilwoneetz territory. He explains that the people of the Kilwoneetz House were also the people of the House of Ginehklaiya. By using this range of names, the Witsuwit'en were able not only to identify houses but also to distinguish between those at the main villages or out on the different territories.[37]

A last source of confusion over houses is worth pointing out. The rendition of the name of the house of Gisdaywa / Alfred Joseph that Johnny gave was transcribed in the court records as Yahoneetz. Linguist Sharon Hargus has pointed out in the glossary that this is a variant of the name Yawinits, 'House in the Middle,' which is a shorter version of Kaiyawiniits. Translation across very different languages and cultures is not straightforward. Johnny David tried to make the issues clear by saying repeatedly 'there are three main Chiefs' and 'The three main Chiefs speak for the Houses,' although the topic continued to be a source of misunderstanding for the Crown.

Another area of cross-cultural confusion is exemplified by questions asked by John Milne about Johnny David's work for wages. These were asked with the tacit assumption that if a Witsuwit'en earned a living from non-traditional labour, he or she no longer had rights to traditional territory, to the land base. Perhaps this relates to the original Indian Act stipulation that Indians could not be paid wages or run a business and remain registered Indians. Mooseskin Johnny, the Kweese, referred to above, was renowned among local settlers for operating a bed and breakfast at his homestead. The founder of Smithers's *Interior News*, Joseph Coyle, stayed at the Bald B and wrote: 'Mooseskins' was a oneroom self-service stopping place equipped with a sheet metal stove, tin cooking utensils, a table, a couple of long benches, and two sets of narrow sleeping bunks ... Such items as tea, sugar, etc., could be purchased at Johnny's dwelling nearby ... It was a well kept, popular place' (Cassidy and Cassidy 1980: 32). Mooseskin Johnny's business was shut down by the Indian agent because Indians were not permitted to own or operate a business.

There is a perception that Natives are not 'Native' unless living in some kind of unchanging time warp. Revealingly, of course, the dominant society is not subjected to such static and narrow measures of identity. This issue is related to a definition of Aboriginal rights as the right to subsistence activities that existed at the time of contact – a narrow definition, but one used by Chief Justice McEachern in the initial decision in *Delgamuukw I*. Fortunately, this position was largely reversed by the Supreme Court of Canada.

Problems in cross-cultural understanding between the Witsuwit'en and the Crown were not limited to the courtroom. The Witsuwit'en are very hospitable. For them, the correct way to treat people, even those with whom you are having a major struggle or difficulty, is to invite them to a feast, where issues can be openly and officially discussed. Before *Delgamuukw* commenced, the Gitxsan and Witsuwit'en put on an opening feast. Initially they had intended to invite the lawyers for the opposition as well as Chief Justice McEachern, but they were advised that such an invitation would be considered inappropriate. The Witsuwit'en and Gitxsan found it hard to accept that the gesture was not proper, that it could be construed as a way to influence the judge and the lawyers for the opposition or make them feel indebted to the people launching the court case. Eventually, however, they were persuaded not to invite their opponents.

During Johnny David's commission evidence, when the court would break for lunch, the lawyer for the opposition would typically go to Smithers to eat, although this involved almost an hour of travel. Not only to save him time, but because it is considered so basic a form of hospitality, John Milne was invited, with the rest of the participants – Johnny David, the translator, the court reporter, the video recorder, Peter Grant, and me – to have lunch at the home of a Witsuwit'en couple who are elders and hereditary chiefs. Although we all went, the event became more complex when the lawyer for the opposition learned that he was eating bear meat. In Witsuwit'en the hosts asked if Milne was concerned whether the game was taken on territory that the hunter had rights to use (which is the Witsuwit'en concern), or whether it was taken with the proper licence and at the time when hunting bears is allowed. The complexities of these issues were both amusing and disarming: an act of typical Witsuwit'en hospitality and generosity had the potential to become another legal duel over indigenous rights to hunt on traditional territory. We hurried back to the commission evidence, glad to leave these questions unanswered. The answer lies in the totality of *Delgamuukw*.

Jagged World Views Colliding: Testifying to Injustices

The difficulties of communicating the nature of the Witsuwit'en house system in Johnny David's commission evidence, cited above, are nothing in comparison to the conflicts Johnny David describes between his people and the settler society that burned down cabins and smokehouses and confiscated First Nations property and land, oblivious to the Witsuwit'en land tenure system and using colonialism as an excuse to treat First Nations unfairly. Johnny David's commission evidence describes poignantly how the total failure of cross-cultural communication over these issues escalated into what Leroy Little Bear calls 'jagged worldviews colliding' (Little Bear 2000).[38] The Witsuwit'en were silenced with no recourse by those who called them 'friends.'[39]

At different stages of his testimony, Johnny David spoke eloquently about what happened to the Witsuwit'en homesteads at the beginning of the twentieth century. In volume 2, for example, he describes how Round Lake Tommy was removed from his land, and how cleared farmland was taken from Johnny David's father. Of particular import are Johnny's comments on the lack of recourse available to the Witsuwit'en: 'The white people had no respect for us. In their eyes, we were poor for them. They just fooled around with us. Whenever we spoke against them, they would call the law and they would put us in jail' (8: 381). Johnny bolstered his general statements with information about specific individuals who were kicked off their land, jailed, and/or fined.[40]

The theme of lack of recourse for the colliding worldviews resurfaces in Johnny's description in volume 6 of how his father's smokehouse was burned down after his father had died:

MR MILNE: Did you tell any person in authority, such as the Indian agent, about what had happened?
MR DAVID: The Indian agent didn't care about us. He was the one that put us back on to reserves and he was a white man ... And the white people even though they stole things from us they would turn the story around and say the Indians stole it first, and [we] would be threatened to be taken to jail, and that is one of the reasons why [we] didn't speak up too much. (6: 291–2)

It is worth noting that, in Johnny David's description of the smokehouse incident, he referred to the men who burned his father's smokehouse and stole his axes and guns, and to the person who stole a valuable black fox from his father's trap, as 'neighbors' and 'friends.' When asked if the fox skin incident resulted in a fight, Johnny replied, 'no, there was not a fight. Considered each other good friends' (6: 291). Clearly, injustices were perpetrated not only by remote governments, but by the Witsu-wit'en's neighbours and supposed friends, who carried out such acts with impunity. These neighbors and officials were presumably 'good Christians,' aware of Christ's counsel to 'Love thy neighbor as thyself.' Johnny David's testimony unmasks the colonial ethic endorsed by the government and its citizens as one that condoned and legitimized behaviour these same people otherwise acknowledged as immoral, illegal, and unethical.

John Milne seemed reluctant to accept the fact that the Witsuwit'en had no recourse against such injustices. He returned repeatedly to the question of how the Witsuwit'en responded to such acts.

MR MILNE: What did the Wet'suwet'en do in circumstances when they were asked to leave? Was there any attempt by them to go before the men who spoke for the white man and ask them not to remove people from the land?

MR DAVID: At that time most white people didn't like Indians and when they spoke up against the land they were threatened to be taken to jail and they would leave, and the white people would take over the land, and it is still the same way today. The white people still don't like the Indians ...

MR MILNE: Do you remember any resolutions or actions that people at the feasts when they were discussing this decided they should do? And what was done as a result of the discussions at feasts? (7: 333)

It is ironic that John Milne asks Johnny if the chiefs took these issues to the potlatch for resolution. The potlatch was outlawed. Johnny's response was, 'When it was discussed at the feast, these problems were brought up with the Indian Agent but he just continued to let white people take the land and he never did anything for our people' (7: 333).

Johnny describes how white law enforcers were of no help to the Witsuwit'en, but rather inspired fear: 'I was afraid of the law. As soon as we talk about something, they put us in court and jail us' (8: 381). And, in later testimony: 'About 1902, 1903, the white people began arriving in our territory. And there was at that time Mr Loring [the

Indian agent] had begun working, and when our people would speak about their land they were put in jail, and it is these people who did that' (8: 400). In volume 7, Johnny amplified the role played by the Indian agent: 'The Indian agent would take the advice of the white people and that is how he went about moving Indian people around' (7: 333).

The Indian Agent and settler society condoned the takeover of Wit-suwit'en land and the destruction of their cabins and smokehouses. *Delgamuukw* case itself was the first time that people like Johnny could get a court of law to listen to them about the atrocities and injustices that they had experienced.

The Indian agent was obviously not an advocate for the Indians who tried to explain to the government and the settlers that the Witsuwit'en had an ancient system of hereditary chiefs with rights to traditional territories. The Indian agent, be it R.E. Loring or those who followed, endorsed the Eurocentric, *terra nullius* concept. Loring believed it was appropriate for the Canadian government to give land rights to Boer War veterans. In addition to being an Indian agent, Loring was a justice of the peace, the enforcer of law. In his dual capacity, he felt he had the right to remove the hereditary chiefs from their land and homesteads. He was among those who sought to move Jean Baptiste off his land. In Volume 5, Johnny David eloquently described the extreme measures this Witsuwit'en chief had to take to resist being forcefully removed in that incident:

MR DAVID: Mr Baptiste had about 160 to 300 acres and he had set up a farm, had cows and horses, and the Indian Agent asked him to move off the land but he defied that order and stayed on the land.

...

He kept resisting the government and they asked him to remove himself from the land. He refused and the government got their own lawyers to try and remove him from his land. The Indian Agent had also asked him to leave the land he was on. He refused, he stay on there. Kept growing hay for his cattle. The people from the government told him that he was to leave the land, he refused again, so they told him to go somewhere and he dressed and got ready. He had two race horses and he got the fastest one and saddled it up, and he had two revolvers and he stuck them on his sides. There were people who were sent to pick him up, were all lined up, and he came by on his horse and as he neared them he jumped off his horse, pulled his revolver out and stuck it to the head of one of the people and asked him if he wanted them both. The people who were sent to pick him up talked to him, told him to get off the land. The Indian Agent told him to get off the land but he refused. When he refused they finally gave in and made that land a Reserve ... It was the Indian Agent who made the land into the Reserve ... that's how the white people fooled around with us ... The way the people have threatened Jean Baptiste, that is the same way other white people have threatened our Indian people. The same is done regarding our trap lines, the white people have been taking them. That's all. (5: 250–1)

Although, as Johnny David reported to John Milne, such problems were – and continue to be – discussed at feasts, they had no way to obtain redress for these grave injustices.

Johnny David also described how resources such as minerals were taken from the territory, even when it was the Witsuwit'en who found them: 'In the eyes of the white man we are poor. They just come and take the land, they put everything in their pockets and they're gone. There was some mining that has taken place near the Hudson Bay Mountain. The Indian people were the first to find the minerals but they were told that it was no good and some time later white people stake claims and they went mining. The white man consider the Indians poor; they took everything including their lands and put it in their pockets' (5: 268).

Johnny David's testimony clearly sets out the devastation suffered by the Witsuwit'en as a result of the failure of settler society to acknowledge Native rights to their lands and to the buildings and resources on those lands: 'Around 1907 the white man came and the game warden began to give the traplines to their own white people which had originally belonged to us. And the game warden told the white people, you see any Indians crossing into your territory let me know and I will arrest them. That is how these people looked at us – also during this time as they were taking our traplines, also began blasting the beaver dams, which reduced the number of beavers ... Our traplines were all gone. The resources on our territories, the trees, were all gone. That's it' (3: 142).

The Babine Barricade War: A Well-Documented Example of Jagged World Views Colliding
Sometimes, as exemplified by the case of Jean Baptiste described above, Native people actively resisted encroachments on their rights and territories. One such incident described by Johnny David is known as the Babine Barricade War. In 1906 Fisheries officers tried to dismantle the

fences or barricades used for salmon weirs near Fort Babine, an area inhabited by the Lake Babine First Nation who are closely interrelated with the Witsuwit'en. Johnny David described what happened next: 'when they came, three or four of the women grabbed the Fisheries officer and dumped him in the water and let him out ... [T]hose three or four women, who had dumped the Fisheries officer, the husbands were arrested. These three or four husbands of the women were sent to jail in Vancouver' (3: 125).

Johnny goes on to relate that an Oblate missionry, Father Coccola, who knew the Babine / Witsuwit'en language, helped the Babine in their conflict with the government, arranging for the chiefs to go to Ottawa to try to settle the matter. According to Johnny, the chiefs were offered 'a large container of silver and a large container of gold,' but the missionary warned them not to accept the money or they would lose their land. As Johnny concludes, 'the Chiefs did not accept the silver and gold, therefore they did not lose their land. That is how it was told to me ... The Chiefs themselves told me this' (3: 125).

It is significant that the result of the Barricade War signalled to Johnny David that the Babine chiefs had not lost their land. From the government's point of view, by 1891 Babine land had been reduced to nine small reserves (D. Harris 2001: 89).[41] At the time of the conflict, the issue was fish, not land *per se*. The conflict, which has been very well documented, (D. Harris 1997, 2001; Mills forthcoming), erupted when the cannery owners at the mouth of the Skeena River mistakenly attributed a serious decline in the number of sockeye to traditional Babine means of catching salmon. In fact the reduction in the number of fish was caused by development of the salmon-canning industry at the mouth of the Skeena River (D. Harris 1997; 2001). In 1902, the cannery industry at the mouth of the Skeena was flourishing. The next year, strikes by the fishers, with the support of the women who worked in the canneries, reduced the profits. At the same time, increased fishing by Japanese as well as Canadians and Americans reduced the sockeye supply in the Prince Rupert–Port Essington area, where by 1904 some eleven commercial canneries had sprung up to process the fish that travelled up the Skeena to spawn.

As Douglas Harris (2001) says, 'The role of Fisheries in the dispute is relatively transparent. By 1904, fishing was big business on the Northwest Coast and the enforcement of the Fisheries Act reflected a business agenda, notwithstanding the rhetoric that removing the barricades was a conservation measure in the interests of all users' (89). The cannery owners convinced the Fisheries officials to attribute the sharp reduction of sockeye to the Babine Lake Native practice of catching the salmon in weirs as they ascended the river to Lake Babine. Their use of the term 'barricade' implies their belief that the Babine kept all sockeye from passing through to spawn. In this belief, they failed to recognize that the chiefs carefully regulated when the fences and weirs were put in place and when they were taken out. In 1904 Fisheries official Helgesen told the Lake Babine chiefs that they were forbidden to use the barricades: they had to fish with gill nets, which he promised to give them. Helgesen recorded Chief Atio's reply:

> The chief advanced many points and some were well taken, he said they have had an indisputable right for all time in the past, that if it was taken away the old people would starve, that by selling salmon they could get *iktahs* [or basic supplies such as flour, sugar, ammunition], and he wanted to know to what extent the government would support them, he thought it unfair to forbid them selling fish when the cannerymen sold all theirs, and I had to promise him to tell the government to compel the canners to let more fish come up the rivers, as some years they did not get enough, that the canners destroyed more spawn than they, that formerly he could not see the water below his barricade for fish, that they had been so plentiful that some of them were forced out on the beach, but latterly they had diminished, little by little every year. (D. Harris 2001: 98)

Needless to say, Helgesen did not compel the canners to let more fish come up the river. Moreover, the nets supplied by the canneries to the Babine in 1905 were rotten, so the Babine were not able to catch an adequate supply of sockeye for the winter. The next year, when Helgesen, now Fisheries overseer, in the company of Indian Agent R.E. Loring, went to distribute nets to the Babine, he discovered that the head chiefs had sent out men to confiscate the nets and had re-established their fences and weirs. In response Helgesen sent out summonses and, when these failed to impress the chiefs, warrants for their arrest on 20 August. Helgesen's account of 23 August 1906 describes the conflict at the site of the barricade with greater detail than Johnny David's account sixty years later:

[Re] August 23rd. [1906]
The fishery Guardians again repaired to the place of action, being determined to remove the barricade if possible, but they found the Indians

well organized, the men drawn up in line on the river bank, the women armed with clubs, had gathered in a semicircle close to the beach, and some Indians immediately behind them, amid a tumult, the Chief could be heard saying, 'If any one touch the dam it will be at his peril, that it was not to be removed.' The Officers tried to persuade them to pull down the barricade, telling them it would greatly mitigate their offence but they would not listen to reason. Guardian Wells then made an attempt to destroy the barricade, placing Norrie and Rosenthal to guard the east bank, no sooner than Norris had stepped close to the barricade than he was dragged back by the Squaws. Wells went to his rescue and the two received blows from the clubs right and left, the Squaws then tried to drown them, but failed in the attempt ...

At this time the noise and turmoil became fearful, the Guardians being almost pulled to pieces, and the Officers knew that if they pushed the women aside or used them roughly it would have been the signal for the men to attack them, and Norrie saw that the Chief had all he could do to keep the Indians from attacking our men, who realized that if they carried matters any further that worse things would happen, as they elbowed their way out of the excited mob. Wells coat was all torn and he was otherwise bruised. Norrie had received a blow on the back, that disabled him for a couple of weeks. The Officers stated that the humiliation and indignities heaped upon them was beyond description. (Helgesen letter of 21 October 1906 copy in the possession of Taché Band)

The two sides were at a major standoff, characterized by conflicting interpretations of 'the law.' For the Babine, the law was the council of their chiefs. For the government, the law was Department of Fisheries regulations. Easy resolution seemed unlikely.

A telegram was despatched to the federal Fisheries minister, L.P. Brodeur: 'Fishery Guardians Babine Lake Assaulted by Indians who have erected barricades prompt action necessary *if laws are to be enforced*' (Berger 1990: Appendix; my emphasis). The assistant commissioner of the federal fishery telegraphed local authorities asking 'What do you suggest to have law respected?' C. Sweeney, the provincial Fisheries commissioner replied, in part, 'Prompt action necessary. *Authorities here unable to cope with situation.* One hundred militia will be required ... Non-capture of recent murderer has encouraged Indians to defy law' (1990: Appendix; my emphasis).

Local industry bolstered the call for action, as a telegram from Peter Wallace, manager of the Wallace Bros. Packing Company attests: 'Babine Indians erected barricades resisted arrest and assaulted Fishery Guardians. Spawning ground must be protected or canning industry will be paralyzed on Skeena River situation beyond control of Government Officials here. Magistrate at Hazelton afraid of serious trouble unless Government takes strong action. Militia will have to be dispatched to cope with situation' (D. Harris 2001: 105–11).

While telegrams flew back and forth between Ottawa and the province, the Babine were preventing Fisheries officials from removing the barricades by having the women guard the fences. Finally, on the invitation of two chiefs – Big George Dyer and William Dzu'k – Father Coccola intervened. The two chiefs then gave themselves up to the authorities and were sent to prison in Victoria for defying the Fisheries regulations. However, the Department of Indian Affairs sometimes took a stand different from Fisheries and defended the Aboriginal right to fish. Father Coccola accompanied the two chiefs to Ottawa to act as translator. The chiefs met with representatives of the Ministry of Fisheries and of Indian Affairs. Father Coccola asked that the Babine be granted more land on which to raise crops. Fisheries ruled that the Babine would not be allowed to use their weirs, fences, or barricades but, recognizing that some concession must be made, granted them the right to catch salmon by using nets (which in general they prohibited in rivers).

After the two chiefs had returned home, the Department of Indian Affairs continued to lobby the Department of Fisheries for the right for the Babine to sell fish, arguing that trade and barter in fish had been a part of their culture from before contact and had kept traders, trappers, and other newcomers alive for many years. The superintendent general of Indian Affairs agreed, in a letter dated 9 February 1907, to terms put forth by the superintendent of Marine and Fisheries: 'On the understanding ... that the Department of Marine and *Fisheries will permit the catching of food fish and their sale without restriction as to numbers, having regard to the extent to which the practice has been previously pursued by them; but subject to reasonable restrictions, as to times of fishing*' (Berger 1990: 7; emphasis in original). Berger notes that, while this letter exists, 'No signed treaty as such has been found. Father Coccola was asked by the Minister of Marine and Fisheries in a letter dated 21 February 1907 to convey to the Indians all of the terms as outlined above and to seek their support. The Indians' response at the time is not known.' If the Barricade Treaty indeed granted the Babine the right to sell fish, a right Johnny David assumed all First Nations had, it is not a right that the Department of Fisheries now acknowledges.

Issues of selling fish have been as contested by the Department of Fisheries as issues of control of land. It is significant that what Johnny David was told about the incident was that the two Babine chiefs had not lost their land because they had not accepted the containers of gold and silver offered to them, which in his eyes would have extinguished their rights to their land. Douglas Harris concludes: 'By sending its Fisheries officers, the Canadian state was asserting its jurisdiction – enforcing its laws – and denying the legitimacy of the existing social order ... Perhaps the most important question in the colonial setting is whose conception of the social order would prevail? ... This dispute was more than a dispute over fishing technology, or even a dispute over fish. It was part of the larger story of colonization and resistance. At its root was the question of whose law would prevail, whose social order would be legitimized, justified and in the end imposed on the other' (1997: 1).

The Babine Barricade War is another chapter in the long, sad tale of Eurocentrism. Johnny David's testimony on this event is an invaluable expression of an indigenous perspective that is all too often unheard. It starts with the assumption that chiefs have the right to the land and to the fish and to their ecologically sensitive way of catching them, regulated through their systems of chiefs. Johnny is very explicit that those rights cannot be extinguished without due consideration and permission from the chiefs. Yet government representatives, with the support of industry, disregarded these rights time after time. (See Sherry 2002 for a contemporary model of creating communication between First Nations and government representatives.)

Repeating the Pattern: Further Illegal Action, Taken without the Permission of the Chiefs

The destruction of the Witsuwit'en fishing sites at Kya Wiget / Moricetown in 1950–1 repeats the same errors made at Lake Babine in 1906.[42] There is the false assumption that Native practices (and in this case even the natural formation of the river bed) are responsible for the reduction in the supply of fish. Again Native rights and governance were completely disregarded. Johnny describes that rights to specific fishing spots in Moricetown Canyon belong to the head chiefs: 'it's true that each Hereditary Chief had their own fishing spots and when they die the name is passed on. The person who takes the name gets the fishing spot' (4: 179–80).

Johnny states clearly that the chiefs had not given their consent to the construction of fish ladders by the Department of Fisheries in 1952, which destroyed many of the traditional fishing sites: 'Louie Tommy as the Head Chief had spoken against the fish ladder and when they first started building the fish ladders police came with their guns, they were on top of the hill and to this day they don't know who had signed the paper for the Government to go ahead to start building the fish ladders ... [Louie Tommy] was Wah Tah Kwets as well as Chief ... And we never did find out who signed his name to get the fish ladders built' (4: 181). Note the tacit assumption on the part of Johnny David, as on the part of all the Witsuwit'en, that the Department of Fisheries would know they did not have the right to tamper with, let alone destroy, the chiefs' traditional fishing sites without due consultation and consent.

When Peter Grant asked Johnny, 'Did Government officials come and speak with Wah Tah Kwets or with yourself or the other Head Chiefs before they built ... the ladders?' he answered, 'They did not talk to them ... The people from here would ask Fisheries – the Fishery people – "who gave them permission to start building" and the Fishery people just told our people they didn't know' (4: 181).

'They did not talk to them' sums up the kind of interaction that all too often took place between various levels of government and the Witsuwit'en. Johnny assumed that someone must have signed Louie Tommy's name. He assumed that he must have been consulted: it breached all Witsuwit'en law, custom, and culture if he was not. Unfortunately, the Department of Fisheries, like Indian Agent Loring, did not feel that they needed to consult with the Witsuwit'en in order to destroy their fishing sites or remove them from their land:

MR DAVID: It was Mr Loring, the Indian Agent, who had tried to convince me to move off the land and he had promised me some land in Hagwilget which I never got, and he did the same with Round Lake Tommy. Mr Loring was on the side of the white people.

...

[H]e was the Indian Agent. He tried to deceive us by promising us other land so we could move off our lands, and I didn't. I resisted him.

...

When Mr. Loring had promised me land in Hagwilget in exchange for my father's land, that didn't happen. I did not get the land in Hagwilget so I moved back to my father's land. I got the land through preemption. (5: 231)

Lane (1987: 8) reports that 'The Province eventually allowed some of the Indians who had been dispossessed of their lands through the use of South African War Land Grant scrip to take land under the preemption provisions of the Land Act.' Apparently this applies to Johnny David's preemption. Ironically, Johnny David secured rights to a small portion of his father's traditional territory by staking the same kind of preemptive claim as the white people. This was necessary because, as Johnny says, 'They did not talk to them.'

As Johnny David's testimony makes clear, such differences in world views were not limited to those between the Witsuwit'en and the government, but also included institutions such as the Roman Catholic Church. Johnny David, like the Witsuwit'en in general, was baptized as a Roman Catholic.

Leroy Little Bear (2000) refers to differences in cultural evaluation of rights as 'jagged worldviews colliding.'

Other Arenas of Conflict, Misunderstanding, and Injustice

In his testimony Johnny David produced a book of Catholic Prayers written in the Babine / Witsuwit'en script devised by Father Morice; the book as an endorsement of Christianity is important to Johnny David. He melded the best of both traditions: he was a healer in the Witsuwit'en tradition and a Christian. His endorsement of aspects of Christianity does not mean that there has always been effective communication about the meaning of various symbolic acts. A telling example of miscommunication is contained in Johnny David's redirect testimony in volume 8, where he relates an incident in 1901 involving Father Morice, a missionary who had arrived in the region in 1885, and the bishop, Augustin Dontenwill:

> In 1901, Father Morice and [the] bishop came from the east, and that is when the Wet'suwet'en quit potlatching because they were going to become Catholics. In the summer, in July, Father Morice and the bishop came to Moricetown. And at that time my father became church Chief. He was first known as Chief David. After he was baptized by the Catholic Church, he was given the name Chief Roosevelt. When he was baptized, I knelt beside him and the bishop baptized us all at once. And the bishop told me that the reason he had me kneeling beside my father is that I would speak after my father had died. And Father Morice was interpreting for the bishop and the bishop called all the Elders together and he had a document and he told all the Elders to come and sign with an 'X.'

Now, the Elders and the Hereditary Chiefs, as well as myself, all signed this document with an 'X.' And our people were not told why they were signing this document. And the priest covered the eyes of the Elders and Hereditary Chiefs while they were putting their 'X's' on the document.

After our people signed the document, the priest told them that they had become good people now and not to talk about anything. And shortly thereafter, about 1902, 1903, the white people began arriving in our territory. And there was at that time Mr Loring had begun working, and when our people would speak about their land they were put in jail, and it is these people who did that. (8: 399–400).

What had the bishop encouraged the chiefs to sign? Johnny relates the incident as a cautionary tale: signing an X to a paper when you do not know, or are kept from knowing, what you are signing is how rights are lost. It is worth noting, again, Johnny's assumption that Witsuwit'en rights could not have been extinguished without consultation and the consent of the chiefs, even if consent was given unknowingly, when blindfolded.

Father Morice's description of the 1901 event does not include the incident of signing a paper when blindfolded. However, his depiction reveals some ambivalence towards his condemnation of the potlatch and towards the burning of the potlatch regalia. He remarks that 'superficial observers' may see the potlatch as a 'legitimate and quite innocent organization.'

Yet Father Morice [the author] and his superior and model, Bishop Durieu, passed year after year thundering against it, and the latter preferred to lose the northern Coast Indians, Kwakiutl, Haidas and Tsimsians, who would not part with it, rather than admit into his Church what he picturesquely called 'washed (that is, baptized) pagans' ... There is at the base of the system, properly understood, a concept which borders on idolatry, since it attributes to animals regarded as patrons, or protectors, a consideration which is nothing if not superstitious. (Morice 1930: 115–16)

Superstition is a term often used to describe practices one does not understand. After decrying the practices of the medicine men or shamans, which the Witsuwit'en called *kaxluhxhkm* and he called sorcerers, Morice became deathly sick and was healed by a shaman. Morice described this episode in a letter to his superior. Morice briefly appreciated the wisdom of their practices, but instead of becoming a member of the healing society, like Johnny David, he soon reverted to his position of seeing such skills as of the Devil (Mills 1994a: 94–6). Morice describes the 1901 incident of which Johnny David spoke, thus:

> By this time (1901), the river Babines, that is those of Rocher Déboulé [Hagwilget / Tse Kya] and of Moricetown, were the only ones who, after sixteen years of insistence on the part of their spiritual guide, had not yet yielded to his pressing advice. Father Morice [the author of this statement] had even gone to the length of segregating at the place which came to take his name [Moricetown, the name he insisted on giving to Kya Wiget] those who were willing to do away with their old ways. He did so much that finally the others resolved to fall into line with them and become good Christians and full Catholics, not Indians with a mere varnish of civilization ...
>
> They had been told that the new Catholic Bishop, the Rt. Rev. Augustine Dontenwill, was soon to come north. To render their conversion all the more memorable and proportionately lasting, they had resolved to profit by his visit in order to give a visible expression to their change of heart ... When he reached Rocher Déboulé, Bishop Dontenwill and a young priest who accompanied him could, at the close of the retreat preached by the former, 'assist at a ceremony which had hitherto been without precedent. At a given signal, on a fine summer evening, each of the hereditary "nobles," members of secret societies and the medicine-men then present, issued from their respective abodes and brought on the lawn either a crown of grizzly bear claws, a cedar bark magic cinture, a painted wooden mask, a rattle of the same material carved to the arms of the owner, plus drums, ceremonial batons or gambling bones, in a word, all that which was thereby formally abolished. All these paraphernalia had soon formed a big heap on the public place: and in the midst of the deepest silence, a bonfire was made of them.' Quite a few readers may be unable to appreciate the drastic nature of the proceeding. Father Morice himself, with his archaeologist's and sociologist's tastes, confesses that he felt a pang at the sight of this miniature museum going up in smoke. He was acting, however, in his capacity as a missionary from whom the savant had disappeared. (Morice 1930: 116–19)

In a footnote Father Morice explains that this 'drastic measure' did not stop the potlatch, which 'would have remained abolished if the extreme imprudence and ignorance of the real import of these paraphernalia had not prompted Father Morice's successor (who never asked his advice on any point) not only to unwittingly restore that old pagan system at Rocher Déboulé, but even to introduce it in places where it had been forgotten for many years: a disaster from every standpoint' (ibid.: 118).

This resurrection of the potlatch happened after Father Morice left the Carrier in 1902 to convert the Nahanais to the north (ibid.: 119–20). Missionaries and colonizers and the settler society failed to appreciate that the Witsuwit'en, and other First Nations, could be good Christians without relinquishing their rights to their land or fish or spiritual traditions. Johnny David's description of the blindfolded signing of a paper highlights the distinction between free choice to become Christians and a forced agreement made without their consent. John Milne's questioning about Johnny David's being a Christian underscores the erroneous assumption that Johnny and his descendants had relinquished their culture and spiritual concerns by their conversion. Colonization in all its forms is resisted because it does not acknowledge that free will and liberty is a universal right. The sad legacy of colonial, imperial, and evolutionary thought is that it continues to be used to justify abrogating the right to free choice and treating others illegally, inhumanely, and without respect, in terms of rights to land, culture, and religion. Father Morice began a dialogue with the Witsuwit'en but reverted to unchristian practices that justify dominance rather right to free choice.

A Culturally Inappropriate Response: Johnny David and His Father's Territory

Important as Johnny David's testimony is, it is not without its problems for the Witsuwit'en. Two Witsuwit'en chiefs with whom I consulted were concerned that Johnny David, despite his understanding of the matrilineal Witsuwit'en system, was affected by colonization to the extent that in his commission evidence he maintained that he had rights to his father's territory beyond Witsuwit'en law. Johnny explained that, typically, a man has the right to hunt, trap, and fish on his father's territory until his father dies. In Johnny's case, his rights were extended with the permission of his father's brother, who took over the chief's name Smogelgem after Johnny David's father died. Yet, it goes against Witsuwit'en tradition for Johnny David to pass those rights on to his son, and his son's son, since they (like Johnny) are not members of Smogelgem's Laksamshu / Fireweed Clan. To reiterate this matrilineal principle, in Witsuwit'en law, one has permanent rights to one's mother's and mother's brother's territory, as that territory belongs to one's own House and Clan. Yet Johnny resisted letting go of the territory (in the form of the rights to the trapline) even after his son Samooh / Moses David predeceased him. Because Johnny was going against the laws of his people, this issue was raised in the feast hall. Why was he so tenacious when he knew it was not the Witsuwit'en way? Sometimes he gave reasons other than those in his commission evidence. Previously, he had mentioned paying the funeral expenses of his uncle as the reason he was allowed to remain caretaker of Smogelgem territory after the death of his paternal uncle, David McKenzie. In the commission evidence this was not mentioned. Was this because there are some things that can be said informally but not officially, a part of Witsuwit'en protocol? Did it have anything to do with his advanced age? Johnny David was old, but his mind was generally crystal clear. Perhaps he did not mention paying the funeral expenses because he knew that no matter how much he paid it did not result in a territory transfer from Smogelgem's Laksamshu (Fireweed) Clan to Johnny's Laksilyu (Small Frog) Clan.

Johnny gives several explanations, both explicitly and implicitly, for holding on to his father's land. His frustration is clear when he states:

> The trees that they have taken off our territory, the government has been receiving the money and they're putting it in their pockets – now we want the stumpage fees. We want the stumpage fees from all the traplines they have logged.
>
> Where do they get the money to be driving nice cars, to have a railroad system, or to be flying in the air? This is our money that they're using and I am walking on my feet.
>
> In the old days these people that trapped each territory, they protected the trees in the blocks so that the animals would flourish. Now the government has trapped all our territories and they have all the money and the way they treat us, they throw us little bits and pieces of things to eat. That's it. (3: 142–3)

This is eloquent expression of the injustice that Johnny and his people have experienced in the way their rights have been handled by the settler society and the government. It is clear that Johnny wanted to maintain indigenous control of his father's traditional territory. At the same time, the game warden awarded the right for sons to inherit their father's traplines: white authorities allowed Johnny to have trapline rights to his father's territory. This was preferable to having white settlers lay claim to Witsuwit'en territory.

Johnny also explains some of the intricacies that meant that his own traditional territory was looked after by Satsan / David Dennis, his maternal uncle's son. Johnny David's mother's brother was Dikyannualat / Old Dennis. Old Dennis held the rights to the Kilwoneetz territory. Johnny was his heir. In Johnny's case, his right to Kilwoneetz territory was doubly confirmed because his mother's brother was his father-in-law.[43] As Old Dennis became blind, Johnny and Old Dennis's son, David Dennis, together trapped his territory. Satsan / David Dennis was necessarily in his mother's Gilseehyu (Frog) Clan, but he had rights to trap his father's Kilwoneetz territory while his father was alive. Traditionally Johnny David, as Old Dennis's nephew and heir, would have had rights to the territory confirmed in the feast hall, and the territory would have been transferred to him on Old Dennis's death.[44]

Johnny identifies this maternal uncle, Old Dennis, as Chief Dikyannualat, describing the name as meaning 'a grizzly clawing away at a tree' (2: 103). Jenness (1943: 493) gives the meaning as 'Grizzly that Bites and Scratches Trees.' Johnny says that Old Dennis 'was a strong Christian' (2: 103). Jenness, on the basis of his 1924 fieldwork, confirms this and adds: 'The present holder of the title [Dikyannualat], since becoming a Christian, does not attend potlatches' (ibid.), thus revealing another way in which the two jagged world views collided. Old Dennis had been affected by the bishop's visit in 1901 described above. He had accepted that his being a Christian meant that he was not to conduct business in the feast hall.

The bishop's visit did not stop the rest of the Witsuwit'en from conducting potlatches after 1906. Yet, with Old Dennis not attending potlatches, he would not have stated in the feast hall that the Kilwoneetz territory belonged to the Ginehklaiya (the House of Many Eyes) and to Johnny David, his heir. Old Dennis's absence may have helped perpetuate Johnny's being caretaker of the territory of Smogelgem, Johnny's father. Because Old Dennis lived much longer than Smogelgem, Old Dennis's son, Satan / David Dennis was legitimately trapping his father's territory while Johnny David was, by Witsuwit'en standards, extending beyond his father's and his father's brother's lifetime, his rights to Smogelgem's territory. Johnny David had probably been registered on the Smogelgem trapline during his paternal uncle McKenzie's life; the anomaly in Witsuwit'en law is that these rights should have extended beyond McKenzie's lifetime. If Johnny's maternal uncle

Dikyannualat / Old Dennis, had chosen to play his traditional mentoring roles as maternal uncle in the feast hall, Johnny would have been clearly designated as the heir to his Kilwoneetz territory, and Old Dennis might have clarified that Johnny's rights to his father's territory could not be passed on to Johnny's son.[45]

Because of this confusion, when Johnny was asked who made decisions 'about who can use your territory for hunting, fishing, and trapping' (4: 158), he first identified himself with Smogelgem's territory, answering, 'When my father was alive he was the one that gave permission for other people to use the territory. Now that my father is gone it is me myself who would give other people permission to use the territory' (4: 158). He then was referred back to his own Kilwoneetz territory.

Although the feast and its procedures were influenced by the opposition of the Christian churches (for the Witsuwit'en, initially the Roman Catholic Church), it is important to note how completely the feast system continued. Johnny says, 'It was about 1906 when they began potlatching again, where they start giving each other food and materials' (8: 401). Other Witsuwit'en chiefs also document this, as does Jenness (1943). Similarly, the Gitxsan persisted in their potlatch ways, as their testimony and the recent publication of *Potlatch at Gitsegukla: William Beynon's 1945 Field Notebooks* (Anderson and Halpin 2000) attest. Despite the official outlawing of the potlatch and the opposition of the church, the system has persisted. Now that it is again legal under Canadian law, the question remains how non-Native governments and agencies will acknowledge this system of passing on rights to territory.

I think we need to see the discrepancy between the Witsuwit'en tradition and Johnny's wanting to hang on to his father's territory as an example of the kinds of problems created when two different cultural systems become interspliced. In the Western system, passing property rights from father to son is standard. As the caretaker for his paternal uncle, McKenzie, Johnny had permission to use his father's territory. During this time, the territory in the form of the trapline was apparently registered in their names. Johnny knew that the Witsuwit'en system did not allow him to keep his father's and his father's brother's territories, but the trapline registration, which the white authorities took (and take) seriously, gave him rights to use that territory after his father died. With all the difficulties the Witsuwit'en have had in maintaining rights to their lands and their traplines, Johnny became reluctant to give up or pass on to successive Smogelgems his registered trapline right to

Smogelgem's territory. He was having a hard time giving it up to its rightful owners, although he acknowledges very clearly that it was the territory of Smogelgem.

Several chiefs – namely, Wah Tah Keght in the Laksilyu (Small Frog) Clan and Namox in the Tsayu (Beaver) Clan – were concerned that future generations reading Johnny David's commission evidence would be confused by his position on his rights to the Smogelgem territory. Johnny does address the issue rather emphatically:

> MR DAVID: Leonard George wants to get this trapline and I am saying no. I want you to hear this. Right now, Peter David [Johnny's son's son] has got some papers with the game warden and he is looking after the trapline for me. If Leonard was talking about the trapline, tell him no, tell him to wait till all the business is done then we'll discuss it.
>
> MR MILNE: Why does Leonard George want that trapline, do you know?
> MR DAVID: Because he holds my dad's name and that is why he wants the trapline.
>
> MR MILNE: This is in the territory of Smogelgem?
> MR DAVID: Yes.
>
> MR MILNE: You are the caretaker of the territories of Smogelgem?
> MR DAVID: Yes, I'm looking after Smogelgem's territory as he asked me to do. I grew up on the territories as a young man. Now Peter David is looking after the trap line. (7: 336)

Wah Tah Keght and Namox were rightly concerned that this aberration from Witsuwit'en tradition not be used as an excuse to transmit territory or trapline rights through the father's side in the future.

I discussed this issue with Smogelgem / Leonard George, and he felt that it was not a problem if Johnny's statement were published as long as it was clear that his views did not reflect Witsuwit'en law. Moreover, by the time of our discussion, the issue of the rights to Johnny's father's land had been worked out. Peter David – Johnny David's grandson and Moses David's son – in whose name the trapline was registered, has signed the trapline over to one of the current Smogelgem's brothers. Thus the white man's trapline system has at last been brought into conformity with Witsuwit'en law.

There is another way to look at Johnny's stubbornness on this issue. After his father was dispossessed of some of his land, buildings, and worked fields, after his father's smokehouse was burned and his axes, and guns, and valuable furs were stolen, after he was not given the land at Tse Kya / Hagwilget that the Indian agent had promised, and after his fight to see that other white people did not lay successful claim to his area as *their* trapline, Johnny's tenacity can be seen as a struggle to support, not undermine, Witsuwit'en society. Ultimately, it is highly appropriate that Johnny David's grandson has corrected the trapline discrepancy and turned the rights back to a member of Smogelgem's house. This matrilineal principle is expressed over and over again in the rest of Johnny's testimony. In general, he is very clear that rights to territory pass through the mother's side. In essence, eagle down has been distributed over this issue of Smogelgem's territory.

How the Testimony Came to Be Presented as It Is

I conceived of the project to publish Johnny David's commission evidence before I had a copy of the transcript of his testimony. My memory of his commission evidence was dominated by the words of Johnny David. My memory was also affected by the experience of having read, in preparation for writing my 'expert' report, the transcriptions of the audiotapes made by Gisdaywa / Alfred Joseph of Johnny describing the boundaries of the territories and talking about his experience on the land. Thus when I first read the official transcript, I was dismayed to be reminded that Johnny's testimony was couched in the tedious question-and-answer format of legal proceedings. Peter Grant, one of the lawyers representing the Gitxsan and Witsuwit'en, would ask a question, and Johnny would reply. Later, John Milne, a lawyer representing the province of British Columbia, followed the same procedure for the cross-examination, and finally Grant asked additional questions in this format for the redirect examination. At first my response was to try to edit the evidence so as to minimize the court aspect and 'give voice to Johnny David.'

The original commission evidence looks like this:

Original: EXAMINATION IN CHIEF BY MR GRANT:

Q   You are Johnny David?
A   (In English) Mm – hmm.
Q   And you are a Wet'suwet'en?
A   Yes, I'm Wet'suwet'en.
Q   And you were born on March 8th, 1894?
    (Portion of question interpreted to Witness)

Q   1894?
A   Yes, that's when I was born.
Q   And your Indian name is Maxlaxlex?
A   (In English) Yeah.
Q   This is your feast name?
A   Yes, that's my feast name Maxlaxlex.
Q   And can you tell us what Maxlaxlex means in English?
A   This is – he doesn't understand.
Q   Okay. Can you explain the word Maxlaxlex in other words?
A   Okay. Name means a person jumping over – over something and it's
    a feast name and it's been used for many years.
Q   Are you a member of the House of – the House Gineeklaiya? G-I-N-E-
    E-K-L-A-I-Y-A for the record.
A   Yes.
Q   And is the High Chief in that House Gut-dum-ska-neese?
A   He answered yes, his House.
Q   Okay. Did you ask him the next question, did you get that
    Is the High Chief in that House Gut-dum-ska-neese?

The first time I attempted to change the transcripts from the original,
I transformed the question component into part of the answer and put
quotation marks around the transformed question and answer. The
above-quoted section then read:

> 'I am Johnny David. I'm Witsuwit'en. I was born March 8th, 1894. Max-
> laxlex is my feast name. The name Maxlaxlex means a person jumping
> over – over something and it's a feast name and it's been used for many
> years.'
> 'I am a member of the House of – the House Gineeklaiya, and the High
> Chief in that House is Gut-dum-ska-neese. He is the High Chief.'

The text is considerably shorter in this version, which I initially considered an asset.[46] I showed a sample of the transformed transcript to a
number of Witsuwit'en to see if they thought the transformation was
acceptable. Understanding that it was better to have a shorter manuscript than the original 347 pages, they said that they were satisfied.
My research assistant, Lisa Krebs, and I then began transforming the
commission evidence into this format. I was about to transform the
fifth volume when another research assistant, Travis Holyk, a graduate
student in First Nations studies at the University of Northern British

Columbia, pointed out to me that it is inaccurate to put quotation marks around the text because it is not exactly what Johnny David said. I was faced then with a question: do I just present the testimony as the court record stands, or do I use some other method?

I tried to change the transcript so that the original question was in italics and Johnny David's answer in roman type.[47] Transformed this way, the same opening of the commission reads as follows:

> *I am Johnny David,* Mm-hmm. Yes, I'm Witsuwit'en. Yes, that's when I was born, *March 8th, 1894.* Yeah, that is my feast name, *Maxlaxlex. The name Maxlaxlex means* a person jumping over – over something and it's a feast name and it's been used for many years.
>
> Yes, *I am a member of the House of – the House Gineeklaiya, and* yes, *the High Chief in that House is Gut-dum-ska-neese,* his House. Yes, he is the High Chief.

Again I consulted with Gisdaywa / Alfred Joseph, Smogelgem / Leonard George, and Gyologyet / Darlene Glaim to see what they thought best. Again they were amenable to the change. I then worked steadily on this transformation, seeking the help of Travis Holyk and Ellen Huse to complete the process. Again, Travis and Ellen pointed out that something was lost from the original: they noted that Johnny David's voice was not as clear as when it was just what he had said.

Around this time, Sheila Peters, author of the book *Canyon Creek, a Script* (1998) suggested to me that Johnny's statements be presented as blank verse. She has described in her book that Johnny David had known that she was going to visit him before she arrived: 'I dreamt about him before I went to visit him. I dreamt him wrapped up tight in blankets, right up to his chin, seated in a chair. The next day, awake, I drove to his niece's to find him sitting in the sun, cane in hand, hat shading his head ... His niece told me he'd insisted on clean clothes that morning because he'd dreamt someone was coming' (Peters 1998: 33).

As a poet, appreciative of blank verse as narrative, Peters provided me with the following example of some of the highlights of Johnny David's testimony:

Johnny David

Maxlaxlex
A person jumping over

over something

When someone is saddened
they perform their dances.
That is our Indian law.

The otter is a very dangerous animal
and people who laugh at it
will be affected the most.
And the otter may be considered
a devil.
I don't want to speak about that anymore.
All the other animals
in the forest our people have no problem
talking about.
Those animals
the otter
they don't like talking about
because it's so dangerous.

After 1907 we began
to lose everything.
Where do they get the money to be driving
nice cars, to have a railroad
system or to be flying
in the air?
This is our money that they are using
and I am walking on my feet.

There are many of us
in the feast hall
we sit in twos
and there are many of us
and I sit in the middle.
There are many of us.
We sit along the wall as well
as in front
and I don't know the exact
numbers. I don't know
the numbers.

And he said in Smogelgem's territory
there were cabins
they used for hunting
and trapping
and when those rotted
down or were burnt
down they would build
another one.

And when the white people
came that's when the cabins
started to be burnt
to the ground.
And then there was a big building
and that was again burnt
by white people.
You can see the outline
of it still
on the ground.

In the earlier days our people
would give salmon
to the white
people for no charge.
And once there became
law by Fisheries
this was all
outlawed.

You kill a few
and you don't
kill them all
and at certain times
of the year
you don't kill
the female
and at certain times
of the year
you don't kill
the male

so that they are able
to reproduce.

There is something very affecting about having Johnny David's voice presented in this way. Moreover, it reflects the growing recognition that First Nations speakers use inflection and rhythm in a very poetic form, and that their words are aften best read as blank verse. Thus, Julie Cruikshank presents some of the transcriptions of Angela Sidney, Kitty Smith, and Annie Ned as blank verse in *Life Lived Like a Story* (1990). She also discusses aspects of presentation in *The Social Life of Stories* (1998). Dell Hymes (1996) and others have noted both the value and difficulties of presenting indigenous voice in such a form. Translations across cultures and languages require intimate knowledge of the intricacies of linguistic forms.

However expressive it might have been to represent Johnny David's voice through blank verse, I could not imagine how it could convey the tenor of the legal struggle that his commission evidence represents. Moreover, in the two prose transformation processes I had tried, I had reached a complete impasse when it came to the cross-examination. One could attempt to transform the questions that were put to Johnny into his answers for the direct evidence led by Peter Grant. But the cross-examination was a totally different situation. The tension in exchanges between Johnny David and John Milne was palpable. Yet, if the text read as if it came from Johnny David, it was impossible to incorporate the questions put by Milne. The court within a home had vibrated with tension when Johnny David had said to John Milne, 'It is just like you, you don't care about Indian people' (7: 370). As in any court of law – and as in Witsuwit'en potlatches – strong words were uttered. Since it is important to hear those words in their exact context, I concluded that it was important to present the evidence as it was recorded.

With the able help of Travis Holyk and Ellen Huse, the commission evidence was edited only so that the court proceedings were slightly condensed. In the original, the speaker was identified, as 'MR GRANT' or 'JOHNNY DAVID' much of the time, or the question was marked with a 'Q' and the answer with an 'A'. For the purpose of making the text less lengthy, I decided to include the 'Q' and 'A' only at the beginning of each volume, and eliminate identification of the speaker unless it was necessary for clarity.

I also decided to put the question in roman type and Johnny David's response in italics, shortening the text by eliminating the space between the question and the answer. This format stays true to the original, makes the manuscript shorter, and has the advantage of setting off Johnny David's words – or the translation of what he actually said in Witsuwit'en – in italics. In the end, that seems particularly appropriate because italics are typically used for words in a foreign language.

This version emphasizes Johnny's words while preserving the court format. That format I had come to see as strategic, for it is the context that formed the questions and answers. What I had initially felt was distracting court procedure I began to see as an important exposition of that very court process. These were historic moments. Furthermore, I respect the integrity of both Peter Grant and John Milne. It is only fair that their words be clearly represented. This final version has the definite advantage of doing so.

Those same opening lines that were given above for the original court transcript look like this in the final version:

EXAMINATION IN CHIEF BY MR GRANT:

Q   You are Johnny David?
A   (In English) *Mm-hmm.*

Q   And you are a Wet'suwet'en?
A   *Yes, I'm Wet'suwet'en.*

Q   And you were born on March 8th, 1894? (Portion of question interpreted to Witness)
A   *1894? Yes, that's when I was born.*

Q   And your Indian name is Maxlaxlex?
A   (In English) *Yeah.*

This is your feast name?
Yes, that's my feast name, Maxlaxlex.

And can you tell us what Maxlaxlex means in English?
THE INTERPRETER: This is – he doesn't understand.

Okay. Can you explain the word Maxlaxlex in other words?
Okay. *Name means a person jumping over – over something and it's a feast name and it's been used for many years.*

Are you a member of the House of – the House Gineeklaiya [House of Many Eyes]? For the record.
Yes.

And is the High Chief in that House Gut-dum-ska-neese?
THE INTERPRETER: He answered: *Yes, his House.*

This exchange, while much longer than either of the versions I had tried, was still shorter than the original. Most significantly, it preserves exactly what all the parties said, be they the lawyers, the interpreter, or Johnny David. I am satisfied with this version, and so are the Witsuwit'en. As an additional tool, the notes to Johnny David's commission evidence contain explanations of how the text has been edited to make it clearer. They also provide additional information from other sources about the events in question.

Changes to the Text
In addition to the pattern of presentation laid out above, I have made several types of changes to the text. First, I have corrected some typographical errors. Second, I have placed some of the formal proceedings in the notes. Because I have transformed the transcript somewhat, I have taken out the certification that the foregoing is a true and accurate transcript of the court reporter. Third, with the consent of the translator, I have made a few changes to the presentation of the translation. Sometimes Misalos / Victor Jim would switch from the usual translation procedure of simply stating in English what Johnny had said in Witsuwit'en, and instead would begin by saying, 'He said ...' In these instances I have sometimes edited the text so it is presented as Johnny David's words. Again, I have included these changes in the notes.[48] I did not change all of these third-person shifts back to the first person because it seemed that leaving in some of these interjections by the interpreter better represented the flavour of the translation process that was integral to Johnny David's commission evidence.

There were a few other puzzles to deal with: the interpreter, Victor Jim, would sometimes say 'Okay' at the beginning of his translation, after having listened with great concentration to the question, translated it into Witsuwit'en for Johnny, listened to Johnny's response, and translated it into English. Peter Grant also would often say 'Okay,' marking the steps in this translation process, and Victor Jim's 'Okay' often paralleled Peter Grant's usage. In an earlier version, I took out most of these 'Okays' because this was what the translator said rather than what Johnny David said. However, after reflection, it seemed best to leave them in, without italics, because they mark the drama of the exchange in which Victor Jim would link the translation of the answer

Johnny gave in Witsuwit'en to Peter Grant's question by beginning with a reverberation of Peter Grant's 'Okay.'[49]

It seemed useful to clarify the transcript on some other matters that had nothing to do with the court reporter or the translator. For example, at one point a question arose about whether Johnny was referring to the person who was sitting on his left or on his right side (because he said right but pointed left). In the interest of presenting the material as clearly as possible, I have taken the liberty of eliminating such unnecessary confusions. As always, such changes have been described in the notes.

Johnny David's testimony includes fourteen exhibits that are in the public domain and hence available. Unfortunately, eight exhibits are not currently accessible: they are under lock and key in the Vancouver courthouse in a collection of the copious exhibits submitted in the *Delgamuukw* case. The evidence that follows indicates where the exhibits were placed; if the exhibit is unavailable, that is noted.

Finally, I should note two other relatively minor stylistic matters. First, at the suggestion of the copy editor, I have inserted additional punctuation to help clarify the meaning of the questions and responses. Second, the three court reporters were not consistent about capitalization of words such as *House, Head Chiefs, commission,* and *counsel.* These terms have been made consistent throughout the eight volumes. I have followed the Witsuwit'en and the *Canadian Journal of Native Studies* guidelines of capitalizing *Head Chief, House, Clan,* and *Elder.* Such minor changes are not recorded in the notes.

Note further that as a consequence of presenting Johnny David's words in italics, I have not used italics for Witsuwit'en, Gitxsan, or other foreign words when used by the lawyers. The meanings of such words and the multiple spellings that occur in the transcripts are in italics in the glossary.

THE COMMISSION EVIDENCE OF WITSUWIT'EN CHIEF MAXLAXLEX / JOHNNY DAVID

VOLUME 1

**Direct Examination of Johnny David by Peter Grant,
20 September 1985**

PROCEEDINGS COMMENCED AT 10:05 A.M. 20 SEPTEMBER 1985 [in the home
of Johnny David].

VICTOR WILLIAM JIM, Wet'suwet'en interpreter, sworn.
JOHN DAVID, witness called on behalf of the plaintiffs, sworn, testifies
as follows:

MR GRANT: For the record this is the commission evidence of Johnny
David or Maxlaxlex, and the interpreter at this is Victor Jim, who has
just been sworn to translate from English to Wet'suwet'en, and Johnny
David is present. John Milne is present representing Mr Goldie, who is
acting for the province of British Columbia. Stuart Rush is present as
well as myself, Peter Grant, acting on behalf of the plaintiffs. The
person assisting with Wet'suwet'en names and their spelling is
Antonia Mills. [Also present are Linda Malinowski, the court reporter,
and Michael McDonald, who is making a video recording of the proceedings.]

EXAMINATION IN CHIEF BY MR GRANT

Q   You are Johnny David?
A   (In English) *Mm-hmm.*

Q   And you are a Wet'suwet'en?
A   *Yes, I'm Wet'suwet'en.*

Q   And you were born on March 8th, 1894? (Portion of question interpreted to Witness)
A   *1894? Yes, that's when I was born.*

Q   And your Indian name is Maxlaxlex?
A   (In English) *Yeah.*

This is your feast name?
Yes, that's my feast name, Maxlaxlex.

And can you tell us what Maxlaxlex means in English?
THE INTERPRETER: This is – he doesn't understand.

Okay. Can you explain the word Maxlaxlex in other words?
Okay. *Name means a person jumping over – over something and it's a feast name and it's been used for many years.*

Are you a member of the House of – the House Gineeklaiya [House of Many Eyes]? For the record.
Yes.

And is the High Chief in that House Gut-dum-ska-neese?
THE INTERPRETER: He answered: *Yes, his House.*

Okay. Did you ask him the next question; did you get that 'Is the High Chief in that House Gut-dum-ska-neese?'
Yes. He is the Head Chief.

What does the name Gineeklaiya mean?
Okay. *You see the pole out there, it's got eyes on the pole and on the houses used to be a lot of eyes. And from that it got its name, House of Many Eyes.*

He was indicating a pole outside. This is a pole that is across the street from your house and is erected, is that right?
Yes. (Further response by witness in Wet'suwet'en)

Okay. Where were you born?
(In English) *Here, right here.*

At Moricetown?
(In English) *Moricetown. Right here, the ground.*

Right on this place?
Here in Moricetown.

And you were baptized in Hagwilgate, is that right?
(In English) *Yeah.*

In 1896?
(In English) *Father Morice. [I] was baptized in Hagwilgate by Father Morice.*

Was your mother Suwitsbain?
(In English) *Suwitsbain, yeah.*

And which House was she in?
She came from the House of Many Eyes [Ginehklaiya].

And was your father Chief Smogelgem?
(In English) *Mm-hmm.*

You should answer that?
Yes, Smogelgem.

MR GRANT: Can we just go off the record a moment.

(OFF THE RECORD DISCUSSION)

MR GRANT: Back on the record.

THE INTERPRETER: He was just talking about that book he showed us earlier this morning.[1]

MR GRANT: Okay. For the record the mother's name is spelled S-U-W-I-T–S-B-A-I-N. The father's name is spelled S-M-O-G-E-L-G-E-M. What House was your father from?
Owl House [Midziya].

And what tribe was your mother from or Clan?
She came from Laksilyu [Small Frog] Clan.

And your father, what Clan was he from?
He was Laksamshu [Fireweed Clan].

Who was – do you know the name of your mother's mother?
Her name was Joenassbain.

Is – I'll ask you this. You don't have to ask him, does *bain* mean something translated from Wet'suwet'en?
THE INTERPRETER: Mother.

So she was Joe Nass' mother?
Yes.

Okay. What Clan are you in?
I'm from Laksilyu.

Do you get that Clan from – do you go into the same Clan as your mother or as your father?
I follow my mother and not my father.

Is this the same with all the Wet'suwet'en?
Yes, they are. They go according to their Clan.

Did your mother die when you were born?
She died about 1936.

And where did you grow up?
North Bulkley.

And can you describe where North Bulkley is?
North Bulkley is just above Houston. (Further response by witness to interpreter) *Where we were when we did the filming, where McInnis used to live.*

Is that near Perow?
This side of Perow.

Okay. Whose territory was the North Bulkley?
That was my father's territory, all that area behind.

Okay. Did you – is there a Wet'suwet'en name for that territory?
Goes we bay winee is the name for the whole territory.

Now, when did you move to your father's territory, how old were you then?
He said: *I was raised there, where – that's where I did my trapping.*

Did you first go there when you were a very young child?
Yes, I moved there when I was a child. I stayed there most of the time.

I would like to ask you some questions about your House. (Interpreter speaks to witness) Are you the Head Chief or one of the leading Chiefs in the House of Gineeklaiya?
Yes, I am today. Before it was Gut-dum-ska-neese and now Sylvester William and I are.

Who holds the name Gut-dum-ska-neese today?
Willy Sims. Willy Sims from Hagwilgate.

And what name does Sylvester Williams hold today?
He is now Hag Wil Negh.

MR GRANT: For the record that's paragraph forty-six of the Statement of Claim, the Amended Statement of Claim.[2]

Was there a big House of Gineeklaiya in Moricetown or Hagwilgate?
There was a big building for the House of Many Eyes but it's no longer standing.

Where was that building?
In Hagwilgate, uh, where Sylvester George presently lives, near that area.

Was it on top of the cliff in Hagwilgate or down at the bottom of the cliff in Hagwilgate?
Before it used to be down in the bottom and later on it was moved up to the top.

Okay. Did he — was this house standing when he was a young man?
Yes, I've seen it all.

When did you get the name Maxlaxlex?
I forgot the date but I got the name when Old Sam died.

How were you related to Old Sam?
My uncle, my mother's brother.

Okay. Who held the name Maxlaxlex before you?
Okay. Old Sam held the name before and before Old Sam it was his uncle and I have the name presently.

It was Old Sam's uncle before him is that what he – you said it was his uncle. When you refer to his is that Old Sam or –
Old Sam before and then before Old Sam was Old Sam's uncle.

Okay, thank you. Do you remember how old Old Sam was when he died?
About eighty, ninety, or ninety-five. He said: *He was pretty old when he died.*

Who decided that you would take the name Maxlaxlex?
Okay. I got the name when Old Sam died and they had arranged for me to take the name years before he died.

Is it normal for a Wet'suwet'en Chief to pass the name to his sister's children? Is that – is that what – is that always done with the Wit – is that usually done with the Wet'suwet'en? (Interpreter to witness, no

response from witness) That the Chief will pass the name to his sister's children?
Yes, that's the way it's done. And I will be giving my name to Pat Namox. That's the way it has been happening for many years.

Do you remember how old you were when Old Sam died?
I was about fifty or sixty when Old Sam died.

Did you have a child's name that you were given when you were born?
Yes, when I was born I was given the name Yaybestee.

And who gave you that name?
It was given to me by a woman whose son had Yaybestee before.

Had the person who held Yaybestee's name died before you got it?
Yes. He died many years before that.

And were you just a baby when you got that name?
I got that name when I was born.[3]

You said that Old Sam held Maxlaxlex before you, and his uncle before him. Do you know when Old Sam got the name Maxlaxlex?
I don't know. Old Sam was put in place by his uncle, Old Sam's uncle or Maxlaxlex.

Was that before you were born?
Yes, way before.

Do you still hold the name Yaybestee?
Yes, I still hold the name. The person I gave it to does not live up to it and I want to give it to someone else.

Okay. Who is the person that you gave the name to before?
Okay. *I gave the name to Thomas Naziel. He does not live up to the name, and according to the old ways I could take the name back and give it to someone who lives up to the name.*

Okay. I understand your concern. Just so that we understand though, how is Thomas Naziel related to you?
Okay. *He's not really related to me. And I still want to give the name to someone else because he does not live up to the name.*

Will you give the name to a person in the House of Gineeklaiya?
Yes, and it will go to one of my relatives.

Is the man who held the name Yaybestee before you, was he in Gineek-laiya?
Yes. From the old days he was from the House of Many Eyes.

Besides Yaybestee and Maxlaxlex, did you hold any other names?
No. (Further response by witness to interpreter) *I had Yaybestee until I got Maxlaxlex.*

Did you hold the name Dikyannualat?
I never had it.

Is that a name in the House of Gineeklaiya?
Yes, it's from there.

Who held that name?
Old Dennis held that name.

MR MILNE: Old who?
MR GRANT: Dennis.

What does that name mean?
Okay. *An animal that grabs, grabs a piece of wood and pulls it off. That's what that name means.*

Is it a particular animal?
Okay. *Grizzly bear.* (Further response by witness to interpreter) *That's the way the old law was. It's a high name and that's how the – that's how the business ran in the old days.*

You mentioned that you have decided who will take Maxlaxlex from you. Just to be clear, is that a Chief's name?
Yes. It is a High Chief name and I've already mentioned that it's going to Pat Namox and that he will use my words when he's speaking.

Have you announced at any feasts that this name will go to Pat Namox?
Yes, I have and I've done this quite a while ago.

Is Pat Namox related to the House of Gineeklaiya?
Yes, he's related to that House and when he gets my name he'll be back in the House of Many Eyes.[4]

Is he a – you said that you were Laksilyu. Is Pat Namox Laksilyu?
Yes, he is.

Did you have any sisters?
No, I had – (Further response by witness to interpreter) *I have no sister or brothers but today people in our Clan we consider brothers and sisters.* (Further response by witness to interpreter) Okay. *Topley Mathew Sam's wife Rose was my half-sister and Mabel Sam now holds Rose Sam's name.* (Further response by witness to interpreter) *Kela is the name that Mabel Sam now holds.*

Where's the territory of the people of Maxlaxlex?
Copper River, Kilwoneets, and the Telkwa River area.

Is – what is the Wet'suwet'en name for that territory?
Okay. *The name for the territory is Kilwoneets. That was where we went and it's in the Telkwa River area.*

And did people – did people from your House live up on the Kilwoneets territory?
Yes, they lived in the territory. They hunted the territory and when the hunting season was over they would come back to the village.

And the village you're referring to is Moricetown?
Yes. This village and some would go back to Hagwilgate.

Are those – the people from the Kilwoneets area known as the Kilwoneetsweten?
Yes, they are known as Kilwoneetsweten.

Was your mother a Kilwoneetsweten?
Yes, my mother was a Kilwoneets.

And he gave a number of other names?
THE INTERPRETER: He gave a bunch of other names; they were all people from Kilwoneets.

Can you say which those names are? Ask him if necessary to go through them slowly.
Old Sam. (Further response by witness to interpreter) *Old Dennis.* (Further response by witness to interpreter) *Joe Nass.* (Further response by witness to interpreter) *Thomas Holland.* (Further response by witness to interpreter) *Julia Holland.* (Further response by witness to interpreter) *Basil Holland.* (Further response by witness to interpreter) *David Holland.* (Further response by witness to interpreter)

   Okay. *Those are the names from the Kilwoneets area, and they are all dead and no one can just go and take their name, it's not right.*

Have their names been passed on to other people?
No. Nobody holds their names.

Are you the last of the Kilwoneetsweten people?
Yes, I am the only Kilwoneets left. Those people I named are all dead and what I am talking about today is very important. Things have been carrying on for many years and this is why it's important.

Did the people of Gineeklaiya who were Kilwoneetsweten have a house in the Kilwoneets territory?
Yes, they did. (Further response by witness to interpreter) *They all have land.*

Where was their house, where was it located?
In Hagwilgate.

Okay. Is it correct that everyone at the feast from one Clan sits together?
Yes, that is right. People from the same Clan all sit in the same area and when somebody dies people from the Clan all help with the cost.

Does this still happen today?
Yes, it's still happening today.

Do you sit with the Laksilyu Clan?
Yes, I do. When the young man shot himself it cost me money as well as members of my clan, the Laksilyu Clan.

Is this the person who shot himself recently and there was a funeral in the last few months?
Yes. (Further response by witness to interpreter) *That is how all the money works. People from our Clan all contribute towards the expenses. That is how things have been happening in the past.*

Who has the right to sit at the Wet'suwet'en feasts?
Okay. *When there's a feast the chairs are there and these people that have names are the ones that sit in them, in those chairs.*

Does Maxlaxlex have a place to sit at the feast?
Yes, he does. He sits in the middle.

And who sits on your right side, right to your right-hand?
Hag Wil Negh sits this way, on this side.

You're indicating the left-hand side, for the record.
THE INTERPRETER: I'm just trying to visualize the hall where they sit. He said: 'This side,' so that's the right side.

Oh, that's the right side. Hag Wil Negh sits on the right-hand side? Yes?
He sits on this side. (Further response by witness to interpreter) Okay. *He sits on the right side of me. I sit in the middle because I am one of the Head Chiefs.*

And does Mabel Sam or Kela sit near you?
Yes, she does. She always sits next to me. She has a very big name.

And does John Namox – just a second. Do you have, uh – we can go off the record for a moment.

(OFF THE RECORD DISCUSSION)

MR GRANT: Mabel Sam, who is Kela, sits right beside you?
(In English) *Mm-hmm.*

And if you were in the feast hall now, would she sit there or there?
This side, on my left.

He indicates on his left but he's pointing to his right-hand side. And does John Namox sit beside Mabel Sam?
Yes, he does. (Further response by witness to interpreter)

And that – I'm sorry, does he want to go on? Go ahead if he wants. Tell him – he started to say something more, so if he wants to say something more –
Okay. *Mabel Sam and John Namox and then Hag Wil Negh.* (Further response by witness to interpreter). *And then there is three more on –*
THE INTERPRETER: I'm getting confused with my directions here.

He's going down on the same side as Mabel Sam is what I'm asking.
Okay. *Three more are sitting, the opposite of Mabel Sam, the opposite side and they have their own High Chiefs and they – when they want to speak they talk amongst themselves and then they pick one Chief to speak for all of them.*

Okay. I'll – I'll – If you can tell him I'm going to go through them individually and he can tell me if it's correct or if it's wrong who does sit there, okay?
(Interpreter speaks to witness)

Is John Namox known as Wah Tah Kwets?
Yes.

Does Willy Sims sit beside John Namox?
Yes.

And is John Namox known as Wah Tah Kwets?
Yes.

MR GRANT: Paragraph forty-six of the Statement of Claim.

Does Madeline Alfred sit beside – I'm sorry no. Does Henry Alfred sit beside Sylvester William?
Yes.

And he is Wah Tah Keght?
Yes.

MR GRANT: That name is referred to in paragraph forty-seven of the Amended Statement of Claim. For the record I'm referring to the June 12th 1985 Amended Statement of Claim – it was filed on that date.

Does Madeline Alfred or Dsee'h sit beside Henry Alfred?
Yes, he does. She does.

And her Wet'suwet'en name is Dsee'h[5]?
Yes, her name is Dsee'h.

Does Basil Michell sit beside Madeline Alfred?
Yes, he does.

And his Wet'suwet'en name is H'Kahk? Oh, I'm his name is – Basil Michell's name is Hottamaneh'k, I made an error in my reference.
Huttakumay.

Is that correct, Huttakumay? Does George Holland sit beside Basil Michell?
Yes.

And is his Wet'suwet'en name H'Kahk, and I apologize for the pronunciation.
Yes, that is right.

MR GRANT: I think we'll take a five-minute break now.

(PROCEEDINGS ADJOURNED AT 11:08 A.M.)

(PROCEEDINGS RECONVENED AT 11:25 A.M.)

EXAMINATION IN CHIEF BY MR GRANT CONTINUING:

I was asking you before the break of the names of the people that sat on your right-hand side and I had got as far as George Holland. Does Mary Mitchell sit beside George Holland?
Yes.

And does Christine William sit beside Mary Mitchell?
Yes, that's right.

And does Mary-Ann Austin sit beside Christine William?
Yes, that's right.

And does Esther Holland sit beside Mary-Ann Austin?
Yes.

And does Charlie Austin sit beside Ester Holland?
Yes.

Are all these people we've just described Laksilyu?
Yes, they're all Laksilyu.

We have described who sits on one side of you. Now Johnny I would like to ask you about the people on the other side of you.
Yeah.

Does Frank Patrick sit right beside you on your left side?
Yes. He sits next to me.

And is he from the Babine?
Yes, he is from Babine. (Further response by witness to interpreter) *He is our relation.*

Does he hold the name Wah Tah Kwets in the Babine?
Yes, he is called Babine Wah Tah Kwets.

Does Stanley Nikal Senior sit beside Frank Patrick?
Yes, that is right.

And is his name Knhuux Noo?
Yes, that's right. His name is Knhuux Noo.

Does Nora Van Tunen sit beside Stanley Nikal Senior?
Yes, that's right.

And is her Wet'suwet'en name Skokumlesas?
Yes, that's right.

Does Agnes Basil sit beside Nora Van Tunen?
Yes, that's right.

Do you recall her Wet'suwet'en name?
By God, I've forgotten her name.

Okay. Does Lucy Basil sit beside Agnes Basil?
Yes, that's right.

And is her name Goohheak?
Yes, her name is Goohheak.

Does Violet Gellenbeck sit beside Lucy Basil?
Yes.

Is her Indian name Tah Galain?
Yes.

Does Sarah Tait sit beside Violet Gellenbeck?
Yes.

Do you recall Sarah Tait's Wet'suwet'en name?
Weehalite is her Indian name.

What does that name mean?
Okay. That name means when an Indian doctor is blowing on a sick patient and he's giving his hand movements for the eagle feathers when blowing on the person.

Okay. Does Agnes Tait sit beside Sarah Tait?
Yes.

And does Lizette Naziel sit beside Agnes Tait?
Yes, that's right.

And is her, Lizette Naziel's, Indian name H'laughkhak – Sorry?
Yes.

In the olden days did the Chiefs have tables in front of them when they sat at the feast?
No, they ate on the ground.

And did certain people sit in front of the Chiefs?
Yes. People sat in front of the High Chiefs and when the High Chiefs die, the person sitting in front of him would move back to take on the High Chief's name. And that is the case with Pat Namox today.

Okay. Who did you sit in front of before you took your present name?
I sat in front of Old Sam. (Further response by witness to interpreter) *He was Maxlaxlex.*

Who sits in front of you today?
Okay. *Pat –* (Further response by witness to interpreter) *– Namox sits in front of me because he is going to be taking my name.*

You indicated that there are other Chiefs in the Gineeklaiya House and I would like you to tell me the meaning of their names. One of those Chiefs you mentioned was Gut-dum-ska-neese. Can you explain what that name means in English?
Okay. *Gut-dum-ska-neese refers to a mountain.*

Do you know where that mountain is?
Okay. *Gut-dum-ska-neese refers to all the mountains and Gut-dum-ska-neese refers to or means mountain man.*

Okay. Another name that you referred to was Wah Tah Kwets as a Chief. Can you tell us what that name means?
He says: *I want to tell you but the language is not too clean.* (Further response by witness to interpreter) Okay. *When – when a person or an animal takes a shit.* Okay. *Wah Tah Kwets means big shit.* (Further response by witness to interpreter) *And some of these names are from the Skeena River area.*

MR GRANT: Just for the record you can tell him that it is all right whatever the translation is because it's important that he can explain those translations.
Big shit. (Further response by witness to interpreter)

THE INTERPRETER: He was asking me: *[Are] they were going to hear that on tape?* And I told him yes. (Further response by witness to interpreter)
[THE WITNESS:] *And that's from the Skeena River language.*

Okay. When did you start sitting in front of Old Sam at the feast?
A long time ago when I was a small boy.

Could you tell us the reasons, that is, the types of feasts that the Wet'suwet'en hold?
Okay. *They have a feast when someone dies and when somebody is going to be taking on a name.*

Are those feasts sometimes combined?
This happens – (Further response by witness to interpreter) *about three times.* (Further response by witness to interpreter) *This used to happen three – you would have three feasts in the old days but now that does not happen, it is combined.*

Okay. Okay, can he describe what each of the three feasts was for in the old days?
Okay. *When someone dies a feast would be held and a song would be lifted up.* (Further response by witness to interpreter) Okay. *The person whose feast is being paid for and the person who is going to be taking the name is brought in front of everybody to witness.* (Further response by witness to interpreter) Okay. *This person who is going to take over the name, he goes out to his hunting territory and a date is set. When the date is set, he brings all the animals that he has killed and this is distributed at the feast.*

Okay, go on?
Okay. *After the name is given, another feast is held to pay for the expenses of fixing up the graveyard.*

Is this also known as a pole-raising or a headstone-raising feast?
Yes.

Okay, go on. He can explain some more.
Okay. *I have done that. The pole you see outside is considered a grave pole.*

This is – you are pointing outside the window, for the record. And outside the window is visible one pole and outside of your house there are two poles. Looking outside, looking from here, which of the poles is he – are you referring to?
The one on the left as you're looking out the window.

MR GRANT: For the record, I've arranged with the video person that we will all go outside after the lunch break and Johnny will be able to point to the crests on the pole and describe those crests.[6]

MR GRANT: You were describing that – the different types of feasts and you've described the naming feast and the pole-raising or the headstone-raising feast. Are there other feasts of the Wet'suwet'en?
That completes everything.

Is there a feast for the clearing away of shame?
Okay. *There were – in the old days a lot of money was spent on the shame*

feast or if someone took a name he wasn't supposed to – a feast was put up for that as well. And this has been happening for many years.

Was there a recent feast for someone to clear his shame?
Yes, there was. (Further response by witness to interpreter) *Yes, there was one just recently. Lawrence Michell had a feast at the hall and at the feast what he did was like wiping the blood off his face and this is how it was done from the old days.*

What is the Wet'suwet'en name for a shame clear – a feast called Clearing of Shame?
(Interpreter speaks to witness. No English response)

If you can just say the Wet'suwet'en name?
Ka nee yet li means shame.

What is Lawrence Michell's Wet'suwet'en name?
Wistace is his Indian name, means Big Hand.

What House is he in and what Clan?
Okay. *He is from the House of Many Eyes and he is from the Laksilyu Clan.*

Why did he put on this feast, what happened?
Okay. *He was hit in the face and his nose was bloody.*

By whom?
Okay. *The person that hit him was Pat Namox's son, the one that – the one that is handicapped.*

Who was invited to this feast?
Okay. He said: *People from the village were invited and I wasn't involved in it. And I think they used the radio to invite the people.* (Further response by witness to interpreter) Okay. *Lawrence had told all the people from the Laksilyu Clan that he was going to put up this feast and everyone was ready for it.*

Did you help with this feast?
Okay. *I did not go; I was still in bed.*

You were not feeling well at the time?
Yes, I was sick.

Did all of – did the Laksilyu Clan help Lawrence with this feast?
Yes. (Further response by witness to interpreter) *Yes, all the Laksilyu people were there and I was supposed to go there and speak but I was not feeling well.*

Were other Clans invited to the feast?
Yes, they were all invited.

Could you tell us the names of the other Clans? *All the other Clans were invited and when their names were called they would put in some money.*

Okay. We have – Johnny, we have not asked you today the names of the Clans other than the Clan you belong to, which is Laksilyu. I would just like to be – you said all of the other Clans were invited and I just would like for the court for you to tell us the names of those other Clans.
Okay. *All the Laksilyu people helped Lawrence Michell was, when he was bloodied up.*

Okay. Did this feast happen this summer?
Yes, about a month ago.

Did people from other villages also come to the feast?
Yes, there were some people from Old Hazelton.

And that is the Gitanmaax people?
THE INTERPRETER: Gitanmaax people.

Were there people from Hagwilgate?
Yes, there were people from Hagwilgate.

Were there people from Kispiox?
I don't know. (Further response by witness to interpreter) *I wasn't there, people were telling me about it.*

Does – do the other, the person who hit Lawrence, does he have to do anything now?
I don't know at this time but the person that hit Lawrence is getting ready to have his feast.

What Clan was he from?
He's from a different Clan. He's from the Gilserhyu [Frog] Clan.

And what is the crest name of that – name of that Clan, Gilserhyu? Is there another name? How does that Clan translate into English?
Okay. *Their crest is the frog.*

Was the person who hit Lawrence at his feast?
[I don't] know if he was there because [I] wasn't there.

Okay. According to Wet'suwet'en tradition, should he have been there?
Yes. In our tradition he should have been there and listened to what was said.

You started to tell us what some of the people did at the feast. Did Lawrence – did the people from Lawrence's father's side have any obligations at that feast?
His father's side did not do anything. It was just the people from Lawrence's Clan.

And that would be his mother's side?
Yes, mother's side.

MR GRANT: I'm going to adjourn for a few minutes because the video, you can tell him the video camera is out so we'll go off the record.

(PROCEEDINGS ADJOURNED AT 12 P.M.)

(PROCEEDINGS RECONVENED AT 1:42 P.M. OUTSIDE JOHNNY DAVID'S HOME IN FRONT NEAR POLES)

MR GRANT: For the record, we are outside of Johnny David's house. John Milne acting for the province is not taking an objection at this time to the explanation of the pole. However, he reserves the right to object to the admissibility of this evidence at the trial. Because of the unavailability of the other reporter or the other translator we were going to have Alfred Joseph translate. However if we go off the record for a moment, I note that the other interpreter is here and this will avoid the requirement for swearing in a new translator.

(OFF THE RECORD DISCUSSION)

MR GRANT: Going back on the record.

I'd like to ask you, Johnny, this is your house?
Yes, it is my house.

And is the pole to our right the pole you were describing before?
Yes, that was the pole I spoke about earlier this morning.

Is that the pole of Maxlaxlex?
Yes. That pole belongs to Maxlaxlex.

Can you describe from the top down the crests on that pole?
Okay. *The two figures on the top are otters.* (Further response by witness to interpreter) *And the one on the bottom is a dog.* (Further response by witness to interpreter)
THE INTERPRETER: And then he asked if he had mentioned the dog and I told him he did.
And then the bottom figure of the man is – (Further response by witness to interpreter) *Gut-dum-ska-neese. He's referred to as the Mountain Man.*

Is this the pole of Maxlaxlex?
(In English) *Yup.*

I notice that there is another pole in your – in front of your house.
Whose pole is this?
THE INTERPRETER: For the record, I told him just to think about it. (Witness responds further to interpreter)
Okay. *This pole belongs to Kela.*

And is that Mabel Sam?
And that's Mabel Sam.

And she's in the House of Gineeklaiya?
Yeah. That's the daughter of Mathew Sam and that's from the House of Gineeklaiya. Mrs Mathew Sam. Pardon me.[7]

Can I – can you explain the crests on that pole?
Okay. *These three figures on there depict the House of Many Eyes.*

Yes?
Okay. *And the figure on top of the human figures with the eyes is the dog crest.*

And you indicate that dog crest is the same as on your drum?
And the dog crest is the same as the one that's on the drum.

Okay, who is the figure on the top of Kela's pole?
Okay. *It's the same – it's the same figure as this one, they're all in one.*

Is that Gut-dum-ska-neese?
Yes, that's the same name.

Now, we can stand back a bit. I notice you're wearing a blanket. Is this
the blanket you wear at the feasts?
Yes, that's the blanket [I wear] at the feasts.

You've turned around and I notice that there is a crest on the blanket
that appears to be an animal. What is that animal on your blanket?
That's an otter – nilchick in Wet'suwet'en.

And that is the crest of Maxlaxlex?
Yes.

You told us that – you told us that you – at the feast is there a dance
performed by Maxlaxlex to show his name?
(Interpreter speaks to witness, no English response) I'm sorry, to show
his crest of the otter?
Yes, he does.

Can you perform that dance for us now and the song that goes with it? *Yes.* (Further response by witness to interpreter) Okay. *In the old days, that's what our ancestors did and this song goes with the name.* [Johnny David performs his dance and sings his and Kela's songs.]

And that is the name Maxlaxlex? *Yes, that's his name.* (Further response by witness to interpreter) Okay. *This tradition has carried on for many years and it's the same thing that people with other names do.*

You're wearing a headband as well. Is there a reason you wear that headband? Okay. *That's the way it's done.*

Okay, I notice, for the record, it's getting a little cold out here so we'll go inside the house to ask you the rest of the questions. THE INTERPRETER: He said: *Okay.*

MR GRANT: Thank you. Go off the record.

(PROCEEDINGS ADJOURNED OUTSIDE JOHN DAVID'S HOUSE AT 1:53 P.M.)

(PROCEEDINGS RECONVENED INSIDE JOHN DAVID'S HOME AT 2 P.M.)

MR GRANT: We've now come back into your house, Johnny, from being outside and I would like to thank you for performing that dance outside for us. (Interpreter speaks to witness, no English response)

I note, for the record, you mentioned before we went outside and after lunch that you were feeling tired and you may want to stop a bit early. Do you feel you can answer some more questions now or would you like us to stop now? Okay. *I can't speak too long. I'm feeling tired and I've finished everything I have to say.*

Okay. In that circumstance then I would like to adjourn this discovery [*sic*] and we will come back when you are feeling better, Johnny, to finish speaking with you about these matters. Okay. He said: *That's fine.* He said: *I'll do it when I'm feeling better.*

Thank you. And he said: *Let me know.* (Further response by witness to interpreter) Oh. *[I'll] tell [him] and [he'll] let you know.*

MR GRANT: Okay, we'll talk with Victor, who is interpreter here, and

arrange another time when the other lawyer and myself can be here to finish these questions. Thank you Johnny.
He said: *[I] will say yes when [I'm] feeling better.*

MR GRANT: Okay, thank you. We'll adjourn the discovery and go off the record, adjourn the commission and go off the record.

(PROCEEDINGS ADJOURNED)[8]

VOLUME 2

**Direct Examination of Johnny David by Peter Grant,
26–27 September 1985**

UPON RESUMING AT 9.00 A.M. 26 SEPTEMBER, 1985[1]

MR GRANT: On the record then. For the record, this is the continuation of the examination of Johnny David which adjourned one week ago on September 20th, and Johnny has been sworn in his own language, in Wet'suwet'en. The interpreter, Victor Jim, has also been sworn in his language to translate from Wet'suwet'en to English and into English from Wet'suwet'en. The other persons present are Mike McDonald, who is doing the video work; Veronica Harper, the court reporter; Antonia Mills, who is here to assist by writing out Wet'suwet'en words for the reporter; Don Ryan, who is here as one of the people assisting Mike McDonald; John Milne, who is here as counsel for the defendant; and myself, counsel for the plaintiffs.

EXAMINATION IN CHIEF BY MR GRANT (CONTINUED)

Q   Last week, just before we adjourned, you performed one of your dances and songs out in front of your totem pole; could you tell me when that song and dance are performed in Wet'suwet'en feasts?
A   *I sing my song and I dance to the song whenever there is potlatch. You can't tell when exactly potlatch is going to be.*

Q   The song that you performed last week, and the dance, what did they signify?
A   *The songs and dances happen whenever there's a feast and that's how we have been doing it.*

Q   Who owned that song and dance?
A   *It belongs to me and that's my dance. Further to what is saddened by an occasion, and the song and dance are performed to lift the spirits of the people. It is done by all the Clans.*

Q   Does each Chief have particular songs and dances which belong to them?
A   *Yes, the Hereditary Chiefs each have their own songs and dances, and when someone is saddened they perform their dances. This is our Indian law.*

Would you perform that dance only at the feast of Laksilyu [Small Frog Clan]?
Yes. It is only done at the Laksilyu feast and this is [the way of] all the Chiefs.

Would you only perform it at a funeral feast or would you also perform that dance at a pole-raising feast?
Songs and dances are performed when someone dies or when a pole is raised. The pole is like telling a story about our people.

You also showed us the poles in front of your house and I understand one is the pole of Maxlaxlex and the other the pole of Kela. You referred to the fact, I believe it was Gitdumskanees was on those two poles; why is his figure on the bottom of Maxlaxlex pole?
Because that is the law of our people. Figures [are] not put on there for any reason. Serves the purpose and Gitdumskanees is referred to as Mountain [Man].

Is Gitdumskanees on the pole of any other Chiefs in the Laksilyu Clan?
He is on the other poles of the Laksilyu but not the other Clans.

You also showed the otter and the dog crests on your pole; is the otter crest on the pole of any other Chiefs in the Laksilyu Clan?
The otter and the dog are only on the Laksilyu pole.

Are they –
THE INTERPRETER: And he said that: *[I] was boss of the Laksilyu.*
– Are they only on the pole of Maxlaxlex?
The figures are on my pole and I am the boss.

Does the otter crest relate to the territory of the Maxlaxlex?
The otter crest comes from our hunting territory, which we own.

Is this crest a very old crest or was it something that Maxlaxlex acquired recently?
The crest has been in existence for many years, many years before I came

along.[2] It's been in use for a lifetime. In Hagwilget, where Old Sam is buried, on his headstone you see the figure of the otter.

Did the otter crest exist before Old Sam in the earlier Maxlaxlex days?
Yes, they use the crest before Old Sam and people before him as well.

So the crest existed long before the white man came?
Yes, hundred years before the coming of the white man.[3] Okay. Old Sam used it. [I can] remember the age, between 80 and 90 and the uncle before Old Sam was about 90. Now I'm using it and that gives you an idea of how long it's been used.

Last week, you showed the otter crest on your blanket and it's hanging up on the wall there behind you. Is that the crest that's on the wall behind you, on your blanket, that is the otter crest?
Yes. Yes, it is the otter crest.

Is there a particular history with the otter crest that you know?
Yes there is. The people act out the movements of the otter and amongst our people the otter is considered a very dangerous animal.

That is, the otter is considered dangerous amongst your people?
The otter takes on the form of the human and again attaches itself to a male or female and once he does that, the people would lose their mind and just go anywhere.

Is there a history of this happening on any occasion a very long time ago?
The person whose name I took over, Old Sam, it happened to him, and it took our people a long time before they finally rescued him from the grasp of the otter.

Just for the Interpreter, he referred to some grabbing?
THE INTERPRETER: *Yes, they had to tie him down.*

Tie who down?
THE INTERPRETER: *Tie Old Sam down so he wouldn't injure himself.*

You know the otter dance and you have performed it at the feasts?
Yes. Doesn't matter when we perform the dance. The otter is a very dangerous animal and people who laugh at it will be affected the most. And the otter may be considered a devil. I don't want to speak about that any more.[4] All the other animals in the forest our people have no problem talking about. Those animals, the otter, we don't like talking about it because it's so dangerous.

Does anybody hold the crest of a caribou?
Peter Alfred's wife [Madeline Alfred, Chief Dzee'h] has the caribou crest.

Is she a Laksilyu?
Yes. There is a pole that is in Hagwilget on the way to the graveyard.[5] You see a figure on top and that is the figure of the caribou.

Whose pole is that?
Madeline's uncle's pole.[6]

What was Madeline's uncle's Indian name? Feast name?
Madeline's name is now Dzee'h, her feast name. And her children's blankets all have the caribou crest on their blankets.[7] And it's similar to this blanket but with the caribou crest on the back.

You're indicating your own blanket, for the record? That's on the wall? ... Just for the record, the blanket on the wall, that is the same blanket as you were dancing with last week? Is that right?
Yes.

What was the feast name of Madeline Alfred's uncle who owns the pole at Hagwilget?
I didn't mean the totem pole, I meant the gravestone of Madeline's uncle in Hagwilget. Which had the caribou crest. It is on the way to the graveyard at Hagwilget.

I asked what his name was?
That was Madeline's uncle's name and that is the name that Madeline now holds. Dzee'h.

Does anyone hold a crest of the skunk?
That is the crest of Peter Alfred.

What Clan is he in?
He is Gitdumden [Wolf Clan] and at the hall you will see the plaques of all the crests of our people.
THE INTERPRETER: He asked me: *If you have time, to open the hall to show you the crests of our people that are on the wall at the community hall.* He is describing all the crests that are on the walls and some haven't been done properly but you can recognise the crests.

Did he just go through the list of the crests around the walls now? Did he just tell you which they were? I am asking you whether he did that or not?
THE INTERPRETER: Yes, he did.

Because I would like you to translate what he said then and that is, if you have to ask him to do it more slowly.
Where we sit, above us you could see the otter crest and to the left of that crest you see the frog crest. Then on the two walls are the ones that belong to the Beaver [Tsayu] and Fireweed [Laksamshu] Clan on this wall.

The first wall you referred to is one of the long walls along the side?
THE INTERPRETER: Along this side.

[MR GRANT:] And the second wall, where there was the two crests is the end wall?
If you go [to] the hall I'll show you.

Okay.
Then you can put it right. Bring the video camera in and film the crests.

Then he can describe them when we're in the hall?
THE INTERPRETER: Yes.

[MR GRANT:] Can we go off the record for a moment?

OFF THE RECORD DISCUSSION

We can go back on the record. You don't mind if I lead a little, just to get into the area?
MR MILNE: Not at all. Not at all.

MR GRANT: Last time you told us that Jimmy Michel announced your name at the feast when you got the name Maxlaxlex; did Jimmy Michel get a name at that feast as well? If so, what was the name he got?
Yes, he got the name Samaxsam.

Do you know the history of the name Samaxsam and how it came to the Wet'suwet'en people?
Yes, it came from the Nass River.

Could you tell us that history and what happened?
THE INTERPRETER: *I don't know if I can remember all that he said.*[8]

You should stop him as he goes along. Tell him it will take time to interpret.
The name came from the Nass River. It is given to Old Tiljoe's uncle, and after a period of ten years that name was given to Old Sam, and that was when I received the name Maxlaxlex.

You want to ask him the same question again? Are you finished?
THE INTERPRETER: Yes.

The first Wet'suwet'en to get the name Samaxsam, was that before Old Tiljoe?
It was during the time when Old Tiljoe was alive. Old Tiljoe and Jimmy Michel went to Kitsegukla.

Who gave the name Samaxsam to them?
There is a Chief from Nass River who is in Kitsegukla when Old Tiljoe and Jimmy Michel went to Kitsegukla and that was when the name was given to them.

Had there been a dispute or killing of a Wet'suwet'en by someone from the Nass?
Old Tiljoe's brother was killed in the Nass and Old Tiljoe went to avenge the death of his brother. This was when he was given the name. Jimmy Michel ran through the village on a pair of snowshoes and Samaxsam was notified that Jimmy Michel was in town to avenge his death – to avenge Old Tiljoe's brother's death. When Samaxsam found out that Old Tiljoe and Jimmy Michel were in town [they] called a feast, and Old Tiljoe and Jimmy Michel were also invited, where a song and a head-dress were given to Old Tiljoe. The head-dress was painted red, red cedar bark. The song he sung is Samaxsam that was given to Old Tiljoe along with the name. [Johnny David, Chief Maxlaxlex, sings the song that was given.]
THE INTERPRETER: And he acted out the part where he is using the spear.

Who would use the spear?
THE INTERPRETER: The dancer.

That is the song that Johnny just sang that you're referring to?
THE INTERPRETER: Yes.

Is that sung in Wet'suwet'en?
That song that I just sung, it is sung in the language of the Nass River peo-ple.[9] And I don't know the translation of it.

It doesn't have Wet'suwet'en words?
THE INTERPRETER: No.

I would like to move back. You said that the name was given because Old Tiljoe's brother was killed; who killed him and why?
Halfway between Kitwancool and the Nass River there was a grave marker of the Old Samaxsam, [who was a Nisga'a Chief. The grave marker] was the size of this table, and on this big log was a big stone and that was knocked over. When the two people had come to this grave marker, they were playing around

on it and it tipped over and Samaxsam avenged this by killing one of the We'suwet'en and it wasn't Old Tiljoe's brother that knocked this rock over, but somebody else. There was [a Nisga'a Chief who was] Samaxsam's uncle whose grave was marked with this big tree and this rock.

You said there were two Wet'suwet'en. Was one of those Wet'suwet'en that was around the marker Old Tiljoe's brother?
It was not Old Tiljoe's brother who knocked the rock over, it was people from –
THE INTERPRETER: – Pointing in that direction –
– the people from there they have gone back and Old Tiljoe's brother was coming through that area and he was the last person going through and he was killed.

Can you describe this marker? Was it a rock on top of a log or was it a rock with some wooden markers in it?
It was big rock similar to what you see in the graveyards today.

Did it have wooden markers in it?
I don't know. It is over a hundred years ago.[10]

You said that some people from 'over there' knocked this rock over. Were they from the Babine?
These people from this area and my father has seen the rock and that was how he described it to me. My father had seen the rock when he was a young man. He had told me, that is what I am telling you now.[11]

Do you know if this marker was also a marker of the border of the Nishga territory?
I don't know whether that was the boundary marker but I knew it was a marker for a grave.
THE INTERPRETER: *And [I] would like somebody to find the location where that stone is and [I] would like to see it as well.*

Was Old Tiljoe alive when you were young?
Yes, and they had brought his body back to Joe Nass' house over here.

They brought Old Tiljoe's body back?
THE INTERPRETER: Yes.
And when Old Tiljoe was buried I spoke at the feast, as well as Jimmy Michel.

Is that when Jimmy Michel took the name of Samaxsam?
Yes. That was the same time he got the name of Samaxsam.

Was the song of Samaxsam that you just sang, was it sung at that feast?

Yes. Everybody witnessed. And the regalia that he used was also shown at the feast but I don't know where they are now.
THE INTERPRETER: He said that he is getting tired.

Can we go off the record for a moment please?

OFF THE RECORD DISCUSSION

You have told us that your father was Smogelgem or Chief David, is that right?
Yes.

And Smogelgem held territory on the North Bulkley, is that correct?
Yes, he did own territory where we had been in North Bulkley where I was brought up as a child.

You have indicated that you moved there from Moricetown soon after you were born and you were raised there?
Yes, I was born there and then later on we moved to North Bulkley.

Just so we understand, the land that we are talking about, can you describe it in relation to Houston or Perow or Topley, which are three towns in the area now?
The area we are talking about is where we have been –
THE INTERPRETER: He is talking about us and Don, Tonia, and I asked him further how far from Houston and he said: *It's about 11 miles east of Houston, the area we are talking about.*

How big an area is Smogelgem's territory there?
It's a big territory but it's just a small area that – cleared an area that my father, Smogelgem, lost.

At some time when you're rested we'll talk about the big area but I would just like to ask you now about this small area. Was this on – did he say how far it was from Houston?
THE INTERPRETER: He said: *It was 11 miles from Houston.*

Is that on the other side of Houston?
THE INTERPRETER: East.

Can you tell me what your father did on that land?
He did a lot of trapping. He did some haying and I personally know where all his traps were.

Now, did you grow up on the area where he was haying?

Yes. I was brought up in the area where he did his haying and I know all the areas where he did his trapping.

Did he have a house or farm there?
In the area of North Bulkley my father had a big smokehouse and when he died the white people burnt it down and they kicked me off the land.

Can you tell us how old you were when that happened approximately?
My dad died and [he] must have been around 30 or 40, and I got a letter from Mr Loring, who was the Indian agent at Hagwilget. I received a letter from him telling me to get off the land and he was going to give me some acreage in Hagwilget, which he never did.

Do you still have that letter?
No I don't have it any more. The area around the present ballpark in Hagwilget, he had promised me 160 acres and I helped survey that land. I asked Mr Loring if he was going to give me that 160 acres in Hagwilget and he said to wait a while. He said the land commissioner from Ottawa was coming and that they would give you the 160 acres in Hagwilget. I was never given the land. The land commissioners never came and Mr Loring lied to me. About two years later Round Lake Tommy was given a letter from Mr Loring where he was kicked off his land and Round Lake Tommy was given some property just next to the community hall.

In Moricetown?
THE INTERPRETER: He's pointing to the area down here which is the area near the community hall.

[MR GRANT:] For the record, that's in Moricetown.
Round Lake Tommy, he was a very good man, worked hard, and when he was kicked off his land some of the non-Indian people took Round Lake Tommy to an area east of Houston, where he was given a small portion of land. The non-Indian people were angry at Mr Loring for treating Round Lake Tommy in a deceiving manner.

Where was Round Lake Tommy's land that he was thrown off?
Round Lake area where the present community hall is situated is where Round Lake Tommy had his home.

Which community hall?
THE INTERPRETER: *Round Lake community hall.*

Okay.

Round Lake Tommy's father died in Round Lake and he is buried not too far away from the area I just described.

Yes? What happened? Go ahead.
He even – Round Lake Tommy's father was buried on his land. Mr Loring still kicked him off his land similar to the way he kicked me off my land.

Did you ever go back to your father's land to see what had happened?
Yes, I have been back to the – to North Bulkley, I was there with you guys –
THE INTERPRETER: He's referring to Don and myself, the film crew and Tonia –
– I have talked about it for many years; there seems to be nothing I can do.

When did you first go back there after you got the letter from Mr Loring?
I went back immediately because I was doing my trapping in that area.

What had happened when you first went back there?
They never talked to me or anything about the territory. They knew I was trapping on the territory. It was only the cleared farmland that was taken from my father.

When you went back there to trap, was there somebody living on that cleared farmland?
When I went back Mr McGuinness was living on the property that my dad had cleared.

How many years was that after you had left? After you had moved off it with Mr Loring?
THE INTERPRETER: He said: *It was a long time.*

You said a few minutes ago that you were getting tired, about 15 minutes ago. Would you like to stop now and rest?
THE INTERPRETER: Yes, he said: *[I'm] getting tired and would like to rest.*

Go off the record.

THE INTERPRETER: He said: *[I have] told you everything that [I] know.*

Go off the record now.

OFF THE RECORD DISCUSSION[12]

UPON RESUMING AT 9.00 A.M., 27 SEPTEMBER, 1985

MR GRANT: This is the continuation of the examination of commission evidence of Johnny David which was adjourned yesterday, September 26th, because Johnny was getting tired. The same persons are present as were present yesterday. I asked you about the feast in which you obtained your name and I would like to know under Wet'suwet'en laws does anyone call out your name when you received it and, if so, how are they related to you?

When I got my name all the Hereditary Chiefs from the other Clans would call my name.

They did call his name?

They did call my name.[13] They would go right around the feast hall.

Is there a Wet'suwet'en tradition called Niggiyotsi which relates to your father's Clan?

There is a system in Wet'suwet'en which is called Niggiyotsi and it is where all the High Chiefs are called around the hall. They mention your name and say something about your crest. It is only the High Chiefs that are called to do this. When the High Chiefs holler out the names they are given some money for witnessing it, and it's like signing your name on a piece of document.

Are they also given food and other gifts at the feast?

The ones that holler out the names are given money and for all the other people in the feast hall food is distributed to them.

Do you know how much money was given out when you received your name Maxlaxlex?

THE INTERPRETER: He said: *Money is spent when you receive a name.* And then I asked him if he spent a lot of money and he answered: *[I] did. Couldn't remember the amount.* He said: *If somebody there named me then he would receive some money.*

When these Chiefs call out your name do they relate it to their name and refer to your crest?

They mention [my] name and then something to do with his crest. They are paid what amount is decided by the people.

I'm sorry, they're?

THE INTERPRETER: They are paid the amount that is agreeable to the people who came there.

Are they paid a different amount depending how high a Chief they are?

The Chiefs with the bigger names are given more money than the ones with the smaller names.

Were the only two names given out at your feast, Maxlaxlex and Samaxsam?
Yes, just the two names.

Did they talk about your territory at the time of your feast?
THE INTERPRETER: *When [I] got [my] name, along with the name went the territory.*

Was that announced at the feast?
THE INTERPRETER: *When [I] got [my] name [I] was given the area around Copper River. And the whole hunting territory is shared by the Clan except for the fact that the Head Chief is the one that decides who goes on there.*

Is he the one who decides who goes on the territory?
Whoever is the head of the hunting territory can decide who hunts and traps in that territory, and if other people want to go there they would have to come and see him, the Head Chief, to get the okay to hunt there.

When you say 'him,' you are referring to Johnny?
THE INTERPRETER: Referring to Johnny. He also talks about the area he had at North Bulkley and his father's trapping land in the North Bulkley area.

Who provides the money at the feast to give out to the Chiefs?
The people from the Clan all put in money and a certain amount is set aside for witnessing of the name and that is the money that is distributed to the High Chiefs.

When you're referring to people you're referring to the Laksilyu?
Yes, Laksilyu, we all help one another.

Are the people who put the money in the same people who have rights to use your territory?
The people from Laksilyu could use the territory with permission from the Head Chief, and this is how it has been done in the past, and this is the same system of helping when someone has died and the casket needs to be paid for. Even when a small child has died they are treated in the same manner as an adult where money is collected and expenses paid for.

When Old Sam died what relations of his were responsible for obtaining or making the casket and preparing him to be buried?
Not just the family puts in money, it's the whole Clan. They all put in money so that he gets a decent burial.

Is the Beaver Creek area in your territory?
McDonnell Lake is here, Beaver Creek runs this way, and my territory is on this side of the lake.

On the side opposite Beaver Creek?
Yes.

And he said something about Kitsegukla?
THE INTERPRETER: *The McDonnell Lake area belongs to Big John from Kitsegukla.*

Was Old Dennis Wet'suwet'en and, if so, which Clan?
Old Dennis was my uncle and he was from Laksilyu Clan.

Did Old Dennis get the rights to use Beaver Creek area?
Yes. Beaver Creek area was given to Old Dennis.

Can you tell us why? Who gave it to him and why?
Big Charlie from Topley Landing had given Beaver Creek area to Old Dennis since Old Dennis has spent a lot of money on Old Charlie's brother at a feast.

Was the Beaver Creek area, did it originally belong to Big Charlie?
Yes, it did belong to him. His brother had died, Old Charlie's brother had died –

Big Charlie's brother?
Big Charlie's brother had died and Old Dennis had spent a lot of money on him at the feast.

Just to be clear, Big Charlie gave Old Dennis the rights to use the Beaver Creek area?
Yes.

For how long did Old Dennis have those rights? Would they go on to Johnny or any of the other people in his House or Clan? Or did they stop when Old Dennis died?
He used it for many years, and Jack Joseph, who was a strong Head Chief, after Old Dennis had died, he took over the territory.

What Clan was Big Charlie in?
Laksilyu Clan. Old Dennis was his half brother and that was why he was given the territory.

Did Old Dennis use that territory while you were alive?
Yes, I seen him using the territory, and David Dennis and I also walked the territory. Old Dennis went blind, was blind for about 35 years, and David Dennis was the person who did most of the trapping in this territory.

Now, was the territory that David Dennis trapped in including the Beaver Creek area?
Yes, it was Beaver Creek area and all the money that he made from the furs, that money was given to his father, Old Dennis.

Were you alive when Big Charlie gave Old Dennis the rights to the Beaver Creek area?
THE INTERPRETER: Would you repeat that again?

Were you alive when Big Charlie gave Old Dennis the rights to the Beaver Creek area?
Yes.

Was it given to him at a feast?
He was given probably at the feast. I wasn't there but everything is done according to our Indian law.

If it is done according to Indian law, is it given at the feast?
Yes, it was announced at a feast.

Was any name given to Old Dennis along with the territory?
Just the territory was given to him, he already had a name, and I was a small boy when this took place. What I am telling you now is information Old Dennis told me. Old Dennis was a strong Christian and he did not lie to other people and it is his words I am telling you now.

What was Old Dennis' Chief's name?
Since he was a strong Christian he had an Indian name before – since he was a strong Christian he just used his European name which was Dennis Clark.

Was his Indian name Dikyannualat?
THE INTERPRETER: Can I see the spelling?
His name was ... I forget that name.

You're reaching out, maybe you can tell us what that means?
The name means Grizzly clawing away at a tree.[14]

Before you translate is he giving any sort of explanation or just talking about –
THE INTERPRETER: He's just talking about some people.

Can we just go off the record. I just want to know what this is about.

OFF THE RECORD DISCUSSION

We can go back on the record now.

You gave an answer on the record and it was translated off the record, and just to summarize, you were referring to some other people you would like to be here when you talk about Smogelgem. I did indicate yesterday we would be asking about Smogelgem's territory, and depending how well we do today, we'll probably do that when those other people are present. Okay, I would like to ask you about the feast at which the pole outside your house which you described on this Commission was raised. Your pole, that is the pole of Maxlaxlex, was carved by Thomas George, is that right?
Yes, it was Thomas George who did all the carvings on the totem pole.

And Thomas George was the husband of Mary George?
Yes, he was the wife of Mary George.

Husband?
Husband of Mary George and since Mary George could not carve the pole, Thomas George carved the pole and when the moneys were paid for carving the pole, all the money went to Mary George.

Mary George was related to your father, Smogelgem?
Mary George was my father's grandchild. That is how the business is done.

Just to clarify that, is that the Wet'suwet'en tradition that your father's relations are responsible for carving your pole?
Yes, they are the ones, yes. And Thomas George's sons are alive today, Leonard George and Andy George.

And Leonard George presently holds your father's name Smogelgem?
Yes he does.

Is the Wet'suwet'en word for the responsibility of the father's relations to carve the pole called Wastyelgilsut?
Yes, that is right. It's right. If I want anything done I go to Thomas George's children. That is why I want them here –
THE INTERPRETER: –
– so Peter can listen.

Your father was in the Gitumden Clan?
No, Laksamshu.

What was the name of his House?
He was from the Owl House. –
THE INTERPRETER: Midziya, which is translated Owl House.
The people from the Owl House who are related to my dad, when Leonard and

Andy are here I want to mention all those names and have them written down so that they know who all my relatives are.

Now, referring back to your pole raising, before you actually arranged to have the pole carved, did you announce this at a feast?
Yes, it was mentioned at the feast and the pole was taken four miles west of here, up the mountain following one of the creeks, and it was brought down here to this site here when it was carved.

Do you know the name of that creek?
There's a small creek or spring comes from under the ground and where that spring is directly behind near the mountain is where the pole is taken from, and in the spring many people went up there and brought it down and they were paid for bringing the pole down.

Is there a name for that particular ceremony of cutting the tree in Wet'suwet'en?
It is called dikanteztsias – it means tree falling over.

Is a song sung and the history told when a tree is cut down?
Yes, before the tree is felled the song is sung with the drum called tegul and it took many people to bring it to the road.

Who actually cut the tree down for your pole?
The person I hired to fell the tree is dead and I can't remember his name.

Would it have been a relation of Thomas George?
The person that was hired to fall the tree was Dick Naziel, and he is from the Gitumden Clan.

When was the pole raising feast?
It is marked on the top of the totem pole, 1948.

Why did you as Maxlaxlex raise the pole?
When I got Maxlaxlex I got the totem carved to pay for Old Sam's name that I have now.

Is that the completion – you said last time there were three feasts, is the pole raising feast the completion of the feasts in which you get your name?
Yes, that is the final feast for getting the name.

Where was the pole carved?
Right in this area. Thomas George.

Was there a special ceremony when the pole was brought from the mountain to this area here? You're indicating by your House.
Once Thomas George peeled the bark off, songs were sung.

Were those the songs of your clan or Thomas George's?
THE INTERPRETER: He was having trouble remembering it and so I asked him if it was the song from the Laksilyu Clan and he said: *It was.*

Was that the same song you sung outside when you performed outside last week?
Yes, it was the song that was sung.

For the record, I am referring to the song that was performed on these commission hearings outside by his poles.
And the process that I just described it is done right throughout the Skeena River area.

Before the pole was carried down the mountain, did Thomas George sit on the pole and sing songs?
When it was brought here is when he sat on the pole and sang the song.

Did you invite other people here when that was done?
Yes, I invited the people to come.

Would those have been people from other Clans in this village and your own Clan?
Yes, all the people from all the Clans brought the pole here.

Did it include people from other villages like Kispiox, Hazelton, and Kitsegukla?
Yes, there are people from Kispiox, Hazelton, as well as some of my relatives from Fort Babine. They stayed in the old log house that was next door.

How long was the ceremony here when the pole came down the mountain?
It took them two weeks to carve the pole. After the pole was completed I invited people to the hall where I paid for it.

Did the other people in the Laksilyu Clan help you?
Yes, all the Laksilyu Clan helped me, even the small children who put in their little quarters.

Did you invite people from other villages to that feast?

Yes. I wear my blanket and went around to the different villages and invite people and they all showed up.

Is that what is supposed to be done under Wet'suwet'en laws?
Yes, that is how it is done and Jimmy Michel went around with me.

What is that called in Wet'suwet'en?
That is called Wuyaniyay, which means inviting people.
THE INTERPRETER: He said: *Now you can speak our language!*

How long did the feast last for your pole raising?
It was all done in one night when everybody went back to their homes.

Before the feast was the pole actually raised? If it was, could you tell us how it was raised?
When the pole was laying on the ground ropes were put on it in three different directions and people were singing while they were pulling it up.
THE INTERPRETER: He said: *Everybody had a good time.*

Is this the way all Wet'suwet'en pole raisings are done?
Yes, and the Skeena River people do the same.

Was there an old pole of Maxlaxlex that you used as a model for this pole?
Yes, there was one pole many years before this one.

Do you remember a pole – you also have the pole of Kela up in your yard. Was that raised at the same time?
Kela pole was raised just recently, whereas mine was raised before that.

Was there an old pole of Kela located somewhere else that you remember?
There is a pole in the canyon area in Hagwilget, just the one pole but now we have the two poles to represent that one.

I'm showing you a photograph of two poles. Could you take a look and see if you recognize either of those as the pole of Kela?
THE INTERPRETER: While he was looking at it he asked me: *Is there a figure of a man?* And I told him this pole did, and he said: *That is the pole of Kela. It is only one but now we have two poles to represent this one pole.*

You're indicating, for the record, the pole on the right-hand side of the picture with the figure of a man on the top. That may be marked as Exhibit 1 on this commission please. Off the record.

Back on the record. We have now marked as Exhibit No. 1 a photograph of two poles that has the National Museum of Canada stamp on the back, dated October 25, 1976 and negative number 59526, for the record. At this time I only have one copy of that photograph but in due course will provide copies to counsel for the province.

Do you know when the pole of Kela in Exhibit No. 1 was raised?
I don't know. I probably wasn't even born.

Did you ever see that pole when you were alive? In the photograph?
No, I did not see during my life. People have just told me about it.

I take it from your question that you recognize that pole of Kela's because of the crest of Gitdumskanees on the pole?
Yes, Gitdumskanees is on top of the Laksilyu Clan's poles.
THE INTERPRETER: He was saying: *Gitdumskaneese and Hag Wil Negh are some of the Head Chiefs from Laksilyu. All the people in the back row are Head Chiefs.*

You have described that back row when we went through that chart?
Yes.

Now, was a song made for you at the time of your pole raising?
Yes, the song was made for me but I have forgotten the song. Alec Michell was the one who made the song for me.

What Clan is he from?
He is from the Gilserhyu [Frog Clan].

Was a feast dish made for your feast when your pole raising occurred?
There is just a pot that was put there and that's where the money went in.

Do you recall a dish with a dog on one end and a frog head on the other end?
Yes. The dog dish was carved by Thomas George for both Kela and I.

Was this done at the time before the pole raising?
It was after the raising of the pole.

Do you have that dish now?
THE INTERPRETER: He says – I asked him if he had the dish and he said: *Yes, in the ... the storage house. And the crest on the pole is the dog – on the dish one is the dog and one end is the frog.*

Exhibit 1

Who holds the crest of the dog?
Mabel Sam, who is Kela, who holds the dog crest.

Does the frog head refer to your Clan of Laksilyu?
Yes. That frog belongs to all the Laksilyu Clan.

Maybe go off the record for a minute.

OFF THE RECORD DISCUSSION

Go back on the record. For the record, you have instructed the people here to get the dish which is now in front of you; is this the dish you were talking about?
Yes. It's the dog plate we call it.

Prior to this dish being made was there another one that was used in the old days by Kela and Maxlaxlex?
Before this one there was another one shaped like a boat and on the end the dog crest and on the back the frog crest.

Was the other one bigger than this one?
Yes, a lot longer than this. It was about ten feet long and all the berries were put in there, and this is where the people dipped their berries from the feast.

The bigger dish was used at feasts, is that correct?
THE INTERPRETER: *Yes.*

Now on the side to the camera there are frogs, three frogs – you want to turn it around – and also on the other side and three frogs; can you tell us why those three frogs are on both sides?
The frogs are painted on these, the crests that belong to the Laksilyu, and this bowl is used to put in the money, and the money from here is what is used to pay the people in the feast hall.

Have you used this bowl at the feasts of Maxlaxlex or Laksilyu?
I used it once not too long ago.

On the side closest to you at the end is what appears to be a dog. Is this the dog that you were referring to when you described the crest of Kela?
Yes, this is the crest of Kela.

On this other side is a frog – just turn it – what appears to be the head of a frog. Is that the frog you were referring to earlier?

When Thomas George carved this he was paid $40. That was paid by myself and Kela.

Did Thomas George carve it because he was related to your father and in the same Clan? I'm sorry, his wife was.
Because Thomas George was related to logalgut Rose Sam [Kela], because he was related to them, it means it is not ...

It means what?
THE INTERPRETER: *Thomas George logalgut Rose means Thomas George is related on – related to Rose.*

On which side?
THE INTERPRETER: *On the father's side.*

Could you just stand it up so there's a sense of the size.

Okay. Go off the record.

OFF THE RECORD DISCUSSION

Go back on the record.

THE INTERPRETER: He said: *You did the right thing by taking the picture of it. If there is ever to be a feast of great importance, this would be taken out where the money would go in.* He said: *[I'm] tired now, [I've] spoken long enough.*

Could you ask him, I will stop after one or two more questions. I just want to finish this section then I will stop. Behind you is the blanket, that is your blanket you wore last week; was that blanket made by Mary George?
Yes, Johnny and Mary George are lexalzut.

Translate that? What does that mean? Is she on his father's side?
THE INTERPRETER: *Yes, she is on his father's side.*

Again, is that the Wet'suwet'en tradition that your relations on your father's side make your blanket?
Yes it is. That is the same system with the Skeena River people, yes.

Do you want to stop for today or do you want to take a break for ten minutes and then go for a little longer?
THE INTERPRETER: *He said to finish it and he wants to go to bed.*

We'll stop now and he can go to bed. Go off the record now.

THE INTERPRETER: Next time he is speaking about his father's side coming.

He wants to speak about his father's side and he wants them to be here.

OFF THE RECORD DISCUSSION

EXAMINATION ADJOURNED AT 10:45 A.M.[15]

VOLUME 3

**Direct Examination of Johnny David by
Peter Grant, 17–19 October 1985**

UPON COMMENCING AT 9:40 A.M. 17 OCTOBER 1985

MR GRANT: We'll go on record then. You've been sworn on oath on this commission evidence and you are still under oath, do you understand that?

And you, as an interpreter, have been sworn to translate? You are still under oath to translate to the best of your ability from Wet'suwet'en to English.

EXAMINATION IN CHIEF BY MR GRANT

Q   Mr David, you described to us the funeral feast and when you received the name Maxlaxlex and the pole raising feast that you held to raise the pole in your yard; do the Wet'suwet'en people hold feasts for other reasons?
A   *Three feasts are held, after the third feast everything is completed and whatever is done remains with you for the rest of your life.*

Q   Are these three feasts held when a Chief dies?
A   *Yes. When a Hereditary Chief dies it is announced at a feast and this is done for the rest of the Chief's life.*

Q   You also described what I will refer to as a shame feast that was held. Are there feasts for other purposes, such as weddings amongst the Wet'suwet'en?

A *There used to be feasts for weddings and again this is to set things for the life of people involved.*

Q Did you attend any of the old feasts for weddings?
A *I've attended many of the feasts when people got married and the feast is a kind of meeting lunch for the bride, and to this day hasn't been happening as much as in the past.*

Did your Clan hold such a wedding feast at any time that you remember?
Yes, many have and I went through the process as well.

Where was the marriage feast for you held?
Hagwilget old church.

And how old were you when that happened?
I can't remember offhand, somewhere in around 20 or 25 years old.

Did you have to do anything for your wife's parents before you married her?
I did many things for my in-laws. I hunted for them, gave them meat and I was working, I made money, I gave the money to my wife and my wife gave it to her parents. – I just remembered, we got married in 1913 and my son Moses was born in 1914.

What was your wife's name, what House was she in, and what Clan was she in?
My wife's name was Miriam Dennis, she was from the Kilwoneetz Clan [on her father's side]. She is from the same House as Mrs Lucy Namox who is Goohlaht.

Do you remember Alfred Joseph coming and talking to you about marriage?
Yes, I told him everything.

This was when he was researcher with the tribal council, is that right?
Yes.

Now, I'm going to read to you something that you said to him about marriage and I would like you to tell me if this is correct. You said, 'When the Wet'suwet'en get married and leave their home that is final. The girl's parents and the man's parents have meetings before the marriage: they prepare an agreement and only then the girl is allowed to leave them.' Now, do you remember telling that to Alfred Joseph, and is that correct?

Okay. He said: *That is right and there is no way I can change what I said in here. The interviews I did with Alfred, it is all written down and what I have said will remain with tribal council, and when you ask me further questions about what I told Alfred I get confused.*

When the Chiefs in the old days decided whether or not to allow their sons or daughters to marry, what did they look for in terms of the proper woman for their son to marry?
When man and woman want to marry the parents of both the man and the woman have a meeting. They discuss thoroughly whether they are meant for each other and if it is agreed upon by both parents then the marriage is allowed.

At any of the wedding feasts that you've been at, including your own, did your parents, your father, or your wife's parents talk about the territories that each of you would be able to use?
When we got married both our parents, our aunts and uncles met and after they said that it was okay to marry, we got married and we had no trouble after this.

I'm afraid he may not have ... Did anyone talk about the territories of your House or your wife's House at the marriage?
My wife's uncle – Francis Lake John – said that I could use my wife's hunting territory which is called Nanika. This was done at a feast that was held here and Francis Lake John got up and announced it at a feast. My brother-in law also got up and said that I could use my wife's hunting territory.

When you say your brother-in-law, was this your wife's brother?
My wife's uncle. Alexander. Alexander Stevens.

Is that always the rule with the Wet'suwet'en that you have the right to hunt on your wife's territory?
This is how it has been done in the past and it is still happening today where the man can hunt in his wife's territory. When I use my wife's territory any game that I shoot or any money I make from the furs this is all spent at a feast that my wife would put up. It is how things were done in the past and it is still happening today even if some of the younger people don't understand the system. Our young people are scattered all over the place and no one is teaching them the ways because they're scattered all over the place.

Is your wife's territory around what we know as Nanika Lake?
It is near Nanika Lake but more towards Ootsa Lake.

When did you last use your wife's territory?
I can't remember the date when I last used the territory but after my wife's uncle Alexander died, I never went back there. I continued to use my own territory. Ever since Alexander died I haven't gone back to my wife's territory. After this I continue to farm near Topley. There's a creek near Topley which bears my name. It's called Johnny Creek and it's on a map.

You attended a funeral feast in Burns Lake a few weeks ago, is that right?
A few weeks ago, yes I did.

Whose funeral was that? Whose House put on that feast and for whom?
Skaxllee name was passed on and that is why the people were invited to the feast.

Was that a Wet'suwet'en feast?
They're people from – the Babine people.

But they are Wet'suwet'en?
We are all one group known as Wet'suwet'en but we live in different villages.

What Clan was that feast put on by?
Gitdumden [Wolf Clan].

Is it correct that you were seated along the side with your Clan?
Yes, that's correct.

You were seated, just as you have described to us at one of these sessions, with the other Chiefs beside you, is that right?
Yes, they did. Pat Namox sat in front of me.

And Pat Namox sat in front of you?
Yes, he sat in front of me. And he sits in front of me at a feast in Moricetown as well. If I should die, Pat Namox will move back to my chair.

How were you invited to this feast: Did people come to your House?
People from Burns Lake came to the House, they were wearing their regalia – and they all came to the House. They spoke to me and after they were done I got up and I spoke to them. When they were here, I gave them some money and when I went to Burns Lake they gave my money back plus interest, and that is how it has worked from the past and it still happening today. They did the same throughout the village. They went to all the High Chiefs, invited them, and the people who were invited gave them money and this was returned to them with interest.

What is this tradition called about them coming to the village and personally seeing each High Chief?

The tradition about them coming to the village and personally seeing each High Chief is called Waganadeex. In the very old days when people went out to invite people to a potlatch, they would stay in these people's homes for six days. The men and also the women. It was like a short marriage for six days and those wives who could not bear children would sometimes bear children within that six days.

This happened to Abraham Nikal whose wife could not bear children, was within that six days the ladies that came to invite him, one of the ladies –

THE INTERPRETER: How can I say this? –

THE WITNESS: *– one of the ladies was fertilized and this was one way of Abraham getting a son.*

How old were you approximately when that –

Maybe ten years old but I distinctly remember it happening, and there is many people that know about that.

Abraham and I were playing in my dad's house. My dad would sing his song and through listening to my dad, both Abraham Nikal and I learned the song that goes with Smogelgem. You learn the song at my dad's house.

When these people came from Burns Lake, did you sing any song or perform any dance, or do anything else as well as give them money?

When they come I did not sing. I spoke to them and while I was speaking to them I played the rattle.

Aside from the repayment of the money you gave – how much money did you give to them and how much money did they return to you?

I gave them each $5, there were three of them, and when I went to Burns Lake I received my $5 back from the three plus $5 interest.

Aside from that money were you given any other money at the Burns Lake feast as witness to that feast?

When this person that received a name collected money, he collected quite a bit of money and those that travelled on the road to Burns Lake, depending on their status, their name status, they were given anywhere from $10 to $20 for witnessing the taking of the name.

Aside from money were you given anything else at that feast?

I received a lot of grocery goods and I still have 20 lbs of sugar left. This is how they do things in the past, and it's still happening today.

Did you receive that sugar and those groceries because you were a Chief?
Yes. This is another way of counting how many people were invited.

Do you know how much money was collected by the House and the Clan? And how much was distributed at that feast?
I can't remember the exact amount but it was quite a bit of money. There was about a ton and a half of sugar and all that was bought by the Clan to be distributed to the witnesses. The same with the grocery goods. All the Clan would bring in some to be distributed.

Who received the name Skaxllee at that feast?
I can't remember the person's name, but it was witnessed by all the High Chiefs in the House.

What House and what Clan was the person in who received that name at the feast?
He was Gitdumden and he came from Kasya or Grizzly House.

Did young girls receive names at that feast?
Yes, young women also received names and the names are usually given to the husband, who has high rank, and the names don't go to just anyone.

Were the names given to these young girls children's names?
It is not children's names, it is High Chiefs' names.

Do you know why they were given those names?
These ladies that received names, they lived the good life, they're fairly well off, and they have been brought up right, and the names just don't go to anybody.

Did they dance in the feast with money in their hair?
Yes.

Is that part of the Wet'suwet'en tradition?
Yes. We do the same as they do because we are all one.

There were gravestones or headstones that were unwrapped at the feast; was it the father's side of the person who died who unwrapped those gravestones?
Yes. That is what happened. They're Bezageelzutgitnee and they were also paid for doing that chore. When they do things it is done for a lifetime and it will never stop. It will continue on.

Many people came in and they danced with blankets on or leather like

moose-skin, and they threw that down in front of the Chief; how were those people related to the Chief who was putting on the feast?
The people that came in to dance with the blankets and the moose hide and the money, these people are called Andamanuk. They're kind of lifted up to show their status.

Are they from the father's side of the Chief who died?
These people that came in to dance are people from the Clan – they're all from the Clan on the female side. Or the wife's side. All these people that come in to dance are married to either the Gitdumden man or Gitdumden woman. These people who are called Andamanuk are dancing to help this person who is taking on the Skaxllee. All these people that come in to dance are married to either the Gitdumden man or Gitdumden woman. Peter Alfred's wife came in to dance because she's married to Gitdumden. Her husband is [Chief Madeek of the] Gitdumden.

Did those people provide – the blankets they threw down, were those blankets given by the Andamanuk to the Clan who put on the feast?
These Andamanuk that come in to dance with these blankets or moose-hides, it is theirs, they've bought themselves, but it is given to the Clan and when the expenses are paid back, the blankets and moose hides is used to add on as interest. In the old days, about 100 hundred years ago, the Andamanuk would come in with rifles, canoes. These would be used as interest to pay to people in the other Clans. I've seen this happen in the Skeena River area.

At the Burns Lake feast a week and half ago there was a rifle given by Andamanuk, wasn't there?
Yes.

Now, did you see Michael McDonald, who's the video operator here today, at that feast using his camera?
Yes, I seen him – focusing his camera. He took pictures of people walking around and where they were seated and they might know now how the system works.

That feast was held at the hall, the community hall at Burns Lake, of the Babine band, is that right?
Yes. It's their own hall, Indian hall.

In your Clan is it correct that you, Maxlaxlex, Gitdumskaneese and Wah Tah Kwets discuss matters before one of the Chief[s] speaks at the feast?
Yes, this is how it is done and in Burns Lake I did not get up to speak because I was feeling very weak and therefore I didn't speak.

Did Gitdumskanees or Wah Tah Kwets speak?
We did not speak at the feast. There were too many people there and there was a person by the name of Dick Alec who spoke about the particular name that was given away and he told the stories that went with it.

What clan was Dick Alec in?
Dick Alec's Indian name is Hohn and he is from the Laksilyu [Small Frog Clan] in Burns Lake. Alec Joseph used to have that name, and now Dick Alec has that name and he is the Head Chief of the Laksilyu in Burns Lake and that is why he spoke at that feast.

Did he speak for you as well?
Yes, he spoke for all of the Laksilyu. When I die Pat Namox will speak.

You have described on previous times here about your blanket and about the crests on your poles. Do you have an amakloo or head-dress?
I had one and they're all gone now.

Do you have a rattle?
I had one and that is gone too.

What netseyeee was shown on your amakloo? That netseyeee refers to crests.
It was human figure, human face figure.

Did it cover your face?
Yes, up to my neck.

Does anyone else in your House own nulwass or rattle?
Yes, there's many Laksilyu who had the rattles. Some have been lost, and there's some who still have rattles.

You said that you shook a rattle when these men came from Burns Lake; whose rattle was that?
It was Wagtahdeexx own rattle. Had bear design on it.

These are people from Burns Lake?
From Burns Lake.

Aside from the things you have shown to us, is there any other regalia that belonged to your House –
THE INTERPRETER: He says: *[I'm] finished now.*
– that exist today, that is what I was referring to?
I've got one but it's one the children use to play with.

I notice you seemed to be a bit tired Johnny, do you wish to take a bit of a rest now or can I go for few minutes more, or do you want to stop? *I'm very tired and I would like to quit.*

We'll adjourn this commission hearing. Go off the record.

EXAMINATION ADJOURNED UNTIL 9.30 A.M. TOMORROW.

UPON RESUMING AT 9.50 A.M., 18 OCTOBER, 1985

MR. GRANT: We'll go back on the record. This is a continuation of the examination on commission evidence which was adjourned yesterday when Johnny David became tired. Johnny David, the witness, is still under oath, as is the interpreter with respect to translation.

OFF THE RECORD DISCUSSION

EXAMINATION IN CHIEF BY MR. GRANT (continued)

A few weeks ago in this commission evidence you sang some songs outside which were performed at the time of the pole raising, as I recall. Could you tell me what these songs tell your people about the power and strength of your House? *That is how things are done when the pole is raised, has been done in the past and still continuing today.*

At the feast when you took the name Maxlaxlex were your netseyeee performed? *Yes, I did and the crests are on my blanket and my drum.*

And there's a performance that goes with those crests? *Yes.*

MR GRANT: Just for the record, I am just asking the Interpreter this question; to explain that word netseyeee: would you translate netsey-eee as meaning performance of the crests? THE INTERPRETER: Netseyeee is the crest.

Why were these performed at your feast? *That is how it is done traditionally. Everybody witnesses the crests on your totem poles and on your blanket.*

Just to clarify, when you are saying the word crest, Interpreter, that's the same as the Wet'suwet'en netseyeee? THE INTERPRETER: Yes.

Yesterday I asked you if you had rights to hunt on your wife's territory after you married her; I would like to ask if your marriage to your wife also gave you rights to hunt on her father's territory?
Yes.

Was your wife's father Old Dennis?
Yes.

Was the territory that he used known as the Kilwoneetz territory?
Yes.

Can you explain the relationship between Old Sam, the man from whom you took the name Maxlaxlex, and Old Dennis, your father-in-law?
They were brothers.

When you received your Chief's name at the feast, Maxlaxlex, did anyone speak of the territories of your House and about your fishing sites?
Yes. Some Chiefs spoke about the territories and if a person is not feeling well or is too old someone else is appointed as trustee.

Is this trustee of the territory?
Trustee of the territory.

Was Jimmy Michel the person who spoke about this at your feast?
Yes, he was the one that got up and spoke at the hall.

And his Wet'suwet'en name was Samaxsam?
Yes.

Did he say who had the rights to use your territory or your fishing holes?
Samaxsam mentioned that I had the right to use the territory. When I got my name he also had a feast.

He then took the name of Samaxsam at the same time?
Yes. He was older than me, that was why he did the speaking and he knows the histories of our people.

As I recall, the feast occurred at the death of Old Sam; do the Wet'suwet'en have a system in which there is succession of the territory from one Chief to another, without break?
Yes, it does.

Did you receive the right to the territory at the time of the death of Old Sam? On the death of Old Sam?
Yes. When the feast happened he [Jimmy Michell] mentioned that I would get the territory and all the other Chiefs in the feast hall were there to witness it.

Has your House ever lost territory because another House paid for the burial of a Chief in your House?
If a person is too old, a person who is worthy is put in and it isn't given to just anyone. Has to be person who is worthy.

I'm not certain he understood my question. Are there circumstances amongst the Wet'suwet'en where a House cannot afford the cost of burying a Chief so people from another House help pay for the cost of that burial?
The wife's husband's, the Chief's husband's relatives help pay for expenses and that is how things are done. And the people that help pay the expenses are the ones that are called Andamanuk.

[Has] your House ever gained any territory because the people of your House helped pay for the [burial of] a Chief of another House?
No. The only people that help are the wife's [or] husband's relatives. They're the Andamanuk.

You say again the wife's husband's relatives. Do you mean the Chief's husband's relatives?
THE INTERPRETER: The Chief's husband's relatives.

Is it correct that the Andamanuk have rights to use their spouses' territories and fishing sites?
Yes, that is right. That is why the men and the women who are married to a certain Clan are able to use their spouses' hunting or fishing sites.
Okay. The people that were called the Andamanuk, depending on how many feasts they attend, how much money they put out – the people there witness these occasions and the people are able to determine how high this Andamanuk person will be in the feast hall. The husbands of the wives are also allowed to go to the hunting territories and do their hunting, and whatever they receive from the hunting territory is brought back to the feast hall, where it is distributed, and sometimes they are allowed to use the territory.
As this process continues, the more the Andamanuk contributes the stronger his name will become in the feast hall. This Andamanuk, once he builds up his or her name in the feast hall, when a person dies he is the person that is

sent out to invite people to feasts and when he does this he's increasing the strength of his name in the feast hall.

Since I am one of the Elders in the community and I know the ways of our people, I am usually invited to go around to bring the person, who is called the Waneeyeh, which means the person who goes around to invite other people to feasts for his Clan. I also do this with the Gitksan people. I go there to invite them and they know me, and since they know I know the ways of our people, most of them usually come. I know the words that are used for inviting people. I know all the songs and this is why I get invited to invite people to feasts. Even when I go to Burns Lake, even if it's a different clan than mine, I'm usually invited along to act as the official inviter to feasts. At the feast, if it is a Clan that is different than mine, at the feast the hosting Clan amongst themselves will decide how much I will be paid as Hereditary Chief for inviting people for them. That's it.

To clarify one point that you made, you said that the more the Andamanuk contributes the stronger his name will become in the feast hall. Are you referring to the name of the Andamanuk or the name of the Chief for whom he's contributing?
When the Andamanuk helps out at the feast in terms of money or bringing meat from the hunting territory, the Andamanuk is building up his or her own name.

Does this still go on today that the Andamanuk who help the feast have the rights to use the host territories of their spouses?
Yes. That is still happening today and any time one of these Andamanuk enters the house, the wife serves them food or tea.

Do the people that use your territory today contribute at the feasts of your House?
Yes they do. This is the how the Andamanuk build up their name.

Is it correct that in the Wet'suwet'en system the Chief's name goes with the territory? That is, they are linked, your name is linked to the territory that you hold?
Yes, the name and the territory go together. That was how it was done in the old days.
THE INTERPRETER: He is describing: *The land that Hereditary Chiefs hold today has been logged. There [are] no more trees and where are Hereditary Chiefs to go trapping?*
THE WITNESS: *Now the timber has been removed and the squirrels and other animals have nothing to feed on and we don't have anywhere to go trapping. They had done the same with the salmon, they give it to us in little bits. In the*

Babine area, the Indian people from there had their own fence and then they came along and took it away and now they use it for counting salmon.

About three or four years ago three trucks came from Prince Rupert. They told the Indian people that they can't take any more salmon and they loaded up the trucks and took it to Prince Rupert where it was sold. That is how they look at us. They have taken the trees away and now we want the stumpage money.

You said that they took the – the Indian people had a fence at Babine and they took it away. Are you referring to people from the Government of Canada or British Columbia?
Yes, the Fishery people, the people who look after salmon.

MR MILNE: When?

MR GRANT: Do you know when that happened?
I can't remember the exact date but when they came, three or four of the women grabbed the Fishery officer and dumped him in the water and let him out. Four Chiefs from Fort Babine and Old Fort had gone to Ottawa to straighten this matter up and when they came back, those three or four women who had dumped the Fisheries officer, the husbands were arrested. These three or four husbands of the women were sent to jail in Vancouver and Father Coccola arranged for the Chiefs to go to Ottawa. When they were going to court – or when they went to Ottawa – Father Coccola had prepared the Chiefs. There's a large container of silver and a large container of gold and he informed the Chief from Old Fort not to take silver and gold, that if they took the silver and gold, they would take all their lands. The Chiefs did not accept the silver and gold, therefore they did not lose their land. That is how it was told to me.

Was this silver or gold in Ottawa or was it brought to them here?
In the Ottawa courthouse. And that's how it was told.

Who told you about this?
The Chiefs themselves told me this. The Old Fort dyee – and dyeez is another word for – the daughter of the Old Fort dyee had some correspondence and she lost it.

Is dyee a name of a Chief or is that the name for Chiefs?
Dyee is a person who looks after the land and whatever on behalf of the people.

Do you recall the names of any of these four Chiefs?
THE INTERPRETER: He remembers the names – *Big George dyee, William Dzu'k' who's Chief, and he couldn't remember the third name.*

Did he say where they went on the way to Ottawa? He didn't say their route to Ottawa?
They went from here by steamboat to Vancouver, and from Vancouver to Ottawa they went by railroad.

Do you know if this trip happened in your lifetime?
Yes, I was alive, I was big. My father was going to go with them but he was quite a ways out in his hunting territory at North Bulkley.

You described this history that happened at Babine. Did the people here in Moricetown use a fence or other methods of fishing that were stopped by Fisheries?
In our village they used the gaff and the gonzay, which is the fish trap, and the fence was the one that got the Babine people in trouble.

Did the Fisheries stop your people from using the fish traps in Moricetown?
They did not prevent us from using the gonzay. It was just that the people that used the fish trap had all died off. When Louie Tommy had his fish trap in the canyon, whatever fish he took out he distributes it to the people and if the people he distributed it to wanted to pay him for that salmon it was up to them to do that at the feast. Blair McDonald was the person in charge of looking after the salmon and all he did was prevent children from going into the canyon area.

Was he with Fisheries?
Yes. He was one of the better persons from Fisheries.

Was there anything wrong with people paying Louie Tommy for fish, in the Wet'suwet'en tradition?[1]
There was nothing wrong with it; it was fine. The people themselves would give him money; he did not ask for it. When he had his fish trap in the canyon, I helped him.

Did he use a specific fishing site in the canyon?
He used his own fishing hole.

Did he have a Chief's name and did that fishing hole go with that Chief's name?
Yes, the name – the fishing hole went along with his Chief's name.

What was his Chief's name?
His Chief['s] name was Wah Tah Kwets.

Was Louie Tommy the only person that used the fish trap in the canyon while you were alive?
Yes, [it] was only Louie Tommy. The ones that had fish traps on the other side had all died off.

THE INTERPRETER: He said he's getting tired.

MR GRANT: We'll go off the record for a moment.

OFF THE RECORD

MR GRANT: Go back on the record. We were off the record and I want to put on the record what he just said. For the record, we just went off the record and the witness, Mr David, was explaining the drum that's behind him and is beside his blanket. That is a drum that appears to have a dog on it. It's a circular drum, which is obvious from the video, and he was indicating that the crest on that drum belongs to Kela. Is that correct?
Yes.

THE INTERPRETER: He asks: *[Let] Kela stand beside [me] so that she can be pictured with [me].*

MR GRANT: Yes, Go off the record for moment.

OFF THE RECORD DISCUSSION

MR. GRANT: On the record. For the record, Mabel Sam Critch, who is now standing beside John David, has been present in the room although of course she's not giving evidence. She hasn't been here on any previous day of the examination and Johnny David, the witness, requested that she stand beside him.

I understand that this is Kela whom you have referred to on this commission, is that right?
Yes.

Mr David wanted to record for the record that she's here.
The name Kela is near Topley. There's a lake called Sunset Lake; there are two graves there, and one is the grave of Kela and his brother.

Thank you.
The white people have taken the area where the two graves are.

MR GRANT: Does he wish to go on? Okay.

Is this the Kela who held the name before Mabel or was this Kela from an earlier time who is buried there?

THE WITNESS: *The name Kela has been passed on through five people and the sixth person now holding the name Kela is Mabel Sam.*

Is it the person sixth before Mabel Sam who is buried at Sunset Lake?
Yes, the first Kela is the one that is buried at Topley[2] ... The first one. After Kela was Big Thomas Nikal. The third person who held that name was Thomas Holland. The fourth person was Jim Holland. The fifth person to hold that name was Mabel's mother, Rose Sam, and the sixth person to hold this name is Mabel Sam Critch.

MR GRANT: Just go off the record for moment.

MR GRANT: On the record.

Before the break this morning I asked you if your name Maxlaxlex goes with your territory and you said it did; can you tell us where the territory is that goes with the name Maxlaxlex?
The area that went with my name is in the Copper River area. I also did some hunting and trapping in the area known as North Bulkley. And Kela's territory is in the Telkwa River area.

Is your territory also known as the Kilwoneetz territory?
Yes, it is known as the Kilwoneetz territory and not just anyone is allowed to go into your territory.

Is Kilwoneetz a Wet'suwet'en name for the Copper River?
Yes. There's some copper in there and that is where the white man got the name from, Copper River.[3]

Did you visit the Kilwoneetzen territory with Marvin George?
Yes, went by helicopter.

Do you recall driving into the Kilwoneetzen territory with me?
THE INTERPRETER: *Yes. He says he remembers going out there with you. He has been on so many trips and he really gets confused with all the names and trips.*

That was in September of this year, that you drove out there with me?
Yes.

Do you recall showing me, and the other people on that trip, the boundaries of the Kilwoneetzen territory?
Yes, I showed them the territory.

Now, in the Kilwoneetzen territory is there a place known as Six Mile Flats where your mother's people used to live?
Yes, there is a place called Six Mile Flats and it is a grassy area.

Was there a big longhouse there of your people?
Yes. There was a longhouse there and Paul – and his wife know where the longhouse was. David Dennis has showed Paul and Dora where the place was. David Dennis was raised under the roof of the longhouse.

Did you see this house when you were a small boy?
No, I didn't. The only thing I saw was the ashes from the fire that burned the house down.

Did the white people that came into that area burn the house down?
Yes, it was the white men. The prospectors, people that are looking for minerals.

Can I refer to your mother's people as the Kilwoneetzen people?
Yes, they can be referred to as the Kilwoneetzen people. My mother and my grandparents were all brought up there.

And Old Sam?
THE INTERPRETER: *And Old Sam.*

What time of the year – what part of the year would the Kilwoneetzen live at Six Mile Flats?
Usually in the summer months and through the fall, and when the snow flies that is when people move back here.

MR GRANT: I think he may have answered, I'm not just clear. When did the people move back, when the snow flies?
THE INTERPRETER: Yes.

They lived up there in the summer months?
THE INTERPRETER: In the summer months.

And the early fall?
THE INTERPRETER: Yes.

Yes. Did the people hunt and fish in the Kilwoneetzen territory in the summer and early fall?
Around 15th August they would go into the Kilwoneetzen territory for salmon

and for mountain goat and other animals. When the snow gets too deep in the mountains that is when we come back here.

When you refer to when they came back, did they come back to live in Moricetown or in Hagwilget?
The Kilwoneetzen people would come back to the village in Moricetown and to Hagwilget.

Did you – you told me earlier that Old Dennis, your father-in-law, was Old Sam's brother. Did Old Dennis trap and fish and hunt in the Kilwoneetzen territory?
Yes, he did.

Did you hunt, trap, and fish there with Old Dennis?
I did not go with him as I was at a different territory. After he went blind, David Dennis and I would go to the Kilwoneetzen territory to hunt and trap. The money that we made off the furs and the meat, we gave to Old Dennis. That is how we did things. David Dennis is an Elder here and he knows the things he does about the territory from his father, Old Dennis. He is too old today to speak about the Kilwoneetzen territory. Old Dennis was blind for 35 years. During that time David Dennis and I hunted and trapped for Old Dennis.

David Dennis was Old Dennis' son, is that right?
Yes, his son. My wife's brother. That is how business was done and what I am telling you now, I have not made it up.

Did you start trapping with David Dennis for Old Dennis after you were married?
It was after.

Did you stop when Old Dennis died?
After Old Dennis died, David Dennis continued to hunt and trap the area, and David had leased or loaned –
THE INTERPRETER: He can't remember exactly how it happened.
THE WITNESS: *– it was leased to white people.*

Did you hunt and trap there after Old Dennis died?
I continued to hunt and trap with David Dennis and after David Dennis got old and could not walk any longer the story goes that it was leased or loaned to a white person.

Did David Dennis build a cabin on the Kilwoneetzen territory while you were trapping and hunting with him?
Yes, he did build one at Six Mile Flats and I showed you when we went there.

That cabin is still standing?
It is still there, you guys saw it.

I understand what I saw, but you have to say it for the record. Now, is it correct that the people, the Kilwoneetzen, had feasts at Six Mile Flats when they lived up there?
They did not have feasts in the Kilwoneetzen territory. They had feasts when they came back here.

Do you recall a history of a man who was killed by a grizzly bear when he left the longhouse at Six Mile Flats?
There is a foot trail leading from Six Mile Flats; it is about one or two miles. Along the foot trail there's a creek that comes from the mountain; that is where this man was killed. They told him not to go alone but he did, and they found his body about two or three days later and his body was decomposed by the grizzly bear.

Was Old Dennis a teenager when this happened?
Yes, he was a young man when that happened. It was a long time ago.

Did Old Dennis or David Dennis show you where this happened?
My uncle Joe Nass had taken me up there and showed me. There's some marks on the trees.

Were these blazes that they marked where he died?
THE INTERPRETER: He said: *The trail was marked with blazes.*

Where did this foot trail lead to from the Kilwoneetzen territory?
The trail led to Moricetown and he was killed when he was on his way back to Moricetown.

Does the Kilwoneetzen territory go as far as McDonnell Lake?
The territory does go up into McDonnell Lake. You remember we stopped at a creek and [from] the creek down is all Kilwoneetzen territory; the area above the creek belongs to the Kitsegukla people.
 There is a Chief from Kitsegukla, his name is Big John, who lived at Tseet-saytuk, and he was the boss of the territory above the Kilwoneetz. There's an area they call Lead Canyon and that is where the area starts that belongs to the people from Kitsegukla.

THE INTERPRETER: He wants to stop now because of his throat.

MR GRANT: We'll adjourn now. Off the record.

OFF THE RECORD DISCUSSION

RECESSED FOR LUNCH AT 11.35 A.M.

UPON RESUMING AT 2.00 P.M. – OFF THE RECORD DISCUSSION

MR GRANT: You showed this creek, which is the boundary of the Kilwoneetzen, to myself and the other people that were there in September, is that correct?
Yes, that is the place.

Where does the boundary – that is the far boundary when you go down to the McDonnell Lake, isn't it?
Yes, that is the far boundary. The area above the creek belongs to Big John.

Where is the boundary on this side of your territory? Is it at a creek and if so do you know the name of the creek?
THE INTERPRETER: Below?

When you're starting to drive into the territory, where does the boundary start for your territory?
There's a little mountain in behind Hudson Bay Mountain, on the west of Hudson Bay Mountain, and there's a lake. The name of it is Guksan Lake and that is where the boundary starts.

Does your territory go as far as the Telkwa River?
Yes, where the boundary is.

Now, this small mountain that you referred to, on the west side of Hudson Bay Mountain, is it known as the Cut Box or Cutoff Box Mountain in Wet'suwet'en? I'll try to pronounce the word and I'll give the spelling. Khenegasxgunxgut.
THE INTERPRETER: He's described: *On this piece of paper, Hudson Bay Mountain would be here. There's a smaller mountain here where there is the lake, that is called Guksan Lake, and McDonnell Lake is in this area. This whole area is known as the Kilwoneetz area and the area above that belongs to the Gitksan people.*

Are there Wet'suwet'en names for the creeks and the mountains in your territory?
They all have Wet'suwet'en names and the white people have names as well for these creeks and rivers and mountain peaks.
THE INTERPRETER: *The area behind Hudson Bay Mountain, the boundary [I] described, belongs to the Gitksan and they also have names of their own.*

OFF THE RECORD DISCUSSION

MR GRANT: Go back on the record.

Is there a mountain within the territory, near Hudson Bay Mountain, that would be known as Cutoff Box Mountain?
Khenegasxgunxgut, that's it.

Now. There is a creek within your territory that goes near the road to McDonnell Lake which is known as a creek where the salmon come up?
The name of the creek is called Kloktuktulgwes.
THE INTERPRETER: That is salmon jumping the falls.

OFF THE RECORD

Is there another creek which has a name which refers to lots of salmon in the creek?
Below or above the McDonnell Lake area, in this direction, the Gitksan people own the territory and they have their own names for the rivers and the mountains. One mountain is called Wonsamoos and this mountain can be seen from Kitsegukla. When you're driving along Highway 16 it is past Khenegasxgunxgut, you see the peaks; the white people have named that the Seven Sisters and in their own language the mountain is called Wonsamoos.

Is it one of those peaks or is it all of the peaks?
All the seven points.

Is the area that we talked about at Six Mile Flats called Kilwoneetz kloohkut?
Yes.

Did people from Gitsegukla come there to trade with Kilwoneetz people?
When the salmon are running all the Gitksan people would gather at Six Mile Flat and prepare their salmon, and once they're done they go back to their own villages.

To be clear, the Skeena River people would come there and fish with the Kilwoneetz people?
Yes. They all fished for salmon as one and, once they have enough salmon, the Gitksan people would go back to their own villages and there was no trouble between the Gitksan people and the Kilwoneetz.

The Gitksan people never claimed the Kilwoneetz territory as their own?
No, they didn't. All they came was for the salmon.

MR GRANT: When the people fished there, would they catch them by fish traps?
MR MILNE: Which people?
THE WITNESS: *They used a sharp stick with a hook on it and it was easy for them to get the salmon since the water table would be quite low.*

MR GRANT: Did the Kilwoneetz people and Gitksan people fish the same way there?
Yes, they did. They also were able to speak to each other.

Did they speak in both Wet'suwet'en and Gitksan or did they only use one of the languages?
Our people were able to speak both languages. My mother, my grandmother, and even when I was young I spoke the language and I've forgotten most of the Gitksan language.

Is it correct that this territory which is held by Maxlaxlex was held by Old Sam before you and was held by Old Sam's uncle before him?
Yes, that is how it went. Old Sam's uncle had the name Maxlaxlex, and Old Sam had it after his uncle, and after Old Sam died I was given the name.

Besides fishing did people trap for small animals with baskets in the Kilwoneetz territory?
They used guns to hunt the animals and whoever was the Chief of the territory, he was given a portion of the meat and the Chief of the territory would distribute it amongst the people as he wished.

Is there a creek called Willow Creek in that area, and if so, what is its Wet'suwet'en name?
Kloncheetoygikwuh. That refers to the lake being near the grassy area and the creek coming. The white man gave the name Willow Creek since the creek comes from the part where there's willows.

When you drive down to McDonnell Lake on the road and you see McDonnell Lake, you can see to the west of McDonnell Lake a mountain and it's on the Kilwoneetzen side of Willow Lake. Is there a Wet'suwet'en name for that mountain?
THE INTERPRETER: He is asking directions from the lake. From where the lake is.

If you are at the end of the lake, at the Kilwoneetzen side, the mountain would be on your left side, if you're looking at the lake, on your left side and little behind you.
South?

Yes, south.

THE INTERPRETER: He says: *There's a mountain here, and along here, and one here, and the one that's here, [I don't] know the name.*

MR GRANT: No, the one I'm talking about. This is the lake and you're at the Kilwoneetzen end of the lake, the mountain on this side?
The middle one is Kelzil. That is second mountain, Kloooguseye Mountain. Cars can drive up that mountain now.

MR GRANT: Just for the record, the description was given from standing at the end of McDonnell Lake and although I don't want to be bound by this, if this lake is a long lake – and this is what I don't want to be bound by – we'll assume that the lake goes in an east–west direction and you're at the east end, if that's the description, the use of Johnny's hands and the interpretation given is that you are talking about the mountains along the south side of McDonnell Lake?

Let's go off the record for moment, just so I can explain what I'm saying.

OFF THE RECORD DISCUSSION

MR GRANT: Go back on the record.

For the record, the description that was given and the names of the mountains that were given were based on Johnny David standing on the Smithers end of McDonnell Lake, facing McDonnell Lake. From that end, I believe counsel and I can agree for this purpose that would be where the road comes down from the Smithers side. Just to put that position in some geographical context, Smithers would be behind Johnny David as he's facing the lake and the Hudson Bay Mountain would be on his right side and to his rear. The mountains that he has described would be the mountains along McDonnell Lake on the left side as he's facing the lake.

What is the Wet'suwet'en name for McDonnell Lake?
THE INTERPRETER: He says: *[I know] the name but [I have] forgotten.*
MR GRANT: Okay.
THE WITNESS: *Tsayxingls is name for McDonnell Lake.*

Now, in that same position as you are, looking at these same mountains at the south side, is it correct that at the far end of the lake is Big John's territory?
That area I described belongs to the Gitksan people and Big John had a big cabin built in that territory.

When you say 'area I described,' are you talking about the far end of the lake?
THE INTERPRETER: The far end of the lake.

MR GRANT: There is a ranch on the Smithers end of McDonnell Lake called the Copper River Ranch. Is that in the Wet'suwet'en territory?
Jeff or Jess Iceman was the first farmer that moved there. Later was somebody – Mr Garden. Yes, it is within Kilwoneetzen territory. He did not trap, he just put up the farm.

Coming back towards the Smithers area within the territory, is there a lake called Dennis Lake and, if so, is there another Wet'suwet'en name for that lake?
Tsilgutznaytie, that means road leading into Dennis Mountain. Tsilgutznaytiebun, that is also a name of a lake.

Is it correct that Tsilgutznaytiebun is Wet'suwet'en for lake?[4]
THE INTERPRETER: Yes, it is.

MR GRANT: You talked earlier, when Kela was standing behind you, about the territory where Kela was buried. Is there a Wet'suwet'en name for that territory?
Alxkat.

Of course, I was referring to an earlier Kela.
Alxkatbun [Alxkat Lake].

I understand that Kela is in your House. Is this correct?
Yes.

Do you have authority within Kela's territory as Maxlaxlex?
Yes, I'm able to speak on the territory and as a young man I also trapped the territory.

You've described one territory next to the Kilwoneetzen as Big John's territory. Do you know what his Gitksan Chief's name was?
I don't know his Hereditary Chief's name.

Was he a hereditary Gitksan Chief?
Yes, he was Hereditary Chief in the village of Tsaytseetsuk.[5] He was the moo'tie for there, which means that he was the person who overlooks the affairs of that village.

What is the Wet'suwet'en word you used?
THE INTERPRETER: Moo'tie.

What other Wet'suwet'en House had territories around the Kilwoneetzen territory you have described and who were the Chiefs?

THE INTERPRETER: Maybe I phrased it wrong – he said: *There was no people that were immediately close by.*

MR GRANT: Okay. Who held the territory next to Maxlaxlex, on the south side of Maxlaxlex territory?

THE INTERPRETER: Which direction is south? He said: *West side was Gitksan.*

MR GRANT: Yes.

THE INTERPRETER: *This side, the east side, belonged to the Wet'suwet'en.*

MR GRANT: Yes. Does he know which Wet'suwet'en Chief held the territory to the east of his territory?

THE WITNESS: *Gyoluget. Gyoluget, who lives in Smithers. The whole area near the Smithers area all belongs to Gyoluget. There's a station near Topley, there's a creek that runs by there, that is the boundary for Gyoluget, and the area above that belongs to – belonged to – Tyee David which now belongs to Woos.*

MR GRANT: I'm sorry, I wasn't clear. Does Woos have territory immediately adjacent to Maxlaxlex or is it territory beyond Gyoluget's territory?

Gyoluget's traditional territory is adjacent to Maxlaxlex.

And Woos is – ?

THE INTERPRETER: *Woos [is] further east.*

MR GRANT: Of Gyoluget?

THE INTERPRETER: Of Gyoluget.

Who holds territory to the north of Maxlaxlex? He has said that Gyoluget is on the east side and Kilwoneetzen on the west side, so who would be north of them?

The area north of the areas I've described belongs to Peter Alfred's wife's grandfather and is now in the name of Wah Tah Keg'ht. And Henry also has that name.

How long ago did David Dennis stop trapping in the Kilwoneetzen territory? And hunting?

Ever since he was not able to walk and when he was feeling sick.

How long has it been since you have trapped or hunted in that territory yourself?

A long time, ever since I was unable to walk and I got too old.

So is it correct you trapped and hunted there until you became too old?
Yes, that is correct. I trapped with David Dennis. David Dennis is alive but is unable to talk because of his advanced age.

Does Maxlaxlex own fishing sites in the Kilwoneetzen territory?
Yes, they are.
THE INTERPRETER: *[I do] have fishing spots there but [I let] other people use it and [don't] say anything about it.*
MR GRANT: Do you let people from your House use those fishing sites?
THE INTERPRETER: *[I let] anyone who wanted to prepare salmon, to smoke it, go up there and use it.*

Can you tell us some of the people who use those fish sites now?
I don't know.

Do you have fishing sites or a fishing site in the Moricetown Canyon as Maxlaxlex?
Yes, there is, on this side of the river.
THE INTERPRETER: That would be ...

MR GRANT: Did you go with Alfred Joseph and other researchers to show them those fishing sites a few years ago?
Yes.

Did your House use fish traps either here or in the Kilwoneetzen territory?
In the – people prior to us did use fish traps but in my time people from my House did not use fish traps.

Did they use those fish traps in the site in the Moricetown Canyon?
I can't recall. It was Gitksan used the fish trap the most.

MR GRANT: Go off the record for [a] moment please.

OFF THE RECORD DISCUSSION

On the record. Who would have the authority in your territory to decide who uses that territory? Is it only Maxlaxlex or is it all the members of your House?
They would ask whoever was the head of the territory. The people would ask him if they could hunt in his territory. The same with the Andamanuk people.

Who? The Chief or the House members or both are considered the owners of your territory?
That is correct. The people who are the Andamanuk can also use the territory. The territory is for the benefit of all the people in that Clan.

I am not certain whether there is something missed in the question or the answer but I gave him three options: who were considered the owners of the territory – the Chief, the members of the House, or both the Chief and the members of the House?

THE INTERPRETER: He explained again what he had explained earlier: *Where people from the Clan, people from the spouses' clan, or people from spouses where there is a husband or wife are also able to use the territory.* Then he went on to say that: *When the person is going to be taking the Chief's name, he is allowed to go out into the territory and hunt and trap. When he takes on the name he distributes the meat amongst the witnesses. And the territory belongs to the Chief.*

Now, has the Kilwoneetzen territory always belonged to the House which Maxlaxlex is in?[6]
Yes, the territory belonged to the Kilwoneetz all that time.

Did this belong to the Kilwoneetz long before the white man came?
Yes, the territory belonged to the Kilwoneetz long before the white man and since the white man came they have destroyed everything.

Did the fishing site of Maxlaxlex at Moricetown belong to Maxlaxlex before the white man came?
Yes. The fishing hole in the Moricetown Canyon belonged to Maxlaxlex long before the white people came and now everybody is using it.

Was the Alkut territory of Kela always held by Kela?
Yes, it belonged to Kela all this time.

You talked about six Kelas this morning and you talked about one who was buried at this lake, before the Kela who was buried, was there another Wet'suwet'en Kela?[7]
As far as I can remember is from the Kela that is buried in Topley and the way our system works there's probably more Kelas before my time.

Okay.
I'm telling you the truth and while Kela before Mabel was alive Mabel took on that name.

Are you finished? Okay, so there would – is it your evidence that there would be Kelas before the white man came and those Kelas had control over their Alkut territory?
In the very old days these names have been carried on, and some are even buried in their territories, and some were cremated, and these names have been carried on for generations.

Is that the same with Smogelgem?
Yes, the same. It is the same with our other hereditary names; not anybody can just come in and take a name. These Hereditary Chiefs' names are not given to just anyone. Some people have been brought up to take on these names.

Was any part of Kilwoneetz territory or the Alkut territory given as compensation by some other House or Clan to Maxlaxlex and Kela?[8]
No, this was not given by anyone. It was the people who had these names prior to us who have handed them down.

Is there any other territory of Maxlaxlex or Kela other than Kilwoneetz or Alkut?
There's – Kela has some territory in Topley area and also Telkwa River area. We do not hold land in any other territory.

And the Topley area is the one known as Alkut, just to be clear?
Alkut, yes.

Is there a name for the Telkwa River territory?
That just goes by Telkwa. Old Sam looked after the area near Telkwa River.[9] The Telkwa River area was looked after by Old Sam and Old Dennis, Joe Nass and myself, Maxlaxlex, and now the land has reverted back to Mabel Sam, who is Kela. This is done right and you can never reverse that.[10]

Is the territory at the Telkwa River, is that close to the Kilwoneetz territory? I mentioned all the mountains, Telkwa River on one side and Copper River on one side. So the territories you are talking about are right beside each other, is that right?
THE INTERPRETER: Kilwoneetzen and Telkwa River?
MR GRANT: Yes.
THE WITNESS: *Yes, they were side by side. We hunted and trapped in the same area.*

Are there any other territories which Maxlaxlex or Kela gave away as compensation in the old days?
It does not seem that way but now white men are trying to take the land.

I notice from what we've talked about that you know the names of many of the places in the Kilwoneetz territory: Is this part of your role as Chief, to know the names of the mountains, the lakes, and creeks on your territory?
Yes, it is because I am a Hereditary Chief.

You talked about Kela's pole outside and the netseyeee on Kela's

drum. Is her pole and her netseyeee connected to her territories? That is, does she own all three?
Yes, all the things we mentioned belong to Kela.

How are the netseyeee and the pole connected to her territory? What is the relationship between those and her territory?
The dog crest belongs to Kela. Gitdumskaneese is on the pole, the human figure. There are some of my crests on that pole.

All right. I would like to ask you a few questions about how you used your land in the old days, when you were younger. Could you tell me what animals you hunted and trapped in the spring in the old days and where you did that?
Me'dzee – caribou – is what I hunted for in the spring, and the meat was smoked and dried.

Was that in the Kilwoneetz territory?
Yes.

What animals if any did you hunt in the summer, in the old days?
There were many animals we hunted and ones that were fat. I did this in my territory and that was for feeding myself and others.

Did you trap marten and beaver in your territory when you were younger?[11]
It is this time of the year that we start trapping for beavers and marten, and other animals.

Can you tell me what other animals you trapped for?
Some of the other animals were yis – which is timber wolf; nastl – which is wolverine; and all the other animals that happen to be in that territory.[12]

You described that you hunted some animals in the olden days, in the summer, and you said you hunted the fat ones. Can you tell me some of the kinds of animals you hunted in the summer time?
Some of the animals we hunted in the summer who were fat was the sas – the bear; latlad – which is deer; me'dzee – which is caribou; ggikh – which is rabbits.

Did you do any trapping in the summer?
No, I didn't. Just went after the animals.

What animals do your people hunt nowadays in the territory?
Nowadays, they hunt and trap for all the animals I mentioned before, the ones that are fat.

Did you hunt or trap in the winter months in the old days?
I started trapping when I got strong.

What animals did you hunt and trap for in the winter in the old days?
In the early days we hunted or trapped for me'dzee when there was no deer and the marten –[13]
MR GRANT: Were there other – sorry?
THE WITNESS: *– and a lot of other animals. Around 1907 the white man came and the game warden began to give the traplines to their own white people which had originally belonged to us. And the game warden told the white people, you see any Indians crossing into your territory let me know and I will arrest them. That is how these people looked at us – also during this time as they were taking our traplines, [they] also began blasting the beaver dams, which reduced the number of beavers.*

During the same time there were many horses and the white man came –
THE INTERPRETER: *– and he refers to Dutch people –*
THE WITNESS: *– and they came and they began to eat the horses, which again reduced the number of horses in the territory. There were a lot of horses and they were all gone.*

Our traplines were all gone. The resources on our territories, the trees, were all gone. That's it.

Just to clarify when this happened, you say this was in 1907 so this would have been when you were a young man or actually a boy, is that right?
Yes, I was a child. After 1907 we began to lose everything.

Johnny, you've outlasted some others today. The lawyer for the province has to go back to his office. He assumed we would be finished or that you would want to stop earlier, so we're going to adjourn today because he has to get back to his office for some other commitment.
What I am telling you now, I have not made it up. What I am telling you now I've learned from my Elders from the early days. I told you about how we were treated by the white man. The game wardens had sticks which they threatened us with, similar to the stick I have behind the door.

The trees that they have taken off our territory, the government has been receiving the money and they're putting it in their pockets – now we want the stumpage fees. We want the stumpage fees from all the traplines they have logged.

Where do they get the money to be driving nice cars, to have a railroad system, or to be flying in the air? This is our money that they're using and I am walking on my feet.

In the old days these people that trapped each territory, they protected the trees in the blocks so that the animals would flourish. Now the government has trapped all our territories and they have all the money and the way they treat us, they throw us little bits and pieces of things to eat. That's it.

I would like to ask one brief final question. Is Hudson Bay Mountain within your territory or is it in another territory?
THE INTERPRETER: Within whose territory?
MR GRANT: Within Maxlaxlex's territory.
THE WITNESS: *The area behind Hudson Bay Mountain is within my territory. Where they used to have the ski jump, all that area is in Gyoluget's territory.*

MR GRANT: As I said before, the lawyer representing the province here, Mr Milne, has made other commitments and so he has requested that we adjourn early today, so we're going to adjourn now.
THE INTERPRETER: He is asking what time you want to start tomorrow.
MR GRANT: Eight thirty.
THE INTERPRETER: *Eight thirty, fine.*

EXAMINATION ADJOURNED AT 3.40 P.M. UNTIL 8.30 A.M., 19 OCTOBER, 1985.
OFF THE RECORD DISCUSSION

UPON RESUMING AT 8.50 A.M., 19 OCTOBER, 1985

MR GRANT: This is a continuation of the commission evidence hearing which we adjourned yesterday afternoon.

EXAMINATION IN CHIEF BY MR. GRANT (continued)

I was asking you yesterday about some of the animals that were harvested, Johnny: Can you tell me what fish you harvested in the spring time and where you harvested them from?
In spring the people would fish for testlee – steelhead – when the ice melts people go to lakes and fish for the fish that are in the lake.[14]

Would this be trout?
THE INTERPRETER: Lake trout.

Did you fish in lakes like McDonnell Lake?
Yes. There is various kinds of salmon in McDonnell Lake. Then in the winter is when we eat the steelhead. We set nets for [them] under the ice.

Would this be in the river or in the lakes?
Yes, at the outlet of the lake.

What fish did you harvest in the summer months, and where did you harvest them from?
They would set nets and they would get testlee *– that's the steelhead;* buguy *– which is lake trout; and sabay – which is Dolly Varden.*[15]

I am not sure, did he [you] say where these fish [are]?
McDonnell Lake. Sagwendax. Which is Wet'suwet'en name for McDonnell Lake.

Did you fish in the summer months in the Moricetown Canyon as well?
Yes.

What did you fish for there?
In the Moricetown Canyon we fished for k'aas, which is the spring salmon; tsamon, which is the pink salmon; tylook, which is the sockeye; and stelkay, which is the eels.

People still fish at the Moricetown Canyon now, is that right?
Yes.

Do people still fish at McDonnell Lake and in the Kilwoneetz River for these other species that you were talking about?
Yes, some people still do get salmon from there. Nobody prevents them going there.

Did you fish in the fall time and, if so, where and for what species?
We did fish in the autumn and this was for some of the stronger salmon that were spawning – some were turning red. They were the older ones.[16]

Where did he do that fishing?
Same area, McDonnell Lake. Where they did most of the fishing was in the Kilwoneetz territory.

Was most of this fishing by gaffing or did you use fish traps or other means to catch fish up there?
They use gaff hooks, which were about six or seven feet in length.

Did your mother's people fish the Kilwoneetz territory the same way as you fished, from before your time?
Yes, they did because it belonged to them.

Do you know if this fishing went on before the white man was here?
Yes, they did fish for salmon ever since they were born.

Ever since who was born, I'm sorry?

THE INTERPRETER: *Ever since our people were born.*

Did you have berry grounds in your territory, in the Kilwoneetz territory, and, if so, did you use those berries and what kind of berries were they?

Yes, our people did have berry patches in their territories and they were that much more valuable when the tahkee – huckleberries – were ready for picking.[17]

What time of year was that?

The area near Dennis Mountain is where a lot of huckleberries were picked, and people from Babine also came to pick the huckleberries. This would be around the month of August.

Do you have a name in Wet'suwet'en for the month of August?

Yes. Buningasxkas is for the month of August. This refers to the small birds being born and they're unable to fly and they're just running around on their legs.

Aside from the huckleberries, did your people harvest other plants in the old days?

The huckleberries were dried on a rack, about two or three feet long. They were dried for the winter months.[18]

Aside from the huckleberries, did your people harvest other plants in the old days?

Berries that were picked was nawus – which is the soapberries, and blueberries – the Wet'suwet'en word for that is yintoewee'.[19] *These berries were dried and these berries were used whenever there was a feast.*

Were there particular places in your territory where you would pick huckleberries or soapberries or blueberries?

The area on the other side of the Hudson Bay Mountain where all the berries grew. Yes, on the slopes of the mountain.

Are these berries still picked by the Wet'suwet'en people today?

Yes.

Are they still used at the feast today?[20]

One of the mountains near Hudson Bay was called Kengitlow't. That's the area near Dowdey, about five [or] six miles from here. That area belonged to Mrs Peter Alfred, who's known as Dzee, and when the berries would ripen she would invite all people from the village to go pick berries.

Before Mrs Alfred held that name, did the previous Dzee also do that and invite the people from the village to go and use the berry grounds? *Yes, they did. This was Madeline's predecessors; they did the same thing as she had done. It went quite a ways back.*

Was this done before – did the people pick berries and use these berries at the feasts from the time before the white man came to this area? *They did harvest the berries long before the white man came.*

Did you and your mother's people use any plants and pick plants for medicine purposes?
THE INTERPRETER: He's gone to get a sample of plant medicine.

MR GRANT: Go off the record.

OFF THE RECORD.

THE INTERPRETER: He's lost it.

MR GRANT: On the record.

There's one plant, that's called the 'konyay [Devil's Club].[21] It grows near the mountain. The roots of that plant is used for medicinal purposes.

Just for the record, I understand that when Johnny left he had some of this plant and he went to look for it and he can't find it now?
THE INTERPRETER: Yes.

What is that plant used for? Curing what ailments or can it help people?
This konyay plant, the roots are separated or crushed and it is used for your back, and it is also used to clean your guns. Our people also use it for good luck charms. If you miss an animal with your gun, you take this plant and you pass the root through the barrel three times, and after this process, it brings you luck and you should not miss another animal with that gun.

Has this plant been used by your people in these ways since before the white man came?
They did use it before the white man came, and [I'd] give an estimate of at least 500 years that it's been in use.

When you say 500 years you mean a very, very long time?
Yes, and we are still using it today. [I] wanted to show you guys but [I] can't find it.

Possibly he will be able to find it some time before we're through.
Yes.

Did the people use this plant before the time of guns to help them in their hunting?
It was used before the gun was introduced. If this plant is touched by people who are not lucky, if they touch this plant they would get ill.

In the days before the arrival of the white man, did your people use cedar or other trees from your territory?

MR MILNE: Mr Grant, I think I should just mention for the record at this point, you're asking questions for periods obviously before the Witness was alive. His only possible answer could be what other people have told him. If that answer is being offered for the truth of the statement then you're entering into a hearsay area. I raise that now, for the record, in that there may be some objection taken when the evidence is being introduced at trial.

MR GRANT: Your objection is noted.

In the days before the white men, did you harvest trees or use wood from trees for any purposes?
The bark from the balsam tree was used for medicinal purposes, as well as the spruce which in our way we call wa'tsoo. Again the bark was used for medicine. The Devil's Club which was described earlier. There is another plant that grows in the swamp back in behind us. It is called gaxlowk. This is a very dangerous plant, and only people who know how to use it should use it. When they eat this plant it brings them great luck. This last plant, when a person is going to go hunting, he would take some of this plant and this plant would bring him luck during his hunt.

This is gaxlowk?[22]
Yes. [I] will remember some more as we go on.

Now, did you use trees for other purposes, other than what you have described where you used the bark of certain trees for medicinal purposes? Did your people use them for other purposes? For example, building or using them to make tools or to make weapons?
Besides using the bark for medicine, some of the trees we used for building smokehouses. We have used the trees in this way for many years. We did it in our time; so did the people before me. The winter when our people go trapping and snow gets too deep, they would place logs in that manner and they would

cover these logs with the branches and these would be half buried. These were called 'half-buried branch house.'

THE INTERPRETER: He also mentioned: *These branches were all facing down this way on both sides.*

MR GRANT: Yes.

– When it snowed, the water would not run into the building, it would run off the branches.

Is this the type of construction that he was looking at that you've drawn, that the interpreter has drawn? For the record?
Yes.

MR GRANT: Okay.

THE INTERPRETER: And he said: *[I have] used this structure [my] self as well.*

For the record, the interpreter has in giving the explanation of this drawn on a plain piece of paper a diagram which is triangular in shape and it assists in describing what the witness is describing. I would like to have it marked as an exhibit as he has put it to the witness and it assists in explaining what the witness has described.

MR MILNE: No problem.

MR GRANT: Go off the record for a moment.

OFF THE RECORD DISCUSSION

EXHIBIT NO. 2 – Pencilled diagram of half-buried branch house [unavailable].

MR GRANT: For the record we have marked this diagram as Exhibit No. 2 on the commission evidence of Johnny David, and the Wet'suwet'en word for this structure is *alxbainy* – can we describe this as a half-buried branch house in the winter months?

THE INTERPRETER: Yes.

We interrupted you, Johnny, to mark that exhibit. My question was: what you had used – your people had used – trees for aside from medicinal purposes in the old days, before the arrival of the white man?

MR MILNE: For the record, I'm not opposed to you leading on that. If you want to ask him if he used trees for this or that, that's fine.

MR GRANT: Is there any other purposes that he can recall at this point in time?

THE INTERPRETER: He described: *Our people had to fell trees before metal was introduced. They used the form of rock which was shaped in the wedge and they would chip away at the tree till it fell. When the tree was felled, they would light fires underneath it to get them to the length they were required and this wood was used for heating purposes.*

Did your people use cedar bark to make necklaces in the old days?

Go off the record for moment.

OFF THE RECORD DISCUSSION

MR GRANT: On the record.
THE WITNESS: *Yes, they did. Used it for necklaces as well as for headbands.*

MR GRANT: Off the record for a moment.

OFF THE RECORD

MR GRANT: On the record.

THE INTERPRETER: He is describing how: *The cedar bark was woven, something like this, and it was worn around your neck as well as around your head. It was red and this was used by the kaxluhxhkm [Wet'suwet'en Healers Society].*

Can you explain what that means?
The headband is called deesgut' and it's red in colour, and that's used by the kaxluhxhkm, and some of this regalia can be seen at Ksan.

Was the necklace and headband of cedar bark, were they woven. That is, braided?
Yes, it was braided and some were the width of your hand.

Did you ever see this being used yourself in your lifetime?
Yes, I did. I watched them.

As far as you know, were they used from the time before the white man came?
Yes, they were used before the white man came and since they have come we don't use it as much.

I've asked you – Mr Milne has reserved the right to object to things you talked about before your lifetime – I've asked you on many occasions this morning about what was done before your lifetime and before the white man came. (Do you want to translate that before I go further?) When you talk about what your people did before the time of the white man, were you told or taught these things by other people?

THE INTERPRETER: He said: *The business we are talking about is very important.*

THE WITNESS: *Before I was born, this disgus [cedar bark] was used. After I became strong enough I watched the people use it. It was used all along the Skeena River. When I became old enough my father made me one and I joined them [the kaxluhxhkm]. This disgus, along with that all went the blanket.*

THE INTERPRETER: He's getting tired.

MR GRANT: Let me follow through.

The Wet'suwet'en people and the history of the Wet'suwet'en was taught by word of mouth from one generation to another, isn't that right?

I was taught by my mother, my father, my uncle, Old Sam. They taught me the old ways of our people. They told me the history that I am telling you now, and what I am telling you now, I have not made it up.

Old Sam would have been told those things by his uncle and so on back in time, is that correct?

Yes, his uncle before him would have taught him.

In those days your people did not write down their history, is that right?

THE INTERPRETER: He said: *In those days our people did not write.* And he was asking me whether he should tell the story about Father Morice introducing the writing system.

Okay, but the question I am asking you is: as I understand, before Father Morice, your people did not write and they did not write the history down?

No. The school teacher came from the coast, he came to Hagwilget. The village was down by the river in the canyon. He came to my father's smokehouse, and that is where he began teaching our people. That House was called Misdziah or Owl House. That is when Father Morice came; he was a Frenchman, and he came in and he watched this teacher trying to teach our people. He used the slate board. He talked for a long time and our people couldn't understand him. Then Father Morice grabbed the slate boards, broke them in pieces, and the schoolbooks that were in the smokehouse, he threw them out. After he was done, he grabbed the school teacher and threw him out. One of our people gathered up the books and packed it down. After Father Morice cooled down, he told the people in the smokehouse being taught by this teacher that this teacher is a devil, don't listen to him.

Even though Father Morice told them not to listen to this teacher, some of our people did learn and one was Pat Namox's father. The reason Father Morice chased the teacher away from here was because he [Father Morice] did not want our people to learn, he wanted to push his religion on us. That's it.

I understand this happened at your father's smokehouse at Hagwilget?
Yes. Down in the canyon.

Was your father there when this happened?
Yes, he was.

Did this happen –
And they were just young men at the time.

Was this before you were born?
Yes, way before I was born.

Your father told you what had happened?
I was told by my father as well as Pat Namox's father.

Who was Pat Namox's father?
THE INTERPRETER: Alfred Namox.
THE WITNESS: *Through his learning his children learned the ABC's.*

Through Pat Namox's father's learning?
He encouraged his children.

Who did?
THE INTERPRETER: *Alfred Namox encouraged his children to learn the ABC's.*

Do you remember how old you were when you first saw a white man in here? That is, first saw a white man yourself?
The telegraph wires came through here in 1901 but I had seen white people before this, maybe five years before 1901.

Did your people use trees to make their totem poles before the arrival of the white man?
THE INTERPRETER: He said that: *Our people made poles from these trees long before the white man came.* And he threw out: *About 100 years before they came.*

Did your people use wood or trees to make houses other than the alxbainy that you've already described before the white man?
Yes. The trees were used for houses long before the white man came and they

split the logs which was used for part of the buildings. There was a wooden wedge about so long –
Can you describe that?
THE INTERPRETER: About two feet long.
THE WITNESS: *– Wooden wedge that was used to split the logs. And the bark from these trees, which is called gilluy', was used for the roof.*

Just to clarify, was the bark called gilluy' or the trees?
THE INTERPRETER: The bark was called gilluy'.
MR GRANT: Okay.
THE WITNESS: *It was very similar to the way we use tarpaper today. They were strong, for the smokehouse. The logs were cut into two-feet lengths to heat the house, the smokehouse in the winter.*

What kind of trees were used to build the smokehouse?
They used all species of trees.
THE INTERPRETER: He mentioned two – *which is birch, and kandew, that is jack pine.*

Was cedar used as well?
Yes. They used all kinds of species for firewood.

Were the trees split when they were standing up or were they cut down first?
Yes, the tree was felled first then split.

How did you people fell the trees in the old days?
I was told before my time, the tree was chipped away at until it fell and after the Hudson's Bay Company came they introduced the ax.

Are you finished? Okay. What did they use to chip away the tree? What kind of tools?
Dayweetz.
THE INTERPRETER: Dayweetz is rock which is shaped into a wedge.

Did your people get the trees that they used from their House territories, such as Kilwoneetz, Kela's territory, and the other Chiefs' territories?
They used the trees wherever they could get them.

Was this the same in the days before the white man came?
Yes.

Did your people always take the trees from the territory or did they go to the Gitksan territory to take trees?

They used the wood as one people. The Gitksan and the Wet'suwet'en, they would all work together as one and use the wood.

Do your people still use trees from the land today for building the smokehouses, for making the poles and for firewood for the smokehouses?
Yes. They're still doing that and they don't prevent or argue with each other about the trees.

When your people want trees for these purposes do they go to the Forestry to get licences to cut their trees?
Now, sometimes we do go to the Forestry to get licence for woods but in the old days we didn't have to.[23]

When the people of your House get wood today, do you know if any of them go to Forestry?
When the white man came, he fenced off the lands and when we had to make wood, we had to get permit in order to make wood for ourselves. It was like that around here, as well as in North Bulkley. The white people did not like us cutting down their trees. They fenced it off and claimed it as their own.

Who do you say now has the right to the trees on your territory in Kilwoneetz, your people or the white people that have moved there?
The land should be used by us. It belongs to us and it shouldn't be used by the white man.

Have you ever been compensated for trees that were taken by the white man from your territory?
No one has compensated me yet. I have mentioned this to Forestry people on several occasions and they have just told me to wait.

You talked about the people using dayweetz or rock ax. Where would they get the stone or the rock for those axes?
I don't know where they got the rock from but I have seen it. They probably made it themselves and some of these wedges you can see at Ksan.

Did your people use particular rocks to make arrowheads in the old days?[24]
Dayweetz was used; they were chipped on the ends and those were used for – chipped rocks – they were used for arrowheads. The way they chipped it, they used another rock. For the bow and the arrow part, they would use the species that grows near where Thomas George used to live.
THE INTERPRETER: I know what it's called but I can't remember it.

MR GRANT: Is there a Wet'suwet'en word he used?
THE WITNESS: *Gitsugun?*
THE INTERPRETER: That's used for the arrow and bow.
MR GRANT: Is this a type of wood?
THE INTERPRETER: It's a type of wood.
THE WITNESS: *Some of them are good size.*

You say this was gathered from where Thomas George used to live. Where was that?
Just east, about five miles east of Telkwa. The area is known as Pencil Mountain. That's the name that is given by the white man.

Is there a Wet'suwet'en name for that mountain?
Tutdeenah, and the white man calls it Pencil Mountain. That is the mountain you see near where Thomas George used to live.

Is there a Wet'suwet'en name for the rock, the type of rock that was used for the arrowhead?
Beez. They're very difficult to find. It's difficult to work with and sometimes shaped like a knife. It is wrapped around the arrow portion and it is made strong and this is used to kill me'dzee or caribou.

You said this rock was hard to find. Did the Wet'suwet'en people dig in the ground for this rock?
They were chipped from – they had to be chipped out and it is very difficult to do. This was in the early days and I don't know where they went to get this rock.

Would they use the same kind of rock to sharpen these arrowheads or would they use a different kind of rock to sharpen them?
Different kind of rock is used to sharpen the point.

Do you know where those rocks were obtained from?
These rocks are found just anywhere, and the rock has to be flat and that's what is used to sharpen.

Did your people use things like clay or red ochre in the old days?
   Do you want to go off the record?
THE INTERPRETER: Yes.

MR GRANT: Off the record for moment.

OFF THE RECORD DISCUSSION

MR GRANT: On the record.

Did people use clay in the old days?
Yes, they did use it [tsaste'l].
THE INTERPRETER: Tsel'ste – I think I pronounced that wrong. Tsel'ste, that's berry. He said that we still use.

MR GRANT: Go off the record.

OFF THE RECORD DISCUSSION

MR GRANT: Go on the record.
    For the record, it was noted by Mr Milne, and I agree, I should put on the record why we've gone off the record on numerous occasions this morning. Many of these words are technical terms and the interpreter is requesting assistance for the correct phrase for these technical terms, such as clay or species of trees and for that reason that we are going off the record so he can consult with another Wet'suwet'en person to try and get the correct pronunciation so the witness is not confused.

Now, I believe my question was: Did your people use clay in the old days? And, if so, what for?
This clay was mixed with sand and it was used to paint the Houses.

Where did you get this clay from?
From various areas and wherever it is found, it is mixed. They also use this for stove and also the pipe that goes up. It was built the same way the brick chimneys are built today, and they would last a long time.

Did you see any of these stoves in your lifetime?
Yes, I did. My own father had built one, and the people before him had done this as well.

MR GRANT: Just for the record, before the last break you had asked him about the clay and you indicated that he had interpreted what you were saying was about berry. Now, is there a Wet'suwet'en word for berry that's very close to the Wet'suwet'en word for clay?
THE INTERPRETER: Yes there is.
MR GRANT: What is that?
THE INTERPRETER: Tsel'ste, which is cranberries; the word is very close to how you say clay.
MR GRANT: For the record those words: the word for clay is tsaste'l; the word for cranberry is spelled tsel'ste.

THE WITNESS: *This clay stove when it is built, rocks are used and clay is put*

around these rocks, and it is built up until it reaches the roof and when the house burns down this remains standing. It was just like cement.
THE INTERPRETER: He said: *That's it.*

Did your people use paint and did they take things from the ground to make paints with?
There's a plant, wild rice or kungalx and wilgus, which is wild rhubarb, these were used for food.

They were used for food?
THE INTERPRETER: They were used for food.

Did you have places in the Kilwoneetz territory where you took these from?
Yes, our territory, and these plants grow in many parts of the world and people use them for food.

Did your people trade those plants with other Indian groups?
People knew of these plants and they would pick them themselves and use it for food.

Did they trade them?
And the other people used it the most and I did as well. There's still a lot of it around.

I raised the question earlier and I'll ask it again: did you use paints? I'm not sure we got an answer to that question?
THE INTERPRETER: No, we didn't.
Did you use any materials from your territory or did your people or your mother's people use materials from your territory to make paints? That is, for colours?
The plant that grows near a swamp, called yinsaylx, the bark of that is where – the fungus from these plants are ...

OFF THE RECORD

THE WITNESS: *The fungus from these plants are dried, and made into powder, and it is mixed and used for paint.*

What is that paint used for?
This paint is used for painting the designs on the houses.

Would these be the crests?
Yes, the crests.

Was the paint used in the old days by the people to paint themselves in preparation for certain ceremonies or for war or for other reasons?
Yes, there was. Before they would dance they would streak it on their face and on their forehead.

Did they use any materials from the ground for paints as well? Like clay?
No, they did not use clay for paint.

Did they use other materials from the ground for paint?
No, just the barks from the trees.

Do you know what kind of trees those were that they used that fungus from?
I have forgotten the name of the species but it comes from a tree and feels like rubber. Gibsco(?) And this is – They heat it up and then they pound it and it becomes powder. They would add water to it and it is just like the paint that we use today. They use this to paint the ammeelow'k, which is your head piece.

Did you see this being used in your lifetime?
Yes, I did. This paint that I'm telling you about is found in the Nadina River area, near the lake. Nadina Lake. You can still find it today.

Was this paint used in the old days before the white man arrived?
Yes. We knew about this for a long time.

We're going to adjourn the examination at this time, for the record – does he have more to say on that answer?
I would like to ... about mining: The Indian people found the minerals –
THE INTERPRETER: He mentioned Dowdy mine.
– my father had found some minerals. My father would show these rocks to the white people and they would say this is no good and they would leave. Year after they would start up the mines. This is how they started Dowdy mine. This is not the only time white people have told Indian people these rocks are no good. This is how the white man has been lying to us. That's all.

MR GRANT: We will adjourn now and will endeavour to complete the discovery next week, starting next Thursday afternoon.

EXAMINATION ADJOURNED AT 10.40 A.M. UNTIL 1.30 P.M.
25 OCTOBER, 1985.[25]

VOLUME 4

**Direct Examination of Johnny David by Peter Grant,
19–20 December 1985**

PROCEEDINGS COMMENCED AT 9:46 A.M. 19 DECEMBER 1985

VICTOR WILLIAM JIM, Wet'suwet'en interpreter, previously sworn.

JOHN DAVID, witness called on behalf of the plaintiffs, previously sworn, testifies as follows:

EXAMINATION IN CHIEF BY MR GRANT:

Q   I wish to confirm you have been sworn to give evidence on this commission and this is a continuation of the commission (interpreter speaks to witness) – which was adjourned on October 19th 1985? Yes?
A   *Yes.*

Q   Now, I'd like to ask you a few questions about your territory, the territory of your House. Who decides who can use your House territory for hunting, fishing, or trapping?
A   *When my father was alive he was the one that gave permission for other people to use the territory.[1] Now that my father is gone it is me myself who would give other people permission to use the territory. And those people that use the territory through our old system would give parts of the money or meat to whoever is the head of the territory, the same with the fishing spots.*

Q   Now, in this case I'm referring to – I'm referring to the Kilwoneets. Who says that – who gives the permission for people to use the Kilwoneets territory?

A   Okay. *For the Kilwoneets territory at this time the head man for the territory is David Dennis and myself while I'm alive and we let other native people use the territory but not white people.*

Q   Does everybody in your House, in the House of Ginehklaiya [House of Many Eyes], have the right to fish at the Kilwoneets territory?
A   Okay, um. *Today a person who is honest and trustworthy is able to use the territory with our permission. If a person is not trustworthy he is not allowed to go into the territory.*

Can a person from another House in the Laksilyu tribe [Small Frog Clan] use the Kilwoneets territory and if so does he require permission?
Yes, that happens. Other members of the Laksilyu houses, can use the territory with the permission of the – with the Head Chief.

If they do, do they have to, um, give – let us say they take some furs off the territory. Do they have to pay the Ginehklaiya people for their use of the territory by giving some of those furs to them?
Okay. *The other House members from the Laksilyu Clan when they go out hunting or trapping at a feast they would get up and distribute some of the meat or furs that they got from the Ginehklaiya territory and they would distribute these to the Ginehklaiya people.*

Is that practice still done today?
Yes, this is still happening today. The practice has never stopped. It will continue on as long as the people are here.

If a person who is not a Laksilyu wants to use the Kilwoneets territory of Ginehklaiya, would he ask permission?
Yes, that can happen. And the way it works is the spouses of the Ginehklaiya Laksilyu people with the permission of the Chief can go and hunt in the territory, then give parts of the money or the meat to the people from the Ginehklaiya.

Do the Ginehklaiya Chiefs give the members of the House permission to use parts of the territory for hunting and fishing so that all members of the House have somewhere to hunt and fish?
Okay. *This is done sometimes when they are invited and not for the – that isn't done for the white people.*

Okay. Um, let me rephrase my question, I think you may have misunderstood. If a person in your House was not given part of the territory

to hunt and fish, how would they get their food? Maybe I should back up. Were there situations in which a member of the House was not – was denied the right to use the territory?
Okay. The Chiefs decide if a person is not trustworthy or honest they are sometimes denied access to the territory; ones that are trustworthy are given permission to hunt and trap in Kilwoneets territory.

Okay. Was there a name for those people who the Chiefs believe were not honest and who would deceive people?
Okay. These people are called nanilate nee. Nanilate nee means people who sneak around.

And were those nanilate nee denied access to the territories?
Yes.

Were they allowed into the feast hall?
No, they don't.

Were the nanilate nee allowed to redeem themselves or to mend their ways by the Chiefs?
Okay. The, um, nanilate nee, sometimes if they hunt on someone else's territory without permission, if they want to mend their ways they are invited to the feast where they are spoken to by the High Chiefs where they sometimes kloxnayklus – means straighten out – and then are given permission to hunt in the territories.

Okay. When you say – you said at the beginning of your answer when they go and hunt in someone else's territory. Is this as an example of what makes a person a nanilate nee?
Yes.

This method of scolding or of criticism by the Chiefs at the feast and the opportunity for the nanilate nee to correct themselves, is there a name for that ceremony?
It's called sonanadeenlate li. (Further response by witness to interpreter) Sonanadeenlate li, and that means to sit down properly.

Can you say that again just so the –
Sonanadeenlate li.

Now, if the person doesn't correct himself, the nanilate nee, can his name be taken away from him, his feast name?
Okay. Their names are taken away and they are never allowed to attend a feast again.

Okay. Did Old Sam tell you about this process?
Using the words of Old Sam, I also observed it at the feast that I attended and Mabel or Old Sam was the Head Chief of the Copper River area and now Mabel – (Further response by witness to interpreter) – Telkwa River, and one of Mabel's children's name – he is one of the persons that holds territory in the Telkwa River area.

Old Sam was? Sorry, I just –
THE INTERPRETER: *No, Old Sam was the Head Chief for the Telkwa River area and now one of Mabel's children has rights to territory in the Telkwa River area.*

Now, you say that you saw this process at a feast. Who – who was involved? Can you recall who was involved and about how old you were when that feast occurred or, if it was a funeral feast, who had died? Okay, just go through the first part. Can you recall who was involved at that feast in the nanilate nee and the sonanadeenlate li?
Okay. *He was – he was at a feast – (Interpreter questions witness further)* Okay. *The process that they use is that the nanilate nee is brought into the feast hall and he is spoken to by all of the Head Chiefs of the different Clans and if he does not listen to the words of the Head Chiefs then his name is taken away and he is not allowed back into the feast hall.*

Okay. Do you recall how old you were when you saw this happen?
Okay. *I was about ten years old when I seen the – seen this process. I have seen it here and in the Kitwancool area.*

When you refer to here you're referring to here in Moricetown?
THE INTERPRETER: *Here in Moricetown.*
MR GRANT: Just for you, the judge may read this anywhere so it's good to be clear where we're referring to, for the record.
THE INTERPRETER: Okay.

Now, in normal cases who does the Head Chief – who would the Head Chief of your House allow to use your House territory? Would all members of the House usually be given the right to use the territory?
Okay. *The different members of the House or the Clan are allowed to use the territory with the permission of the Head Chief and the person who is given permission to use the territory at a feast redistributes the meat or the money to members of the House and this is our own Indian law and it is not the white man's law.*

Would the husbands or wives of members of the House be allowed to use the territory?
Okay. *The spouses – spouses as well as the relatives who are honest and trustworthy are allowed to hunt in the Laksilyu territory.*

Okay. Would the women, the children of the Ginehklaiya women, be allowed to use the territory?
Yes. The children are allowed.

Would the children of the men of the House of Ginehklaiya be allowed to use the territory?
THE INTERPRETER: Want to repeat that, Peter?
Would the children of the men be allowed to use the Laksilyu territory, of the men of the Ginehklaiya House? I'm sorry.
Okay. *These – the children of the men from Ginehklaiya are allowed to use the territory and they are called basalkanutzlee.*

Does that – does that mean something? What does that word mean? Okay, maybe you can ask Johnny ... (Interpreter speaks to witness) ... if this is just a special name for the – okay, we'll just go off the record. We're going to go off the record for a moment. Before I go off the record I just want to confirm.

MR MCDONALD (video technician): We're off the record.

(OFF THE RECORD DISCUSSION)

MR GRANT: Okay, for the record I just asked for a break so that the – the witness has referred to Mabel Critch who is Kela, who is present, in his last answer. For the record Counsel for the province objects to the witness referring to another witness to determine the meaning of the word basalkanutzlee. I would just – on that basis there was no discussion. I would ask you again if the word basalkanutzlee can be explained by other words, if you can ask the witness that. Just ask the witness that.
Okay. *The men's children –*
Just go ahead?
Men's children, offspring are the ones who are called basalkelzut.
That was basalkanutzlee?
Basalkelzut.

MR GRANT: Okay. Can you explain to the witness what I explained before as to why he could not speak with Mabel due to the objection? (Interpreter speaks to witness) I just wanted him to understand what happened.

If someone in Ginehklaiya's House is too old to hunt or fish, how would they get their food and who would provide it to them?

Okay. *If a member of the House is too old to hunt or fish, a strong person would go out to hunt or fish for the elderly Chief and this person would give all the meat or the fish to the Chief and the elderly Chief – and the elderly Chief can and does sometimes give half back to whoever has done the hunting for him.*

Okay. Is this usually done by a person in the same Clan or on the father's side, that is a different Clan?

It can be members of the same Clan or a member from the father's side.

If it's a member from the father's side, is he repaid by the elder Chief or by the House of the Chief?

Okay. *The person who does the hunting or the fishing for the elderly Chief would bring all the fish or the meat to the Chief and he is – the elderly Chief gives half or whatever amount he decides back to the person who has done the hunting for him. And even today this is happening with Mabel Critch always bringing me food, the salmon in the summer, and same with my grandson Peter David.*

Does your House hold any fishing sites at Moricetown?

Okay. *Each of the different Clans or Houses had their own fishing spots and if someone wanted to use that fishing spot, he would ask the Head Chief of that Clan or House before he is allowed to do any fishing in those particular spots, and yes, my House does have their own fishing spots.*[2]

Are your fishing spots in Moricetown Canyon or are they outside of the canyon itself?

Yes, it is in the Moricetown Canyon.

[THE INTERPRETER:] And then he went to explain again that: *You ask permission first before you go fishing in those holes.*

Okay. Do the people in your House have to ask the Chief for permission – that is, the people of Ginehklaiya – to use the fishing site?

The members of the Ginehklaiya do have to ask the Head Chief of that House – Head Chief or Chiefs of that House – and when they get their salmon they would give half or whatever amount to the Head Chief or Chiefs of Ginehklaiya.

Is the Ginehklaiya fishing sites on this side of the canyon or the other side of the canyon? I'm talking about – when I say this side, I'm referring to the highway side, Highway 16 side, of the Moricetown Canyon, for the record.
Okay. *It was on both sides of the river and the smokehouse was on the highway side of the river.*

Did you show Alfred Joseph the location of your fishing sites at Moricetown Canyon?
Yes. I showed him – showed him all the fishing holes of all the other clans as well.

And you showed him all the fishing holes in the Moricetown – that's in the Moricetown Canyon?
Yes, I showed him all the – the whole area in the Moricetown Canyon and there were many people who came to ask for that information and I told them all that I knew.

Did you show Alfred Joseph the Wet'suwet'en fishing site and the location of those sites at Hagwilget Canyon?
Yes, I did take Alfred to the Hagwilget Canyon. I showed him where all the platforms were, who they belonged to on both sides of the river, and Alfred has all this information.

Okay. Did Alfred to your – did Alfred show you a map on which he put this information?
Okay. *Alfred did have a map and I told him where all the fishing sites were and he hasn't given me a copy of those maps.*

Okay. Can you tell us which Chiefs, which Wet'suwet'en Chiefs, owned fishing sites, fishing stations, in the Hagwilget Canyon? Without telling us the location, just tell us which Chiefs held fishing sites at the Hagwilget Canyon? (Interpreter speaks to witness, no response by witness) Maybe you can go – can you translate what he's given you thus far?
Okay. *Old Muldoe ...* (Interpreter speaks further to witness) ... *Old Muldoe had a fishing spot across from Hagwilget. He probably had the best spot. He caught a lot of salmon and he would give it away to the people and the people that he gave it to themselves would sometimes repay him with – repay him with money; he did not ask for it. And on this side Paul Lawelxges..*

What is that again?
Paul Lawelxges had a fishing spot. (Further response by witness to interpreter)

Okay. *Alfred has all the information on who had fishing spots in the Hagwilget Canyon.*
And that's Alfred Joseph?
THE INTERPRETER: Alfred Joseph.

Was Old Muldoe Gitksan or Wet'suwet'en?
Yes. He was Gitksan.

Do you know what his feast name was, his Chief's name?
Tsaykya.[3]

Was Paul Lawelxges Gitksan or Wet'suwet'en?
He was part Gitksan. Along with Old Muldoe they were the High Chiefs.

Okay. Do you know what his feast name was, Chief's name?
Welxges was his feast name. (Further response by witness to interpreter) *Okay. Paul Lawelxges used a belt that was from the Queen, that's what he used.*

You mean he wore it?
THE INTERPRETER: *He wore it.* (Further response by witness to interpreter) *And [I don't] know who has that now.* (Further response by witness to interpreter) *And Spoaks also had a belt and [I don't] know who has that.*

Was Paul Lawelxges' mother Gitksan or Wet'suwet'en?
She was Gitksan. (Further response by witness to interpreter) *And the land at Mud Creek, across from Mud Creek all belonged to Paul Lawelxges.* (Further response by witness to interpreter)

Is that Wet'suwet'en or Gitksan territory?
It's Gitksan territory.

Okay, were there any Hagwilget or were there any Wet'suwet'en Chiefs who owned fishing sites at Tsaykya. (Interpreter speaks to witness; witness responds, no response by interpreter) Okay. What is he saying to you?
THE INTERPRETER: Okay. I was just clarifying whether Stephen Alexander was Wet'suwet'en.
Some of the Wet'suwet'en Chiefs that had platforms or fishing holes were Stephen Alexander – Stephens Alexander, he was from the Morice Lake area – and another one was Dzikens Williams who is the grandfather of Peter Williams who is still alive today.

Are those the two that he's given?
He says that: *Alfred Joseph has all the information on who owned all the platforms.*

Okay. Did Stephens Alexander have a Chief's name and if so what was it?
Noostel. (Interpreter speaks further to witness)
MR GRANT: For the record, you're asking if Dzikens Williams has a feast name?
THE INTERPRETER: *Yes.*
Okay. *Stephens Alexander's feast name was Noostel and Dzikens was the name used, and that was his feast name.*

Can you explain what Noostel means?
Okay. *Noostel when you translate it means wolverine.*

Is that a Wet'suwet'en or Gitksan name?
It's a Wet'suwet'en name.

Did you see any of these fishing platforms or – being used in your lifetime?
THE INTERPRETER: At Hagwilget?
[MR GRANT:] Yeah.
Yes, I did see them. I also got fish from the platform.

Okay. How did the people – can you just describe for us how the people fished at Tsaykya?
They used to gaff, gaffed it.

Do you – did people used to use baskets or weirs at Tsaykya?
Okay. *Old Muldoe had a fish basket, they called it wee and we call it gonzay, and then it was fairly long. It had a box at the end and when it would fill up he would take it out and he would distribute it amongst the people and the people themselves would pay him with money or if they went trapping in the winter they would give him meat as payment for their fish. He did not ask for it, the people did it themselves.*

Okay. When the people repaid Old Muldoe, did they do that at the feast or outside the feast hall?
Okay. *They would – they would repay Old Muldoe with money or meat at any time, whenever the people had the money or the meat. It wasn't done only at the feast.*

When you were talking with Alfred Joseph, you showed him the locations of these platforms at the canyon?
Okay. *I showed him where the platforms were. His grandfathers showed him where the platforms were and Alfred knows all the information about the canyon at Hagwilget.*

Okay, just – you went to the canyon with Alfred Joseph, is that right?
Yes, we did go there. We stood on the bridge and I pointed out the locations.

Are there some cases where you're – a Wet'suwet'en Chief may transfer a territory to another Chief or to another person when that person has helped, for example at a feast.
Okay. *After a person spends a lot of money at the feast he is sometimes given a territory forever, it never goes back.*

Okay. Is that the answer?
THE INTERPRETER: Yeah.

Do you recall a situation of Tom Alex's wife, um, doing this?
He wants to know her name.

Okay. I understand that Tom Alex's wife was the older sister of Mrs Long Charlie and she was from Babine?
Older one, right?

Okay. I'm not certain.
Okay. He says: *There were two sisters. He wants to know whether it was the older one or the younger one.*

MR GRANT: Okay, just go off the record for a moment please.

(OFF THE RECORD DISCUSSION)

MR GRANT: We'll go back on the record.

(witness speaks to interpreter)
Okay. *[I think I remember] Tom Alex's wife. It is the older sister of Long Charlie.*
[MR GRANT:] Um-hmm?
She was a lady from Kilwoneets territory.

Now, I understand that she asked Halzbun for some money, a feast, and – and in return she – I'm sorry that she, just let me get this straight here. I understand that Tsadzalh gave her permission to use his hunting territory for one year. Do you recall anything about that? Okay. Do you want to just –

ANTONIA MILLS (writer): Tsadzalh.

MR GRANT: – Tsadzalh. Tsadzalh gave her permission to use his hunting territory for one year, gave Tom Alex's wife that permission?

THE INTERPRETER: Tom Alex's wife asked?

MR GRANT: Tsadzalh gave Tom Alex's wife permission to use his, that's Tsadzalh's, hunting territory for one year. Ask him if he recalls the circumstances of that?

He wants to know: *Which territory?*

[MR GRANT:] It may have been Beaver Creek. (Interpreter speaks to witness, no response by interpreter) Okay. If he doesn't, can't recall –

MR MILNE: The witness gave an answer, we don't have a translation.

MR GRANT: Go ahead, what did he say?

THE INTERPRETER: He can't remember or he doesn't recall. (Further response by witness to interpreter)

[THE WITNESS:] Okay. *Tom Alex's wife was Klatden or married to Klatden and they spent most of their time –* (Interpreter questions witness further) *– Manson Creek. They spent most of their time at Manson Creek and when they got old is when they moved back to Hagwilget.*

Was she – Okay, go ahead? (Witness responds further)

Okay. *While they were hunting Tom Alex's wife found gold and that creek is now called Tom Creek.* (Further response by witness to interpreter) *Tom Alex's wife was taking water from the creek and she saw something red and she dipped it and it was gold and she put it in a pail.* (Further response by witness to interpreter) *And when Tom returned she showed him what was in the bucket and Tom knew that it was gold.*

What did he do, what did they do with the gold?

Okay. *A camp was set up and gold was produced there.*

Who – did the Wet'suwet'en produce the gold or did the white men come in and take the gold?

Okay. *He was part – he spoke some Sekanne.*

Who, Tom?

Tom did, he spoke some Sekanne and Tom himself had set up the line.

Um-hmm?

And they worked it for two or three years and then they quit and he said that's how it was told.

Did this happen before you were born?
It might have been the time when I was born, I can't remember. But I remember Tom's own wife telling me.

What was her – was she Wet'suwet'en?
She was – she was a Wet'suwet'en woman from the Kilwoneets territory.

And did she have a feast – what was her Wet'suwet'en name?
Hakasbaine is her feast name, Hakasbaine.

MR MILNE: I think I should mention for the record at this point again something I had mentioned in the October sitting – that we're dealing again with information that was told to the witness and not information that he has of his own personal knowledge and therefore an objection may be made at trial to the introduction of that kind of evidence as hearsay.
MR GRANT: It's not necessary to translate that. Your objection's noted. (Witness speaks to Interpreter)

THE INTERPRETER: He thinks he's starting to remember that earlier question we were asking him about.
Okay, you – your last answer has helped me with it, I'll come back to it. I'd like to finish what you've just talked about first. I'd like you to tell me what Tom – what Tom did with the gold?
When they worked the mine the gold was put into small boxes, they were sent away. And there was a white person whose name was Jack, he was helping Tom. And this white man named Jack received about five thousand and Tom received a lot of money and that's as far as I remember.

Okay. You said you remembered about Hakasbaine, and Tsadzalh gave her permission to use his territory. Can you describe that to us, what happened?
[THE INTERPRETER:] He's asking me if Hakasbaine used his territory. (Further response by witness to interpreter) Okay. And he also wants to know where the territory was.

I cannot clarify the location of the territory but I understand that your father, Smogelgem, was involved in having it returned to Tsadzalh. Does that help you to remember?
He said: *If you guys can give [me] an idea of where the land was [I] would probably remember.*

Okay. Tell him we'll return to that after we – at some other time, okay. I'll check that and see if I can help you with that.

Okay. *[I think I'm] starting to remember when [my] father, Smogelgem, helped someone give the land back. And [I remember] a court in Hagwilget, and it was in [my] father's house, Smogelgem's house where they had their court.*

Was this a court of the Chiefs?
Okay. *[I remember] it was the High Chiefs who were trying to settle the dispute on a trapline but [I want] to know where the territory was.*

Okay, okay. Bear with me, Johnny, and I will – I will ask you about that tomorrow. I will find out where it is and try and ask you about that tomorrow. I don't want you guessing and trying to guess what we're referring to, we need to help you.
Okay. *[I remember] being there listening to them; all [I want] to know is where the territory was, whether there's a lake or a mountain peak and describe the territory.*
[MR GRANT] Okay, we understand.
Okay. He's saying: *[I remember] them talking about it and [I don't] want to guess as to where the territory is.*
[MR GRANT] That's correct, okay. I'd like to ask you about another area now, we'll return to that tomorrow. (Interpreter speaks to witness)

Okay. Did the Kilwoneetsweten people trade with the Nishga and Gitksan in their territory, in the Kilwoneetsweten territory?
Okay. *When there was – in the Kilwoneets territory there used to be a lot of salmon. When the salmon started running people from Kitselas as well as the Skeena River area as well as the Babine Lake people would all converge into the Kilwoneets territory. There were so many fish there that they just used a stick to kill the salmon. They were prepared for winter and then everyone would in their – go back to their own villages. They never disputed over who the salmon belonged to, the salmon was for everybody.* (Further response by witness to interpreter) *There were no people from Fish – federal Fisheries Department – there was no one like that around. The Indian people themselves looked after the management of the salmon.*

Did the Kilwoneetsweten people give – did these people from the other areas ask the Kilwoneetsweten people for permission to come into their territory?
Okay. *People from the different areas did ask the Kilwoneets if they could fish there and they were given permission and when the people from the different areas had prepared their salmon for the winter they would all disperse back to their own villages and the same was done with the berries.*

Okay. Did the Skeena River, the Babine, and the other people that came to the Kilwoneetsweten territory, did they give gifts to the Kilwoneetsweten or pay them for using their territory?
Okay. *They did not give them gifts. They just took their salmon and left and nobody was paid for anything.*

Did they feast at the Kilwoneetsweten territory when the other people were there?
Okay. *They did feed themselves and when these people returned to their villages they would tell stories about who helped them get their salmon or the berries and then they were distributed to other people from the other villages.*

And was this fishing in the Kilwoneets territory by all these people, this occurred in the summer time?
Yes, in the summer.

And the use of the berry grounds, did that occur in the late summer as well?
The berries were done the same time. All the salmon and the berries were dried and they were taken back to their villages where they would gather the people, and the fish and the berries would be distributed and the people would be told the fish and the berries came from certain areas such as Kilwoneets.

Okay. Did the Kilwoneets people return to Moricetown in the winter?
Okay. *They would – the Kilwoneets people after the fishing season would return here in Moricetown. And at this time of the year – which means now in December – in December they would move to Hagwilget.* (Further response by witness to interpreter) Okay. *Mabel owns territory in Telkwa, Telkwa River area.* Okay. *The same thing would happen: all her wild game or whatever they took from her area would be taken to Hagwilget and distributed amongst the people. And she is the only one left now from – she's the only one left now that holds territory in the Telkwa River area.*

And that's Kela's territory?
Yes.

MR GRANT: Okay. We're going to take a few minutes break so there can be a new film put in the camera.

(PROCEEDINGS ADJOURNED)

(PROCEEDINGS RECONVENED)

I've been referring to Maxlaxlex's territory and the Ginehklaiya terri-

tory. When I refer to those that is the Kilwoneetsweten area, the same as the Kilwoneetsweten territory around McDonnell Lake and Dennis Lake, is that right?
Yes.

Okay. Which is the territory you described earlier in these commission hearings?
Yes.

Yes. Okay we're only asking that again because of the length of time and counsel's, the province's lawyer, wanted to clarify the area we were talking about. (Interpreter speaks to witness) Now, since the break and just before we started again, you indicated you remember this territory that Hakasbaine used from Tsadzalh. Can you – do you remember that now, and do you want to explain what happened?
Okay. *There was – [I remember] the incident with Hakasbaine. There was a person named Klayslahtl – he was from Cheslatta – and the area [I'm] going to tell [you] about is around Ootsa Lake.* (Further response by witness to interpreter) Okay. *Hakasbaine's father had given Klayslahtl a box of berries which had some oolican grease mixed with it. He had given it to him because there was starvation.* (Further response by witness to interpreter) Okay. *And Klayslahtl told Hakasbaine ['/you can use my territory for one year for giving me the berries and the grease.[']* (Further response by witness to interpreter) Okay. *And Hakasbaine's sister Jeannies Kyo – means big Jenny – they made trouble with each other, and Klayslahtl came into the House of Smogelgem which is my father.*[4] (Further response by witness to interpreter) *And then they talked about the land in question and Smogelgem helped Klayslahtl get his territory back.* (Further response by witness to interpreter) *After Klayslahtl died Jeannies Kyo had registered the line in her name and now [I don't] know who has that territory registered.* (Further response by witness to interpreter) *And that's as much as [I] can remember.*

Okay. Do you recall which House and what tribe Hakasbaine belonged to?
Okay. *Both Hakasbaine and her sister Jeannies Kyo were Laksilyu and both were from Ginehklaiya.*

What about Klayslahtl, which House and which tribe?
Klayslahtl was from Cheslatta. I can't remember which House or Clan he came from.

Was Klayslahtl Witso –
THE INTERPRETER: *Klayslahtl.*

Was Klayslahtl Wet'suwet'en?
Klayslahtl was not a Wet'suwet'en, and Hakasbaine's father was also from the same area and that's where the problems started.

And Klayslahtl is a Nutsenee?
Yes, they were Nutsenee.

And the Nutsenee are the tribe to the east of the Wet'suwet'en, is that right?
Yes, they do live east of us. (Further response by witness to interpreter) And that's as far as I remember and I wanted to talk about it and I've told you now.

Okay. This happened – you remember when they came to your father's House?
Yes, I remember.
Okay?
[I remember] the process they went through. Klayslahtl come into the House with Smogelgem and when it was okay with him they invited the ladies in. They talked about it and the ladies lost and Klayslahtl got his territory back.

Was Smogelgem the only Chief that mediated that dispute or were other Wet'suwet'en Chiefs involved as well?
There were other Hereditary Chiefs involved and since Smogelgem was the Head Chief at that time the other Hereditary Chiefs told him that the land should go back to Klayslahtl and that's what happened.

Do you know who the other Hereditary Chiefs were that were involved when they told that to Smogelgem?
Chief Kal. (Further response by witness to interpreter) Okay. [I remember] two other Hereditary Chiefs that were there. There was Chief Kal, he was the second leading Chief and also Francis Lake John, and the others [I] can't remember.

Okay. Was Chief Kal – was that his feast name, Kal?
Yes. That was his feast name and he was the second leading Chief.

After Smogelgem?
THE INTERPRETER: *After Smogelgem.*

And what – what House and tribe did he belong to?
He was from the Ginehklaiya. (Interpreter speaks further to witness) *Laksilyu. He was from the Laksilyu.*

Okay. And Francis Lake John, did he have a Chief's name, and what tribe and House was he from?
Kosteeget, Gilserhyu.

Okay, the first thing he said was, just for the record, was Kosteeget his Chief's name?
THE INTERPRETER: *Kosteeget was his Chief's name.*
Yes?
THE INTERPRETER: *And he was Gilserhyu.*

That was his tribe or Clan?
THE INTERPRETER: *That was his tribe or Clan.* (Interpreter speaks further to witness)
And he was from Ya'tsowitan, which means Thin House.

Okay, and that was his House?
THE INTERPRETER: *That was his House.* (Interpreter speaks to Antonia Mills)

Did the Kilwoneetsweten people trade with the Gitksan people at any time of the year?
They did no trading but they were in close contact with the Gitksan people who had a village near Carnaby called Tsi'tse'gut. Big John was the Chief there. (Further response by witness to interpreter) Okay. *Big John was Laksamshu [Fireweed Clan, also a Clan of the Gitxsan].*

And he was a Gitksan Chief?
Yes.

Did the people of your House trade with the Gitksan or the Nishga at Hagwilget or at Moricetown at other times of the year?
THE INTERPRETER: I'm just trying to find a better word for trade.
Okay.
(Interpreter speaks to unidentified party)
THE INTERPRETER: That's what I've been saying.
[MR GRANT:] What is the Gitksan?
THE INTERPRETER: Ketneeayelgee is trade.
[MR GRANT:] Okay, and there is a problem understanding what he's referring to?
THE INTERPRETER: And he said: *They haven't been trading but they would invite each other to the village where they would feed each other.*

Okay. Do you know if the Wet'suwet'en ever went to Mission Flats near Hazelton to trade with the Nishga or the Gitksan?

[THE INTERPRETER:] He wants to know what they traded.

Okay. That's what I'm asking – I'm asking you if they traded for things that the Gitksan had or if they traded for oolican grease with the Nishga?

Okay. *They did trade seaweed and oolican grease for the different animals that the Wet'suwet'en had such as marten or goat; goat meat and this is what they traded for.*

Okay. Now, what other tribes did they trade with? For example, who did they trade with for oolican grease?

Okay. *The people from the Nass. They would trade with the people from Moricetown as well as from Hagwilget and Babine.*

Okay, and what did – what did the Wet'suwet'en people give the Nishga in exchange for the oolican grease   in other words, what was it traded for?

Okay. *The – our people would trade furs from the marten and beaver as well as other animals.*

Did you trade for seaweed from the coastal tribes, and if so which tribes?

Okay. *The swinak or seaweed, that was traded with the coast Indians, and the xha or the oolican grease was traded with the people from the Nass River area.*

And what did you give to the people from the coast in exchange for the seaweed?

Okay. *The – in the old days we, as I said before, we traded marten and other animal furs for the seaweed and nowadays it is money.*

Okay. Did the Wet'suwet'en people go to the coast and up to the Nass to trade or did the coastal people and the Nishga come here to your territory?

Okay. *They – the people from the outside would bring it in.*

Okay. And did you give – trade fish, smoked fish, or other fish products with these people or did the Wet'suwet'en mainly provide meat and furs to the Nishga and coastal people?

No, they did not trade, trade dried salmon or fish.

Okay. Did you – did the Gitksan and Wet'suwet'en trade, and if so what did the Gitksan give to the Wet'suwet'en?

Okay. *They did trade with the Gitksan people and it was for basically the same items as the coastal people and it was the same, same things they traded for.*

Okay. Do you – you know the village of Kisgegas, which was a Gitksan village on the Babine River?
Yes, I remember the village. My father had taken me there for three winters.

Did the Wet'suwet'en people provide moose or caribou hide to the Kisgegas people to your knowledge?
Okay. *What little moose hides there were all came from the North. They were sold to the Hudson Bay Company, and Native people would buy the moose hides and that was what they used at the feasts because at that time there were hardly any moose in this territory.*

Okay. What furs other than moose did the Wet'suwet'en and Gitksan use at the feasts in the old days?
Okay. *The meat was used at the feast. When the Hudson Bay Company became established people would buy the Hudson Bay blankets and this is what was distributed amongst the people.*
THE INTERPRETER: And he also mentioned: *The datnee was used. Datnee is groundhog.*

Okay. Did the Wet'suwet'en provide groundhog to the Gitksan? Did they trade with the Gitksan and give them groundhog furs?
Okay. *The furs of the groundhog was given by the Wet'suwet'en to the Gitnay or the Gitksan people and the groundhog fur made good blankets.*

What did the Gitksan people give in exchange for these groundhog furs, to the Wet'suwet'en?
Okay. *They would trade different furs. As well blankets were exchanged for the furs.*

When you went to Kisgegas with your father, did your father trade with the Chiefs at Kisgegas then?
Okay. *The people of Kisgegas would invite the Wet'suwet'en people and all the Wet'suwet'en would go up there. There would be a feast, they would be given blankets and other things. And about two years later the Wet'suwet'en would invite the Kisgegas people and they would be given blanket and other materials to repay them.*

Okay. Did you attend any of the feasts that your father went to at Kisgegas?
Yes, I did go with him. He had his regalia on and I would sit between his legs and look between the – between his regalia.

Okay. Do you recall how old you were about then?
About nine years old. (Further response by witness to interpreter) *And I*

heard all their words. (Further response by witness to interpreter)
And I would listen to each of the Chiefs getting up to speak, and I would ask my father what they were saying and my father then would tell me what was being said.[5] *And that is how I am telling you this information.*

Did – do you remember any of – the names of any of the Chiefs that put on those feasts that you attended?
No, I can't remember their names. (Further response by witness to interpreter) *But I know that they were Hereditary Chiefs that would get up to speak, there was always three of them.*

Were those feasts – do you remember why they were holding those feasts? Were they because somebody had died, or was there some special – or was there a pole raising or was it something else?
Yes, the – some of the feasts I attended were, were for a person who had died. People from that House would come in to invite the people.

Where were you – was your father in Moricetown or on his territory when he was invited to these feasts?
Okay. The – the people from Kisgegas would come to Hagwilget, where they would spend three days inviting all the people, and it was when most of the people were back in Hagwilget that people would come to invite them.

Okay. Was this usually in the winter months then?
Yes. It was during the winter months, not in the summer.

Okay?
This was usually after the Christmas season, when the river and lakes were frozen over.

Okay. And how did you travel to Kisgegas with your father?
Okay. It was by a dog team with toboggans, and my father had eight dogs, and most of the people would go along with him.

Okay. I wanted to ask you something about the medicine that you used in the old days?
[THE WITNESS:] *Dicanyu.*

Do you recall – do you recall an old person from Kispiox who became very sick when he went into an area where there was a lot of devil's club and he was brought back to the Wet'suwet'en territory and was cured with cedar bark or disklas? The word was given to me.
THE INTERPRETER: I remember that word the last time but I'm having the same problem. You were the one that told us –

MR GRANT: Off the record for a moment.

(OFF THE RECORD DISCUSSION)

Go back on the record. Do you have my question? You've lost it?
THE INTERPRETER: If he remembers the man from Kispiox who –
[MR GRANT:] Do you want the question read back?
THE INTERPRETER: Yeah, please.
(Court reporter reads last question back to interpreter)
(Interpreter speaks to witness)
[I remember] a story. Alusinuk was his name. That was when the devil first got him. (Further response by witness to interpreter) Okay. *This man [I'm] talking about – we all know where the bridge is in Kispiox where it crosses the river. He had gone upriver from the bridge, he had gone up another trail and he had come to this large devil's club, it was quite large. And he had chopped it down and once that –* (Further response by witness to interpreter) *– then the big devil's club had fallen to the ground and he was working on the limbs when he had fallen on the big plant.*

He fell onto the plant?
THE INTERPRETER: He fell on top of the big plant.
Okay?
(Further response by witness to interpreter)
And people had found him at this place and he was brought back to his house and he couldn't breathe very well and they don't know how many days he had been laying there. (Further response by witness to interpreter) *When he was brought back to the house he was laying down. A song was sung with a drum. And slowly, he slowly woke up and came normal again.* (Further response by witness to interpreter) *And it was the people who are called the diyenee, medicine man in the English language. There were many of them there and they were the ones that had sang these songs and did the drumming who woke him up.* (Further response by witness to interpreter) *And the song that they sung [I] can't sing it but it was the song this sick person was singing himself, that's what they were singing as he woke up.* (Further response by witness to interpreter) And he said: *The story is very long but I can't tell it all.*

Okay. Did this happen – where did this happen that he fell on the devil's club?
THE INTERPRETER: He told you all that.
Okay. He described the territory?
THE INTERPRETER: Yes, it was above the bridge, above the present day Kispiox bridge.

Oh. Okay. I'm sorry. (Witness responds further to interpreter)
And this man that was cured, this man who made the disklas, and that is what the people from here as well as along the Skeena use today.

The *disklas* is the cedar bark headdress?
Yes, and that's cedar bark headdress and he painted [it] red from s'wah' is what they used to colour it.

Did the people, the medicine men when they cured this man, did they also use spiritual – did they rely on a spiritual cure as well as the physical medicines they were giving him? That is, did they invoke some, did they – for example – did they pray for him in a traditional way? (Interpreter speaks to witness, witness sings song)
Okay. *That song [I sang], that is the kind of song they would sing as the medicine man does his physical thing with his hands on the body and that is how he was cured and he did not do any spiritual prayers for the sick person.*

Okay. Did this happen before you were born, this particular incident, or did it happen after you were alive?
This was – this was before I was born.

Okay, and who described what happened to you, who told you what happened?
Old Bill and Old Satsan, he was the person that told me this and he also got the song. And I was – I was a – I was a big person when Old Bill or Old Satsan had died.

And what House and what Clan were Old Satsan in?
Okay. *He was Gilserhyu [Frog Clan].* (Further response by witness to interpreter) *Which is Birch House [Kaiya].*

And that was Wet'suwet'en?
Yes, Wet'suwet'en.

You referred to the man who was cured as Alusinuk. Was he Gitksan or Wet'suwet'en?
He was Gitksan.

Do you know what Clan he belonged to and what House?
No, [I don't].

Okay. I'd like to return for a few moments to the fishing sites at Moricetown. Is it correct that each Chief had his own specific fishing sites at Moricetown Canyon?
Yes, it's true that each Hereditary Chief had their own fishing spots and when

they die the name is passed on. The person who takes the name gets the fishing spot.

Okay. In the old days was there one Chief who caught a lot of the fish in the Moricetown Canyon?
My uncle – my uncle whose name was Wah Tah Kwets was the person who was the best fisherman in the Moricetown Canyon.[6]

And did he – how did he fish?
Okay. He had a fish basket, and it is on the highway side of the river where the fish ladder is now situated.

Okay. Was his fishing site destroyed by the fish ladder?
Yes.

Was there a name for his fishing site?
Okay. There are names for the fishing spots and [I] can't remember the proper name for it, but the area you're asking me about was called – (Interpreter questions the witness further) *– Gonzayeegutz. Gonzayeegutz means place where the fish basket is. There was a long – there was a pole which would raise the – raise the fish basket, then a gaff would be used to take the salmon out and he would – Wah Tah Kwets would – distribute the salmon amongst the people.* (Further response by witness to interpreter) *He would give a lot of the salmon to people who were going to go out trapping and when these trappers would return they would give him some of their furs as, as repayment for the salmon he had given them.*

Okay. Earlier today you described that the Ginehklaiya fishing site was on this side of the canyon. And was this a site that was used by Hag Wil Negh and by yourself, Maxlaxlex?
Yes. (Further response by witness to interpreter) *There were many smoke-houses in the canyon area. Hag Wil Negh had a smokehouse. Wah Tah Kwets had a smokehouse, and Wah Tah Keght had a smokehouse where the salmon was dried.*

Okay. And what was the name of Hag Wil Negh's fishing site in Moricetown Canyon?
[I] can't remember.

Okay. Was Smogelgem's fishing site on the other side of the canyon from the highway?
Okay. That was on the other side of the river where Hag Wil Negh and Smogelgem used it as one company – (Further response by witness to

interpreter) – *Hag Wil Negh's father [and Smogelgem used it was one company]. And it was at a place where it is called Gilloo kluk, means where the fish jump up.* (Further response by witness to interpreter) *And below that was Mooseskin Johnny's. And there is three different areas, I can't remember their names. And there's one, one area the name is not, it's a vulgar name, was a fishing area.*

It's all right if you say whatever names they are.
Tsantat'lay was the name of that fishing area [I] was talking about and that, that means 'shit falling in the water.' And that was the name of the area.

Do you remember when the government of Canada put in these fish ladders at the canyon?
[I remember] when they were doing it, but [I] can't remember the exact year when the fish ladders were built.

Okay. Did you or the other Chiefs to your knowledge consent to them putting those fish ladders in there?
Okay. *The Chiefs had not given their consent to the Department of Fisheries to put in the fish ladders. Louie Tommy as the Head Chief had spoken against the fish ladder and when they first started building the fish ladders police came with their guns, they were on top of the hill, and to this day they don't know who had signed the paper for the government to go ahead to start building the fish ladders.*

Was Louie Tommy Wah Tah Kwets?
Yes. He was Wah Tah Kwets as well as Chief. (Further response by witness to interpreter) *And we never did find out who signed his name to get the fish ladders built.*

Did government officials come and speak with Wah Tah Kwets or with yourself or the other Head Chiefs before they built the can – or built the ladders?
They did not talk to them.

Thank you.
(Further response by witness to interpreter) *The people from here would ask Fisheries – the Fishery people – who gave them permission to start building, and the Fishery people just told our people they didn't know.*

Okay. You said earlier that Wah Tah Kwets's fishing site was destroyed by this fish ladder. Were other Chiefs' fishing sites destroyed by these fish ladders?

That was the only area that was destroyed. (Further response by witness to interpreter) *And on the other side where the area that is known as fish jumping.*

That's Smogelgem's site?
Smogelgem.

Okay, was Smogelgem or Wah Tah Kwets ever compensated for the loss of their fishing – the destruction of their fishing sites to your knowledge?
They never received anything at all.

Okay. Do you know – sorry?
There was people that were supposedly looking after fish, Fisheries Department people. They didn't – they didn't care about what we said to them or they didn't care for our Indian people. (Further response by witness to interpreter) *And the Department of Fisheries people had said that a carload of salmon or truckload of salmon would be brought from the coast which would be distributed to the people in Moricetown, and to this day we haven't even seen a half a can of salmon.*

Did – when the ladder was put in, did it destroy – can you tell me how it destroyed the fishing sites of Wah Tah Kwets and Smogelgem?
Okay. *The area where they fish it was blown with dynamite so the cement would be poured. So their fishing area was destroyed by removing some of the rock.*

Did the fish used to rest in these spots where you fished?
Yes. It was the place where the salmon rested. It was like a home for the salmon, and now the ladders have been put in – very few people are able to get salmon from those areas. (Interpreter speaks further to witness)
THE INTERPRETER: Okay. He's asking if you're going to quit because I noticed he was getting tired, I asked him.

Um-hmm. Okay, I'd like to stop – I'd like to just finish this area. If I can ask you just one or two questions more then I'll stop, is that all right?
(Interpreter speaks to witness) *Just to finish this area?* He asked me: *If that was it, that was it period.* I told him we were going to continue tomorrow, and he said: *What's going on?*

Prior to Louie Tommy, Wah Tah Kwets, providing fish for the people, did his uncle or the previous Wah Tah Kwets do the same thing?
Yes, the previous Wah Tah Kwets had done the same.

The final question for today, Johnny, is did you see the smokehouses on the banks of the Moricetown Canyon?
Yes, I saw them and I was in them.

Okay. Maybe we'll try to get a picture to show you those, maybe you can tell him that, tomorrow.
THE INTERPRETER: Maybe tomorrow?
MR GRANT: Um-hmm.
THE INTERPRETER: Okay.

I want to thank you for all the time you've put in today and we'll meet again, adjourn to tomorrow. What time do you want us to start tomorrow?

(OFF THE RECORD DISCUSSION)
(PROCEEDINGS ADJOURNED AT 1:10 P.M. UNTIL DECEMBER 20TH 1985)

DECEMBER 20, 1985
(PROCEEDINGS RECONVENED AT 9:50 A.M.)

VICTOR WILLIAM JIM, Wet'suwet'en interpreter, previously sworn, testifies as follows:
JOHN DAVID, witness called on behalf of the plaintiffs, previously sworn testifies as follows:

PROCEEDINGS COMMENCED AT 9:50 A.M. 20 DECEMBER 1985

MR GRANT: This is a continuation of the examination adjourned yesterday and you the interpreter are still under oath and the witness is still under oath and he understands that, is that right? (Interpreter speaks to witness)

EXAMINATION IN CHIEF BY MR GRANT CONTINUING:

Yesterday we were talking about the fishing sites at Hagwilget and I have some photographs here and I would like to show them to you and if you could recognize any of those fishing sites that you could tell us whose they are.
He asked me: *Where the – if these were the fishing spots.* And he was saying: *[I'm] having difficulty seeing the photographs.*
Okay. Oh, he has some difficulty seeing them?
THE INTERPRETER: Yes.

Okay. If you cannot recognize any of the pictures or you have a hard time seeing, don't worry; just say so and we won't worry about it.

Okay? The first one for the record is – National Museum of Canada negative number 34615. Do you recognize the fishing site that is in that photograph?
It's Hagwilget.

This is at Hagwilget? (Interpreter speaks to witness, witness responds, no English response) Okay, if you have any – if he can't see it that's all right. (Interpreter speaks further to witness) Okay, I'll show – (Witness responds, no English response)
MR MILNE: I think we better have a translation.
THE INTERPRETER: Okay. What he's described is that there were –
Turn it so we can see.
THE INTERPRETER: He's describing: *There were three fishing spots or fishing holes on this side.*

You're indicating the bottom of the picture, for the record?
THE INTERPRETER: *The bottom of the picture. And three more across the river, there was six total.* And he's saying: *[I'm] having a lot of difficulty seeing the pictures clearly.*

Um-hmm. Did he indicate whose sites were across the river – that is at the upper part, the far side of the river from the photograph?
THE INTERPRETER: *The first site [I] indicated was Paul Lawelxges', then John Nabistes' and William Dzikens' on the other side.*

Okay, and that's going from the right to the left of the picture on the far side of the river?
THE INTERPRETER: Yes.

MR GRANT: Could that picture be marked as an exhibit please, Exhibit number 3.

EXHIBIT 3 – Photograph National Museum of Canada negative number 34615

MR GRANT: While that picture is being marked I'd like to show – could the witness look at the next picture. I'm sorry, could the witness look at the next picture which is National Museum of Canada negative number 34612. Just go off the record for a moment please.

(OFF THE RECORD DISCUSSION)

Okay, I'm showing you a picture which is numbered 34612. I would like you to – which appears to show in the picture some, one or more

Exhibit 3.

fishing sites. Can you – do you recognize those fishing sites in that pic-
ture and do you recognize what the picture is of?
He says: *[I] can't see the photographs too well.*
Okay. Okay, if you can give me that one back.
[I] just recognize the poles they're going across.
He indicated the lower part of the picture –
THE INTERPRETER: Yes.
– for the record.
He said: *If [I] could see the picture clearly [I] would recognize it right away.*

Is it his eyesight that is the problem?
Yeah, it's [my] eyesight.

MR MILNE: Would a magnifying glass help?
(Witness responds further to interpreter)
MR MILNE: What did the witness say?
THE INTERPRETER: He asked me if it was the Skeena River. I told him it
was the Bulkley.

MR GRANT: Okay. Um, it may be apparently because of the light shin-
ing on these pictures that makes it hard which is difficult because um,
if you look at these, these are glossy pictures. We maybe should not –
I'm just wondering if we should show him these pictures with the
lights off.
MR MCDONALD (video technician): Could I have the picture and see
how much glare he's getting, hold it in front of him. No, there's a little
glare but not a lot. (Witness responds further to interpreter)
THE INTERPRETER: He's still asking me where it is.
MR GRANT: Okay, is that still, is that still causing you some trouble with
the light off? (Witness responds further to interpreter)
MR MILNE: What did the witness say?
THE INTERPRETER: He asked me if it was the Bulkley River and I told
him that it was.

MR MILNE: I think the witness should give the evidence and not the
interpreter as to what's in the photograph.
MR GRANT: Well, okay for the – for the record I mean, I'm putting, I'm
putting the witness – I am putting to the witness some photographs.
There are numerous photographs that are quite old of different locations. These pictures could be taken anywhere in Canada or northern
British Columbia. I think that there's nothing wrong with me attesting
to the witness, subject to the fact that we would have to prove it later,

that these photographs are photographs of Hagwilget Canyon. This witness wants some form of direction as to where the photographs are of so that he knows what we're talking about and I don't see that there is any reason to object to that so long as we, at a later time, establish that these pictures are actually of a particular canyon.

MR MILNE: As long as you establish later where the photographs were taken and where they are from, then fine I don't have any objection to that. But the issue is where these photographs were as well as what sites that may show in the photographs. So if the interpreter is giving answers to the witness as to where it is, then certainly that is not evidence as to where those photographs were taken from.

MR GRANT: Okay. I'm going to ask you another question –

MR MILNE: I think you could preface your remarks by saying, if this was in Hagwilget Canyon, then are these the sites that you recognize.

MR GRANT: That's what I was going to do. I'm going to –

MR MILNE: But I certainly object to the photographs being tendered as evidence that they are photographs of Hagwilget Canyon. You'll have to prove that later. These will be marked for identification, not as exhibits.

MR GRANT: They'll be marked as exhibits and they can be dealt with later as –

MR MILNE: They'll be marked as exhibits for identification not as exhibits at the trial.

MR GRANT: I understand that these photographs are at Hagwilget Canyon. Can you – if you were told that these were photographs of Hagwilget Canyon, would that assist you in recognizing whose fishing sites they are?

[I] still can't see it.

Okay, you can give me that photograph back. I'm showing you another photograph, which is from the defendant's own archives, catalogue number 28541, negative number B-705. On the face [of the reverse] of the photograph is written Indian Salmon Trap, Hazelton B.C. Did you ever see a salmon trap such as is in that photograph?

He said: *[I've] seen one in Hagwilget and [I] referred to it yesterday. They called it wee. Wee.*

Um-hmm, go on? Who owned that trap in Hagwilget you saw that was like the one in the photograph?

Old Muldoe. (Further response by witness to interpreter) He's describing the photograph saying: *Salmon get in the other end –*

[MR GRANT:] Pick it up so you can show it to us.
[THE INTERPRETER:] He's describing the photograph.
The salmon would come in from the top end and into the basket at the bottom and they would be gaffed out by the people to get the salmon out.

MR GRANT: Okay. Could that photograph be marked as Exhibit number 4 please?

MR MILNE: That photograph is being tendered for what purpose, simply to show that is a salmon trap that was being used or that that is like a salmon trap that was being used?

MR GRANT: It was – I'm asking – I asked him – we will, we will demonstrate where that photograph was taken in due course.

MR MILNE: Well, but the purpose of the photograph, you said have you seen this, have you seen traps like this in Hagwilget.

MR GRANT: Okay. I want to mark it as an exhibit and we will proceed from there.

MR MILNE: Well, just a minute. I'm taking some objection to it being marked as an exhibit right now. I think we should clarify for what purpose it is being entered as an exhibit. Is it simply to show that he has seen salmon traps like that in Hagwilget? If that is what is being marked as an exhibit then fine. But it shows nothing further than that at this point.

MR GRANT: Well, it can – it only connects to his evidence. He's referred to this photograph in giving a description and therefore I want it marked as an exhibit because it's part of the record.

MR MILNE: But it's an exhibit that is simply showing a salmon trap. And it could be a salmon trap that was made anywhere and placed anywhere.

MR GRANT: Theoretically one might say that. Mark it as Exhibit number 4 please.

MR MILNE: Now, the salmon trap photo then is being marked as an exhibit for identification?

MR GRANT: It's being marked as Exhibit number 4.

MR MILNE: For what purpose is it –

MR GRANT: And you can reserve your right to object to its admissibility at trial. And I think that your objection's noted.

MR MILNE: Now, from the defendant's point of view, this photograph is being submitted, for the record, simply to show that it appears to be a salmon trap which appears to be like the ones that the defendant, or witness rather, has seen in Hagwilget and nothing further.

MR GRANT: Mark it as an exhibit please.

EXHIBIT 4 – Photograph entitled Indian Salmon Trap Hazelton B.C., catalogue number 28541, negative number B-705

(OFF THE RECORD DISCUSSION)

MR GRANT: Go back on the record. Just for the record I note that the exhibit stamp does have the standard exhibit stamp the reporter has for identification. These are exhibits proper on the commission evidence and counsel for the province has taken a position as to the purpose for which Exhibit number 4 will be used.

I'd like to refer the witness back to Exhibit number 4 now. Do you recognize that photograph, do you recognize that particular trap as one you saw?
He said: *It looked – [I've] looked at the photographs,* and he says: *[I recognize] all the features of these. [I recognize] all the features of the fish trap,* and he says: *[I] used to take the salmon out of the basket that is on the end.*

Okay. I think you – I believe you said that that trap was like Old Muldoe's trap, is that right?
He said: *Yes.*

Can you tell us if that was Old Muldoe's trap, that picture was actually his trap?
He says: *It is his and Old Muldoe had built it himself.*

Okay. Was that the only trap like that in the Hagwilget Canyon?
Yes.

MR MILNE: For the record, I've never seen any of these photographs before and you presumably will be providing copies to counsel for the province well in advance of any trial.
MR GRANT: For the record some of these, including exhibit number 4, are actually extracted from the province so the province already has possession of them.
MR MILNE: There are a great many photographs in the possession of the province and you will hopefully provide copies of the ones that you are tendering as exhibits at trial, well in advance of trial, is that correct?
MR GRANT: Yes. Hopefully some of them will come out in our – in the – in our disclosure, the defendant's disclosure of documents as well so that there may be other photographs of which we are not yet aware. For the record as I recall, the list of documents provided by the defen-

Exhibit 4.

dant to date, that is to December 20th of '85, does not disclose any photographs in their possession, although clearly these are photographs in their possession.

MR GRANT: I would like to show you another photograph –
MR MILNE: As I recall, Exhibit number 4 was a photograph that was created by the defendant, and it's in the defendant's archives, so it's clearly in their possession and not in the province's. In fact I think I will also –
MR GRANT: The defendant is – the defendant is the province.
MR MILNE: Oh, I'm sorry you're correct.
MR GRANT: So it is in the defendant's possession.
MR MILNE: Quite right, quite right.

EXAMINATION IN CHIEF BY MR GRANT CONTINUING:

Okay. I'd like to show you another photograph that is in the defendant's possession. Catalogue – Province of British Columbia Provincial Archives catalogue number 18992 negative number A-6843. The cataloguing indicates that this was a photograph taken at Hazelton. And on the basis that this is a photograph at the Hagwilget Canyon, can you recognize any fishing sites in that photograph? (Interpreter speaks to witness)

MR MILNE: Again for the record, I reserve the right to object. This is asking the witness to speculate. In the event it is at Hagwilget Canyon, the witness shouldn't be asked to speculate. He should simply be asked if that is a photograph of Hagwilget Canyon. I simply state that for the record.

(Witness responds) *[I'm] having problems seeing this picture clearly.*

MR GRANT: Okay. The final photograph is again from the defendant's Provincial Museum Archives, negative numbers PN13465 and it shows a man doing something with respect to a fish. Do you recognize where that photograph was taken and do you recognize the man in the photograph?
[THE INTERPRETER:] He's asking: *Where [is] this photograph [from?]* –

Okay, do you recognize the location of that photograph yourself?
He says: *[I] can't see too clearly.* (Further response by witness to interpreter) He said: *If [I] could see the pictures clearly [I] would identify who those fishing spots belonged to.*

Okay.

[THE INTERPRETER:] He's asking if it's wood.

He's asking if what?

THE INTERPRETER: If this is a piece of wood that's coming down.

Just a second, what is he asking?

THE INTERPRETER: He's asking if this is a piece of wood coming down.

Okay.

(Witness responds further to interpreter, no English response)

MR MILNE: Now, I hope you're not going to give evidence as to what that is or what it is not, Mr Grant.

MR GRANT: You should wait until I ask a question before you object. I understand that this is at Hagwilget.

MR MILNE: Objection for the record.

MR GRANT: Your objection's noted.

On the assumption that this is at Hagwilget, do you recognize – if you were told that this was at Hagwilget, do you recognize – does that help you to recognize anything in the picture?

MR MILNE: Objection. You're asking the witness to speculate, for the record.

MR GRANT: Go ahead, ask the question.

[I'm] having trouble identifying – (Further response by witness to interpreter) Okay, he's saying – he's saying: *If it's a photograph of a platform across the river that would be the spot of Peter John.*

Okay, when he's referring to across the river he means on the Hazelton side of the Hagwilget Canyon?

Yes, he's saying: *On the Hazelton side and that side was used by the Gitksan.*

And Peter John was Gitksan?

THE INTERPRETER: Peter John was Gitksan.

MR GRANT: Okay, if you could mark that as Exhibit 5, please, subject to the objections my friend has already noted.

EXHIBIT 5 – Photograph, British Columbia Provincial Museum negative number PN13465[7]

(OFF THE RECORD DISCUSSION)

MR GRANT: Do you recognize the person in the photograph?

[I] just – [I] just see the white of the shirt in the photograph.

Okay, fair enough. Did you see platforms like that at Hagwilget Canyon yourself, referring to Exhibit 5?
He said: *Yes I – I played on them as well as fishing off of them.*
Okay.
He said: *I used to gaff salmon off the platforms.*

I'd like to refer you to Moricetown and I'm showing you a picture numbered 88705 from the Provincial Archives in the custody of the defendant, negative number E8399, and I'd like you to tell me if you can recognize the buildings in that picture.
He said: *It's a picture of Kya Wiget which is Moricetown.*

MR GRANT: Okay. For the record, did you translate to him my – that I was referring to Moricetown before he gave that answer?
THE INTERPRETER: No, I didn't.

Okay, go ahead?
THE INTERPRETER: And then he said: *This used to be called Kya Wiget.*
MR MILNE: Just a minute. Just a minute. Your question was, 'I'm now referring you to Moricetown.' Did you translate that to the witness?
THE INTERPRETER: No, I didn't.
MR MILNE: Why not? That was part of his question.
MR GRANT: Well, don't – you're not questioning – you have no right to question the interpreter. I'm asking for the record if the witness –
MR MILNE: I'm clarifying a previous question, and you said did you translate. The witness has been sworn to translate everything.
MR GRANT: He did not translate that, that wasn't part of my question. Can you go on with the description please?
MR MILNE: If it wasn't part of your question, why did you make the statement? You said, 'I am now referring you to Moricetown.' I object to that procedure, Mr Grant. I think the photographs can be put to the witness without any coaching as to what they are or where they are from.
MR GRANT: I agree with you. I have two piles of photographs. I have numerous photographs, for the record, Mr Milne. I was speaking possibly out of turn myself because I was referring to a second pile of photographs. That – when I noted how short the question was of the interpreter, I wanted to clarify whether the interpreter had referred to Moricetown. The interpreter has answered me that he did not refer to Moricetown when he asked the question. Because he asked a brief question and my question was longer, I wanted to know whether he had referred to Moricetown.

MR MILNE: Well, it raises the issue of what you wish the translator to translate. If he's going to translate portions of what may or may not be questions, then it concerns me. It concerns me a great deal – the accuracy of the translation. I think that in the future we should make sure that the question in total is being translated to the witness.

MR GRANT: Your objections are not being translated, my comments are not being translated, and I'm referring to the fact that that was a comment. I'm not asking him to translate that. Now, the witness was going on describing the photograph. First of all, I'd like to have that photograph marked as Exhibit number 6 before the witness explains it.

EXHIBIT 6 – Photograph, Provincial Archives of British Columbia catalogue number 88705, negative number E-8399

(OFF THE RECORD DISCUSSION)

EXAMINATION IN CHIEF BY MR GRANT CONTINUING:

I'm showing you Exhibit number 6 which you have in front of you. I'd like you to tell me what that is and if you recognize any of the buildings? He says: *That's a photograph of Moricetown and [I] recognize that there – there are smokehouses.*

Okay, can you recognize who the owners of those smokehouses would be, like which smokehouses they are?

MR MILNE: What was the answer?

[I've] identified one as being Alfred Namox and [I'm] straining to have a good look at the photograph. And he's saying: *[I'm] having difficulty seeing it clearly.*

MR GRANT: And, okay. In relation –
He's identified two of the smokehouses.

You're starting – is this the lower line?
THE INTERPRETER: This is the lower line of the two rows of buildings.

Starting from the left-hand side?
THE INTERPRETER: Yes.

Could you tell us which ones are –
THE INTERPRETER: The first one on the left has been identified as Alfred Namox's.

Yes?
And the smaller one beside Alfred Namox's is Old Dennis's and [I] couldn't – Old Dennis, and then [I] had trouble seeing the photograph clearly.

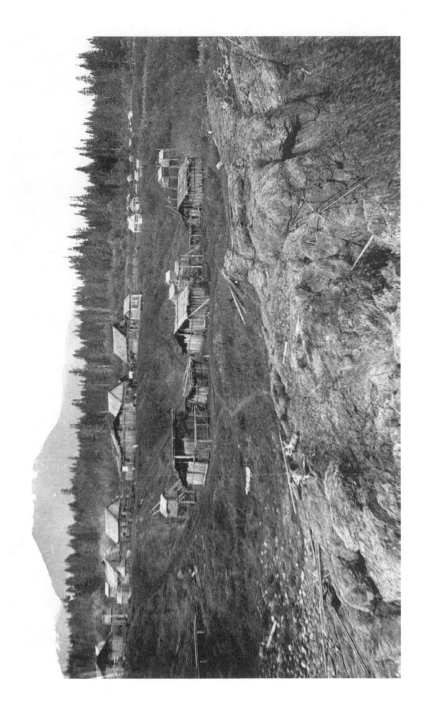

Exhibit 6.

Did you see the smokehouses in your lifetime?
Yes, I've been through all the smokehouses.

And these ones you're referring to, were they on this side of the canyon – of Moricetown Canyon – or on the other side?
On this side of the highway.

On this side of the canyon?
The smokehouses were directly below where the present day handicraft store is.[8]

Okay, and for the record, the handicraft store is on the southwest side of the Bulkley Canyon at Moricetown and also known as Highway 16 side of the canyon.

Now, also for the record, in light of the exchange we had, I wish to confirm that Mr Milne indicated off the record that he was not challenging the credibility of the interpreter but only the question of what was being interpreted.
MR MILNE: Mr Grant, I think it most inappropriate to put our off the record comments on the record.
MR GRANT: I want that on the record.
MR MILNE: I strictly object to that, strenuously.
MR GRANT: Okay. I'm showing you another photograph –
MR MILNE: There is not much purpose going off the record if those comments appear on the record, Mr Grant.
MR GRANT: They can stay on the record then.

I'm showing you another photograph. Do you recognize where that is? I'm sorry, Just a moment. It is Public Archives of Canada PA21434 for the record.
He's indicated: *That photograph is of Moricetown.*

MR GRANT: Okay. Can we mark that as an exhibit please. Exhibit 7. You can just tell him that she's marking it.

EXHIBIT 7 – Photograph, Public Archives of Canada number PA21434

MR GRANT: Just go off the record.
MR MILNE: I think we should stay on the record, Mr Grant.
MR GRANT: Stay on the record.

Do you recognize the structure at the bottom of Exhibit 7 and the buildings that are beyond it?

Exhibit 7.

He said: *That's the bridge and that's one of the few things [I] can see clearly in the pic – in the photograph.*

Okay, and what does that – did that bridge cross?
He said: *It crossed the canyon.*

Was it at the same location as the present bridge that crosses Moricetown Canyon?
Yes, the same place. (Further response by witness to interpreter) *And this bridge in this photograph was taken apart when the new one was built.*

Do you know who built the bridge in the photograph?
It was the white people who built the bridge, the government. The people who built the bridge are probably all dead.

Okay?
And [I] remember – [I] remember an Al Banister who used to haul logs with the wagon team.

Did – can you recognize – oh, I'm sorry. Before – do you – do you know if there was a bridge there before, across the canyon before the bridge in the picture?
[I] remember before this bridge –
[MR GRANT:] Referring to the bridge in the picture, for the record.
– the bridge in the photograph there was, excuse me, there was another bridge that was built by the Indians themselves.

Okay. Do you recognize any of the buildings behind that bridge in Exhibit 7?
[I] can't see the buildings too clearly.
Okay?
[I] can't see the houses.
Okay?
[I don't] want to make a mistake and give the wrong names to the houses and it could be used against us.

Okay. Let me ask you this, were there smokehouses on the far side of the Moricetown Canyon, that is to say on the side opposite the side that the highway now goes, in the old days?
Yes, there were three smokehouses on the other side of the river. One person identified as Mooseskin Johnny.
Um-hmm?
He said: *If I could see the photographs clearly I could identify the people that belonged there.*

That's all right Johnny we'll just – you're doing a very good job. We'll just do it as we can. I'm showing you another photograph –
MR MILNE: Now, is that supposed to be translated, that question?
MR GRANT: Yes, you can translate that. It's not a question. (Interpreter speaks to witness) The – the other – the next photograph is Public Archive of Canada PA82992. Do you recognize anything in this photograph?
[I] recognize it's a photograph of the old bridge that the Indians themselves had built. And the word he uses for the – he was pointing this out when he said that: *This is what they used to call wa'tso'tee.*

That you're indicating – just for the record – you're indicating a wooden or what appears to be a log or wooden structure that sort of arches out over the centre of the picture?
THE INTERPRETER: Yes.
MR GRANT: Okay. Can that picture be marked as Exhibit number 8 please?

EXHIBIT 8 – Photograph, Public Archives of Canada number PA82992

(Further response by witness to interpreter) And he also said: *[I] remember when the bridge was being built.*

MR GRANT: Okay. Now, where was that bridge located, Exhibit 8?
THE INTERPRETER: He's trying to –
What was his answer to the question where the bridge was located?
THE INTERPRETER: It was located in Moricetown.
Yes?
And from the photograph – from the bridge [I] was trying to gauge whether this was a smokehouse or not.

And he's – you're referring and pointing, for the record, to a picture which is in about the centre mid-ground –
Yes.
– on the right off the bridge structure?
He said that: *If that is a smokehouse, then that belonged to Wah Tah Kwets.* (Further response by witness to interpreter)

You said you remember when that bridge was built. Do you recall how old you were when it was built?
About ten or twelve, ten to twelve years old. I was strong.[9]

I'm going to show you another photograph, again in the possession of the Defendant from the Provincial Archives catalogue number 30393,

Exhibit 8.

negative number B-1717, and I would ask you if you can recognize that photograph as to where it was – where that photograph was taken.

[THE INTERPRETER:] Then he was asking me if that was Kya Wiget, Kya Wiget. He said two names for Moricetown: Kya Wiget and Moricetown.

Okay. Ask him if he can recognize where it is, does he know where it is?

[THE INTERPRETER:] He's asking me if that's a house and I answered no. He asked me if that was a picture of a person and I said it was.

Okay, let me show you the photograph. I'm going to try to assist you because it seems it's hard for you to see. It appears in the background of this photograph that there is a structure that looks like a bridge. Can you see that structure and does that help you to determine where the photograph was taken?

[I] recognize that, it's a bridge.

It's a bridge where?
Moricetown.

MR GRANT: Okay. Mark that as Exhibit 9 please. And before – just for the record, on the back of that is labelled that it is located at Moricetown. Throughout these questions I've asked up to this point, I've not referred the witness or the interpreter to the label on the back nor have I made reference to the location. If that could be marked as Exhibit 9.

EXHIBIT 9 – Photograph, Provincial Archives of British Columbia catalogue number 30393 negative number B-1717

MR GRANT: Now, in exhibit number 9 it appears that there is some structure near the river. Do you recognize that structure? The question may not be clear. I'm referring to what looks like vertical poles hanging up and down and a round object which is in about the mid-ground of the photograph. The poles appear to go into the water. Do you recognize that structure?

[THE INTERPRETER:] He's asking me if it's a fish basket.
Okay. I take it you're having a hard time seeing what is in the picture?
Yes. (Further response by witness to interpreter) He – he said: *Where you see the poles that are standing upright, that is the location where Louie Tommy had his fish trap.*

Okay. When we were talking about exhibit 8 you said this was a bridge

Exhibit 9.

that you saw built at Moricetown. Was there a bridge across Moricetown Canyon before the bridge that you saw built?
Okay. *Prior to the photo – prior to the bridge in this photograph, I remember
that there were just trees that were fallen across the canyon and people would
cross on foot.* (Further response by witness to interpreter) Okay. *The
places that I have seen and spoken about I have not made it up. I've been there,
I've seen them.*

I'm showing you another photograph which is again in the custody of
the defendant's Provincial Archives catalogue number 15534, negative
number A-6063. For the record this photograph appears a bit dark but
it appears to be of water, but – can you recognize where that picture
was taken and if you cannot see you can just tell us?
[THE INTERPRETER:] He's asking me – he's asking me what this is.
Okay?
[THE INTERPRETER:] He's asking if it's a bridge.
Okay, I – if you cannot recognize the picture you can just tell us?
He said: *I can see the outline of the poles.*

He's indicating the – what appears to be poles going across the centre
of the picture, from the centre to the right-hand side?
And if I could see more clearly I could tell you exactly where it is.

Okay. For the record the card or the label on this indicates that it is a
picture at Moricetown. So if – if this is a picture at Moricetown, if I tell
you this is a picture of Moricetown Canyon does that help you to identify the items in the picture?

MR MILNE: Same objection again, Mr Grant, for the record.
MR GRANT: Um-hmm.

(Interpreter speaks to witness)
MR GRANT: Okay, just – can you translate what he said?
*[I'm] thinking that that's the area where – where when the water rises they
put a bridge across so people can walk back and forth.*

Across from where to where?
From one rock to another.

And why would people cross over?
Because of the high water.

No, no. Okay, where would people be going to?
Oh, he's saying: *You would cross the bridge to go fishing.*

Okay, I'd like to have that marked as the next exhibit and I note the objection of the Crown.

EXHIBIT 10 – Photograph, Provincial Archives of British Columbia catalogue number 15534 negative number A-6063

EXAMINATION IN CHIEF BY MR GRANT CONTINUING:

Now, you've described that those, what appear to be poles crossing the centre of the exhibit you believe are a bridge for high water. What side of the canyon was that bridge on, the highway side or the far side? (Interpreter speaks to witness)
MR MILNE: This is again assuming that it's in Moricetown, I take it?
He's indicated: *It's on the side of the highway.*

Okay. And whose fishing site did that bridge go to that you were talking about?
Okay. *The area where the footbridge went to belonged to Louie Tommy.* (Interpreter speaks to witness) *Old Bill, Bilna.*
What was that last –
Old Bill, who is also known as Bilna or Madeek.

MR GRANT: For the record, in Exhibit 10 there are pictures in the dark of a couple of people. But given the Witness's difficulty in seeing the detail of the photograph, I'm not going to put those questions to him about those persons.

I'm going to show you another photograph. Now this – the copy that I have is labelled Provincial Archives, again in the custody of the defendants, number 88690-E-8384. Unlike the other photographs, this photograph has been mounted on cardboard with the label on the left-hand side. I have covered over the label so that neither the interpreter nor the witness will be able to refer to the label at this time. I'm showing it to my friend so he is satisfied that I have done that.
MR MILNE: Fine.
MR GRANT: And I would ask if you can recognize the building or buildings in that picture and if so where they were?
He said that: *It's a smokehouse in Moricetown.*
Yes?
THE INTERPRETER: He's indicating a road –
[MR GRANT:] Along the bottom of the photograph?
THE INTERPRETER: – along the bottom of the photograph. (Further response by witness to interpreter)

Exhibit 10.

Okay. He's recognized that: *This is a smokehouse in Moricetown.* He said: *That's a road and this is a place where your dried salmon would be stored and in Wet'suwet'en it's referred to as tsa kan.*

Okay, for the record, the larger building on the right is the one he indicated as the smokehouse?
THE INTERPRETER: Yes.

The smaller building that appears to be on stilts he indicated was a place where you dried salmon?
THE INTERPRETER: Yes.

And he indicated something on – going from the right, the bottom right-hand corner up towards the middle ground towards the building in the background on the far left-hand side as a road?
THE INTERPRETER: Yes.

MR GRANT: Okay. If that could be marked as an exhibit.

EXHIBIT 11 – Photograph, Provincial Archives number 88690-E-8384

MR GRANT: I'd like you to – I'm just going to hold up the photograph which is now marked as Exhibit 11 to show on the record for the video that it's covered over as I indicated, in case it's not clear in the wording. I'd like to ask you, just to clarify: the building on stilts – is that where the salmon is dried or where dried salmon is stored?
THE INTERPRETER: He said: *That's where dried salmon was stored.*
Okay, that's the answer the witness gave?
THE INTERPRETER: That's the answer the witness gave.

All right, thank you. Do you know whose smokehouse that was?
Okay. [I've] *indicated that this is Wah Tah Keght's smokehouse and the building behind belongs to –*
THE INTERPRETER: *What did he say?*
MR GRANT: For the record, the building you're referring to as Wah Tah Keght's smokehouse is the large building in the right foreground of Exhibit 11. Okay, go ahead, and then he gave an answer as to whose building it was behind?
Yeah. (Interpreter speaks to witness) Okay. *The – the smokehouse in the photograph belonged to Wah Tah Keght and there was another one behind this one which belonged to Wah Tah Kwets and this is where the dried salmon was stored.*[10]

Okay, and so you're indicating that the larger building in the foreground was Wah Tah –

Exhibit 11.

THE INTERPRETER: Wah Tah Keght's.

MR GRANT: – Wah Tah Keght, for the record, and that the – that behind that there was another smokehouse that belonged to Wah Tah Kwets?

THE INTERPRETER: Yeah.

MR GRANT: Which may or may not be the one that's visible from behind, he doesn't know?

[MR GRANT:] Do you want me to keep this covered as it is?

MR MILNE: I think we should.

MR GRANT: What I'll do is I've used a clip as I may end up stapling it. We're referring just to the covering we've put on the exhibit. Now, for the record any copies that are made probably won't be mounted in that way.

Do you recall speaking to a woman named Ruth Murdoch who was an archeology student about the location of smokehouses in Moricetown? *Yes, I took her down there.*

Okay. And you pointed out where the smokehouses had been in the earlier days at Moricetown Canyon? *Yes. And she had written down all their names.*

I see. The names of the owners?

THE INTERPRETER: *The names of the owners.*

Okay. I'd like to ask you about your father's territory now for a few moments. Can you describe where Smogelgem's territory is and describe for example a starting point of a mountain or a lake along the border of Smogelgem's territory?

[THE INTERPRETER:] *He's asking if it's the North Bulkley area.*

Yes, I'm referring to the North Bulkley area. I'd like to just go off the record for a moment and ask my friend something, a question.

(OFF THE RECORD DISCUSSION)

(PROCEEDINGS ADJOURNED AT 11:15 A.M.)

(PROCEEDINGS RECONVENED AT 11:30 A.M.)

MR GRANT: Just for the record, it's now 11:30. We took a bit longer break because the witness wanted to have a bit of a rest and counsel and everybody else agreed that that was reasonable and we're going to try to proceed on for a little longer today. Now, before the break I asked you to describe your father's territory. Now, you indicated in an

earlier examination that you hunted – that you trapped with your father on Smogelgem's territory in the North Bulkley, is that right?
Yes.

Now, I understand from your evidence earlier that your father's territory was around the North Bulkley and this is near Perow which is on Highway 16, is that right?
Yes.

Okay. Now, there's a mountain known as China Nose Mountain. What is the name of that mountain in Wet'suwet'en?
Okay. *The Indian name, the Wet'suwet'en name, for China Nose is Tsez zul, Tsez zul.*

Is that mountain on the boundary of your father's, of Smogelgem's, hunting territory?
Okay. *The China Nose Mountain is the corner marker for his territory.*

And would that be the southeast corner of his boundary, approximately?
THE INTERPRETER: Southeast.

Would it be on the Smithers or the Burns Lake side of his boundary?
It's on the Burns Lake side, east side.

Okay, and is it on the – the – okay. Now, can you describe other points on your father's territory which are that eastern boundary? Where would the boundary go from Tsez zul if you were describing the eastern side?
(Interpreter speaks to witness, witness responds, no English response)
Do you want to translate that answer before we go further?
Okay. *From – I've just done a rough sketch.* Okay. *China Nose is located here and then it runs in this direction.*

Okay. That – are we talking about running north?
THE INTERPRETER: *Running north. Or –*

Okay, runs north from China Nose.
THE INTERPRETER: – He mentioned north.

Okay, runs north from China Nose?
THE INTERPRETER: *And then down to Wilson Lake.*

And is that going west or east?
It's in south side.

Wilson Lake is on the south side?
South of China Nose and then it goes back up to China Nose.

Okay. Now, whose territory is on the east side of Smogelgem's?
Okay. *On the Babine side of the territory the person who owns that territory is Kas baine.* (Further response by witness to interpreter) Okay. *and the road passes through Perow on Highway 16 and then according to this the north end would belong to Mabel Sam Critch.*

All right. Okay, now – just a second now. Babine – is Babine Lake and the Babine people to the north of Smogelgem's territory?
Okay. *It would be opposite the side of the Babine, the direction that goes to Babine.*

The direction of what that goes to Babine, the road?
THE INTERPRETER: *The territory. That belongs to Mabel Sam Critch.*

Would Mabel Sam's territory be on the Burns Lake side of Smogelgem's territory or on the Babine Lake side of the territory?
On the side of Burns Lake.

Okay. Now, and I understand that, just to be clear, Kas baine's territory is on the Babine – towards the Babine from Smogelgem's territory, on the Babine side of Smogelgem's territory?
Yes.

Okay. Do you know who holds that name now?
He says: *It is somebody like myself who holds that name and [I] can't remember.*

Okay. If he cannot – if you cannot remember that's all right, don't worry. (Interpreter speaks to witness) I don't want you to guess. Now, whose territory is on the Smithers side of Smogelgem's territory?
Okay. *[I'm] trying to – [I] know she's somehow related to Mary Joseph of Smithers but he can't remember the name.*

Okay. Do you know Mary Joseph's name, feast name?
Okay. *[I] – [I] remember the daughter's name, which is Skokumwaha.*

Okay. Now, do you know who holds the territory to the south of Smogelgem's territory?
Okay. *To the – above the area where [I] had mentioned Mary Joseph's name, that territory belongs to Namox and that is where a mine is situated which had belonged to one of my grandfathers.*

Do you know the name of that? Oh I'm sorry, was that mine a mine that the Indian people ran or that the white people ran?

It is run by the white people and the mine is situated within the territory of Namox.

Do you know the name of that mine?
I – I don't know the name of the mine.

Is this mine still operating?
Yes, it is still operating.

Is this a mine that is near Sam Goosley Lake?
Yes, it is near Sam Goosley Lake and that territory belong to Namox.

Is Namox the Chief's – is that the feast name or is that the name and if it isn't, what is his feast name?
Yes, that is the feast name.

Okay, who holds that name right now?
Okay. *The person who holds Namox is the wife of Sylvester William, who lives in Two Mile.*

That's Two Mile near Hazelton?
(In English) *Two Mile.*

Oh. Two Mile in Moricetown?
THE INTERPRETER: Two Mile in Moricetown.

MR GRANT: Okay. We'll take just a few moments, we'll go off the record so that the tape can be changed.

(PROCEEDINGS ADJOURNED AT 11:45 A.M.)

(PROCEEDINGS RECONVENED AT 11:54 A.M.)

EXAMINATION IN CHIEF BY MR GRANT CONTINUING:

Did you travel throughout Smogelgem's territory with your father?
Yes. I travelled with him when I was small.

Do you recall taking Richard Overstall out to see that territory and show him the landmarks of Smogelgem's territory before a trapline case that was heard in Smithers?
Yes.

And did you see a map that he – did he show you a map that he made of those, of the boundaries of that territory?
Yes, I saw it.

After your father died, who took over Smogelgem's territory?

I look after the territory and stayed there most of the time.[11]

Did you take care of it as a yinanlay or caretaker?
Okay. *I looked after it and it became mine.*

Okay. Is – is – is there such a concept in Wet'suwet'en society of a care-taker of the land?
Okay. *The children of the Chief are entitled to the land and they end up look-ing after it and people from the – other people from the Clan with permission are able to hunt on the territory, hunt and trap on the territory.*

Okay. Did somebody become Smogelgem right after your father died?
Yes. His brother whose name was McKenzie became Smogelgem.

Was that your father's brother?
Yes. He was the older brother of my father.

Okay. Did you help your Uncle McKenzie pay for the feast for your father's death?
Yes, I did pay for my father's burial. I had hunted and trapped and the money we got from the furs I gave to my father and my father put it aside and he said that was what would be used to pay for his expenses and he said, 'Now you're talking,' now I'm talking.

And is this one of the reasons why you became the caretaker of your father's territory?
The gravestones that are on his grave I had ordered them. (Further response by witness to interpreter) *Mr. Loring the Indian agent helped me with the inscriptions on the headstone. He helped me order the headstone.* (Further response by witness to interpreter) *And no one else had helped me. The expenses were paid just from my money.* (Further response by witness to interpreter) Okay. *Since no one had helped me to pay for the expenses the land became mine according to the – to our old laws.* (Further response by witness to interpreter) *And all McKenzie did was speak for me. It did not cost him anything; he was much too old.*

Was McKenzie sick at that time?
He was not sick, he was just too old and he didn't know how to handle money.

Okay, about how old was he?
It was a long time ago; I can't remember his age.

Okay?
When my father had died they had figured his age out at the age of forty-five years in 1908.

Who was forty-five years, your father or McKenzie?
My father at age forty-five.

I see. Did he die of an illness, of a flu or a disease?
Yes. He had a sickness and that's what he died from.

Okay. And when did he die?
He died in 1908.

Okay. So you were just a child when he died?
Yes. I was a young man, I was strong, I worked with horses and that's when the territory was given to me.

Okay. And how long did McKenzie hold the name Smogelgem?
He didn't keep it very long because of his old age.

And who took the name after him?
Abraham Nikal received the name.

Was that at McKenzie's death?
Yes, after he died. (Further response by witness to interpreter) *And people had said that he should take the name and that's why it was given to him.*

Okay. And how long did Abraham Nikal hold the name?
He kept it for some time, about ten years.

Okay, and who received the name next?
After Abraham's death there was some dispute as to who should take the name and Leonard George finally took the name.

Did Mary George, Leonard George's mother, ever hold the name Smogelgem?
She did not have the name. It was her son Leonard George.

Did Leonard George get the name at Abraham Nikal's death?
Yes, after he died.

Okay, and do you recall when Abraham Nikal died?
I know when he died but I can't remember the exact date, and he had a house just across from this house.

Did Abraham die in Moricetown and is he buried in Moricetown?
Okay. *He died at the Hazelton Hospital and he's buried at the Moricetown cemetery.*

And did your father – is your father buried at Moricetown?
No, he's buried in Hagwilget.

Okay. Okay, now I just want to be clear. You said that Leonard George took Smogelgem after Abraham Nikal died. Was it at the time of Abraham Nikal's funeral feast, that is, immediately after his death?
He did not take the name immediately after the death of Smogelgem. It was sometime after.

Do you recall approximately how many years later?
Can't remember. One or two years.

While you were taking care of the land after McKenzie got Smogelgem's name, did he come on the land, that is, did McKenzie come on the land?
Yes, he was on the land. I was with him, I showed him where the territory was and I also trapped for him.

Did you take care of McKenzie and provide him with food?
Yes, I did look after him. I provided food for him as well as looked after the horses that he had.

Did Thomas and Mary George help McKenzie when he had a feast – when he had feasts as Smogelgem?
Yes, they did help McKenzie at the feasts but not as much as I helped him because he was my father's brother.

Is there a name for that relationship between you and the people – your father's relations – (Interpreter speaks to witness) – in Wet'suwet'en?
He said: [I] described the relationship that [I] had with [my] father's brother and [I'm] finding it difficult now.

Okay, he – to remember the word do you mean? Is there a name for that relationship, not just between he and McKenzie but between a Wet'suwet'en person and his father's side?
THE INTERPRETER: *I think I'm having difficulties – Okay? – trying to word it properly, what you're saying, what you're asking.*

Okay, I'd like to ask you Johnny are you getting tired now? I can see that you're having – you seem to be having a harder time answering the questions. Are you getting a bit too tired to answer more questions now?
Okay. *[I] want to finish this section.*

Okay, good. That's a good idea. Now, when your Uncle McKenzie died, did Thomas George come and talk to you about– and help you and did you help put up money for McKenzie's feast?

Okay. *When McKenzie died one of Thomas George's relatives came to me by car and told me about the death. Then I also got in the car and went.*

Um-hmm. Where did McKenzie die and where was he buried?
He is buried next to my father in Hagwilget. (Further response by witness to interpreter) *And he died right in Hagwilget.*

Who – how was Thomas George or Mary George related to your father and McKenzie?
Mary George was my father's second sister.

Was Mary your father's second sister or your father's second sister's daughter?
THE INTERPRETER: Say that again?
I just want to be clear. Was Mary George your father's second sister or your father's second sister's daughter?
Okay. *Mary George's mother was my father's sister.* Okay. *Before my father died he had told me to look after the territory since [he said that] you are the only one that has helped me in looking after me.*

Okay. Did he announce that at a feast?
He did not announce it at a feast. He had told me in front of Mabel Sam Critch's mother.

Did McKenzie know that's what your father wanted?
Yes, he knew and their words are the same.

Okay. In other words McKenzie agreed with your father?
MR MILNE: Um – um –
MR GRANT: Did McKenzie agree with your father?
MR MILNE: Objection. How can this witness know whether McKenzie agreed with or not with his father?
MR GRANT: If he doesn't know – if he doesn't know the answer he can say he doesn't know.
MR MILNE: Objection just made for the record.
THE INTERPRETER: Can you repeat the question please? (Court reporter reads back last question) (Interpreter repeats question to witness)
Yes. Yes, it was okay with McKenzie and my father in his words were like one and he agreed to it because I had helped him a lot while he was living.[12]

Okay. Just to clarify you – he – do you know – did he tell you that he agreed with this at some stage?
Yes. (Further response by witness to interpreter) *He agreed and told me before he died that 'I want you to look after the territory.'*

MR MILNE: That's an objection again to that – it's hearsay, for the record.

MR GRANT: Did this happen at the time – when you say he told me before he died, was this near the time of his death or a long time before?
He told me – he told me before, before he died he was getting old and he was dying so I stayed with him and that is when he told me.

Okay. Did Abraham Nikal agree with you being the caretaker – (Interpreter speaks to witness) – of Smogelgem's territory?
Yes, he knew and he also trapped on the land.

Okay, and he agreed – did he agree?
Yes, it was okay with him. Since I was living right he agreed that this arrangement should continue.

Okay. This concept of taking care of the land for another Chief, do you know of other examples where Wet'suwet'en people have been the caretakers of the land for another Chief?
Yes, there are many examples.

I'd like – do you know of a situation at Morice Lake where there was a caretaker or *yinanlay*?
[I] want to know who.

I'm referring to a situation with Jimmy Antoine and Frank Jimmy.
Okay. *Jimmy Antoine's father had some land near Burns Lake and when Jimmy Antoine had died Frank Jimmy was the caretaker for Jimmy Antoine's father's land.*

And what was the relation of Frank Jimmy to Jimmy Antoine?
Jimmy – Jimmy Antoine was Frank Jimmy's father.

Okay. Is this the Frank Jimmy who is alive today and lives in Smithers?
Yes, he lives in Smithers.

Is he still considered the caretaker of that land or has someone else taken it over?
Yes, he is still looking after the land; it hasn't been handed over to anyone else.

Does Leonard George and his family have the right to – can they go and hunt on Smogelgem's territory now, on the territory that you're caretaker of?
Okay. *When my son was alive he had – he did trapping on the territory.*

Who's he?
Moses David.
Okay?
Okay. *Half of the money he got from the furs he had given that to me and Peter David would do the same.*

MR GRANT: Okay. Okay, how are you feeling now, because we are finished that area and I'm prepared to go into another area if you want or if you are too tired we can adjourn.
Okay. *[I'm] tired now.*

MR GRANT: Okay. Just for the record, before we go off the record, I asked that question at the end because I observed him, some of the – I observed some – that he was tired and another person indicated to me that maybe he was getting tired by the way his answers were coming, was slower. So we'll adjourn it over to the 27th or the 29th of January for continuation.

(PROCEEDINGS ADJOURNED AT 12:32 P.M. UNTIL JANUARY 1986)[13]

VOLUME 5

Direct Examination of Johnny David by Peter Grant, 29–31 January 1986

UPON COMMENCING AT 9:45 A.M., 29 JANUARY, 1986

MR GRANT: This is a continuation of the commission hearing of Johnny David which was last adjourned on December 19th and December 20th, 1985. The witness, Johnny David, and the interpreter, Victor Jim, are still under oath. You understand that?
THE INTERPRETER: Yes.

Q   You recall at your feast Jimmy Michell – or at a feast, Jimmy Michell was given a name and a territory?
A   *When people had gathered for the feast Jimmy Michell had spoken for me.*

Q   Jimmy Michell described that the territory was being passed to you when you received the name?
A   *When the people had gathered all the business was done, then Jimmy Michell mentioned that I was getting the name and the territory. After the business was done I got up so the people could recognize me.*

Q   Your territory around the Telkwa River was talked about at that feast, was it?
A   *They had the feast, the Maxlaxlex territory was described, and the people were there to witness that.*

Q   At the feast today are the territories described?
A   *The same procedure is used as in the past; whoever is taking a name and*

the territory, if the business is run in the right manner, the Chiefs from the various Clans get up and say that it has been run okay, and the person is worthy of the name. They all speak to that today.

Just one moment. Is it correct that before you received the name Maxlaxlex Jimmy Michell looked after the hunting territory that is now in Maxlaxlex's name?
Jimmy Michell did look after the territory that he knew I was the heir to [as] Maxlaxlex. When the time came the feast was given and the named territory was given to me.

At our last day you described how you are a caretaker for Smogelgem's territory; was Jimmy Michell a caretaker for Maxlaxlex's territory or was he the owner of that territory?
Jimmy Michell and I together own the territory.

Did the Kilwoneetz people trade furs with the Gitksan people?
The ladies who belonged to the Kilwoneetz would marry into the – would marry Gitksans and the spouses of the Kilwoneetz ladies were allowed to come into the territory to hunt and trap and there were no problems.

Did the Wet'suwet'en people generally in the old days, that is in the time of your father, trade furs with the Gitksan people?
The people from the Skeena River and the Wet'suwet'en did trade meats from the various animals, and the Gitksan people were also invited to hunt in the territory and so would they. When they went back to their homes, had a feast, they would show the people the meat from the game and say to the people that this is where we got this meat from, so the people could witness it.

What kind of furs did they give to the Gitksan people?
MR MILNE: I am not sure that he did say 'furs'; the word was 'meats.'
[MR GRANT:] I'm sorry. What kind of meats did they give to the Gitksan people, and what did they trade for?
They traded caribou meat, beaver, bear. No, and other game with the Gitksan, and there were no white people who were there. There was no trouble between the Gitksan and Wet'suwet'en people.

Now, I asked two questions. The second part of my question was, what did the Gitksan give in return for this game?
The Gitksan people traded foods that they ate with the Wet'suwet'en and there were no white people to boss the Indian people about how to use the land and how much to take from the land, and there were no problems. At no time were there any white people who would boss the Indian people around.

What specific foods did the Wet'suwet'en receive from the Gitksan in those days?

OFF THE RECORD DISCUSSION IN WET'SUWET'EN

The Giksan people would give the Wet'suwet'en people seaweed, herring eggs, and ooligan grease to trade for the various game meats that the Wet'suwet'en would give to the Gitksan.

Did the Wet'suwet'en trade with particular – with the same House or Clan of the Gitksan when they traded? For example, would Smogelgem's House or tribe trade with a parallel Clan or House of the Gitksan?
There was no particular trading between Houses or Clans. People traded with each other because they cared for each other and, again, there were no white people to tell us how to trade or who to trade with.

Did the Wet'suwet'en also trade with the Nisga people on the Nass and the Tsimshian people on the coast?
Yes, the same way.

Do you use soapberries today?
Yes, it is still used today.

Was it used in the old days, in your father's and grandfather's time?
They did as well. That was one of our main staple food.

Do you use Saskatoon berries today, and were they used in your grandfather's time?
The Saskatoon was also used. It was either dried or made into jam.

Did you use what is commonly known as low bush blueberries in the old days, and do you use those today?
It is still used today, and today it is usually jarred.

Were they used in the old days?
It was used in the old days and blueberries were dried.

Blueberries are also used today?
THE INTERPRETER: Yes, he said that.

I'm sorry. Did you use huckleberries in the old days and are they used today?
Yes, that was used in the old days and it is still used today, and it is usually jarred.

Were any of these kinds of berries traded with the coastal people, such as the Tsimshiam, the Nisga or the Gitksan?
Yes, all the berries that I mentioned have been used in trade with the Nass River people, the Gitksan and the Tsimshian.

Were all of those berries, that is soapberries, blueberries, huckleberries and Saskatoon, dried before they were traded?
Yes, it was dried. All the berries were dried, as well as soapberries.

Were they dried over a fire or were they dried just in the air or in the open, in the heat of the sun?
There was a frame about a foot wide and three or four feet long. The berries all would be boiled first, then leaves would be put on a frame and the berry was poured on the leaves, and the fire was lit underneath the frame and the smoke would dry the berries.

Were they packed in a special way to be traded?
The berries, once dried, would be rolled up and tied together.

Were they put in special boxes?
They were put in wooden boxes and people made sure that the berries were clean, they were not dirty, and they were transported and traded.

Did people have – were the boxes considered one of the units of value? Like, did each box of a particular kind of berries, depending on its size, have a specific value for trading purposes?

OFF THE RECORD DISCUSSION IN WET'SUWET'EN

The berries, once dried, were put in cedar boxes and –
THE INTERPRETER: – and he gave several dimensions –
– these were – this was from cedar, they were carved and painted, and the inside was like the top of this table, it was very clean, and then when they traded people want boxes as well as berries inside, and there was no specific amount of money that was attached to each box.

Did he describe what the dimensions were? I am asking you, as the interpreter?
THE INTERPRETER: He gave the various dimensions, some that high and some that high, and others quite high.
So you're saying –
THE INTERPRETER: *Different size boxes.* He is saying: *They were different sizes again.*

OFF THE RECORD DISCUSSION IN WET'SUWET'EN

The oolikan grease was transported in the same way. In the cedar boxes. Don Ryan knows about the boxes I am talking about.[1]

OFF THE RECORD DISCUSSION IN WET'SUWET'EN

THE INTERPRETER: He is saying: *The cedar was used in the old days to make caskets which people were buried in.*

Where did the Wet'suwet'en people meet the Nisga to trade with them? Did they go to the Nass or did they meet part way between, or did the Nisga come here?
The Wet'suwet'en would go up to the Nass. There was a foot trail near Kitwancool. That is the trail they used to go up to do their trading.

You described in this commission the history of Samaxsam and the rock that came off and some Wet'suwet'en were blamed for it; were those Wet'suwet'en on a trading trip to the Nass when that happened?
Yes, it was during a trading trip that the story of Samaxsam, where the – Samaxsam's grandfather – where the rock was tipped over and two people were killed.

Where did the Wet'suwet'en trade with the Nisga? Not the Nisga, the Gitksan?

OFF THE RECORD DISCUSSION IN WET'SUWET'EN

When they traded with the Gitksan they would meet at Hagwilget, and smoked salmon was one of the items that was traded. And they would meet at Hagwilget.

Who traded smoked salmon? Did the Gitksan give the Wet'suwet'en smoked salmon or [did the] Wet'suwet'en give that to the Gitksan?
Was the people of the Nass River who would give the Wet'suwet'en smoked salmon, and then Wet'suwet'en would give the Nass River people the foods that they ate.

I was referring earlier to the Gitksan –
It was the Nass River people who gave the smoked salmon.

Okay.
Not trading with the Wet'suwet'en.

Okay. Where did the Wet'suwet'en trade with the coastal or Tsimshian people? Where did they meet to trade?

OFF THE RECORD DISCUSSION IN WET'SUWET'EN

The Tsimshian people would come down by canoe. They would meet at an area just this side of where the 'Ksan office is now. It's name was Bisgeebul. This is where the Tsimshian people brought their seafoods and the Wet'suwet'en brought their wild game. That is what was traded.

OFF THE RECORD DISCUSSION

Was that across the river from where the 'Ksan office presently is or was it on the same side of the river? I'm referring to the Bulkley River.

THE INTERPRETER: *Yes.* He said: *It wasn't across the river, it was this side, on the side where the 'Ksan village is.*

[THE WITNESS:] *Southtown would be in this area, and there is a creek that flows through here which is what they call Bisgeebul, Old Hazelton would be here, and that's where the Tsimshian would come ashore.*

Can you from your description – you have said here and there – are you saying they came ashore on the South Hazelton side or on the opposite side of the river? Do you know? Your interpretation?

THE INTERPRETER: He told me it is not on the South Hazelton side, it is on the Old Town side.

[MR GRANT:] Just for the record, I just want to be clear what sides you are talking about. Did the Wet'suwet'en send specific people to trade? Were there specific Wet'suwet'en Chiefs or persons in the House who were responsible to take care of trading missions to this spot?

There was no particular types of people that were sent. It was the people who had the items to be traded.

Did you ever go on any trading missions to the Nass yourself?

I did not myself, but my father did. When he was younger.

Did you go on any trading missions up to Bisgeebul?

I know where the creek is. During my time I did not go there; I was told about this by my father.

Did he go up there? Did your father go up there?

Yes he did. I was not born when the Tsimshian people would come down and trade. I know where Bisgeebul is, we used to play on the sand there.

Was there in your or your father's time a specific thing that was most desired by the Gitksan, Nisga, or the Bisgeebul which you had? That is, of all these things you traded, was there something of special value to them?

There was no particular item that was valued. Berries and wild game were traded. The Nass River people since they had a lot of salmon would bring a lot of smoked salmon for trading.

Do you remember a time when there were caribou in your territories? Either in Smogelgem or Kilwoneetzen territory?
During my time I remember there being a lot of caribou. My territories was Kilwoneetzen territory and there was some caribou behind this mountain peak, in this direction. Just past the power line.
THE INTERPRETER: *Then he describes another peak on this side where there was caribou.*

[MR GRANT:] For the record, from the place where we are in Johnny David's house he and the interpreter were pointing out a mountain which would be – which is visible from the window of his house and generally a northerly [*sic*] direction, of southeasterly direction, I would think. It is on the direction away from the river, which is visible to all that are present here.

When the caribou were here did your people hunt caribou and did they trade either the caribou meat or the furs with these other groups we have been talking about?
The Nass River people, the Gitksans, and Tsimshian people like the meat of the caribou. That's what the Wet'suwet'en traded. The fur was used by the Wet'suwet'en themselves for gloves as well as the webbing for the snowshoes.

The fur was used for the webbing of the snowshoes or was some other part of the animal?

OFF THE RECORD DISCUSSION IN WET'SUWET'EN

It was the hide of the caribou. After it was dried it was cut into tiny little strips. That was called babiche. That is when it was used for webbing for the snowshoes.

Was there other things made out of the furs and used by the Wet'suwet'en?
The hide of the caribou is used for moccasins as well as for tents.

Are there caribou in your territory now?
There are not as many as there used to be. When Alfred Joseph and I [went] through the territory we seen five caribou.

That was flying over the entire Wet'suwet'en territory or part of it?
The area around the head of the Telkwa, that whole area.

Is that the headwaters of the Telkwa River that he is referring to when you say head of Telkwa?

We flew the whole area along the Telkwa River area, and we landed in a flat area, and when the white man came he start shooting all the bulls. Therefore they were unable to reproduce and there aren't as many as there used to be. They are doing the same with the moose, shooting all the bulls and they're not reproducing, and it is the white man that are doing that.

There are moose in your territory now, is that right?

There aren't as many as used to be; most of the moose have been shot by the white people.

When the caribou were more common in your territory, were there also moose there?

When there were many caribou in our territory there weren't too many moose. They started to arrive around 1901, 1902. That is when the moose population started to come to the area. Before that there used to be few moose around. As soon as people seen them – the white people – they were shot.[2]

Did your people after the moose came trade moose furs or moose meat with the Gitksan, Nisga, or Tsimshian?

Not that much, because all the moose had moved into their territories. And the people mentioned would shoot their own moose.

Do you still trade for oolikan grease now?

When I have friends come from the west we still trade. I give them whatever I have and they would give me seafood. Then the bull moose have all been killed; the Americans have come into the territory and they get licence to hunt and they just take the head. Other white people in the area do the same. When the Indians shoot the moose – When the Indian shoots a moose, the game warden is on their backs. And the Indians are scared of the game warden.

Is that the answer?

THE INTERPRETER: Yes.

What kinds – I'll come back to what you were saying about the moose and the hunting of the moose, but right now I would like to continue about this trade for a few more minutes. What kinds of things do you now trade to people from the west for oolikan grease or other things?

The trading is not as much as it used to be but it still happens. I am talking about Americans shooting the moose, just for the heads.

What do you give to the people from the west when you get things from them now?

We trade various meat from the games that we get and we trade for seafood with them.

Do you trade furs or hides still? It should be clear I am not just talking about you individually but you or other people, Kilwoneetzen people? *The hide of the moose is now used to make moccasins, jackets, and other things, and the moosehide itself now is an expensive item to get.*

Do you know if any of the Wet'suwet'en people trade moose hides to the Gitksan, Nisga, or Tsimshian today? *Not as much as in the past. People nowadays use moosehide for gloves, jackets, which are sold.*

Do you still use soapberries? *Yes, still use soapberries, as well as all the other berries. We ate berries. In the old days they were dried and now they're mostly jarred.*

Do other people – do the younger people collect those berries for you today or do you trade for them? *Some people pick berries for me. I also buy some of the berries from other people.*

THE INTERPRETER: He wants to have a drink of water.
MR GRANT: Okay, go off the record.

OFF THE RECORD DISCUSSION

ON THE RECORD.

Are the people who pick the berries for you members of your House or your Clan?

OFF THE RECORD DISCUSSION IN WET'SUWET'EN

Some, mostly ladies, pick berries for me, and others from my Clan as well as House also pick berries for me.
Okay.
When the people – or when the ladies from other Clans pick for me, that is paid for in the feast hall.

Do the Kilwoneetzen people have a specific area where berries were grown or where they harvested berries? *The area that was best for picking berries was the Dennis Mountain area. People from Babine, Hazelton, and here would pick berries up there, and the same was done with the salmon.*[3]

What kind of berries grew in the Dennis Mountain area which were of particular value to your people?

The berry that was of some importance to trade was the dagee, which is the huckleberries.

Did people burn areas in order to help the berries grow better?

OFF THE RECORD DISCUSSION IN WET'SUWET'EN

The fires were usually not started by the people. It was usually by nature. After a two-year period is when your berries would start growing well again. People respected the land and they were very careful with fire.[4]

Earlier on in the commission, not the last time but probably the time before that, you had referred us to a plant that is at – the root of a plant which you had. Where did you collect that plant? Where did you get that plant from?

The root that I was going to show you, I couldn't find it. I dug that myself up on Hudson Bay Mountain, near where they ski.

That's in the Laksilyu territory, isn't it?

Yes.

Does that plant have special spiritual value to you?

This root I was going to show you which I can't find, that root is used to clean a gun when it's not shooting straight. You put it through the barrel three times. And it is also a strong medicine.

What is the Wet'suwet'en word for this particular root?

The Wet'suwet'en word is konyay.

What this root – the root is put through the gun to help the gun shoot straight – I believe that was the last answer, right.

THE INTERPRETER: Yes.

Also for medicinal purposes. Have the Wet'suwet'en used konyay for as long as – for a long time before the time of your grandfather?

The root has been used for a long, long time during my father's time and his father's.

Were you taught how to harvest this root by your father?

I observed my father when he dug the root – that is where I learned from. His father taught him and so on back through the years.

Is his answer through?

THE INTERPRETER: Yes.

Does this root generally grow high up in the mountains?
Yes, usually in the mountain area –
THE INTERPRETER: [He] pointed to this area up around here.
– You could see the leaves on the mountains.
Right.
Of the root.

Is it part of the Wet'suwet'en tradition that you would take this root from a place on your Clan's territory and each Clan, each person, who used the root would take it from their Clan's territory?
The root is taken from anywhere you see it. You just don't dig it in particular areas.

Yes.
They belonged to the Houses or Clans.

Are only certain people authorized or have the right to dig this root and use this? Use konyay?
Everybody uses it.

Is there any other kind of root that has special spiritual value that grows by the rivers?
The ones that grow by the rivers, lakes, or swamp is referred – is called xelxtuk. It's bad medicine. If you don't know how to use it. It's people who don't know how to use it, people who don't know how to use it pick it and they would get sick.[5] Even I don't use it, it's that bad.

In the old days were certain people trained to learn how to use xelxtuk? Were certain people trained how to use it?
There is certain people who knew how to use this plant. The only ones that were allowed to use it. My father told me not to use it in my lifetime since you don't know the plant and how to use it.

Do you know anyone who was trained how to use it?
My father used it. There weren't too many other people who knew how to use the plant.

What did your father do with this plant, xelxtuk?
They ate it. They would chop it into small pieces and eat it. There was some very dangerous medicine. Some used it to wash their hands.

What would it do when they used – why would they eat it or use it to wash their hands?

When the person who uses it to wash their hands, they would touch a woman and the woman would get very sick. Others used it to – for luck when they went out hunting.[6] If Victor Jim took this xelxtuk and used it he would have to stay away from his wife and his child for a month. If he didn't do that – if he sees his wife and child within that month, he will not be lucky.

Do you know of another poisonous – another plant that grows around the lake which is very dangerous? I will try to pronounce the Wet'su-wet'en name, oxyenikyo?
That's poison. Oxyenikyo is poison. If horses or cattle who eat it they would die.[7] It grows basically around the edges of the lakes.

Was it used by the Wet'suwet'en at all in the old days or now?
I can't recall how this was used or what purpose it was used for. It was really bad poison. The horse and the cows can smell this plant.

I wanted to ask you just to clarify the question I asked earlier about your mother. Was your mother quite old when she died?
My mother was very, very old when she died. My father died when he was 45 years old in 1918.

Your mother's name was Suwitsbain?
Yes, Suwitsbain.

Was she given the white name of Monique?
Monica. She was baptized and married with that name.

Your mother had two husbands and her first husband – did your mother have two husbands?
My mother had two husbands. First one was Smogelgem.

That was your father?
That was my father. The second one was Alexander.

Alexander?
Alexander Dzibun.

Where did she live with Alexander Dzibun?
They live[d] at Pack Lake, which is near Francis Lake.

Did your mother marry Alexander before or after your father died?
My mother married Alexander after five or six years after my father had died.

Your mother died in Hagwilget?
Yes, she's buried there.

Just one moment. Did your father or anyone else use his territory for ranching or farming?
No, they did not use it for ranching or cattle. I was the only one who looked after the land. No one else had brought any animals for my father.[8]

So did you use it for ranching or farming?
My father had many horses on the land. Afterwards I also had horses as well as cattle.

Was this on your father's territory?
Yes.

In an area near Perow?
Yes, near Perow. I have been looking after the land as a young man, up to now as an old man.[9] *I taught my son Moses the territory, as well as trapping on the territory.*

When did you farm or raise horses and cattle on your father's territory and when did it stop?

OFF THE RECORD DISCUSSION IN WET'SUWET'EN

As a young man I raised horses and cattle on the land, and my father had raised horses before that.

Is that it?
THE INTERPRETER: Yes.

Did you grow hay on the land for the horses and cattle?
Yes I did. I grow hay and oats on the land.

What did you do with the horses and the cattle that you raised?
I sold the animals after they started growing old.

Were they milk cattle or meat cattle?
Milk cows. Jersey cows.

Did other people in your House or in your Clan or in your father's House or his Clan help you with your farming?
People from my Clan did the haying and they were paid for it.

OFF THE RECORD

When did you stop farming on this territory?
It was about – I quit farming when the hard times came. I sold cattle and horses. It was about 1926.

Did any white government agency interfere in any way with your farming on your father's territory?

OFF THE RECORD DISCUSSION IN WET'SUWET'EN

There were government people around, and I would send my cows to Rupert to be sold.

Did any government agency, like Indian Affairs, [or] the government agent or anyone else try to stop you from farming on your father's territory?
No, they did not prevent me from farming. It was the Indian agent who signed for me when I got the land, just like the white man.

Did the Indian agent interfere with your farming on your father's territory?
No, he didn't. I had been on the land as a young man and was on the land until I grew old.

It was my understanding that you were persuaded to move off your farm by somebody, do you remember that?
It was Mr Loring, the Indian agent, who had tried to convince me to move off the land and he had promised me some land in Hagwilget, which I never got, and he did the same with Round Lake Tommy. Mr Loring was on the side of the white people.

Mr Loring was the Indian agent, is that right?
Yes, he was the Indian agent. He tried to deceive us by promising us other land so we could move off our lands, and I didn't. I resisted him.

How did you resist him?
When Mr Loring had promised me land in Hagwilget in exchange for my father's land, that didn't happen. I did not get the land in Hagwilget so I moved back to my father's land. I got the land through pre-emption.

This is the land we are talking about that is near Perow?
Yes, that's the area we are talking about. There is even a creek named after me called Johnny Creek.

Johnny David Creek?
THE INTERPRETER: Just Johnny Creek. He said: *It's noted on the map.*

Your land was right near that creek?
My son Moses had also a house built in one of the corners of my father's land.

THE INTERPRETER: He wants, since his son has died now, he wants his grandson Peter to have some say about the land.

[MR GRANT:] You said you got this land by pre-emption. Did you ever get any papers saying that you were the owner of any land?

OFF THE RECORD DISCUSSION IN WET'SUWET'EN

THE INTERPRETER: He is saying that he did receive some papers that stated that it was Crown – couldn't remember what word they used – Crown something. That is when he got the land, and which was the land he sold later on.

Was this land formed into part of the reserve, to your knowledge?
Not to [my] knowledge. [I] paid taxes the same way [a] white person [does].

Do you have any papers relating to this land?
No.[10] We'll look for it some other time.
Okay.
THE INTERPRETER: He said: *I paid into school tax. I've got the papers and we'll look for it some time.*

Did you sell this land at some time later or was it taken away from you?
I sold it.

To who?
I sold it, they did not take it away.

Who did you sell it to?
Tom Hall is the person I sold it to. They were – he was the son of a farmer who farmed next to us.

What was his father's name?
Bill Hall. Englishman.

Do you recall how much money you received for this land?
I can't remember, maybe it's $500 or less.

Just before we complete, I would like to show you some photographs. Do you have your looking glass so you can see them more easily?

OFF THE RECORD DISCUSSION

The first picture I would like to show you appears to be a photograph of yourself in front of the house we are now in. I wonder if you could recognize that picture?

It's a picture of the poles outside.

THE INTERPRETER: He says: *The taller one is mine and the shorter one is Kela.*

And the taller one is the one on the right hand side, for the record. If that could be marked as Exhibit 12 I believe is the next exhibit number.

OFF THE RECORD DISCUSSION

EXHIBIT NO. 12 – Small coloured photograph of totem poles.[11]

I would like to show you another photograph, which appears to be a photograph of a totem pole with the numbers on the top 1948. Do you recognize that picture?
Yes, it is my totem pole. Yes, something written on top.[12]

Is that the same pole that is presently outside your house and was in the earlier photograph, exhibit 12?
Yes, that is the same pole.

Is that the same pole that you went outside during this commission and described the crests on the pole?
Yes, the same pole.[13]

For the record, I believe that was on the first day of this commission, which was September 20th, 1985. Could that picture of Johnny David's pole, negative number PN3233 of the B.C. Provincial Museum be marked as exhibit 13?

EXHIBIT NO. 13 – Large black and white photograph of Johnny David's totem pole, negative number PN3233 of the B.C. Provincial Museum.

I would like to show you another photograph, negative number PN3918 of the B.C. Provincial Museum. Can you look at that photograph and do you recognize where that is?
THE INTERPRETER: *He recognizes it as a picture of the canyon in Hagwilget.*

MR GRANT: Okay. Can you recognize – go ahead.
THE INTERPRETER: He is describing this picture. *You see the cliff here, that is where they get the name from, Hagwilget.* Then he said: *Beyond this cliff is the rock that went clear across the river and it was called tse hangel, means split rock.*

Can that photograph be marked as Exhibit 14, then I'll ask some more questions on it.

Exhibit 13.

EXHIBIT NO. 14 – Large black and white photograph of Hagwilget Canyon, negative number PN3918 of the B.C. Provincial Museum.

Now, the rock that you describe, was it in the bottom – going across the river in the bottom of the canyon?
This rock I described was in the river bed. It was quite steep and I don't know how the salmon got over the rocks, and I don't know how long the rock was there.

Do you recognize any of those buildings in this photograph, Exhibit 14?
In this photograph the first building belonged to Old Muldoe.

For the record, you're pointing to a building that seems to be in the centre of the picture and in the mid-ground?
He said: *The second one belonged to [my] father, Smogelgem.*

That is the one that looks like, then, on the base of the cliff, the left of that first building.
That was called the Owl House. [I] can't decipher the other two, each had a name.

Okay.
This pole –

The one furthest to the left of the picture?
– that was the pole that belonged to Old Bill.

Was that Bill Nye?
Yes, Bill Nye.

And the building you have referred to as belonging to Old Muldoe, is that building here?
Yes, this is the building at the base of the cliff; that was Old Muldoe's.

Does he know – there appear to be two other poles there, does he know if there were other poles there and, if so, whose they were?
The first, this one [I] identified as Bill Nye's pole. The last pole in the photograph –

The one furthest to the right?
– The one that is furthest to the right, belonged to [my] House.

OFF THE RECORD IN WET'SUWET'EN

That was the one with the figure of a man on top. That pole was sold.

Exhibit 14.

Is that the pole that belongs to Kela?
Kela's pole was called Kaiget. That was the first pole that was erected in the canyon. There is a figure of a man on top and that is what you see outside.

OFF THE RECORD DISCUSSION

I would like to show you another photograph of a totem pole. Do you recognize that pole?
THE INTERPRETER: He's saying: *[I] think that this is the pole and [I] think that this is Kela's pole and [I] think these are the ones standing outside.*

I would like you to take another look at that picture. Just take a look at it closely; on that pole there seems to be a building behind it. See if you can recognize the location of it?
I can't see very good.

This photograph has it labelled at the bottom that it is a totem pole at Hagwilget, on the face of the picture. Now, having told you that, does that help you to identify that pole and where it was? Where that pole was?
THE INTERPRETER: He is asking me: *[Is it] a photograph of the pole in the canyon[?] Then [I recognize] that it's a smokehouse beside the pole.*

Do you recognize whose pole that would belong to?
THE INTERPRETER: He said he can't see too clear. Said: *The figures on the totem pole, I can't see too clearly.*

That's fine. I showed you one other photograph before we commenced our examination of a number of people. I would like you to look at it and see if you can recognize any of the people in that picture.
In this photograph I recognize this man as my uncle. Chief David.

He is indicating the man in the – second from the left holding a broom in his hand.
The others probably know who they are but I'm having trouble seeing the photograph clearly.

Mark that Exhibit 15 please. That is the National Museum of Canada negative number 59520.

EXHIBIT NO. 15 – Black and white photograph, National Museum of Canada negative number 59520.

For the record, I provided photocopies of these pictures I am showing you. On the back of Exhibit 15 there is some other handwriting, which

Exhibit 15.

I am showing to Mr Milne, and I have not referred that handwriting to the witness and the witness did not look at it when he examined the photograph. Possibly we could go off the record for a moment?

OFF THE RECORD DISCUSSION

Off the record we have had a discussion and the witness has now gone for two and a half hours or slightly over that and is getting quite tired. By agreement between counsel we have agreed to adjourn this matter over until tomorrow until 10.00 A.M. So this commission is adjourned now.[14]

UPON COMMENCING AT 10.00 A.M., 30 JANUARY, 1986
OFF THE RECORD DISCUSSION

This is a continuation of the commission that was adjourned yesterday afternoon.[15]

Do you know who Chief Louie is?
[I] want to know where he lives.

I understand this is a person that lives at the eastern end of your territory, near Ootsa Lake or Cheslatta?
Chief Louie is from Cheslatta.

Do you remember – do you know this man?
Yes, I know him. I've spoken to him.

Has he died?
Yes, he died. His brothers have died also.

Who were his brothers?
His brother's name was Bagee. He became Chief after Chief Louie died.

When you say he became Chief, do you mean he succeeded Chief Louie in the Wet'suwet'en tradition? Or in the Indian tradition?
Yes, it was through the Wet'suwet'en way, he was already in line for this name.

Do you know where Chief Louie was buried?
Right at Cheslatta.

OFF THE RECORD

Is that where his brother was buried?
Bagee was not buried right at Cheslatta. When people were moved off Cheslatta he was given a piece of land near Francis Lake. He is buried on the land that was given to him.

OFF THE RECORD DISCUSSION

When you refer to Francis Lake, it is commonly referred to on the maps as Francois Lake?
THE INTERPRETER: Yes.

Did Chief Louie die before the people were moved [off] Cheslatta?
Before they were moved off.

But his brother died after they were forced off?
His brother had died after the people were moved from Cheslatta and he is buried on the land that was given to him.

Is his brother buried near Grassy Plains?
Bagee was buried on land that was given to him by the government after they were moved off Cheslatta.

What Clan was Chief Louie in?
He is in your Clan –
THE INTERPRETER: [He is] pointing at me, and he said: *Tsayu [Beaver] Clan.*

Where was Chief Louie's territory?
He was a Chief; his land was around Cheslatta since he was a Chief there. His territory ran along Ootsa Lake up near Alf Michell's traditional grounds, and his boundary was Sebola Mountain.

Did you say Alex Michell or Alf Michell?
Alex Michell.
MR MILNE: And the name of the mountain again:
[MR GRANT:] Sebola.

Is any of that territory flooded now by the dam that is near Cheslatta?
The territory around Cheslatta was all flooded. The village was flooded, the church, the graveyard. When it was flooded bodies were floating downstream. This is how the white people have fooled around with us.
Go ahead?
Roy Morris was there. He managed to remove some of the bodies. The ones that he didn't move, he saw the bones floating downstream. Roy Morris was a witness to this.

Has he finished that answer? When you refer to Roy Morris, his Indian name is Woos?
Yes. He is still alive. Roy Morris was there when it was being flooded and he

saw the remains of people who had died many years ago come up with the water. Floating downstream.

This all happened when the dam was put in by Alcan and the government?
Yes, there was a time when Alcan was putting in a dam and I think opened the gates at Skin Dyee territory, and that is where the water came rushing through.[16]

Do you know if this flooding included the flooding of Chief Louie's territory or part of that territory?
His whole village disappeared.

You referred to Sebola Mountain earlier. Does part of that mountain belong to Chief Louie's territory?
Half Sebola Mountain belonged to Chief Louie, and the other half of the mountain belonged to Francis Lake Johnny. All the relatives of Chief Louie have died and I don't know who will be getting the – whose territory now.

You don't know who the successor to Chief Louie is, is that right?
THE INTERPRETER: He wants us to find out who will be getting Chief Louie's territory.

Okay. Does Caspit hold any part of Sebola Mountain as part of his territory?
Caspit did not have territory near Chief Louie. His was more the Morice Lake area.

Would it be closer to this direction than Chief Louie's? That is, further west than Chief Louie's territory?
Yes, it's on the west side of Morice Lake.

Is Caspit a Wet'suwet'en Chief?
Yes, he lives here.

Was Chief Louie a Wet'suwet'en Chief?
He was not a Wet'suwet'en Chief, he was from Cheslatta.

Is there an Indian name for the Carrier people that lived to the east of the Wet'suwet'en?
Nutseni. Nutseni means people that live east of us.[17]
Okay.
THE INTERPRETER: He said: *The Cheslatta people and people from Anaheim Lake are just about the same people. And they speak the same language.*

Was Chief Louie Nutseni?
Yes.

Was he the Nutseni Chief whose territory bordered on the Wet'suwet'en territory?
Yes, he was and on several occasions he just about had a few problems but, since they knew each other, they would talk it over and there were no problems.

Is Sebola Mountain on the boundary between the Wet'suwet'en people and the Nutseni people?
The Sebola Mountain – half is Wet'suwet'en territory, and half is Nutseni territory. I can't see the map too clearly and I can't speak to that.

I am not going to ask to show you this map. It's hard even for us to see this map. What Chief's territory was on the Wet'suwet'en side of Sebola Mountain? In other words, who owned part of Sebola Mountain from the Wet'suwet'en side?
Francis Lake Tommy held part of the mountain and Alex Michell held the other half. I don't know who has taken Chief Louie's name and the trapline. I don't know who has got it.

Do you know what Alex Michell's Indian name is? Chief name is?
Anabel's, that's old Indian name. Alex Michell's uncle held that name before.

What Clan is Alex Michell in?
Gilserhyu [Frog Clan].

Do you know what his Indian name means?
I can't remember. I can't remember what the name means. I think one of Sylvester William's kids may have the name. I am not too sure.

OFF THE RECORD

Alex Michell has died, has he?
Yes, he died a long time [ago].

Now, the other person you said who held part of Sebola Mountain is Francois Lake Jimmy or Johnny or Tommy? You said Francois Lake Tommy also held part of Sebola Mountain. Was he also Wet'suwet'en?
Francis Lake Johnny. He was Nutseni.

Do you know – I'm sorry, were you continuing your answer? Do you know what Clan he was in and what his Indian name was?
It's a Gitksan name and refer[s] to having your fingers severed.

Did he give the name?
THE INTERPRETER: *Gojiget.*

MR GRANT: G-O-J-I-G-E-T. Just for the record, I'm giving those spellings as Ms Mills is writing but I have indicated to her before today started she may want to go back and check them.

MR MILNE: I appreciate your spelling because it is very difficult for me to phoneticize these.

MR GRANT: She may want to review them and in the transcript they may appear slightly different.

Earlier this morning you referred to Skin Dyee's territory as being flooded when the dam was made. Was Skin Dyee a Wet'suwet'en Chief?
He was Wet'suwet'en who lived in Hagwilget.

What Clan was he in?
Gilserhyu. He was the brother of Samooh, the name Moses had held, [in] Gilserhyu [Frog Clan].

You're referring to your son Moses?
Yes.

Do you know what Skin Dyee's Chief or Wet'suwet'en name was?
Gibukun.[18] That refers to a person carrying a stick. That is a Gitxsan word.

Do you know how he got that name, Gibukun?
No, I don't. It was way before, I just know that he is called Gibukun.

Was that a name that he would have received in the feast?
Yes, he did and he got that name when he was a young child.

Was it a name that the Wet'suwet'en used and recognized and has been passed on from Skin Dyee?
Yes, this name is passed on, and Skin Dyee had died in my presence.

Just to clarify that, were you present at his actual death or do you remember when he died?
My wife and I had gone to Skin Lake. Skin Dyee was really sick, he was going out of his mind. Before this he had showed me his territory and gave me the Indian names for the mountain. There is one mountain name that was Nayis-tendie, that is where he did his trapping. When we came back he showed me all the lakes and their names. Afterwards I was still staying with him and he began to lose his mind. The police came and took him to Vancouver.

Did he die in Vancouver?
Before he got sick I talked to his sons. I told Robert Skin that if they were going to take Skin Dyee to Vancouver to write a paper [put in writing] that if anything should happen to Skin Dyee while he is in Vancouver that they are to send his body by train back to Burns Lake, and that is what they did. When he died the hospital phoned my wife. By phone. After the phone call my wife and I went to Burns Lake to meet the body that was coming by train. From the train we took the body back to the Reserve, and on the box there was a note on there which said to not open the casket. I wondered why the note was on the casket stating not to open it, so I got the screwdriver and opened it and had a look at the body, and there was nothing wrong with it. I checked the body thoroughly and couldn't find anything wrong with it, and he was buried afterwards. I paid for the expenses because he was a half brother of mine.

When you opened the casket was the body clothed for burial or did you or your wife have to get clothes for Skin Dyee's burial?
He was just wearing a shirt, so clothes were bought for him. He was dressed and buried.

Who purchased those clothes?
Matthew Sam had bought the clothes and the expenses were repaid at the feast. This is how it's been done for years.

Was Skin Dyee's sister Samooh?
Yes, his sister, David Dennis' mother.

Was [it] David Dennis' mother or David Dennis' wife?
His mother.

It was Old Dennis' wife, I'm sorry?
Old Dennis' wife.

I believe you have already indicated to us that David Dennis was your wife's mother [sic]? Your wife's father?
My wife's brother.

David Dennis was your wife's brother?
Yes, my wife's brother.

So to summarize, Skin Dyee was your wife's uncle on her mother's side?
Yes.

This is why your wife was responsible for his burial?
Yes. That is how the business is done.

In relation to his funeral and in relation to him you were Andamanuk to him?
Yes, I was Andamanuk.

What House was Skin Dyee in?
He was Ya'tsalkas, means Dark House.

So he was in Ya'tsalkas or the Dark House, is that right?
Yes.

I think, I'm just not sure, I want to check the earlier part of that answer. You said Gilserhyu [Frog], was that the Clan he was in?
Yes.

Was he a leading Chief in the Ya'tsalkas?
Knedebeas, or the main Chief of the Dark House.

And Samooh and Gibukun stay close to Knedebeas?
Yes.

OFF THE RECORD

How old were you, approximately, when Skin Dyee showed you his territory?
I was getting pretty old, Moses was pretty big boy then. I forget the age.

Now, to get to his territory did you cross Francois Lake?
Yes.

Did you go by wagon or by horse or on foot?
We used the wagon. The area in his territory is called Skin Lake. It's near Francois Lake.

OFF THE RECORD DISCUSSION IN WET'SUWET'EN

There is a mountain near Skin Lake called Tso'o tay, and you go across the lake and that is where his trapline was. His line was four or five miles from Skin Lake. The area and half mountain belonged to him. Now Francis Skin is looking after the territory. He is Skin Dyee's grandson.

Do you know what the white people call this mountain? I believe you referred to it as Tso' o tay?
I don't know the English name for Tso' o tay. I don't know what they call it.

Aside from Skin Lake are there any other – first of all, is there a Wet'suwet'en name for Skin Lake?
The Wet'suwet'en name for Skin Lake is called Netanlii.

Are there any other lakes that you know of in Skin Dyee's or Gibukun's territory?
This is the only name of a lake that I know.

Do you know why people called Gibukun Skin Dyee? How did he get that name Skin Dyee?
THE INTERPRETER: How did he get Skin Dyee?
Yes.
Skin Dyee got the name from the trapping that he had done. Whenever he trapped he got a lot of skins. As a result of that he got the name Skin Dyee.

Do you recall whether there is a lake or mountain that marks the boundary of Skin Dyee's territory?
There is one lake that is used as boundary and that lake is called Who n duk Bun.

Do you know what white people call that lake or do they have a name for it?
I just know the Wet'suwet'en name.

On the other side of the lake is it Nutseni territory?
Yes, belongs to Wet'suwet'en. There is another lake. In Wet'suwet'en it's called Ma'dzee Bun, which translated into English would mean Caribou Lake.[19] Then that is the, where –

OFF THE RECORD DISCUSSION IN WET'SUWET'EN

– That is the boundary of where the land of Nutseni begins.

Is that also on the boundary of Skin Dyee's territory?
Yes.

Do you know which Nutseni Chief has territory right across from these two lakes you have just described, Ma'dzee Bun and Who n duk Bun?
I don't know who holds the territory near these two lakes.

Do you know if the white people have a different name for Ma'dzee Bun?
It might be called Caribou Lake.[20] That's as far as I know about the territory.

When you say that you mean you don't know the names on the other side of that boundary, is that what you mean?
All I know [is that it] belong[ed] to Big Louie and now I don't know who is holding it.

This is –
Francis Skin knows the territory as well as the names.

Your son Moses held the name of Samooh. Did Skin Dyee talk to your wife about who would get that name, Samooh?
Skin Dyee had spoken to someone about who he wanted the name to go to.

What did he tell – I'm sorry – I said your wife. I should refer to his sister, Agnes. I may have misled you. Did Skin Dyee talk to his sister, Agnes, about who would get the name Samooh?
He had spoken to Agnes and my wife and he had told them that Samooh should go to Moses David. That is what happened and now Moses is dead.

Who held Samooh before Moses? Ask him if he would like to take a break?
Before Moses my wife held that name.

And before your wife did David Dennis hold that name?

OFF THE RECORD DISCUSSION IN WET'SUWET'EN

David did not have Samooh, he had the name Satsan.

Before your wife did her mother Agnes have that name?
Yes.

Just to clarify the record, Agnes was Skin Dyee's sister and David Dennis's mother, and was also Johnny David's wife's mother. I've already referred to that, that is how he described it, is that right?
THE INTERPRETER: Yes.
MR MILNE: Just let me summarize that, I just want to make sure I have it right. Agnes is Skin Dyee's sister, David Dennis's mother?
Yes.
MR MILNE: And Johnny David's wife's mother?
MR GRANT: That's correct.

Johnny David's wife was Marion, is that right?
Yes.

And she was David Dennis' sister?
Yes, David's sister.

Marion David. Johnny's [wife's] mother and father were Agnes Dennis and Old Dennis, is that right?
Yes, that's right.

We had to clarify because some of the people were confused and I didn't want people to misunderstand your answers.

THE INTERPRETER: He said: *The way you write it down here is the correct way.*

[That's] what he just said to you?

THE INTERPRETER: Yes.

So I understand Moses held the name Samooh; before, his mother Marion held the name Samooh; and before her, her mother Agnes held the name Samooh. Do you know or were you told who held the name Samooh before Agnes?

OFF THE RECORD DISCUSSION IN WET'SUWET'EN

I think the name of the person who held Samooh before Agnes may have been –

OFF THE RECORD DISCUSSION IN WET'SUWET'EN

– His name may have been Philip but the headstone is in Hagwilget, and he was the first Samooh.[21]

Is he the first Samooh – was he the first Samooh or the first Samooh that Johnny can remember?

OFF THE RECORD DISCUSSION IN WET'SUWET'EN

As far as I can remember there is only – I can only go back to as far as Philip.

Do you remember a feast at which Agnes received the name Samooh?
No, I was too young. Old Dennis had told me about his wife getting the name.

At the present time is it correct that no one is holding the name Samooh?
The name hasn't been passed on yet. In July his headstone will be here and that is when the person will step forward to take the name.

That's this coming July he is referring to?
Yes. I had spoken to his son, Peter David about this.

Who is the Head Chief – is there another Chief in the same House [or Clan] as Samooh and, if so, who is that?

OFF THE RECORD DISCUSSION IN WET'SUWET'EN

Yes, there are other Chiefs who are the head of the House [or Clan] Samooh is from.

Does this include Knedebeas?
Yes, Knedebeas is also from that House [or Clan].

Is Goohlaht Head Chief of that House [or Clan]?
Yes, same way.

Is Goohlaht the Head Chief of the House or of the whole Clan?
Goohlaht is head of the Clan.

Between the time when a Chief such as Samooh dies and the headstone feast, would the Head Chief of the House such as Knedebeas or the Head Chief of the clan such as Goohlaht take care of the territory until a new Samooh was appointed?
Yes, that is how it is done, and the Chiefs in the House they would decide amongst themselves as to who gets the name. Usually [they] look for a person who is well respected in the community and they would decide who gets the name.

Who is taking care of Samooh's territory now? Which of these Chiefs?
Samooh's territory is now being looked after by Francis Skin from Ootsa Lake.

Is he taking the role of caretaker?
Robert Skin and his son are the grandsons of Skin Dyee and, as a result, they are looking after the land doing their trapping.

Earlier this morning or just a few moments ago we were talking about Skin Dyee's territory. Is that the same as Samooh's territory or is it different?
Yes, it is the territory of Samooh.

Does Samooh also have other territories?
No.

Do you know or have you heard of a person called Canyon Creek Tommy?
Thomas?
Canyon Creek Thomas. Yes.
She knows, Mabel Sam [who] is sitting here right now.
Did white people try to throw Canyon Creek Thomas off some land?
Yes, they did try to kick him off his land.

Do you recall who that was? What [were] the names of the white people?
The people who lived next to Canyon Creek Thomas is Jack Carr and his

brother Bill Carr, and he was good friends with him and they did not talk
about his land. I don't remember –

Just go off the record for a moment.

OFF THE RECORD DISCUSSION

Go back on the record.

– I heard that Jean Baptiste was being troubled by the white people but not
Canyon Creek Thomas, and that's all I remember.

His land, do you know a place known as – called Bulkley Valley Road
that existed a long, long time ago?
Yes. Wah tie ee kie, means foot path. I was raised around there and I walked it
many times.

Was Canyon Creek Thomas's land near a place known as Canyon
Creek on that Bulkley Valley Road or footpath?

OFF THE RECORD DISCUSSION IN WET'SUWET'EN

Yes, he had land near Canyon Creek, and the Wet'suwet'en name is Ken' oo ee
Kwah. All the creeks have names all the way down.

We need to go off the record for a moment to change the video tape.

SHORT RECESS

MR GRANT: Go back on the record.

You referred earlier that Jean Baptiste was troubled by the white people. Was he Wet'suwet'en?
Yes.

Can you tell us what you know about what happened to Jean Baptiste
and his land?
Mr Baptiste had about 160 to 300 acres and he had set up a farm, had cows
and horses, and the Indian agent asked him to move off the land but he defied
that order and stayed on the land.

What happened when he defied that order?
He kept resisting the government and they asked him to remove himself from
the land. He refused and the government got their own lawyers to try and
remove him from his land. The Indian agent had also asked him to leave the
land he was on. He refused, he stay on there. Kept growing hay for his cattle.
The people from the government told him that he was to leave the land, he

refused again, so they told him to go somewhere and he dressed and got ready. He had two race horses and he got the fastest one and saddled it up, and he had two revolvers and he stuck them on his sides. There were people who were sent to pick him up, were all lined up, and he came by on his horse and as he neared them he jumped off his horse, pulled his revolver out and stuck it to the head of one of the people and asked him if he wanted them both. The people who were sent to pick him up talked to him, told him to get off the land. The Indian agent told him to get off the land but he refused. When he refused they finally gave in and made that land a reserve.

Who finally gave in?
It was the Indian agent who made the land into the reserve.

Do you know where that land is?
Yes, I know. It's on the road on the way to Babine at the bottom of the hill.

Is it on the road known as Burnt Cabin Road?
Yes, that's how the white people fooled around with us.

Is that land that is now known as the Jean Baptiste Indian Reserve?
Yes.
Go ahead if you have something to say.
The way the people have threatened Jean Baptiste, that is the same way other white people have threatened our Indian people. The same is done regarding our traplines; the white people have been taking them. That's all.

Was Jean Baptiste related to Old Sam, Mabel Sam's father?
No.

OFF THE RECORD

Was Jean Baptiste told that the army was going to come to kill him if he didn't move off his land?
MR MILNE: It's going to be very hard for this witness to say what he was told if he wasn't there, so I'm going to make the same objection I have been making throughout.
MR GRANT: Go ahead, ask him the question he got ready for.
He was told that, that is why he got ready for them and they didn't bother him. They had all caught all their horses and they were all lined up, and that is when they came to them.

Was Jean Baptiste in the Gitdumden [Wolf] Clan?
Yes, he was the brother of Tyee Lake David and Peter Pierre; the three of them were brothers.

The third name was Peter Pierre?
Yes.

What House was he in?
He came from Kyas ya, Grizzly House.

Did he have a Chief's name?
Tyee Lake David had the name Woos, and Tyee Lake was named after him. And the lake is named after him.

After Tyee Lake David?
Yes. He was big Chief.

Did Jean Baptiste have a Chief's name and, if so, do you know it? If he can remember the name?
THE INTERPRETER: He can't remember.
[THE WITNESS:] *Skallithx.*

Just before moving into another area I just want, for the record, to say, before the coffee break we had this morning the witness went over to speak with Mabel Critch with respect to a name, and I have to come back to that, I believe it was the name of a site. It was with respect to my question relating to Canyon Creek Thomas. Counsel for the defendant didn't object and I didn't make any point of it because the witness was clearly trying to help, appears to have been trying to help refresh his memory. Due to his elderly age I believe both counsel thought it would have been inappropriate to object and try to have the witness remain.
MR MILNE: For the record, I would hate to see that as a regular occurrence but it would seem the witness does recall the names shortly after the question is asked, in any event, but I do agree with what Mr Grant has said.
[MR GRANT:] Thank you.

Did the Wet'suwet'en people use arrows in the old days?
Yes they did.

Can you describe what they used to make the shaft of the arrow and the point of the arrow?
The shaft that was used for the arrow is called tsayx. That is what was told to me. If somebody else tells you they might say another thing.

When you say – I am just clarifying with the Interpreter – is tsayx, is that the name for the shaft or is that the material that was used for the shaft?

It is some kind of root that is used to wrap up the shaft.

Do you know the name of the plant that that root comes from?
It doesn't grow on the ground, it's the veins in your arm, it was usually taken from the caribou.

Is that made out of – a rope that is made out of like the tendons of the caribou that is used to tie up the arrow?
Yes, it is from the caribou and the way they kept it together was the sap from the trees which was used to tie the arrow head to the shaft.

Now, did the people use a kind of rock for the head of the arrow?
There is some kind of rock. I don't know the name for it, I was just told about it and it is a rock similar to material in the glass.

It is similar to glass?
It's not glass but it is white-coloured rock.

Did the Wet'suwet'en people have special places where they would get this rock in their territory?
The rock is very difficult to find and that is the material that [was] used for the arrow head.

Did your father show you a place where you could get this rock?
Yes, my father did show me. I don't want to give the location because white people would destroy the rocks if they knew where it was.

Did your father and others take this rock out by using other rocks to chip it away?
They may have used an instrument similar to a knife and the rock was up quite high and it was very difficult to get at, and that's all I know.

Did many Wet'suwet'en people know where this rock was, in your lifetime?
Not too many.

As far as you know is this rock still there?
Yes, the rock is still available. I was told where you could find it and that's all I know.

Did your son Moses know where the rock was?
Yes, he knew where the place was, I told him and that's all I'm going to tell you. One time David Dennis and myself had gone to the location. We parked close by to where the rocks would be found and it started to thunder and we just left.

Go off the record for a moment please.
OFF THE RECORD (Visitor to see Johnny David)

Johnny,[22] I understand you don't want to describe exactly where the location is and I'm going to respect your wish on that, but can you tell us whether or not these rocks are located within Wet'suwet'en territory?
Yes, my father's territory.

That was Smogelgem's territory?
Yes.

Were they located somewhere near Perow?
Yes, near Perow. If people found out where it was they would destroy the site. I did not see the rocks myself, I was told where it was and people went there and tried to locate the rock, they tried to locate the rock and told me. I am telling the truth.

Just a moment please. Is there a Wet'suwet'en name for Lake Kathlyn, which is a lake near Smithers?
The Wet'suwet'en for Lake Kathlyn is Tas Dleese, which means boiling rock and it is also referred to as Chicken Lake by white people.

Is there a history of that lake?
Yes.

Why it's called boiled rocks?
I know the story of why it's called Tas Dleese.

Can you tell us that story?
In the early days there were two young girls who took off their clothing and began playing in the water. The two young girls had long hair and they held their hair up by a bone which was – which came from the coast. They were quite a ways out in the lake, facing the mountain, a big wave came by and a serpent-like creature came up and swallowed the young girls. The serpent had a den near the railroad tracks, where the serpent was located. There is a person who lived near the lake who heard the cries of the two young girls when they were swallowed by the serpent. About a year later during the winter the person that lived near the lake had made about a thousand moccasins and he invited all the people from the surrounding area, and during the summer all the people had come to the lake, and they walked right around the lake and began building fires with rocks, with hot rocks. The people had surrounded the lake and began heating up the rocks and someone suggested that they throw the rocks into the lake. So they did this and in about half an hour the lake

began to boil. The lake was boiling similar to the way a kettle boils on a stove. The big serpent came floating to the surface. [The serpent] was all boiled by the hot rocks. When the serpent came floating to the surface the people retrieved it and cut open the serpent. In the stomach of the serpent was found the two bones that the young girls had in their hair. That is why the lake is called Tas Dleese. Now, if you look carefully around the lake you can see rocks that are black in colour. They were rocks that were used to boil the water and that is where the lake got its name, Tas Dleese. That is the story of the lake.

Was the person who brought the warriors together, was he a Wet'suwet'en Chief?
He was a Wet'suwet'en Chief. He was the predecessor of Gyologet.

Were the girls who the serpent swallowed his daughters?
I think they were relatives of Gyologet since they were playing there. That is all I can tell you.

Did this happen long before the white man came?
[I] Think it is about 200 years before.

Were the bones the girls wore in their hair abalone shell?

Off the record for a moment.
OFF THE RECORD (Johnny left the room)

Go back on the record. Before you answer the question, the witness went and got something to indicate what it was, to help him with the answer. Could you translate the answer now?
THE INTERPRETER: When I asked him the question he said: *[I] knew what kind of rock or bone it was.* And he went into the bedroom and came out with this. Inside the circular is abalone and he is saying: *This is expensive.*

Is that the kind of bone or rock that they had in their hair?
Yes. I don't know what material that is made of this.
[MR GRANT:] I believe Counsel can look at it but it appears to me this is abalone and I believe defence counsel can examine it as well.
MR MILNE: It looks like abalones that I have seen. Definitely a mother of pearl kind of substance. Not to say that the bones were of that, I don't know.
[MR GRANT:] No.
MR MILNE: Just looking at the pendant it appears as though that is what the pendant is.
[MR GRANT:] He is showing the pendant, we can agree with that.

THE INTERPRETER: *He is asking me what white people call this.*
You can say the white people call it abalone.
THE INTERPRETER: It was the same material that he has been describing. *It was tied to the back of their hair. That was all they found.*

Is that material, that abalone that you have indicated, is that one of the materials that the Wet'suwet'en traded in the old days with the people from the coast?
Yes, they did for that and it was very difficult to get and expensive.

You described in this history that you gave about Lake Kathlyn that the man, Gyologet, made a thousand pairs of moccasins. Why did he make those moccasins and what did he do with them?
He made those moccasins to give to the people who were going to help with the boiling of the water, and the moccasins [are] called baxkay.

Is that the name for moccasins all the time or when they are made for this purpose?
The moccasins are called baxkay because it is similar to the army boots that the present day army uses, and it was called baxkay because we were all considered brothers and that's what baxkay means, brothers.

Were those specially made for situations like this history you have described or when the Wet'suwet'en went to war with another group?
These moccasins were made specifically for this purpose and also when our people were going to war, it was done again. This was done when Kweese went to war, and it is a long story. You see in today's army when they are going to go off to war they put on new boots and this was basically used for the same purpose.[23]

I would just like to ask you a few more questions just to clarify some of the answers you gave earlier in the commission. Volume I of this commission, September 20th, at page two you were asked about the pole which belonged to Ginehklaiya. You indicated that it was the pole across the street from your house. I am going to show you a photograph and ask you if this was the pole you were referring to?
MR MILNE: Is that photograph one I have?

OFF THE RECORD DISCUSSION IN WET'SUWET'EN

THE INTERPRETER: *[I] can't see very well and [I] can't recognize it.*

In Volume II of the transcript, at page eight, which is September 26, 1985, you were describing a situation about Samaxsam and you said –

I'll read the question and the answer – you said that the name was given because Old Tiljoe's brother was killed, and I asked you who killed him, and your answer was: 'Halfway between Kitwancool and the Nass River there was a grave marker of the Old Samaxsam, [which] was the size of this table, and on this big log was a big stone and that was knocked over. When the two people had come to this grave marker, they were playing around on it and it tipped over and Samaxsam avenged this by killing one of the Wet'suwet'en and it wasn't Old Tiljoe's brother that knocked this rock over, but somebody else.' That is how the transcript reads, and I want to ask you, was your answer 'It was not Old Tiljoe's brother that knocked the rock over but somebody else'?
It wasn't Old Tiljoe who had tipped the rock over, it was somebody else.

It was not Old Tiljoe?
No.

I am just asking you to be clear on the record.
THE INTERPRETER: Yes.

At page 17 of that same volume, Volume II, you were asked if Dennis, Old Dennis's Chief's name was Dikyannualat, at line 30. You said you could not remember his name; do you remember Old Dennis's name now?
THE INTERPRETER: *[I] remember his name is Dikyannualat, and the white people give him the name Dennis Clark.*

Clark. Go off the record for a moment.

OFF THE RECORD DISCUSSION

Go back on the record. You raised earlier that these moccasins or baxkay were used by Kweese when Kweese went to war. I would like to ask you that history but if you are too tired to tell it now, I'll leave that question until tomorrow morning.
It's too long and I don't want to talk about it.[24]

I told you I would stop at one o'clock and it is one o'clock so I'm going to stop. Tomorrow morning we'll finish, and Mr Milne will be questioning you tomorrow. We'll adjourn now until tomorrow morning.
THE INTERPRETER: He wants to know: *What time.*

Go off the record.

OFF THE RECORD DISCUSSION
PROCEEDINGS ADJOURNED AT 1.00 P.M.

UPON COMMENCING AT 10.15 A.M., 31 JANUARY, 1986
EXAMINATION IN CHIEF BY MR GRANT (CONTINUED)

Yesterday you spoke with us and explained what happened with Jean Baptiste when he fought for his land. Did this happen in your lifetime? *Yes, I was aware.*

Would it have been before or after you were married or can you estimate how old you were when it happened:
It was before I got married. I think I was about 20 years old.

I am showing you a photograph of a pole. Do you recognize that pole? It is the same picture you looked at earlier this morning.

OFF THE RECORD DISCUSSION IN WET'SUWET'EN

THE INTERPRETER: He is having difficulty seeing it again. *[I] think it is the pole, the one that is in front of the fire hall.*

On this pole in this picture there is writing saying 'Agnes Dennis, died May 8th, 1946.' Do you remember a pole that was related – that was erected in relation to the death of Agnes Dennis?
THE INTERPRETER: *After explaining the printing on the pole [I am] recognizing that as the pole that is now in front of David Dennis's house.*

The witness and yourself pointed down the road from Johnny David's house in Moricetown here in the direction of the church or an easterly direction generally towards Smithers. Is that where David Dennis's house is?
THE INTERPRETER: Yes it is.

I would ask to have that picture marked as the next exhibit.

OFF THE RECORD DISCUSSION IN WET'SUWET'EN

THE INTERPRETER: He stated: *The figure on top of the pole, in our language the figure is called mansilx. [I] can't remember the English name for the figure.*

Can you, as interpreter, do you know what mansilx means when translated to English?
THE INTERPRETER: No, I don't.

I'll have that photo marked as exhibit 16. It is number PN10233, from the defendant's Provincial Museum.

EXHIBIT NO. 16 – Photograph of totem pole, B.C. Provincial Museum negative number PN10233.

Do you recall when this pole was erected in front of – I believe you said it was in front of David Dennis's house?
I remember when the pole was raised but I can't remember the exact date and say when the pole was erected.

Was it in the same year as Agnes Dennis died or was it some time after her death?
It was after, one year after she had died when the pole was erected. She died in my hands. She was brought back to the log house that used to be next to this house, and I had spent money since I was Andamanuk.

Was this the same Agnes Dennis who was the wife of Old Dennis and who held the name Samooh?
Yes.

On top of the photograph is a bird, is that – or appears to be a bird and what you have described as mansilx – is that still on the pole?
The bird may have fallen from the wind, I haven't seen it lately, and the figure of the bird in our language is called mansilx.

I understand it is hard for you to see the photograph on Exhibit 16 but can you describe from your memory the crests that are on Samooh's pole?

OFF THE RECORD

THE INTERPRETER: He was working his way up the pole.
From the bottom?
THE INTERPRETER: From the bottom. He said: *The bottom figure was the figure of a female. The second figure above the female was a porcupine, and two figures were otters, and then [I] couldn't see the other two.*

The two figures you indicated are the otters, you're pointing to the two middle figures on the pole that seems to have a dark bar with white or light markings between the two –
THE INTERPRETER: Yes.
Is that right? And the figures he can't recognize are the figures above that which appear to be fairly large?
THE INTERPRETER: Yes.

Exhibit 16.

The figures just below the figure of the bird on the top of the pole, is that correct?

THE INTERPRETER: Yes.

Just for the record, when he was talking about the figure of the bird in exhibit 16, there is what appears to be a very small thing at the top of the pole separate from the pole, is that what he was referring to?

THE INTERPRETER: Yes.

The other day you described to us that you returned to an area where you had been farming and later you sold that land. How big was that land that you farmed and then later sold?

One hundred and sixty acres.

Was this land within Smogelgem's territory?

Yes.

Was Smogelgem's territory much larger than this farm?

THE INTERPRETER: He said: *The land after it was considered Crown land is when I sold it.*

My question was, was Smogelgem's territory much larger than this farm?

Yes, much larger.

Yesterday –

Smogelgem's territory was quite large. The land I sold was just a small part. One hundred and sixty acres.

THE INTERPRETER: He said: *Smogelgem's territory was miles and miles around.*

– Yesterday you told us Francis Lake Johnny's name and I wondered if that name was Gwatsikyet? Just to be clear for the –

Yes.

– I am referring to the Jenness article, which I have provided a copy of his paper on anthropology, Number 25, dated 1943 on the Carrier Indians, to Mr Milne. I am referring particularly to page 509 under the general title 'The Thin House.' Jenness translates that name, Gwatsikyet, as he that cuts off the head with a knife. Is that what you understand the name to be in Wet'suwet'en or does it mean something else?

Yes, that is the correct interpretation for the name. When this white man came around, he took all the pictures and talked about the Chiefs, and that is what is written in books.

Yes, but you described it, as the name meaning cutting off the fingers.

Is the name more precisely cutting off the head? Or cutting off the fingers with a knife?

Yesterday when I was indicating a movement like this, I was trying to indicate that his head was cut off with a saw. Across this way.
And the movement that you're indicating, both the witness and the interpreter, is a cutting motion across the hand?
THE INTERPRETER: Yes.
Or across the wrist?
THE INTERPRETER: Yes. He wants a doll and he will indicate how he just indicated that Gojiget in here: *And his head was cut off with a cross-cut saw, one people on each end, and when his head was cut off, all the blood was in this area and his head had fallen this way.*
Okay.
THE INTERPRETER: *And that is what the name Gojiget is.*

Johnny just performed that motion with the use of a doll or dummy, for the record, that he had stretched across the table indicating, for the record, cutting across in the neck portion, cutting the head off.
    Did you ever see the performance that you just described when you were young? Or the cutting of Gwatsikyet's head?
No, it was before my time. It was Balna who saw one of the people cut off the head.

Was this before your time – was it your understanding that this was re-enacted at a feast, the cutting off of Gwatsikyet's head?
This happened a long time ago and Balna was one of the people who was involved, and that was way before my time.

Do you know why – I'm sorry?
They [did this] at the hall, when there is a feast –
THE INTERPRETER: He was pointing to Tonia Mills –
– she's witnessed how the name is passed on. The people get up to speak and the people get[ting] the names are identified. That is how it has been done in the past and still being done today.

You refer to Balna as the person who cut off the head. Is that a Wet'suwet'en name and, if so, who is the person that presently holds that name, do you know?
Balna was Wet'suwet'en and he holds the name Madeek.

Madeek?
That is the name that George Naziel now holds.

Do you know why Gwatsikyet's head was cut off?
That was the style. Gojiget is also [a] Gitksan name and in our language it means cutting off the head.

Does Gwatsikyet – has he performed the description of his name at a feast that you know of? Let me rephrase it. For the record, the interpreter is trying to determine how to phrase it rather than the witness. Let me rephrase the question for you. Jenness refers to the fact that this cutting off of Gwatsikyet's head was enacted at feasts before the white men came. Did anyone tell you whether that was so?
I remember this white man coming and talking to our people. I remember seeing him and when our name is going to be passed on people get up to speak, the people who are there to witness, and this is how the name's passed on.

Can you tell us any more about the cutting off of the head and as to why it was done? We understand it happened a long time ago, the history of that cutting of the head, and whether or not it was performed as Naxnox at the feasts?
When [enacted at the feast] Gojiget's head was not really cut off. When they performed – when they first performed it his head was here and the cutting motion was done in front on top of the head. So his head was not actually cut off. It was acted out as if the head was being cut off.

You mean on top of the hair of the head as he was lying down?
Yes.

Was the original Gwatsikyet given that name because he cut off the head of the lover of his wife or the woman he was with?
When the cutting of the head was acted out Gojiget got up and danced.

Was there a song to go with that dance?
When the name was acted out he would get up and dance, and what they were trying to say was the head turning around twice. It's very difficult to explain it. There is a figure of a head has the thread running from it and that is what is used to turn the head. That is how it happened and that's all I'm going to say.

That is just what I was going to ask you. Is there anything else that you wish to tell us about Gwatsikyet's performance or that history?
That's all.

You referred to the fact that the person – one of the persons – cutting

off the head was Balna, whose Wet'suwet'en name was Madeek. Was that person the father of a man known as Old Bill Nye or was that person Old Bill Nye?
Yes, Balna was the same person in the English language who has the name Bill Nye.

Earlier on in the commission you showed us the pole of Kela, which is the large pole with the dog crest on it. Did the father of Old Bill Nye have the original Kela dish made for him?
Yes, there was, the dish was made for the father of Bill Nye, and the dog dish is now held by Mabel Sam, who has the name Kela. Who's sitting over here.

Did you ever see the earlier dog dish that was made for Kela, the father of Old Bill Nye?
No, I did not see it. It was a long time ago. There is a song that goes with the dog dish.

That is Kela's song, is that right?
Yes. The song of the dog dish is still alive today.

I would like to refer to another event. Do you recall a feast of Charles – I'll try to pronounce the name – Teytalwus at which you were involved in the performance of Naxnox?
Yes, I remember, I was alive and I was a young man.

My understanding is that you were down at the river and then you were taken up to be involved in the performance. Do you remember that and, if so, can you describe what was done for that feast in which you were involved?
I was outside and someone, one man, came and got me. And my mother had given a suitcase to some people, and there's an area near the Hagwilget Canyon where people gathered and that is where they took me. Chief Charles was there with his uniform –
THE INTERPRETER: – which you say regalia –
– and he also had my suitcase. He opened it and my regalia was in it, and they dressed me up with my regalia. Before we went into the feast House I was told that someone was being picked on and I was given a stick and I was asked to tell the people to quit picking on this person. Chief Charles was holding my wrist and I was struggling. When I got to the door I poked the door with this stick and the doors flew open. The people who were going to fight Chief Charles were standing there; when they seen me they did nothing. I was acting as the door for Chief Charles and all the participants danced, performed

right around the hall. That is how it is done. Since I was the son of the High Chief Smogelgem I was in front of Chief Charles. Those people who were going to fight him never touched me. That was how it ended.

Where did this happen?
It was at the Dark House. The House of Knedebeas in Hagwilget.

Were you just a boy when this happened?
THE INTERPRETER: He said: *I was a small man at this time and I'm still small today. I was strong and I knew the business.*

What was Chief Charles' Wet'suwet'en or Chief's name?
He was called Gitdumskaneese. He was an old timer.

You described that both you and Chief Charles or Gitdumskaneese were wearing regalia. Do you remember what your regalia was? Was it an animal of some sort or what was that regalia?
I wore a hide of a mountain goat, still had its head and horns and hooves and that is what I used when I performed.

Do you remember what was the regalia of Gitdumskaneese or Chief Charles?
Gitdumskaneese used a button blanket, which was his own.

Was anyone dressed as a grizzly at this feast and in this performance?
No.

Were the people that you stopped dressed in certain regalia, and was there any dressed as animals or other creatures?
They were not dressed in their regalia, they came as if they were going to go to war with Chief Charles, and I got in front of them.

Was anyone given a Wet'suwet'en Chief's name at this feast?
No, the name is not given out at a performance like that.

How long did that performance go on for?
It lasted for about half an hour and when it was over everybody left the House.

I would like to just ask you about how Wet'suwet'en people settled murders, or killings I should say. Is there Wet'suwet'en laws for settlement as to when a person has been killed by somebody else?
There is a way this is settled when someone is murdered. For example, when Mooseskin Johnny killed someone, two of his relatives were given to people who were killed. That is how it was done. This happened way before my time and this is what was told to me, and that's all.

When this happened in this case or generally is there a feast at which the relatives are given over to the victim's family?
Yes, there is a feast.

Is eagle down used as part of the settlement at that feast?
Yes, eagle down is used. Eagle down is our law.

When you say eagle down is our law, what do you mean?
The eagle down is our law. It is blown in the direction of the people and it is similar to white man's way now where they sign their name. Eagle down is our law.

After the eagle down is thrown at the feast is that the sign that there will be no more revenge or killings because of the dispute?
Yes, once the eagle down is blown the revenge or murder is stopped and once that is done you are not allowed to break that law. The same is done with the passing of a mountain or territory.

You referred to when white people sign papers, so the analogy you're making is to a peace treaty between [combatants], for example, after a war?
Yes, they quit.

Now, in the case you referred to of Mooseskin Johnny, was his nephew or his nieces given as compensation?
Mooseskin Johnny's sister's kids were given as compensation.

Who was the person to whom they were given and was there a marriage?
For a man a woman is given as compensation, and for a female a man is given as compensation.

Maybe he has answered that; you don't have to ask him if he has answered it. When you say for a man do you mean when a man has been killed or a person who is harmed?
When a man is being compensated.

Do you know the name of the person who was killed in that incident? His Wet'suwet'en name?
He was Gilserhyu. I can't remember.

Was a woman given to Satsan as compensation in this incident?
It was Satsan's brother who received the girl for compensation.
[MR GRANT:] I'm sorry, would you read that answer back?

THE REPORTER: Answer: *'It was Satsan's brother who received the girl for compensation.'*

Do you recall his name?
Kuminyay.

Was this settlement of Moosekin Johnny's, was this before the white man came?
It was before the coming of the white man, and Father Morice was travelling around when this happened.

Did Mr Loring, the Indian agent, and Father Morice try to stop this practice of settlement?
Yes, they tried to stop this practice. That is all I'm going to tell.

When you speak here giving evidence can you speak for the other Chiefs in the House of Hagwilnegh?
Yes, I'm speaking for other Chiefs from Hagwilnegh's House. I speak for them because I know the histories of our people.

During part of this commission you have spoken, and in between the commission, to Mabel Sam, whose Chief's name is Kela. Can you in this commission, in your evidence, speak for Kela when she authorizes you to?
Yes. It is the old Kela's words that I am speaking right now and younger people are learning from me and they will continue to use Kela's words. Also I use my father's, Smogelgem's words. I do not try to deceive the people, I try to tell the truth.

I have three more questions to ask you. Did you or any member of your House or your tribe agree at any time to give the Kilwoneetzen territory to the white man's government?
We did not agree to give the land. It was the government who took the land.

Did you or any member of your tribe consent to the government taking your land?
MR MILNE: Before he answers I, of course, have to object because you are asking for an answer that can only be hearsay. He can't possibly know what all members of his tribe would say, and that applies equally to the land of the Kilwoneetzen.
[MR GRANT:] I will modify the question in a minor way. To your knowledge did you or any other Kilwoneetzen person consent to the government taking your land?

No. In the eyes of the white man we are poor. They just come and take the land, they put everything in their pockets and they're gone. There was some mining that has taken place near the Hudson Bay Mountain. The Indian people were the first to find the minerals but they were told that it was no good and some time later white people stake claims and they went mining. The white man consider the Indians poor. They took everything including their lands and put it in their pockets.

To your knowledge did your father or you as the caretaker or yingxun-lee or anybody in Smogelgem's House consent to giving up Smogel-gem's territory to the white man's government?
No, we did not. They took it themselves.

If the Wet'suwet'en Chiefs or anyone of those Chiefs ever say to give up Wet'suwet'en territory, would this have to have been announced at the feast?
Yes, it would have to be done at a feast. The Indians pass on lands to other Indians through the feast and they don't give it to white people.

Was there ever an announcement of the transfer of any Wet'suwet'en lands at a feast that you either attended or were told of? Was there ever – just read that question back to me, I may have left something out.
THE REPORTER: Question: 'Was there ever an announcement of the transfer of any Wet'suwet'en lands at a feast that you either attended or were told of? Was there ever –'
MR GRANT: I'm sorry. Was there ever any announcement of the transfer of any Wet'suwet'en territory to the white man's government or to white men at a feast that you either attended or at a feast you were told of?
No. They don't do that.
You have given us – I'm sorry – is there something else he wants to say?
No, land is not given to white people. For our trapline, the police come and jail our people. That is how they lost some of their trap lines.

OFF THE RECORD

You have given much evidence of the histories, the songs, and the territories of the Wet'suwet'en Chiefs. According to the Wet'suwet'en tradition are these histories, the descriptions of these territories and crests and songs the property of the Wet'suwet'en Chiefs?
Yes, it is theirs. It is not the property of the white man. It is our own property.

Did you give these histories, songs, and descriptions of the crests and

the territories solely for the purpose of the Wet'suwet'en Chiefs' court case against the government of British Columbia?
Yes, that is why I told. What I have been telling you will never die, it will go on for a long time; it will never be erased. You will be using it –
THE INTERPRETER: – pointing to [me, he said] I will be using it, and he was pointing to myself.

By telling these histories and the songs and the crests do you still wish to reserve the right that they are the property of the Wet'suwet'en Chiefs and other than the court case are not to be published without the consent of the Wet'suwet'en Chiefs?
Yes. If people are going to be using any of the material other than the court case they would have to get the permission of the Wet'suwet'en Chiefs.

I would like to go off the record for a moment.

OFF THE RECORD DISCUSSION

Go back on the record. I just want to record, for the record, and I took a brief break and now I've asked Johnny to sign Kela's song.

THE WITNESS SINGS THE SONG AND PLAYS DRUM

THE INTERPRETER: He was explaining the song: *There was a dog dish, about four to six feet long, and on the face had the head of a dog, at the end the tail, and that is when this song was made.*

He mentioned there were people on the side?
THE INTERPRETER: *There was an old man standing on the side around the dish and he was the one that made the song.*

And he referred to the dog – that was the drum, is that right?
THE INTERPRETER: Yes. *This is – a picture similar to this was on the dog dish.* [THE WITNESS:] *Whoever takes over my name along with the name will get the blanket that is behind me and also the drum. He will keep it with him.*

Can he explain at what ceremonies the song is sung? Why is that song sung and at what ceremonies?
When there is a big party, whenever there is dancing to be done, that is when it is sung.

Is there anything else you would like to tell us about the song or about the description of the ceremony you just gave?
Another time the song is sung is when the berries are given to High Chiefs. They lift up the berries and that is when the song is sung. The song is sung by

Kela as well as myself. When this is done the other Chiefs sing their own songs –
THE INTERPRETER: – pointing to Tonia –
– she's witnessed that a few times.

When this is done, when the berries are there, is there a dog dish filled with the berries?
No, they're put in small bowls. That's all.

Those are all my questions. I just, for the record, want to put in as exhibit no. 17 a photograph of the drum which was being used, which I have shown to my learned friend, so it is on the record. And as exhibit no. 18, [a] photograph of the blanket which was worn by Johnny David outside the pole early in the commission to which he referred in the commission and which is presently at the commission and visible on the video tape as hanging behind Johnny David.
MR MILNE: I think you had better put those to the witness. I don't know if the witness can see them.

Is that a picture of the same drum you were using?
I recognize it as my drum.

And is this a picture of your blanket to which you referred?
That is the blanket behind me.

Put those, the drum is exhibit 17 and the blanket will be 18. There is handwriting on the back to which I haven't referred the witness, and today I am not making reference for these purposes now. Once those have been put in as exhibits I have completed the direct examination of Mr David, and I understand the lawyer for the province wishes to adjourn to commence his cross-examination on Monday, the 24th of February or such other time as counsel may agree?
MR MILNE: That is correct.

EXHIBIT NO. 17 – Photograph of the drum used by the witness [unavailable].
EXHIBIT NO. 18 – Photograph of the blanket previously worn by the witness, presently hanging on the wall [unavailable].

You could maybe explain to Johnny what's happening. Go off the record.

OFF THE RECORD DISCUSSION
PROCEEDINGS ADJOURNED AT 11.55 A.M.[25]

VOLUME 6

Cross-Examination of Johnny David by John Milne, 24–25 February 1986

UPON COMMENCING AT 10:30 A.M., 24 FEBRUARY, 1986[1]

CROSS-EXAMINATION BY MR MILNE: For the record, this is the start of the cross-examination of Mr David. Direct examination has taken place over the last four–five months starting in September 1985. Mr David has been sworn throughout, as has the interpreter. Would you explain that to him please?

OFF THE RECORD DISCUSSION IN WET'SUWET'EN

MR MILNE: He understands that he is still under oath?
THE INTERPRETER: Yes.

Q   Mr David, I act on behalf of a lawyer called Mr Goldie – he's the lawyer for the province and he's asked me to come here on his behalf and ask you some questions.
A   *Yes.*

Q   When I ask you questions during the cross-examination I'm going to refer to 'you' and when I say 'you' I mean you personally, and when I say 'your people' or in some other context I mean the Wet'suwet'en people. When I ask you questions would you confine your answers to whether or not you're talking personally or whether you're talking on behalf of the Wet'suwet'en. What I want to do then, when you give your answer, if you have not personally seen what you're giving your evidence about, I would like you to tell me you have not personally seen it but somebody else may perhaps have told you about it. Is that all right?

A   Yes.

THE INTERPRETER: He said: *If we don't know about it we don't tell about it.*

Q   What I am concerned about, that you know about it personally and that you have seen these things and if you have not seen them, it's fine to say that somebody else told you, but I want to know when that circumstance arises; do you understand that?

A   Yes.

Now you have had many days of being asked questions by Mr Grant, and I will try to be short so we can finish this up altogether.

A   Yes.

If you get tired, let me know and we'll stop?

Whatever I've been telling you I would like to have it written down properly. The way I tell it it's the way it happened.[2]

I understand that, Mr David.

For the record, the people present are, of course, our able reporter, Veronica Harper; the phoneticist, Tonia Mills; the video operator, Mike McDonald, and the interpreter, Victor Jim.

   Mr Grant, for the record, I previously during the direct examination reserved rights to objections on various points and that, of course, was because there was no commissioner present and to avoid interruptions during the direct examination. Those interruptions would have been normally for a ruling on the objection or on other evidentiary considerations. I just want to again repeat that I reserve the right to object at trial and I assume you make the same reservation at this point in terms of the cross-examination?

MR GRANT: Yes, I'll be noting any objections to any questions here and the answers can be given and they can be ruled on at trial.

Mr David, I just want to go over a few points with you and see if I can tie a few things together. I am going to probably cover some of the things that Mr Grant asked you about. Please bear with me, it's only because I want to get them straight in my own mind.

   You were born in 1894?

Yes.

And you were baptised in 1896?

THE INTERPRETER: He says: *[I've] got baptismal papers [I] want you to see.*

MR MILNE: All right.

OFF THE RECORD (WITNESS LEFT THE ROOM)

THE INTERPRETER: That's not the baptismal, that is certificate of registration of Indian status. And has his birth date on it.

The document that you have shown me has a picture on it as well and says that you were [born] March 8th, 1896?
THE INTERPRETER: He said: *That hasn't been done properly.*
MR MILNE: Did he say what –
They've given the wrong year when [I] was born.

What is the correct year that you were born? I think what he is saying, he was baptised in 1896 but was born in 1894. Is that correct?
THE INTERPRETER: He's saying: *Some people who were born later than, their birth –*
THE WITNESS: *the year they were born is the same as mine.*

When was he born?
THE INTERPRETER: He is saying: *This date is when [I] was baptised.*
MR MILNE: And that date is 1896?
THE INTERPRETER: 1896.

When were you born?
THE INTERPRETER: He is saying: *This is the date that they have given [me] but [I] can't remember the number exactly when [I] was born.*

Do you remember how old you were when you were baptised or has somebody told you how old you were when you were baptised?
THE INTERPRETER: He said: *[I'm] finding it difficult to remember the exact date.*

Was he a baby or a young boy?
THE INTERPRETER: He said: *[I] was about a year old.*

Can you remember the date when the telegraph line was put through this area?
MR GRANT: Before he answers, there were two telegraph lines put through. Which one –
MR MILNE: Either one. I simply want to be able to relate a time in history. Did this occur before or after the telegraph line. I just want to be able to tie that to a time.
MR GRANT: Just for the record, there were two telegraph lines. As I

understand, one was around – the Collins overland, which was around 1865 and the other one was sometime later. Clearly, from the evidence he has given and his appearance I don't think he's 120 years old. I don't think you're necessarily referring to that unless you're asking –
MR MILNE: I would be referring to the one that was later and I just want to know if he knows when that occurred.
MR GRANT: He's asking about the second telegraph – you're asking about the second telegraph line?
MR MILNE: The second telegraph line put in.
THE INTERPRETER: He gave the answer as: *Somewhere around 1901.*

In your examination, Mr David, you said the white man came into this area around 1907. Is that correct? Is that what you said?
MR GRANT: That's two questions.
MR MILNE: I expect two answers.
THE INTERPRETER: What was the first one?
MR GRANT: One at a time.
MR MILNE: Let me rephrase the question. When did the white man come to your knowledge, to this area?
THE INTERPRETER: He said: *There were some white people and it was prior to 1901 but there weren't too many of them.*

When did most of the whites start arriving?
After 1901 was when the white people started arriving when gold was discovered at Manson Creek.

Do you remember when the railway first came through?
About 1908. They came from the west as well as the east and met somewhere.

Was that about the same year that your father died?
Yes.

You were married sometime around 1914?
Yes.

You stated that you sold your land near Perow around 1926, is that right?
Yes.

You called that the hard times, is that right?
Yes, people had a difficult time after the war.

Your mother died in 1936?
Yes.

You remember World War II?

THE INTERPRETER: Yes: *[I] remember the war starting in August 1914.*

MR MILNE: 1940 did he say?

THE INTERPRETER: *1914.*

You're talking of the First World War, do you remember a war after that in 1940?

THE INTERPRETER: Yes. *[I] remember.*

I just want to make sure that I have the names of your family correct and their Houses and Clans. I will try and summarize it and you tell me if I am right or wrong. Your mother's English name was Marion Dennis and her Wet'suwet'en name was Suwitsbaine?

THE INTERPRETER: *[My] wife was Marion Dennis.*

MR MILNE: I'm sorry.

What was your mother's name?

Her name was Suwitsbaine.

Did she have an English name?

She didn't have an English name. Her name was Mrs Roosevelt.

MR GRANT: Sorry, her name was Mrs. Roosevelt?

THE INTERPRETER: Mrs Roosevelt is her English name.

She is from the House of Ginehklaiya [House of Many Eyes] and the Laksilyu [Small Frog] Clan?

Yes.

Your father is Smogelgem. Did he have an English name?

He was Laksamshu. He was first of all called David and after he was given the name Chief Roosevelt.

His House was the Owl House?

Yes.

The Wet'suweten name for owl was?

Misdzi ya.

Your grandmother's name was Joenassbaine?

THE INTERPRETER: He is asking: *[My] father's mother?*

MR MILNE: That was going to be my next question.

What was your father's mother's name?

Basa.

Did she have an English name?
No. Her husband was Big Chief.

Was she alive when you were born?
Yes, he seen me born.

Does he remember when she died?
No, I don't. I was quite small.

What was your mother's mother's name?
THE INTERPRETER: He said: *[I] can't remember.*

Was it Joenassbaine?
Yes, that's right.

Was she alive when you were born?
Yes.

Do you remember when Joenassbaine died?
It has been a long time ago and I can't remember the date.

Do you remember if it was before or after the railroad?
It was way before the railroad came.

Was it before or after the telegraph line in 1901?
Before.

She died then after his birth but some time before the telegraph line, is that what he is saying? Is that what you're saying?
THE INTERPRETER: You want to repeat that again?
[MR MILNE:] Johnny, I understand that you said you were alive when your mother's mother died, is that right?
That's right. I was born right here.

Your mother's mother died when you were a young boy, is that right?
THE INTERPRETER: Yes: *[I] was a baby.*

Your grandfather was Old Sam?
That's my uncle. My mother's brother. Oldest brother.

What was the name of your grandfather? In other words, your father's father?
Gitdumskaneese.

Did he have an English name?
No, he didn't have an English name.

Were you alive when he died?
No.
THE INTERPRETER: He said: *I was alive when he died.*

Do you remember how old you were when he died?
My mother told me that I was walking when he died.

What is the name of your mother's father?
He came from Hazelton and his name was Spookx.

Did he have an English name?
Didn't have an English name.

Were you alive when he died?

OFF THE RECORD DISCUSSION IN WET'SUWET'EN

THE INTERPRETER: I think he's getting confused.

OFF THE RECORD DISCUSSION IN WET'SUWET'EN

THE WITNESS: *No, I wasn't alive.*

You said that you were born at Moricetown and that you spent a lot of time growing up in the area that you describe as North Bulkley. When did you first come to the North Bulkley area?
After I was born here in the spring, we went to North Bulkley. That's where I grew up.

What does the name Wet'suwet'en mean?
It's the name given to people from this area.

Is it true that the people from this area used to be called Gitksan-Carrier?
MR GRANT: Which area are you referring to? Because I think the question is misleading.

[MR MILNE:] Did the Wet'suwet'en people used to be called Gitksan-Carrier?

OFF THE RECORD DISCUSSION IN WET'SUWET'EN

THE INTERPRETER: He's getting confused with the names, and [he said:] *The Gitneys are called Gitksan.*

Has he ever heard the term 'Gitksan-Carrier' before?
Can't recall.

In the document which has been filed in court by your lawyer called an Amended Statement of Claim filed in June of 1985, there are people called plaintiffs and I want to know how many of these people you know, and I want to know their English name if you know it, and I want you to tell me if you know where their territory is, if you know it. Maybe you can explain that to him so far and then we'll go through each one. Does he understand that?

THE INTERPRETER: He doesn't understand the word 'plaintiffs.'

[MR MILNE:] I'll go on anyways and I think he'll probably catch on. The first one is – and forgive my pronunciation – Gisdaywa? Does he know who Gisdaywa is?
Yes.

Is he a Hereditary Chief?
Yes.

Who has that name now?
He's a man from Hagwilget. His name is Alfred.

His last name is Alfred?
Alfred Joseph.

Does he know what Clan Alfred Joseph is a member of?
Gitdumden [Wolf Clan].

Is Alfred Joseph Wet'suwet'en?
Yes, he's Wet'suwet'en.

Do you know how long Alfred Joseph has had that name?
It has been a long time. I think it is about ten years. He got his name at the hall here in Moricetown.

Do you know who Gitdumden was before Alfred Joseph?
MR GRANT: For the record, you were referring to Gisdaywa.
MR MILNE: I'm sorry, Gisdaywa.
Thomas George.

Do you know Thomas George?
Yes, I know him.

The next one I want to ask you questions about is number seven on the Amended Statement of Claim, Goohlaht?
Yes, I know Goohlaht.

MR GRANT: I just want to note for the record that prior to this continuation there has been extensive interrogatories directed to each one of these persons including the questions which you've asked relating to Gisdaywa. I assume you're going to do that with the other plaintiffs, as you have indicated – at least with the Wet'suwet'en ones, it appears – and I just want to point out for the record that there is the interrogatories which are extensive and deal with all of those questions on each of those plaintiffs.

MR MILNE: I haven't seen any interrogatories. If you have a copy, perhaps if I took a moment and take a look it might prevent a lot of duplication.

MR GRANT: Go off the record for a second.

OFF THE RECORD DISCUSSION

MR MILNE: We can go back on the record now. For the record, I have had an opportunity during the break to take a look at Part 2 of some of interrogatories given to me by Mr Grant.

What I'm endeavouring to do here, Mr Grant, is to simply generally find out whether the witness knows the other people set out in the Statement of Claim and who they actually are. It's not my intention – I don't want him to go into detail as to the other Hereditary Chiefs, particularly dealing with information which may already have been requested in the interrogatories. I might add this is the first time I've seen these interrogatories.

MR GRANT: Thus far you have been asking questions with respect to the Wet'suwet'en Chiefs and you're asking him to just find out what he knows about that. I have no objection to that. I do take objection to the defence endeavouring to elicit all this information from one witness when they're actually double-tracking it with interrogatories, massive interrogatories which have been directed to all of the plaintiffs who have been knowledgeable in all areas.

MR MILNE: Your objection is noted and again I repeat that it's my intention to see if he generally knows these plaintiffs and where they are. The interrogatories were delivered to the plaintiffs but I am just trying to determine the extent of the witness's knowledge.

MR GRANT: Just also for the record, the Writ of Summons has on it English names of all of these persons, subject to any changes that may have occurred between the time of filing and now. I note you don't have it in front of you but I presume you do have the writ somewhere. Again, if you are only asking to see if he knows them I am not going to object to that.

MR MILNE: Maybe we can go off the record for a moment, the witness has walked away!

OFF THE RECORD

MR MILNE: Back on the record. The witness has now sat down again.
MR GRANT: He just stepped out into his bedroom for a couple of moments.

We were starting to discuss the Hereditary Chief Goohlaht and I was asking the witness whether or not he knew who that person was. Do you know who that person is? Mr Interpreter, would you translate the name for me, paragraph 7 of the Statement of Claim.
Yes, I know him.

Who holds that name now?
I can't remember who holds that name now.

The next one is paragraph 11 of the Amended Statement of Claim, and that name is Kweese. Do you know who has that name now?
That name is held by Gordon Hall's wife.

Do you know her name? Her English name?
Before she got married her name was Beulah Dennis.

When did she get married, do you know?
No.

Do you know her name now? Her English name?
THE INTERPRETER: He just knows her as: *Gordon's wife.*
THE WITNESS: *Gordon Hall.*

Is this Hall that you're talking about related to this person you sold your land to in Perow?
MR GRANT: Who?
MR MILNE: Gordon Hall.
THE INTERPRETER: Would you repeat that please?
MR MILNE: Maybe you should read that back?
THE REPORTER: Question: 'Is this Hall that you're talking about related to this person you sold your land to in Perow?' Then it went on: 'Gordon Hall.'
THE INTERPRETER: I don't know how you come to that conclusion.

The next paragraph in the Amended Statement of Claim is no. 41 and the Hereditary Chief set out there is –

THE INTERPRETER: He said: *It was an English man named Tom Hall.*
I take it from your answer that Gordon Hall is not English?
No.

In paragraph 41 of the Statement of Claim is the name Woos. Do you
know who has that name now and what their English name may be?
Roy Morris has that name now.

The next paragraph in the Statement of Claim is no. 43, Samooh. Who
has the name Samooh now?
*Samooh was held by my son, Moses David, who has died and no-one has taken
over the name yet.*

In paragraph 44, the Hereditary Chief set out is Smogelgem. Is it true
that Leonard George now has that name?
Yes, he has that name.

Paragraph 45 in the Statement of Claim, the Hereditary Chief is
Kloumkhun. Who holds that name now and what is their English
name?
Johnny Mack, who is now in the hospital.

Is it true that Sylvester Williams has the name Hag Wil Negh, which is
in paragraph 46 of the Statement of Claim?
Yes.

Your evidence is given on behalf of the House of Hag Wil Negh, is that
correct?
Yes.

Paragraph 47 of the Statement of Claim sets out Wah Tah Keght. Who
holds that name now?
Henry Alfred.

In paragraph 48 of the Statement of Claim it's Wah Tah Kwets. Who
holds that name?
John Namox.

Are there any other Wet'suwet'en Hereditary Chiefs other than those
ones that I have asked you?
MR GRANT: As plaintiffs?
MR MILNE: Period. Any at all?
THE WITNESS: *If you have their names down I can answer that question. If
you don't then I can give the wrong name.*

I am not asking for names at this point, Mr David. I am just wondering if there are other Hereditary Chiefs.

MR GRANT: For the record, I think in the evidence it has been clear that there are, if I may say, there are Chiefs and there are Chiefs. I am not certain if you are trying to elicit from this witness whether there are any Chiefs who are the head of a House or if you – it appears that there are more than one Chief in each House and I think that was elicited on direct. This may be confusing and I think you should be clear as to what you're seeking or what you mean by Chiefs when you're asking –

MR MILNE: I am asking about the term used in the Statement of Claim which is, quote, Hereditary Chiefs, and I am just wondering if there are any Hereditary Chiefs other than the ones listed in the Statement of Claim.
MR GRANT: For the Wet'suwet'en you're talking about?
MR MILNE: For the Wet'suwet'en.
Yes, there are others and the example I'll give is, I've already stated that Pat Namox is the heir to my name.

Are there Hereditary Chiefs who currently have names and who are not heirs that are not mentioned in the Statement of Claim?
There are others and the Chief's name doesn't go to just anyone.

Are there other Houses other than those listed in the Statement of Claim for the Wet'suwet'en?
Yes. There's Chiefs that have names, they all come from a House.

Are these Hereditary Chiefs?
Yes. Some, their names are taken away if they don't live up to that name.

I understand that. Do you have any idea how many other Hereditary Chiefs there might be other than those stated in the Statement of Claim?
From each House there are usually three Main Chiefs, from each of the Clans. Also three Main Chiefs at the table when the feast is on.

So the number of Houses is, what?
There were four potlatch Houses.[3]
The number was four?
THE INTERPRETER: Four.

Well, I'm getting quite confused about this whole issue of who the plaintiffs are and who else might be out there that is not a plaintiff but are still in the same position as the plaintiffs, namely they are Hereditary Chiefs of certain Houses.

MR GRANT: Before you go on – could you translate that to Wet'suwet'en?

THE INTERPRETER: He was just talking about: *Just three Main Chiefs from each Clan who get up to speak on behalf of all the Chiefs from their Clans.*

Do you know if some of these people in the Statement of Claim which we've just gone through are those three Main Chiefs?

Yes, they are. Yes, the names we just went over are some of the leading Chiefs of those Clans.

Do you know if they are all of the leading chiefs of those Clans?

Yes.

MR GRANT: For the record, before you go further, you did not refer to Knedebeas which is in paragraph

MR MILNE: Oh, 42.

MR GRANT: – 42.

MR MILNE: You're quite right.

MR GRANT: I think it is only fair, if you are starting to refer to these Chiefs in general terms, you also give him that name so that he knows that is one of the ones listed.

Paragraph 42 of the Amended Statement of Claim sets out the Hereditary Chief in the House of Knedebeas. Do you know who that person is and what their English name may be?

The name Knedebeas is held by a lady from Prince George.

Do you know what her name is?

OFF THE RECORD DISCUSSION IN WET'SUWET'EN

THE WITNESS: *Sarah.*

THE INTERPRETER: He has given the last name: *Tommy.*

Is she Wet'suwet'en?

Yes, Sarah is Wet'suwet'en.

Do any of these Hereditary Chiefs that we have dealt with share the title with anyone, share their name with anyone?

THE INTERPRETER: You mean the Indian name?

MR MILNE: The Indian name.

No.

Do you know the names of the Gitksan Hereditary Chiefs? I'm not asking you to give them, all I want to know [is] if you know them.

I know the older Hereditary Chiefs from before but I don't know who's taken their names now.

For the Wet'suwet'en Hereditary Chiefs which we've gone through in the Statement of Claim, without saying where it is, does he know where their territories are?
Yes, I do.

In relation to the Kilwoneetzen territory, is the territory of Wah Tah Kwets, being 48 in the Statement of Claim, close by? By that I mean is it either right next to it or within a day's walk of it?

OFF THE RECORD DISCUSSION IN WET'SUWET'EN

Yes, it is close by.

Is it within one day's walk?

OFF THE RECORD DISCUSSION IN WET'SUWET'EN

It is about two hours by car you could get there.
MR GRANT: Just for my own clarification, were you referring to Wah Tah Keght or Wah Tah Kwets?
MR MILNE: Wah Tah Kwets, paragraph 48.
THE INTERPRETER: He mentioned: *Wah Tah Kwets territory is near the McDonnell Lake area.*

When you went to your territories in the old days, did you go on foot or by some other means?
We went on foot. With our packs, and went over the Dowdy Mountain and took about two or three days to get there.

Does he know who had the territory – the Wet'suwet'en Hereditary Chief who had the territory the furthest from his territory?
MR GRANT: In which direction?
MR MILNE: In any direction. Who had the most remote territory from his?
MR GRANT: From where? McDonnell Lake?
MR MILNE: From the Kilwoneetzen territory.
MR GRANT: The Kilwoneetzen territory is some distance itself.
MR MILNE: From Six Mile Flats.

OFF THE RECORD DISCUSSION IN WET'SUWET'EN

From Six Mile Flats John Namox hold territory and from there it was the people from Skeena Crossing.

The people from Skeena Crossing are Kitsegukla?
Yes.

Have you travelled to the territories of other Hereditary Chiefs besides
Smogelgem and Hag Wil Negh?
MR GRANT: The Wet'suwet'en?
[MR MILNE:] The Wet'suwet'en, again.
Yes, I travelled to many of the territories. We're all from the same Clan and we
do not cause trouble with each other.

Did you often go to the other territories and, if you did, what were you
going there for?
We travelled the other territories with the permission of the Chiefs who own
the territory so we could hunt for game to eat.

When you're saying 'we' you mean the Wet'suwet'en people?
Yes.

How often would the Wet'suwet'en or yourself personally have travelled to other territories?
Usually for one or two months and when the white man came they would
chase us off with sticks. If you went on their land without their permission.

Is it true that you travelled all the time through the territories of the
other Chiefs?
Yes.

Is it true that for most of the time during a particular year you would
be travelling through those territories?
MR GRANT: Are you talking about all the seasons of the year?
MR MILNE: Yes.
Yes, and only with the permission of the other Hereditary Chiefs who own the
territory. When we trapped we would set out traps and the white man would
come behind us and take the trapped animals out of the traps and steal them.

Mr David, I am going to ask you later about trapping and I am going to
ask you later about being chased with sticks by the white man if you
were on what they call their land but first I want to deal with the travel
aspect of going to and from your territory.
  During a year what would be longest amount of time that you
would spend at any particular spot, generally speaking?
When we trapped we would start in September and then finish up in December.

That was the time that you spent out on your territory, is that correct?
Yes.

Did you spend any part of the rest of the year out on your territory?
They would go back later on with the permission of the Hereditary Chiefs who own that territory.

Which Chief has the territory which is closest to Moricetown?
Wah Tah Keght has territory close to Moricetown.

The person having that name is Henry Alfred?
Yes.

So it's true you hunted not only on your territory but on almost all of the territory of the Wet'suwet'en?
Yes, I did trap in other territories [of] my wife's relatives and when I trapped on other people's territory, half of what I got would go to the Chief of that territory.

Is there any territory of the Hereditary Chiefs in the Statement of Claim that you have not trapped upon?
We trapped most of the other Hereditary Chiefs' territories with their permission and we did not cause each other any trouble. It was the white people who started creating problems for us.

Do you remember if there is any territory of the Wet'suwet'en Hereditary Chiefs that you personally did not trap on?
No, I can't remember not trapping on other Hereditary Chiefs' territory. When I did it was usually with their permission.

Your answer then is that you think you trapped on all of the territories at some point or other?
Yes.

When I say 'you' I mean Johnny David personally?
Yes, I understand when you say 'you' you're referring to me, and I have trapped or hunted in other peoples' territory with their permission.

Have you ever gone to school?
No, I haven't.

Do you know how to read or write English?
No.

Do you know how to sign your name?
I just know how to sign it with the cross.

Have you at other times told people that they can sign your name for you?
Yes, they write their own names down as witnesses.

Do they write your name down at the same time with your permission?
Yes, I cross it; they write my name next to it.

Do you know if other Wet'suwet'en do the same thing?
Yes, they do it, all the old people.

Do the Wet'suwet'en have a written language?
Yes, it is written, I'm getting part way through it. It's written down in a book.
THE INTERPRETER: He wants to ask you: *Do you want to see it.*

When you were growing up, did you write things down or did people that you know write things down?
Yes.

Do you know if people wrote down the history – if your people wrote down the history of the Wet'suwet'en?
The older people that have died before us, they did not write down their histories. After their deaths we're suffering.

Is the Wet'suwet'en language different among different Houses?
We all speak the same.

Is it different among the Clans?
No, the only place it's different is amongst the Skeena River people.
[MR MILNE:] The Gitksan?
THE INTERPRETER: The Gitksan.

Do you speak their language?
At one time I spoke the Gitksan language as well as the Tsimshiam language, and I have now forgotten how to speak the language.

Do you know how to speak the language of the Nishga?
No. Their language is different.

MR MILNE: Maybe we should take a break to change the tape at this point. Off the record.

OFF THE RECORD DISCUSSION
RECESSED FOR LUNCH AT 12.05 P.M.

PROCEEDINGS RESUMED AT 1.50 P.M.

MR MILNE: Before we stopped for lunch, I was asking you questions about language, the language of the Wet'suwet'en and whether you spoke other languages. You said at one time you spoke Tsimshiam and Gitksan. Who taught you those languages?

It was through my mother and father. Whenever people from the Gitksan or Tsimshiam people would come they would speak their own language and I would ask my mother what they were saying, and she would translate for me and that's how I learn the languages.

Did the same thing occur with the people from the east of the Wet'suwet'en?
MR GRANT: Like who?
MR MILNE: Did you learn their language? The Carrier? The Nutseni?
The Nutseni speak our language but it sounds a little different, but we understand Nutseni.

But you didn't learn Nishga?
No. Their language was different. The way they spoke and their words were quite different.

Do you remember Nishga people coming to your House and talking either to your mother or father?
Yes, I remember them coming around to potlatches and Hagwilget.

Do you know other people who are Wet'suwet'en who speak the Nishga language?
No, I don't. They speak a dialect similar to the Gitksan but it's, somehow it's different and I can't understand it.

Have you ever had any contact with people – or during the time that you were growing up – contact with the Tahltans?
I don't know where they come from.

Dees Lake. Telegraph.
No.

Do the Wet'suwet'en have a legend or a story about the creation of the Wet'suwet'en people?

OFF THE RECORD DISCUSSION IN WET'SUWET'EN

The Wet'suwet'en people have always lived here. They weren't just dropped here. They've all grown up in this territory.

Is there a story or history that you know of about where your people came from in a spiritual sense?
No, there are no stories. Our people, the Wet'suwet'en, were always here and it was the white man who came after the Wet'suwet'en.

Have you ever worked for wages?

OFF THE RECORD DISCUSSION IN WET'SUWET'EN

Yes. My father and their ancestors would get money from the furs that they got and sold to the Hudson Bay, and as I got stronger I did work for wages surveying.

Did you work for the government as a surveyor?
Yes.

When?
He said: *I worked for them a long time.*

Do you remember when you started working for the government?
I can't remember.

Was this for the government of British Columbia or the government of Canada?
It was for the government that surveyed, starting surveying the land. The person's name that I remember was Mr Gray.

Do you recall whether that was for the people in Ottawa or the people in Victoria?
I don't know which government it was. They might be from Victoria, the people who surveyed.

Were you married when you were working as a surveyor?
No, I was single.

Did you work as a surveyor after you were married?
No, I didn't.

Then, as I understand your other evidence, you were married around 1914 or so, so you would have been working as a surveyor before that time?
Yes, that's right. Also worked for the railway with a team of horses.

Was this also before you were married?
Yes, before I was married.

Did you work on the survey crew for putting in the railway?
Yes, [it] was both for the land survey as well as the railway.

Were you involved in surveying any of the lands that were set aside as reserves for your people?
No, I didn't. It was Mr Loring who set up the reserves.

Was your surveying job a steady job?
It was just during the summer.

When you were working for the railway, was that a steady job?
It was a steady job.

It was a steady job?
THE INTERPRETER: It was a steady job.

Steady job, is that to mean you worked every day all year round except
for holidays and weekends and that sort of thing?
Worked for ten hours a day.

For how many years did you work for ten hours a day for the railway?
*It was for the summer through Christmas. That's all the time I worked for
them.*

Did you work from the summer to Christmas for many years for the
railway?
Altogether about five years.

I'm sorry if I asked this question already. Did you work for the railway
after you were married?
Before I got married.

Where were you living when you were working for the railway? Or for
the surveyor?

OFF THE RECORD DISCUSSION IN WET'SUWET'EN

I lived at North Bulkley.

Were you living on the land that you owned there?
Yes.

Do you remember if at the time you were working for the railway you
had received the grant from the government for that land?
My father lived on that land all of his life and so did I.

What kind of a house did you have on that land?
Smokehouse.

What kind of a place did you live in on the land? What building?
THE INTERPRETER: He said: *Smokehouse.*

Did you live in your smokehouse?
Yes.

Was that the only building that you had on that land?
No, just my father's house. When the white man came they burnt down all the smokehouse.

Did they burn down your father's house?
Yes, they did burn my father's house down, and they stole all the guns, they stole all the axes.

When did this happen?
It was about 1909. It was after my father had died they stole all the contents of the house and then burnt it down.

Who did?

OFF THE RECORD DISCUSSION IN WET'SUWET'EN

It was McGuinness and his sister's husband, Tom Hagen.

How did you know it was them?
I recognize the stuff they stole from the house. I seen it but I did not say anything.

Why didn't you say anything?
He said: If I spoke up about it the law would come and take me away.

Did you tell any person in authority, such as the Indian agent, about what had happened?
The Indian agent didn't care about us. He was the one that put us back on to reserves and he was a white man. In the fall my father had put aside all the furs that he had trapped for. My father trapped anaydoskee, which is black fox, which was worth in those days about $800. Akai MGuinness had come along and taken it out of the trap and took it home. It was expensive in those days and he may still be using the money.

What did your father do about that?
My father had gone to get the black fox and he was refused so he waited for a while to see if he could get it back again and he never did get it back.

Was there a fight between McGuinness and your father?
No, there was not a fight. Considered each other good friends.

Did McGuinness live near your father?
Lived on the other side. He had a farm there.

How close to your father's house was it?
About two miles.

Was Mr McGuinness living there when you were a child?

Yes, I was a big boy when he lived there. And the white people even though they stole things from us they would turn the story around and say the Indians stole it first, and [we] would be threatened to be taken to jail, and that is one of the reasons why [we] didn't speak up too much.

Did your father ever tell you why McGuinness burned his house?
It was after my father's death that they burnt his house down.

OFF THE RECORD DISCUSSION IN WET'SUWET'EN

There was Tom Hagen who took all the guns, the axes, the knives. I knew about it but I didn't say anything.

Where were you when all this was happening?

OFF THE RECORD DISCUSSION IN WET'SUWET'EN

I was not on my father's property when this happened. I was away.

Were you working on the railway or as a surveyor then?
I was working at a mine when this happened.

What mine were you working at?
Owen Lake Mine.

Were you working for wages then?
Yes.

How long did you work at Owen Lake?
I was working with powder. I didn't work there very long – about one or two months. I worked with powder, load it into the rocks and blow it up.

After you got married, did you work for wages?
Yes, I did.

Where did you work at the time you were married?
I worked all over the place.

Did you work on a regular basis? Were you always working or did you have long times during the year when you did not work?
Worked in the summers and in the winters I did my trapping.

Did you ever work in a saw mill?
Yes, I did.

You said that you worked for about five years for the railway. Did you work anywhere else for that length of time?
No.

Have you ever worked as a guide for wages?
THE INTERPRETER: How do I say that? I'm having problems with the word 'guide' in our own language.
MR MILNE: To hunt animals?
No.

You stated in your examination in chief that you had farmed a property that you lived on near Perow. After your father died, how long after was it that you started farming?

OFF THE RECORD DISCUSSION IN WET'SUWET'EN

I got some land near Topley through pre-emption and that's where I did my farming.

Is that the same land that you lived [on] as a boy?
Yes.

Were you farming before you were married?
Yes, I did.

Did you farm after you were married?
Yes, and I had cows and other animals.

Were you running your farm at the same time that you were working for wages after you married?
Was a different time when farming. I trapped and I also did some logging.

How long did you work as a logger?
Skidded for about eight years for Carl McKenzie. I was skidding.

Was this during the time you owned the land in Perow?
Yes.

And was this after you sold the land in Perow? Did you work as a logger after you had sold your land in Perow?
Yes, after. In those days, they were hard times.

Did you work as a logger skidding for Carl McKenzie or anybody else after your mother died?
Yes, I worked for McKenzie. Also worked for him doing his haying and other things, for about eight years.

MR MILNE: Perhaps we'll just take a break here for a few minutes.

OFF THE RECORD DISCUSSION

Do you remember the first name of the man you called McGuinness?
Akai (?). His brother's name was Neil.
MR GRANT: Named a stereo system after him!

You said that you were afraid that the police would come and take you away if you told them about your father's house being burned down. Do you know of anyone that that had happened to? That is, they complained and the police took them rather than the white man away?
No, I can't remember.

I think we had got up to about 1940 or so in terms of your employment record. Do you remember if you worked for wages other than for McKenzie after your mother died? If so, what did you do?

MR GRANT: Before he answers that question, I just question this on the grounds of relevance. I may be persuaded but I'm not sure. I'm not certain what you're leading to in terms of this evidence of this individual's employment history.
MR MILNE: The Statement of Claim sets out that, in paragraph 55 I believe it is without having it in front of me, all of the types of things which the Wet'suwet'en were alleged to have done in their various territories. This person is a Wet'suwet'en and is a Chief of the Wet'suwet'en and is giving evidence that, in addition, it appears, to what those things were in paragraph 55, he also did other things and those are the things I am eliciting for the record. I think it is relevant to paragraph 55.
MR GRANT: I'm going to maintain the objection, for the record, and I presume you will proceed but I reserve the right to object at trial on the grounds of relevance. Possibly – before you go to your next question – I would like you to translate, if you can, the exchange that occurred so the witness knows what is happening. If you wish, the reporter can read it back to you.
THE INTERPRETER: Would you read it back please?
MR MILNE: Maybe I can put it on the record this way. Mr David, your lawyer has said that he is objecting to the questions I am asking you about your employment because he doesn't think it has much to do with the case your people are making and he may object when it goes to trial on the same basis or some other basis if he sees fit.

OFF THE RECORD DISCUSSION IN WET'SUWET'EN

MR MILNE: What was that answer?
THE INTERPRETER: He said: *[I'm] getting confused.*

MR MILNE: In any event, I think Mr Grant has made his objection and I've noted it.

MR GRANT: Just for the record, I would like the reporter to read back your explanation why you're asking this question. I think it is only fair to the witness [to know] why you're asking these questions and I would ask the reporter to read that answer back now.

MR MILNE: I think he's confused about your objection not my answer.

MR GRANT: I guess he hasn't heard your answer yet in Wet'suwet'en.

THE REPORTER: Mr Milne said: 'The Statement of Claim sets out that, in paragraph 55 I believe it is without having it in front of me, all of the types of things which the Wet'suwet'en were alleged to have done on their various territories.'

OFF THE RECORD DISCUSSION IN WET'SUWET'EN

THE REPORTER: 'This person is Wet'suwet'en and is a Chief of the Wet'suwet'en and is giving evidence that, in addition, it appears, to what those things were in paragraph 55, he also did other things and those are the things I am eliciting for the record.'

THE INTERPRETER: He is saying: *'When we finished our trapping that's when we went logging.'* He asked if that's the information you want?

MR MILNE: Yes.

THE WITNESS: *We stay on the land. Once all our trapping was done we did other things. Logging, haying, and so forth.*

When you were logging, or working as a surveyor, or working in Owen Lake mine, or any other jobs you had for wages, were there other Wet'suwet'en working with you?
No, there weren't too many other Wet'suwet'en worked along [with] me. It was just Topley Matthew Sam who worked with me, working with powder for five years.

During the time that you were working for wages and hunting or trapping otherwise, did you make more money working for wages than from trapping?
I made more money trapping than I did at logging.

Do you know if this was the case with other Wet'suwet'en?
MR GRANT: Just a minute. He said that not many others worked with him. You just asked him that question and he said only two others worked with him.

MR MILNE: Well, they were Wet'suwet'en and the question is do you know if that was the case with other Wet'suwet'en?
MR GRANT: Are you referring to these two?
MR MILNE: No, I'm referring to the Wet'suwet'en people.
THE WITNESS: *Yes, there was other people who did that. Most of them made more money at trapping than they did working for wages.*

I think we have to go back to one of my other questions. We looked after your employment record until about 1940. You earlier stated you remembered World War II. Did you work for wages after World War II?

OFF THE RECORD DISCUSSION IN WET'SUWET'EN

First World War I remember we worked for a dollar a day. Second World War everybody worked for a wage.

You continued to work for wages after the Second World War, is that right?
Yes. That was the time that I did some logging.

As you grew older, from the time that your father died to the time you did logging, did you work for wages more and trap less?
After my father died I did more trapping than I did working for white people.

What about later on?
After that I became a farmer and I got married.

After you became a farmer and got married, did you work for white people more?
After I got married I worked at logging and also haying. I was usually put in that position because I did things right.

Have you ever had a driver's licence?
Yes, I did have a driver's licence and I got my son, Moses, a car licence when he was 15.

Do you remember when you got your driver's licence?
About 1920?

Have you ever had a fishing licence?
No, I didn't have fishing licence. I only did when I was down at the coast.

Do you have a licensed trapline?
Yes.

Do you have more than one?

OFF THE RECORD DISCUSSION IN WET'SUWET'EN

About six traplines that belong to my father. Nobody goes round there except myself.

Are these traplines that are licensed by the government?
Yes, they did.

Are they in your name now?
It was in Moses' name and now it's in Peter David's name.

Peter David is one of your sons?
My son's son.
MR MILNE: Is he through?
THE INTERPRETER: (Nodding affirmatively)

Are these traplines in the territory of Smogelgem?
Yes.

Are they in the Kilwoneetzen territory?
No, it's near Perow.

All of them?
My father's land is near Perow in North Bulkley.

Are all the traplines near Perow in North Bulkley?
Yes. My father's trapline was looked after by my son, Moses. Now that he's dead Peter David is looking after it.

How old is Peter David?
I've forgotten what his age [is].

Is he a boy or a man?
He's a man. He had a wife and he has got many children. His son Philip is standing behind him.

Do you have any licensed traplines in the territory of Maxlaxlex?
His land is in the Copper River area.

Do you have a licensed trapline in the Copper River area?
No, I don't.

Were these traplines in your name at some time?
MR GRANT: Which traplines?
MR MILNE: The six that he talked about.
It was in my name.

Do you have any traplines in the territory of any of the other Hereditary Chiefs?
No, I don't.

When did the six traplines go into your name. Do you remember?
I don't remember.

Do you remember if you had any problem with the government about
getting those traplines?
No. No, I didn't.

Ask him how he is feeling, would you?
THE INTERPRETER: He said: *I'm tired and my throat is starting to feel sore.*

Ask him if he wants to stop and continue tomorrow morning.
THE INTERPRETER: He said: *Yes, and try to finish tomorrow.*
MR MILNE: I will do my best. Go off the record now.

OFF THE RECORD DISCUSSION

MR GRANT: I'm sorry, could you go back on the record for a second? I
want to put something on the record. On the record, I was going to
advise the witness of this off the record, but maybe you can tell him as
he is under cross-examination he shouldn't talk to me or anyone else
about the general nature of his evidence until tomorrow. Thank you.
Off the record.

OFF THE RECORD DISCUSSION
PROCEEDINGS ADJOURNED AT 3:00 P.M. UNTIL TOMORROW MORNING AT
10:30 A.M.[4]

CROSS-EXAMINATION BY MR MILNE (contd):
VICTOR WILLIAM JIM, Wet'suwet'en interpreter, previously sworn.
JOHN DAVID, a witness called on behalf of the plaintiffs, previously
sworn, testifies as follows:
UPON RESUMING AT 11:25 A.M., 25 FEBRUARY, 1986

OFF THE RECORD DISCUSSION

MR MILNE: This is the continuation of the cross-examination of the witness, Johnny David, from yesterday. All of the same parties are present
as yesterday, and the witness and the interpreter are still sworn.
Would you, Mr Interpreter, explain to him that he is still under oath
and make sure that he understands that. Does he understand that?
THE INTERPRETER: Yes, he understands.

Yesterday you were telling us of your traplines and the fact that you had six of them that were licensed, and all of them were in the North Bulkley territory. Do you have or have you ever made a map of your traplines?
There were maps but they've all been lost. I know where the traplines are.

When was the last time you saw these maps?
Was a long time ago, and when we trap the traplines are blazed and this is what you go by.

Have you ever seen a government map of your traplines?
Yes I did. Yes, I did see the map, and through our own laws you see the trees blazed and that's where we go.

Do you know if the government maps were different to what your line was according to your trees being blazed?
Our own laws where the trees are blazed are correct. The government maps are wrong, and our ancestors have trapped and we know where their lines are.

Have you told other people who are doing research for you and for the Wet'suwet'en people where your traplines were?
MR GRANT: I object to anything that is aimed to elicit information gathered for this litigation or in contemplation of this litigation. I claim privilege with respect to that.
MR MILNE: I am not asking what he told them. I am just asking if he told them, and I don't think that's objectionable.
So would you ask if he has told people where his traplines were for purposes of this litigation?[5]

What sort of traps did you use in your territory?
Used three different types of traps that were man-made as well as your normal traps. One of the man-made traps is the dead-fall traps.

When you say normal traps, do you mean steel traps?
Yes. And there's three different kinds. They were traps for bears and – grizzly bears.

For as long as you can remember, have you used only steel traps?
I use the three different kinds of steel traps as well as three different kinds of dead-fall traps.

Where did you get the steel traps from?
Hudson Bay.

Where was the Hudson's Bay?
Old Hazelton.

Was there any other Hudson's Bay around the areas that you went to?
They had stores throughout the territory. They also sold liquor, Hudson Bay rum.

Do you know where in the territory these stores were?
Beside the one at Hazelton, they had a store at Babine, Fort St James, and the last one at Fort Fraser.

Was the store at Old Hazelton there when you were born?
Yes.

Did you trade with Hudson's Bay since the time that you were born? I mean, have you on a regular basis traded ever since you were born?
All the old people traded their furs with Hudson Bay.

Did you also get guns and blankets and other supplies from the Hudson's Bay store?
Yes.

Do you know who the person was when you were growing up as a young man who ran the Hudson's Bay store in Hazelton?
There were many people that ran the stores and I can't remember their names.

Did you or do you know if any of your people asked the Hudson's Bay store to leave? That is, the Hazelton Hudson's Bay store?
THE INTERPRETER: You mean the Wet'suwet'en or –
MR MILNE: The Wet'suwet'en.
Our people did not ask the people from the Hudson Bay to leave. The first store was at the location where 'Ksan Village is, in the area where the campground is. At the site I described, there were three smokehouses and the store was right in the middle and they would bring their materials by steamboat. My father's brother, David McKenzie, when he was a young man, spoke three languages. He spoke Gitksan, Wet'suwet'en, and Chinook. Because he knew the three languages he was made the operator of the store.

For how long was he the operator of the store?
When McKenzie was the store owner, during that time the first store had burnt to the ground. The other buildings from the village had also burnt. That village was called Gitanmaax. And the trees near the village and some of the totem poles had also burned. It was after this incident that the Hudson Bay store moved to the new location.

Were you alive at the time of this fire?
I was not born yet, it was way before my time. McKenzie himself had told me about this.

Was David McKenzie Wet'suwet'en?
He was my father's brother. Older brother.

What was his Indian name?

OFF THE RECORD DISCUSSION IN WET'SUWET'EN

Skitkanu. That was his child's name.

In relation to your territory, what is the name of the nearest other Indian tribe?
MR GRANT: You mean non-Wet'suwet'en?
MR MILNE: Who is not Gitksan or Wet'suwet'en?

OFF THE RECORD DISCUSSION IN WET'SUWET'EN

They were all Wet'suwet'en.
MR GRANT: Just to clarify, are you referring to the Perow or Smogelgem territory or the Kilwoneetzen territory?
MR MILNE: I was referring actually to the Perow Smogelgem territory. What I want to know is: have you heard of the Carrier Indian Band? I don't know what the Wet'suwet'en word for Carrier is.
THE INTERPRETER: Nutseni.
Have you heard of the Nutseni?
Yes.

Did they have a boundary that was shared with Smogelgem's territory?
No, they didn't. They lived further east.

Did they share a boundary with a Wet'suwet'en?
They did live close by to the Wet'suwet'en. They had their own territory.

Do you know where their boundary of their territory is? The boundary closest to the Wet'suwet'en territory?
MR GRANT: Are you referring – just to be clear – the boundary between the Wet'suwet'en – not necessarily between his territory but between the Wet'suwet'en and the Nutseni, is that what you're asking him?
MR MILNE: I'm asking him the boundary between the Wet'suwet'en territory and the Nutseni territory.
MR GRANT: Okay.

The boundary between Wet'suwet'en and Nutseni is at Burns Lake and Ootsa Lake and part of Skin Dyee's territory was the boundary. And Skin Dyee was a man from Wet'suwet'en country.

Do you know if Skin Dyee had any trouble with the Nutseni?
No, they didn't. They lived next to each other and they considered each other good friends.

Do you have any relatives who are Nutseni?

OFF THE RECORD DISCUSSION IN WET'SUWET'EN

My two relatives who are now living in Nutseni territory is Alex Long Charlie and another lady who is partially blind, and the wife of Francis Charlie whose name I think is Louise.

OFF THE RECORD DISCUSSION IN WET'SUWET'EN

There's some ladies from here have married men from Nutseni territory and their kids are brought up in that territory. That's all.

By that marriage, do the Nutseni have any right to hunt in Wet'suwet'en territory?
No. They were born in Nutseni, that's where they were brought up.

Who was born? The children?
The children from the Wet'suwet'en women and Nutseni men.

But do either spouse, if it is male or female depending on the case, who marries a Wet'suwet'en and is Nutseni himself have the right to hunt or trap on the Wet'suwet'en territory?
It's very rare that they come into Wet'suwet'en country. There's a few that come but they go back to their territory right away.

But do they have a right to come to the Wet'suwet'en territory to hunt?
Only if they're invited by the Head Chiefs of the territory. If they do, they give half their catch to the Hereditary Chief who owns the territory.

We're going to have to take a break for a video tape change.

OFF THE RECORD DISCUSSION

Do you know if the Nutseni were ever invited to Wet'suwet'en feasts?
Yes, they're invited and they helped out at Hagwilget.

What sort of feasts were they invited to?
They're invited when someone dies and expenses have to be paid back.

Were they invited regardless of who died? So long as there was a feast?
When their relatives die and when anyone dies for that matter, they are invited and they usually dance and they're Andamanaak. I have pictures of those feasts, I have them in the room.

Is it possible for a Nutseni through his attendance at a feast [to] become entitled to Wet'suwet'en territory?
When the Nutseni are invited to a feast, when they help they're invited for short periods of time to trap on Wet'suwet'en territory but they are not given Wet'suwet'en territory forever.

If they come as [Anda]manaak is it not so that Andamanaak under Wet'suwet'en law can acquire territory?
They're only given the opportunity to trap in the territory for a year. They don't give it to them forever.

Have you known this to occur? That Nutseni has been given the right to trap in Wet'suwet'en territory?
I have seen them and that is why I'm telling you now.

Were the Nutseni ever able to trap on the territory of Maxlaxlex?
No.

Were the Nutseni allowed to hunt or trap on the territory of Smogelgem?
No. They never came around. They trapped for three occasions in the Francis Lake area only after they were invited. That is why the overlap with the Carrier-Sekanni is with us today. When the Nutseni say their boundary goes from Houston east, that is not so, they will not take that land. From Burns Lake to Skin Dyee's territory, that is the boundary of the Wet'suwet'en people. It's got nothing to do with the Nutseni.

Has there always been this dispute with the Nutseni over the overlapping territory?
MR GRANT: Just a moment. I'm not certain that he ever said there was a dispute with the Nutseni. He did say there is an overlap with the Carrier-Sekanni, but I think you're putting words in his mouth. I think you should rephrase the question.
MR MILNE: You have said that Nutseni will never have the territory from Houston to Burns Lake because that is Wet'suwet'en. Have you argued with the Nutseni over that territory?
In the old days the Nutseni and the Wet'suwet'en did not have any problems with the overlap. It is the people that are being born today that are creating the problems with the overlap.

How long has this problem been going on?
The land of the Wet'suwet'en and the Nutseni has been talked about for many years, and it is young people or the people that are born and our young people are the ones who are disputing the land, and they will not get the land.

Are the Wet'suwet'en invited to the feasts of the Nutseni and, if so, are they entitled to any Nutseni territory?
Yes, they do invite us and I have been there many times myself.
THE INTERPRETER: I have to finish the other half of the question.

OFF THE RECORD DISCUSSION IN WET'SUWET'EN

When I'm invited I'm usually asked to speak, as I do here. No, the Wet'suwet'en do not trap on Nutseni territory. When our relatives die that is when we are invited to the feasts by the Nutseni. And that's all.

OFF THE RECORD DISCUSSION IN WET'SUWET'EN

We go down for a feast when our relatives die and expenses have to be paid there.

Have you heard of the Kitwancool Indian people?
Yes, I do.

Do you know where they are in relation to the Wet'suwet'en territory?
The Wet'suwet'en live in this area and then you have the [area] where the road goes to Alaska.

Do you have relatives who live with the Kitwancool?
I just have a granddaughter there, I've forgotten her name.

OFF THE RECORD DISCUSSION IN WET'SUWET'EN

Even though we speak different languages we are still related.

Do the Kitwancool have a boundary in common with the Wet'suwet'en in their territories?
I don't know. The people from Skeena River would know that.

Have the Wetsuwet'en or to your knowledge [the] Gitksan gone to war against the Nutseni or the Kitwancool people?
MR GRANT: When?
MR MILNE: Ever.
THE WITNESS: *Oh boy!*
MR GRANT: I think on reflection that question is actually four questions combined into one and I think it is only fair to the witness that you break it down.

MR MILNE: I don't –

MR GRANT: You're talking about the Wet'suwet'en or Gitksan going to war with the Nutseni or the Kitwancool.

MR MILNE: I'll break it down.

MR GRANT: There's four different groups and, given the time frame, is rather broad.

MR MILNE: Do you know if the Wet'suwet'en have gone to war against the Nutseni?

In the very old days I was told that they did go to war.

Were you told what the war was about?

OFF THE RECORD DISCUSSION IN WET'SUWET'EN

I am not feeling strong enough to talk about that. I was told by my ancestors a long time ago.

Are you feeling strong enough to continue on or would you like to take a break?

OFF THE RECORD DISCUSSION IN WET'SUWET'EN

THE INTERPRETER: He says he's feeling tired and not to take too long this afternoon.

MR MILNE: Let's go off the record and discuss our time frame here.

MR GRANT: Just before we do, I just want to put on the record and I would like to explain to Johnny, there was a delay; Mr Milne had to be in chambers this morning and, for the record, we were scheduled to start at 10.30 and it actually started at 11.30, and Johnny was waiting here patiently from 10.30 on. I am not saying this to cast fault but just that we understand that he was waiting an extra hour and that may well lead to making him feel tried. On behalf of myself, I would like to apologize for making you wait, Johnny.

MR MILNE: Go off the record.

MR GRANT: Just wait till he tells him that.

MR MILNE: Okay.

MR GRANT: Go off the record

OFF THE RECORD DISCUSSION
RECESSED FOR LUNCH AT 12.30 P.M.

PROCEEDINGS RESUMED AT 1.30 P.M.

MR MILNE: Before we broke for lunch, you were going to tell me about the Wet'suwet'en and whether they ever had a war with the Nutseni.

Can you tell me that story now? If you are too tired, I can ask you the question some other time and we can go on to other things now. *I get pretty tired and I can't sit up for too long.*[6]

MR MILNE: Ask him if he's too tired now to go any further today.
THE INTERPRETER: He says: *I'll speak for a little while, and I want you to finish as quick as possible, and I don't want to speak again next time.*
MR MILNE: I'll do my best.
THE WITNESS: *If you are going to finish now, I'll sit up a little longer.*
MR MILNE: Would you tell him I have many more questions to ask him and if he would instead of doing it now he would rather do it later then I can come back and he can have a good long rest. Tell him the next time we meet will probably be the last time.

OFF THE RECORD DISCUSSION IN WET'SUWET'EN

MR GRANT: Maybe go off the record.

OFF THE RECORD DISCUSSION

MR GRANT: For the record, I just want to set out what occurred at this break. It appeared when Mr Milne asked the first question that the witness, Mr David, was tired although he – questions were then asked about how tired he was. I'm concerned as counsel for the plaintiffs on two respects here. One is we seem to have difficulty in setting out another date which is relatively soon. We have agreed between counsel, and I must say with some reluctance on my part, to April 21st, 22nd, and 23rd. I'm further concerned about that given the witness indicated when we were off the record that he is not feeling as well, that he feels he is getting weaker and he's not certain he will be as well the next time as he is now. The reason why we set the date so far is because counsel for the Crown has indicated that he anticipates or estimates two days at the rate we're going, which I would say is between two and four hours when we talk about a day for Johnny's evidence and, therefore, in order not to have this all split up into small pieces, which is just more exhausting for the witness and more difficult logistically, we've agreed to a three-day block of time, which gives an extra day in case we don't have enough time in the first two days. I didn't raise this with Mr Milne yesterday and, of course, the order speaks as it does. Today we have to adjourn because the witness is tired. It's unfortunate that this commission is taking so long but I anticipate from what Mr Milne says that we will be able to complete on that next block of time in April.

MR MILNE: For the record, as I mentioned as well, my estimates are probably about the same as Mr Grant's were on the examination in chief and I too hate to see it go to so far but that's the only time counsel are able to get together on their dates. Hopefully the witness is well rested and able to continue at that time. The order speaks for itself as at whose risk this adjournment is made. We'll adjourn over then until April 21 for the continuation. At nine o'clock.

OFF THE RECORD DISCUSSION

MR GRANT: Just going back on the written record, not on the video because it has been disassembled. Johnny, I want to tell you that you're under cross-examination and I hope this won't be difficult for you given the length of the adjournment but generally you should not talk about your evidence to others while you're under cross-examination. So you won't be interviewed or discuss the general nature of your evidence in this case until we try to complete the cross in April.

THE WITNESS: *Okay. I understand.*

MR GRANT: So adjourned to nine o'clock on April 21.

OFF THE RECORD DISCUSSION

PROCEEDINGS ADJOURNED AT 1:50 P.M., 25 FEBRUARY, 1986 TO BE RESUMED AT 9.00 A.M., 21 APRIL, 1986.[7]

VOLUME 7

Cross-Examination of Johnny David by John Milne, 21–22 April 1986

VICTOR WILLIAM JIM, Wet'suwet'en interpreter, previously Sworn.
JOHN DAVID, a witness called on behalf of the plaintiffs, previously sworn, testifies as follows:

UPON COMMENCING AT 10.00 A.M., 21 APRIL, 1986

MR GRANT: Just for the record, I want to confirm that I have spoken with Mr Milne and we've agreed that we're going to do our best efforts to complete this very extensive examination in the next two days and, if necessary, go over to the 29th April. I want to set out for the record that since the last adjournment, which was on February 25th, Johnny – the witness – has become ill on one occasion and I'm concerned as counsel for the plaintiffs that if we extend this too much longer, it may mean that the commission could not be completed. I have advised Mr Milne of that and he has indicated that he will endeavour to complete his cross-examination as much as possible over the next two days.

MR MILNE: That's correct. I hope not to leave anything out because of the witness's health but certainly there is no desire on the part of the defendant to cause him any undue stress. Again, for the record, this is the continuation of the cross-examination of Mr David. The last time we were sitting was February 25th. The original examination commenced in September of 1985, so it has been some lengthy time. Also for the record, all of the parties that were present during the cross-examination in February as well as during the previous examinations are present. The witness is still sworn, as is the interpreter.

Q Mr David, do you understand that you are still under oath?
A *Yes.*

Q MR MILNE: Mr Interpreter, you understand as well that you're under oath still?
A THE INTERPRETER: Yes.

Q Mr David, the last time I was here I was asking you questions or started to ask you questions about any wars the Wet'suwet'en people might have had with the Nutseni. I am going to leave that area for now and I am going to ask you some questions about the land which you owned in Perow area or Topley area?
A *All right.*

Q You said last time you got some land near Topley through pre-emption and that is where you did your farming. I have some documents from the Land Title Office in Prince Rupert I want to show you. I don't know if you will be able to make out the writing on it but I'll give it a try. The first document is a copy of a certified copy of title no. 18962 I, and it's dated March 8th, 1926 as date of registration. It certifies that John David is the owner of a piece of property known as Block A of Lot 30, 3327, Range 5, Coast District. Have you ever before seen that title from the Land Title Office?
A *I have seen this. I got a similar one when I got the land.*[1]

Q That is a copy of the title to the land that you owned then?
A *Yes.*

MR MILNE: Could I have that marked as the next exhibit?

EXHIBIT NO 19 – Document entitled document, certified copy of title no. 18962 I, date of Registration March 8, 1926.

You also said last time we were here that you got this land through pre-emption or Crown grant: How did that come about?
I got it first through pre-emption. After three years on it then I got it through Crown grant.[2]

I have another document that is order-in-council, it's a minute of the Executive Council dated September 30, 1920, and that says that application was made for that property – I'm paraphrasing – and it is said that Johnny David is a reliable hard-working man and has eight head of horses and five head of cattle. Could you just translate that portion of it to him?

Exhibit 19.

[Image of British Crown over the British Flag with a lion on top, a caribou to the left and a ram to the right]

No. 18962 I

THE GOVERNMENT OF THE PROVINCE OF BRITISH COLUMBIA

From The Crown

Certificate of Indefeasible Title

Date of Application for registration, the 8th day of *March*, 1926.

Register, vol. 57

This is to certify that *Johnny David*

is absolutely and indefeasibly entitled in Fee-simple, subject to such charges, liens, and interests as are notified by endorsement hereon, and subject to the conditions, exceptions, and reservations set out hereon, to *that* piece of land situate in the *Omenica Assessment District* and Province of British Columbia, and more particularly known and described as:-

Block "A" of Lot thirty-three hundred and twenty-seven (3327) Range five (5), Coast District, said to contain ninety-three decimal twenty (93.20) acres more or less.

> In witness whereof I have hereunto set my hand and Seal of Office at *Prince Rupert*, British Columbia, this 11th day of *March*, 1926.

R.M. L. [Initials written to the left of the above. The word *"Cancelled"* is written vertically over the paragraph above].

[Signature and Seal of Registrar]

This Certificate of Indefeasible Title is void as against the title of any person adversely in actual possession of and rightly entitled to the hereditaments included in same at the time of the application upon which this Certificate was granted, and who continues in possession , and is subject to---

- (a.) The subsisting exceptions or reservations contained in the original grant from the Crown:
- (b.) Any Provincial tax, rate, or assessment at the date of the application for registration imposed or which may thereafter be imposed on the land, or which had therefore been imposed and which was not then due and payable:
- (c.) Any municipal charge, rate, or assessment at the date of the application for registration imposed or which may thereafter be imposed on the land, or which had therefore been imposed of local improvements or otherwise and which was not then due and payable including any charge, rate or assessment imposed by any public corporate body having taxing powers over an area in which the land is situate:
- (d.) Any lease, or agreement for lease, for a period not exceeding three years, where there is actual occupation under the same:
- (e.) Any public highway or right-of -way, watercourse or right of water, or other public easement:
- (f.) Any right of expropriation by Statute:
- (g.) Any lis pendens or mechanic's lien, judgment, caveat, or other charge, or any assignment for the benefit of creditors or receiving order or authorized assignment under the "Bankruptcy Act," registered since the date of the application for registration:
- (h.) Any condition, exception, reservation, charge, lien or interest noted or endorsed hereon:
- (i.) The right of any person to show that the whole or any portion of the land is by wrong description of boundaries or parcels improperly included in this certificate:
- (j.) The right of any person to show fraud, wherein the registered owner or wherein the person from or through whom the registered owner derived his right or title otherwise than *bona fide* for value has participated in any degree.

THE FOLLOWING PIECES OF LAND HAVE BEEN TRANSFERRED:

Land: All See 0.2.B Vol. 85, Cert. No.:25895

MR GRANT: For the record, that is dated 28th September 1920, the date of approval on the bottom.
That's correct?
Yes.

It says that you were the son of a former Chief of a Hagwilget tribe, that's correct?
Yes.

And it says that you were some time ago compelled to abandon your tribal lodge ground and fishing site on the south side of the South Bulkley Crossing?
THE INTERPRETER: Does that mean they were asked to leave that area? I would like to be sure.

I don't know what it means. I was going to ask you about that. Just ask him if he was forced to leave that area.
Roy McDonald, he used to look after the Fisheries throughout the whole area and talked to me about this, and we got into a disagreement and we had a little argument. Roy McDonald never came back again to bother me about this area.[3]

Did you have to give up anything to get this land?
MR GRANT: I object. I think that is too general. I don't understand. I think if you want to be a bit more specific, that's fine. I don't understand that question; I can't answer it and I don't know how the witness can.
MR MILNE: I think the question is pretty straightforward.

Were you compelled to abandon your tribal lodge ground and fishing site on the south side of the Bulkley?
The people didn't bother me initially. It was after the coming of the white man that I started being hassled and before there were no white people there were many salmon in the area that you are describing.[4] It was the Dutch people who came in and took all the land and all the horses and everything else.

In the same area since there were many salmon there a lot of the animals would come down to the river to feast on the salmon.[5] Like the grizzly bear, bears. There was this area where my father did a lot of his fishing and he would prepare many salmon. This is two or three years before 1901.

Where is this South Bulkley Crossing?
THE INTERPRETER: I guess CN crossing?

OFF THE RECORD DISCUSSION IN WET'SUWET'EN

It was the area where the McGuinnes had lived; a foot trail went to [Alxkat]
Graveyard Lake.

Did you give up fishing at the South Bulkley Crossing?
We didn't quit fishing but that wasn't the only place we fished. People fish the
area from the North to South Bulkley.

Did you fish in that area after you owned this land?
Yes, we continued to fish. We dried the salmon, we canned it, and then when
the Dutch people came, they blocked the rivers and very few salmon made it
up to the area you are describing.

This document that I have been reading from seems to suggest –

MR GRANT: Before you go further, you could put it in as an exhibit since
you have referred to it.
MR MILNE: I wasn't going to mark it as an exhibit. I will, perhaps,
except for identification; it is only a photocopy and I imagine it will be
proved at trial.
MR GRANT: I am only asking that it be put in as an exhibit because you
have been referring to it and so there is an understanding of what you
have been referring to. I agree it can be an exhibit for identification.
MR MILNE: Exhibit 'A' for identification.
MR GRANT: Go off the record for a moment.

OFF THE RECORD DISCUSSION

EXHIBIT 'A' – For identification only – Copy of Order-in-Council No.
1727 dated September 30, 1920.

MR MILNE: Back on the record.
    The document which has been marked as Exhibit 'A' for identifica-
tion is Order-in-Council No. 1727. This document suggests that you
got the land because you had given up your tribal lodge ground and
fishing ground on the south side of the South Bulkley Crossing; that is
why I asked you if you had given up anything for the land.
MR GRANT: I object. That document doesn't say that. It sets out a number of things and –
MR MILNE: I didn't say it says it, it suggests it. I am about to point out to
the witness, is it his understanding why he got the land?
MR GRANT: I object. I don't think –
MR MILNE: I can ask him whether or not he kept his tribal lodge ground
and fishing ground on the south side of the South Bulkley Crossing

Exhibit A.

1 D.
5 copies   1727

For Identification

Ex No. A Date ____
Witness JOHNNY DAVID
VERONICA HARPER
OFFICIAL COURT REPORTER
BCSRA #263

Copy of Minute
SEP 30 1920
Approved

CG18162-I   53718-I

report;-

THAT application has been made by the
Department of Indian Affairs, at Ottawa, under the
provisions of Clause A, Subsection 2 of Section 7
of the "Land Act", for the granting of a pre-emption
Record to one, "Johnny David", an Indian of the
Hagwilget tribe covering Block A of Lot 3327,
Range 5, Coast District.

THAT it is also represented that Johnny
David is a reliable, hard-working man, and has eight
head of horses and five head of cattle.

THAT he is the son of a former Chief of the
Hagwilget tribe, and that some time ago he was
compelled to abandon his tribal lodge ground and
fishing ground on the south side of the South
Bulkley Crossing.

THAT it is further alleged that this parcel
of land contains no inducement for a white settler,
but that it will suit this Indian better than any
portion of the land to be found on any of the reserve
of his band.

THAT the application is favourably reported
upon by the local Government Agent.

AND TO RECOMMEND that by virtue of the
authority contained in Clause A of Subsection 2 of
Section 7 of the "Land Act", a pre-emption record of
the parcel of land above described be issued to
"Johnny David".

DATED this   28th day of September, A.D. 1920.
                       "T.D.Pattullo."

                   Minister of Lands.

APPROVED this   28th day of September, A.D. 1920
                       "John Oliver."

             Presiding Member of the Executive Council.
     File 017781

and whether that had any, as far as he knows, influence upon whether he got a grant of Crown land. Let me phrase the question then.

This document suggests that you gave up some fishing grounds and something called tribal lodge ground in return for your land. What was your understanding of what happened?
MR GRANT: I object, the document does not suggest that.
MR MILNE: Your objection is noted.
MR GRANT: Don't answer that question.
MR MILNE: You can argue this at trial. You reserve the right to objection, at this point. There's no commissioner to rule on objections and if you want to reserve your objection to trial, that's fine, but I think the witness should answer the question.
MR GRANT: You have my objection.
No, it didn't happen that way. We still continue to hold the lands that we had.

OFF THE RECORD DISCUSSION IN WET'SUWET'EN

That is when they were making up their own words and that is what most people have been going by.[6]

The land that you owned was in Smogelgem's territory, is that correct?
MR GRANT: Which land are you referring to?
MR MILNE: Block A of 3327 Range 5, Coast District.
Yes.

You later sold that land to the Hall's?
Yes. It was after the hard times came and I sold it to Tom Hall.

And the Halls were white settlers?
Yes.

I have got another document here to show you. This one is a little bit harder to see because it's a photocopy of a microfiche. It is deed of land dated October 22nd, 1935 and it's a certified extract showing a transfer between Johnny David and James William Hall and Thomas Hall. Can you tell me, Mr David, if that is your signature on the bottom of the document?
I can't see too clear.[7]

You sold your land –

OFF THE RECORD DISCUSSION IN WET'SUWET'EN

I saw that paper as well.[8] *After I sold the land.*
You saw a paper like this at the time you sold the land?

THE INTERPRETER: That is what he said.

How much money did you get for the land?
I just about gave it away for nothing.

Was it for $300?
It might have been $50, I don't know, I have forgotten.

You can't remember how much money you got?
Yes, I've forgotten.

OFF THE RECORD DISCUSSION IN WET'SUWET'EN

When I gave that contract and signed, that is when they gave me the money,[9]

MR MILNE: Have this marked as Exhibit 20.

EXHIBIT NO. 20 – Three-page document, photocopy of microfiche, deed of land dated October 22nd, 1935, certified extract showing transfer between Johnny David and James William Hall and Thomas Hall.

MR MILNE: May we just go off the record for a minute?

OFF THE RECORD DISCUSSION

MR MILNE: Go back on the record.
    I have another document that is a survey or map and it says that it is in relation to Crown Grant No. 4346514. There's a shaded area on the map which purports to be Block A of Lot 3327. I am going to show that to you, Mr David, and ask if you – the defendant says that is your land, that is what you've got. Are you able to recognize that as being your land?
MR GRANT: I would ask that the interpreter could point out to him the obvious labelled things. There appears to be a river marked, the Bulkley River, and also GTPR, which would appear to be Grand Trunk Pacific Railway. I would ask that that be put to him to assist him.

OFF THE RECORD DISCUSSION IN WET'SUWET'EN

I can't see it too clearly but from the description you have given me it sounds like it is.

MR MILNE: Because you say you can't see it that clearly I think we'll have it marked as an exhibit, Exhibit 'B' for identification.

OFF THE RECORD DISCUSSION IN WET'SUWET'EN

THE INTERPRETER: He says there is a Johnny Creek that runs through

Exhibit 20.

025895

This Indenture

Made the **twenty second** day of **October** in the year of Our Lord one thousand nine hundred and **thirty five** In Pursuance of the "Real Property Conveyance Act"

Between   Johnny David, of the town of Moricetown, in the County of Prince Rupert, in the Province of British Columbia, Indian

hereinafter called the Grantor of the FIRST PART

And   James William Hall
&
Thomas Hall

of the Town of Topley, in the County of Prince Rupert, British Columbia, farmers.

hereinafter called the Grantee of the SECOND PART

Witnesseth, that in consideration of   **three hundred ($300.00) dollars** Dollars of lawful money of Canada now paid by the said Grantee to the said Grantor the receipt whereof is hereby by him acknowledged the said Grantor DO th GRANT unto the said Grantee his heirs and assigns FOREVER:

All and Singular, that certain parcel or tract of land and premises situate lying and being in Range 5, Coast District and more particularly known and described as, Block "A" of Lot thirty three hundred and twenty seven (3327), Range five (5), Coast District, said to contain ninety three decimal twenty (93.20) acres more or less.

TO HAVE AND TO HOLD unto the said Grantee   their heirs   an assigns to and for   all their sole and only use FOREVER; SUBJECT NEVERTHELESS to the reservations, limitations, provisoes and conditions expressed in the original grant thereof from the Crown.

THE said Grantor Covenant s with the said Grantee s that he has the right to convey the said lands to the said Grantee notwithstanding any act of the said Grantor.
AND that the said Grantees shall have quiet possession of the said lands free from all encumbrances. AND the said Grantor Covenant s with the Grantee s that he will execute such further assurances of the said lands as may be requisite.
AND the said Grantor Covenant s with the said Grantee s that he has done no acts to encumber the said lands.
AND the said Grantor RELEASE s to the said Grantee ALL his CLAIMS upon the said lands

In Witness Whereof, the said parties hereto have hereunto set their hands and seals.

Signed, Sealed and Delivered
in THE PRESENCE OF

Donald _____

Johnny David

025895

FOR WITNESS

I hereby certify that ...
personally known to me appeared before me, and acknowledged to me that ... is the person whose name is
subscribed in the annexed instrument as Witness that is ... is of the full age of eighteen years, and having
been duly sworn by me, did prove to me that ... is of the full age of
twenty-one years, did execute the same in ...

IN TESTIMONY WHEREOF, I have hereunto set my Hand and Seal of Office
at ... British Columbia.
this ... day of ... in the year
of our Lord one thousand nine hundred and ...

A Notary Public in and for the Province of British Columbia

Deed of Land

Murphy Bros., Ltd. Printers and Stationers
Prince Rupert, B.C.

DATED October 22nd, 1935

Johnny Myld
-TO-
James William Hall
Thomas Hall

STUATE IN

Range 5 Coast District

AND BEING

Block "A" of Lot 3327

No.25895 Registered the 4th
day of ... 193...
Book, Vol. ... on application
received the ... day of ...
193..., at the hour of ...

25895

Form No. 3. Affidavit for Maker (including Married Women).
L. R. Act 1921.

Murphy & Chapman, Ltd., Printers and Stationers
Vancouver, B.C.

For Maker (including Married Women)

I hereby certify that on the **twenty second** day of **October** 1935
at **Smithers**, in the Province of British Columbia,
Johnny David
(whose identity has been proved by the evidence on oath of
who is) personally known to me, appeared before me and acknowledged
to me that **he is** the person mentioned in the annexed instrument as the Maker thereof, and whose
name is subscribed thereto as part and that he knows the contents thereof, and that he executed
the same voluntarily, and is of the full age of twenty-one years.

IN TESTIMONY WHEREOF I have hereunto set my Hand and Seal of Office at
Smithers British Columbia, this **22nd** day
of **October** in the year of our Lord one thousand
nine hundred and **thirty five**

E. Guy

A Notary Public in and for the Province of British Columbia.
A Commissioner for taking Affidavits within British Columbia.

Note.—Where the person making the acknowledgment is personally known to the officer taking the same, strike out
the words in brackets

A Notary Public in and for the Province of British Columbia

I HEREBY CERTIFY that the paper writing hereto annexed is a
photographic print of a film of an original instrument which was
deposited in the office under #25895-I and subsequently microfilmed,
the said film being in my custody in the Land Title Office, in the
City of Prince Rupert, B.C.

DATED this 19thday of   February, 1986

3 pces

Ex No. 22 Date 21/APR/86
Witness JOHNNY DAVID
VERONICA HARPER
OFFICIAL COURT REPORTER
BCSRA #263

K. Jacques
Registrar

PER:

74AA

the middle of his land and he asked me if it was on that, and I told him
it wasn't.

EXHIBIT 'B' – FOR IDENTIFICATION ONLY – Copy of survey in relation to
Crown Grant No. 4346514, purporting to be Block A of Lot 3327.

Do you know how many acres you had on your land? The title which
has been marked as an exhibit says you have 93.2 acres more or less. Is
that about how large your land was?
It was 160 acres.[10]
You say it was 160 acres?
THE INTERPRETER: He said: *It was 160 acres.* And I told him on the document it was 92.2 acres.

Who told you there was 160 acres?
He said: *When I first got the land the people at the Land Office told me it was
160 acres.*[11]

OFF THE RECORD DISCUSSION IN WET'SUWET'EN

Mr Hart.[12]

Who was Mr Hart?
Mr Hart was the person who did up all the documents for the Land Office and

Exhibit B.

74B
1D

Traced by _____

Compared by _____

British Columbia.

Crown Grant No. 434

RANGE 5 COAST DISTRICT.

Johnny David

Scale, 20 Chains = One Inch.

For Identification —

Ex No. B Date 21 April 88
Witness JOHNNY DAVID
VERONICA HARPER
OFFICIAL COURT REPORTER
BCSRA #263

L.3568

Blk. A

Bulkley River

Blk. A

L.3566

G.T.P.Ry.

L.5722

L.2636

Blk. B

L.3327

Blk. B

he was the one who told me I had 160 acres. He was the person in charge of giving out the land.[13]

When you sold it to the Halls, did you sell them 160 acres?
Yes.

OFF THE RECORD DISCUSSION IN WET'SUWET'EN

I sold them the area that was fenced off, the river property, and I still have the documents where I paid school and land tax.[14]

Do you remember – actually, I can put it to you this way – you got a grant in March 1926 and there was a sale of your land to the Halls in October 1935. That's correct, is it?
I think I first got the property around 1921, 1922, and I have got some old documents which I'll look for tonight.

Maybe you could show them to your lawyer before you show them to me.
Yes.

You say you paid the school taxes and land taxes for each year that you owned it?
Yes.

You have told me at various times that this land was either near Perow or near Topley; Which community is it closer to?
The area we are talking about is three miles west of Topley and there is a creek that was named after me that flows through the territory that we are talking about. The creek is named Johnny Creek.

Why did you buy the land or apply for the pre-emption?
Since I was in the area for many years, they were giving out land through pre-emption and that is why I decided to apply for it.

Do you know if the Dutch settlers were also getting land through pre-emption?
All the white people were getting land through pre-emption and the white people didn't want us Indians to get any land but I still went and applied for it.

Did you apply for the land because you were afraid that they were going to get all the land?
The white people hated us and they didn't want us to get any land and that is one of the reasons why I applied for the land.

You said when Mr Grant was asking you questions you raised milk

cows and you sold some in Prince Rupert I think. Were you a farmer during the time that you owned that land?
Even before I got the land I raised cows, and after I got the land I raised even more cows.

Did you buy feed and, if so, where did you buy it?
I grew my own feed, oats and everything else.

Did you sell your cows or did you use them for your own benefit?
I sold some in Rupert and when the money came, that is what I used to buy food.

How did you get your cows to Rupert?
Railroad.

Was there an agent there or somebody who sold them for you or did you sell them here and they were shipped there?
I would send documents to Prince Rupert and when they come back they said they wanted me. That is when I send the cows to Rupert.

During the time that you owned this land, did you also go hunting and fishing in the Kilwoneetzen area or in any of your other territories?

OFF THE RECORD DISCUSSION IN WET'SUWET'EN

Yes, in the summer.

Who looked after your farm while you were away hunting?
My wife and my son.

Did you ever hire anybody to help run the farm?
Yes, I had many relatives as well as some white people who helped clear the land.

Did you pay them for their help?
Yes, they worked for money. It was during the hard time, and money was hard to come by.

You lived on your farm, I take it?
Yes.

Did you clear the land?
Yes.

Now, I am just a little bit confused as to the time when you went hunting rather than staying on your farm. The last time I think you said that you went hunting –

MR GRANT: Where are you referring?

MR MILNE: I can't find it in the transcript right now but maybe you can clarify that for me. When did you leave your land to go hunting and when did you then return to your land?

MR GRANT: Are you talking about in each year?

MR MILNE: Generally speaking, each year.

I want to know how much time you spent on your land and how much time you spent hunting and trapping in each year.

While I was hunting and trapping I would be out for four five days and while I was away my wife would run the farm.

What time of the year was it when you went hunting and trapping?
From 15 September to 1st May.

OFF THE RECORD DISCUSSION IN WET'SUWET'EN

Before 1st May all the wild animals are bearing children and that is when we stop.

Do you know if any other Wet'suwet'en during the summer in the 1920s bought land in territories which they had the right under Wet'suwet'en law to use?

MR GRANT: I object. Don't answer that. I think it is clear from the documents you have introduced he hasn't bought land. There was preemption.

MR MILNE: There is a distinction, I'm sorry. Maybe you could phrase the question to him. [Were there] Any other Wet'suwet'en who pre-empted land in the territory that they're entitled to use by Wet'suwet'en law?

MR GRANT: To his knowledge?

MR MILNE: To his knowledge.

Matthew Sam. Thomas George. Bill Alex.

Can you remember anybody else?
Those are the only ones I remember.

OFF THE RECORD DISCUSSION IN WET'SUWET'EN

Those three people got the land through pre-emption before I did.

Are they still alive today?
They're all dead. Mabel Sam is still living on the land her dad got through pre-emption.

OFF THE RECORD DISCUSSION IN WET'SUWET'EN

Do you know if they did the same thing that you did, farmed it and went hunting and came back to the farm again?

THE INTERPRETER: Before you asked the question, he said: *Mabel Sam may be here tomorrow and you can ask her, she would be the person to ask.*

MR MILNE: Again that is something your lawyer may want to discuss with her.

Do you know if these people, Matthew Sam, Thomas George, and Bill Alex, also had farms?

Yes, they also did farm. They had horses and cattle. Thomas George's children had gone off to war. Times were tough. The children all came back from the war.

Were any of those three people a Chief?

Yes, they were all Hereditary Chiefs. Thomas George and Matthew Sam, they were Head men.

What were their names, their Wet'suwet'en names?

Matthew Sam was Gyologet. Thomas George had two names and the person who holds one of the names is Alfred Joseph who holds –

Alfred Joseph is still alive?

THE INTERPRETER: Yes.

And he is a plaintiff?

THE INTERPRETER: Yes.

OFF THE RECORD DISCUSSION IN WET'SUWET'EN

Bill Alex didn't have a name.

He didn't have a name?

THE INTERPRETER: He didn't have a Hereditary name.

[MR MILNE:] Is that unusual, that he didn't have a Hereditary name?

He hadn't yet received the Chief's name when he died.

What House would these three men be from?

OFF THE RECORD DISCUSSION IN WET'SUWET'EN

Thomas George came from Yahoneetz [Kaiyawinits: House in the Middle of Many]. He was big Chief and his sons Leonard George and Andy are still alive today.

Is this House represented in this action as a plaintiff?

Yes. The person who holds his name will be asked questions.

As a witness or as a party?

MR GRANT: I think if you want to clarify this matter and save us a little time, I think if you ask him if this is the same House of Gisdaywa you will probably get to the answer you want. Gisdaywa is a named plaintiff and represents a House.

[MR MILNE:] Is this the same House that Gisdaywa is?
Yes.

And what about the other people?
Matthew Sam comes from the Grizzly House [Kyas ya].

MR MILNE: Maybe we can save more time. Mr Grant, can you point me in the right direction?

MR GRANT: What he indicated, Matthew Sam was Gyologet, and if you asked the question if Matthew Sam was in the same House as the present Gyologet you may get your answer.

MR MILNE: Would you [the interpreter] ask that question please?
Gordon Hall is the present name. Gyologet.

And Matthew Sam was in the same House as Gyologet?
THE INTERPRETER: Matthew Sam, he was Gyologet.

And that is a plaintiff?
THE INTERPRETER: No.

Gyologet, is that a House?

MR GRANT: Maybe you can go off the record for a moment here.

OFF THE RECORD DISCUSSION

In what House is Matthew Sam?
He was [There were] three Houses from [or in] the Clan that he is from. I think he is from the Grizzly House.

And the Indian name for Grizzly House is what?
Kyas-ya.

MR MILNE: Correct me if I am wrong, Mr Grant, but I don't see –

OFF THE RECORD DISCUSSION IN WET'SUWET'EN

THE INTERPRETER: *Balna or Bill Nye and George Naziel are from the Grizzly [Kyas ya] House [of the Gitdumden/Wolf Clan.].*

OFF THE RECORD

MR MILNE: Who represents the Grizzly House?
MR GRANT: George Naziel is a plaintiff, for the record.
MR MILNE: George Naziel is a plaintiff?
MR GRANT: For the record.

And his Indian name is?
Madeek.[15]

And the House?
Balna.
MR GRANT: It's referred to as the House of Madeek.
MR MILNE: In the Statement of Claim it's referred to as the House of Madeek? Oh, no. 40? But that's Gitksan.
MR GRANT: It's Wet'suwet'en.
[MR MILNE:] Madeek is Wet'suwet'en?
THE INTERPRETER: *Yes.*
MR GRANT: For the record, Madeek is referred to in paragraph 40 of the Statement of Claim and Madeek is, I believe it is George Naziel, referred to in the Writ of Summons. If you wish to clarify this, you may ask him and I am just doing this to shorten the time and keep you from being misled, if Woos, referred to in paragraph 41, is any relationship to the Grizzly House.

MR MILNE: What does Madeek mean in English?
MR GRANT: You can ask the interpreter that.
MR MILNE: What does it mean, Mr Interpreter?
MR GRANT: Maybe you want to ask the witness?
THE INTERPRETER: I'll ask the witness.
I can't remember what the Wet'suwet'en or English name for Madeek is. I think it's a Gitksan name.

Is the House of Madeek and the House of Kyas-ya, are they separate Houses?
The main House is Kyas-ya.

Are there still members of that House?
MR GRANT: You mean alive?
Yes. George Naziel has the present name Madeek and before that it was his uncle.

Is he from the House of Kyas-ya?
Yes.[16]

So he has, I take it then, two names, or is the Hereditary Chief of two Houses, Madeek and Kyas-ya?
His House is Kyas-ya, and he had the House in Hagwilget, which was called Kyas-ya.

Are members of the House of Kyas-ya also members of the House of Madeek?
Yes, that is the name of the House and everyone comes from the House. It is the name of the House.

But is every member of the House of Kyas-ya also a member of the House of Madeek?

MR GRANT: I think, I believe he has answered that question. He just answered that question.

MR MILNE: I didn't understand the answer. Maybe you [the interpreter] could ask him to give it another go?
    What I am concerned about obviously, Mr Grant, if it appears there's a House, Kyas-ya, that is not a plaintiff and I want to explore that, and it may be that House is somehow tied into the House of Madeek, but that's not what the Statement of Claim says.

MR GRANT: Just for the record –

MR MILNE: What I am asking [is] whether or not the members of the House of Madeek are all members of the House of Kyas-ya or vice-versa.

MR GRANT: And you have asked that question a number of times and he's answered it.

MR MILNE: Is his answer yes or no, I'm not sure of that. Would you [the interpreter] put the question to him again so I can find out whether or not that is true?

Yes, there are other people in that House [or Clan], such as Gisdaywa. In the feast hall Gisdaywa sits next to Madeek. There is another person that sits next to Madeek and they are all from one Clan. One House. When we are at the feast hall there are three main Hereditary Chiefs from each House [or Clan].

Does the House of Kyas-ya have a territory?
Yes.

Is it the same territory as the House of Madeek?
Yes, they all own territories. The territories they have are used for hunting and trapping.[17]

Is that the same territory as held by the House of Madeek?
Yes. They are all one company. All the people from the House help each other in their hunting and trapping, and the meat that they get is what they use at the feast hall.

I hate to ask this question again, but is everyone or are the people who are members of the House of Kyas-ya also members of the House of Madeek?
MR GRANT: I think he has answered that question. His answer was in the affirmative. He said yes about four or five questions back, the third time you asked him. Just after my last objection. You have got the answer. I don't think you have to ask again.

[MR MILNE:] Are there members of the House of Kyas-ya who are not members of the House of Madeek?
Yes, that's how it is and people nowadays are getting all confused.
I can understand why.
MR GRANT: Maybe he's referring to the questions.
MR MILNE: That would be equally true. Let me summarize then.
There are some people of the House of Kyas-ya who do not belong to the House of Madeek, correct?
THE INTERPRETER: That is what he said.

Who speaks for these people?
THE INTERPRETER: Which people?
The people who are members of the House of Kyas-ya and not members of the House of Madeek?
The people that don't belong to Madeek House but are from Kyas-ya speak for themselves. There are usually three main Chiefs that speak for the House [or Clan].

The people who speak for themselves, do they also have territory?
Yes.

Is that territory the same as the territory for these people who are members of the House of Madeek?
THE INTERPRETER: You want to run that by me again?

Let me rephrase if I can. There are some people in the House of Kyas-ya who the witness says speak for themselves, and he also says that they have territory. Is that territory that they have the same as the territory the other members of the House of Kyas-ya who are represented, it seems, or who are included in the House of Madeek?

MR GRANT: What you're trying to ask is, are those persons who are not in the House of Madeek but are in Kyas-ya, is their territory the same as Madeek's territory?

MR MILNE: Yes, or, and is it the same as the territory as the other members of the House of Kyas-ya?

MR GRANT: That's about, at least three questions.

MR MILNE: Well –

MR GRANT: So I think you should –

MR MILNE: The trouble is, we have to label these people as being members of one House or the other, so we have got members of the House of Kyas-ya, who are members of the House of Madeek, and we have people who apparently are not members of both Houses but only of Kyas-ya. Follow me so far?

For those who are members of the House of Kyas-ya but not Madeek and who speak for themselves, okay, is their territory the same – is [it] the same territory as those that speak for the House of Madeek?

MR GRANT: Well, can you refer to that as Madeek's territory?

MR MILNE: I don't know whether or not there is other territory. There may be other members of the House of Kyas-ya who don't speak for themselves, don't belong to the House of Madeek and belong to some other House.

THE INTERPRETER: Now I'm thoroughly confused.

MR GRANT: Maybe we can go off the record for a moment.

MR MILNE: That's fine.

OFF THE RECORD DISCUSSION

MR MILNE: Let's roll.

Now, we've been discussing the House of Kyas-ya and it appears that members – some members – of the House of Kyas-ya are also members of the House of Madeek and are represented by – oh, I forget the fellow's name – who is the Hereditary Chief?

THE INTERPRETER: Madeek.

And the name for that person?

THE INTERPRETER: George Naziel.

Now, George Naziel does not represent the same people as the House of Kyas-ya, is that right?

MR GRANT: I think it would be better if you said he doesn't speak for them.

[MR MILNE:] Okay.

At the hall there are usually three main Chiefs who speak for all the House [or Clan] members. For the Kyas-ya [or Gitdumden/Wolf Clan] there is George Naziel who holds Madeek, Alfred Joseph who holds Gisdaywa, and Roy Morris who holds Woos.

The second name was?

THE INTERPRETER: Alfred Joseph who holds Gisdaywa.

George holds what name?

THE INTERPRETER: Madeek.

And Roy Morris again?

THE INTERPRETER: Woos.

MR GRANT: All three of those parties are plaintiffs.

MR MILNE: Thank you.

These three main Chiefs are similar in all the other Clans.

THE INTERPRETER: You have three main Chiefs in the other four Clans, that's what he's saying.

MR MILNE: Then is it true that each of these Wet'suwet'en plaintiffs set out in the Statement of Claim –

MR GRANT: Are you referring to these three?

MR MILNE: No, each of them. [Do] any of the Wet'suwet'en plaintiffs speak for other Houses that aren't mentioned in the Statement of Claim?

MR GRANT: I would like to go off the record for a moment. I am reserving the right to object but go off the record.

OFF THE RECORD DISCUSSION

MR MILNE: Let's go back on the record. Mr Grant and I have had a discussion to the effect that the Chiefs who are plaintiffs represent Houses that two may, in any event aren't disclosed in the Statement of Claim and rather than going through each and every one of the plaintiff Chiefs I'll ask the witness to produce a list of the names of the Houses for which the plaintiff Chief has the right to speak.

MR GRANT: For the record, I don't wish to imply that the Chiefs are speaking for Houses which are other than the ones which are referred to in the Statement of Claim. What I endeavoured to explain to counsel for the defendant was that the Chiefs – the names of the Houses – that each House for which the Wet'suwet'en Chief speaks has its own name, and the name of those particular Houses is not set out in the Statement of Claim, but that those Houses are the House of that particular Chief as alluded to in the Statement of Claim. I have noted your request and to the extent that this witness can provide that answer I will arrange – we will provide that list. As I indicated while we were off the record, if you produced a Demand for Particulars or interrogatories – an additional question on interrogatories to each of the plaintiffs – I would endeavour to produce the answer on all of them. I may be able to produce an answer for all of them from this witness, but I don't know that until I –

MR MILNE: Obviously something further will be followed up if he is unable to produce a complete list. To that extent, of course, I have no objection to you discussing the matter with him while he is under cross-examination and certainly won't object to that at trial.

I think we left off, before we hit this tangent, dealing with other Wet'suwet'en who've got land through pre-emption and you mentioned three of them. Do you recall any others?
MR GRANT: He has answered that. He said no.

Do you recall any Wet'suwet'en during that same time who purchased land rather than getting it through pre-emption?
MR GRANT: What time are we referring to?
[MR MILNE:] The 1920s.
No.

OFF THE RECORD DISCUSSION IN WET'SUWET'EN

Did any of the Indian agents that you dealt with during that time or any of the white people prevent you from farming?
MR GRANT: Where?
[MR MILNE:] Anywhere.
No.

You said that the white people hated you, particularly you mentioned the Dutch, I think. Were there fights between you and the white people over the land, and I mean you personally or people that you knew?
There was one incident in particular, the incident at Barrett Lake where the family of Lame Arthur Michell and George Naziel's father, Nazel, were kicked off the land because they fought with Charlie Barrett. When they had buried Lame Arthur Michell's father and had buried him in the winter, then he was dug up and moved to Hagwilget and buried properly there. After he was buried Lame Arthur Michell and Nazel were put in jail, that was over the claim at Barrett Lake and I took you there last summer. Pictures were taken of the area that I am talking about.

When you say you took someone there I take it you took someone from Mr Grant' s side?

THE INTERPRETER: Yes.

MR GRANT: Was he referring to the interpreter?

THE INTERPRETER: To myself and other people.

Do you remember any other problems that you had or that other people you knew had with white people?

There was another incident at Two Mile, which is part of this village. Sylvester Williams' grandfather, whose name was Looseeya, he was speaking up against white people about the land, and he was also put in jail and fined.

When would that have been?

I can't remember.

Around 1915?

I can't remember, it could have been at that time.

MR GRANT: I'm sorry, what was the name of that second person?

MR MILNE: Sylvester Williams' grandfather.

THE INTERPRETER: *Looseeya.*

OFF THE RECORD DISCUSSION IN WET'SUWET'EN

The area behind Two Mile, a lot of our Indian people lived there and when the white people came they were moved off the land and the white people moved on. Pete Van Happy was the person who took all the land and sold it to other white people.

What was he?

He was the person who took the land and was paid by the government.

Was he an Indian agent, do you know?

No, white man.

Did he work for the government?

He worked for the government. He told them to get the land and they would buy it off him.

Do you know if this was the provincial government or federal government?

I don't know which government he worked for.

Do you know when this was? Was it during your lifetime?

Between 1904 and 1905.

Do you remember any other incidents like fights or something between white people and the Wet'suwet'en during the same period?

OFF THE RECORD DISCUSSION IN WET'SUWET'EN

There was another person, Peter Michell, and there was Old Happy, who is the same person who chased him off the land around the Glentana area.

Do you know what happened there? Can you tell me more about that incident?
Before the white people came Peter Michell had been haying there many years and Old Happy had threatened Peter Michell if he does not get off the land he would report him to the law, and our people were afraid of the authority of the white people, and they had no respect for us, and when he was threatened Peter Michell left the land.

Other than the story that you have told us about Joseph Baptiste –
THE INTERPRETER: Jean Baptiste.
– Jean Baptiste, do you know of anyone who stayed on their land after they were threatened and told to get off?
    Give the answer while the new tape is being put on. Any objection?
MR GRANT: No, no. I would like the answer recorded.

OFF THE RECORD

It was only Jean Baptiste who refused to leave the land when he was asked to leave.[18] *He cleared the land, built a house on it and he said no when he was asked to leave. I can't remember anyone else.*

What did the Wet'suwet'en do in circumstances when they were asked to leave? Was there any attempt by them to go before the men who spoke for the white man and ask them not to remove people from the land?
At that time most white people didn't like Indians and when they spoke up against the land they were threatened to be taken to jail and they would leave, and the white people would take over the land, and it is still the same way today. The white people still don't like the Indians.

Other than Sylvester Williams' grandfather, whom you mentioned, do you recall anybody else, any other Wet'suwet'en who spoke out against the white people taking their lands?
I can't remember anyone else.

Was the taking of lands that Wet'suwet'en were living on discussed at feasts that you had?

THE INTERPRETER: You mean the lands that they were –
The lands that were being taken by anyone, this Van Happy fellow or
whites generally, was that a problem that was discussed at the feasts,
to your knowledge?
*This problem was discussed at feasts, and the white people didn't have respect
for the Indian people. They would threaten them, if they spoke up against people about the land, and our people were afraid of the white man's laws.*

Do you remember any resolutions or actions that people at the feasts,
when they were discussing this, decided they should do?
MR GRANT: The problem was that it was discussed at feasts?
[MR MILNE:] And what was done as a result of the discussions at feasts?
*When it was discussed at the feast, these problems were brought up with the
Indian agent but he just continued to let white people take the land and he
never did anything for our people.*

How many – how long was the same Indian agent in this area? Was
there somebody here that was here for a long time? How many Indian
agents have you dealt with?
MR GRANT: When?
[MR MILNE:] In the early years up to 1930? Or that the Wet'suwet'en to
your knowledge dealt with? Not necessarily personally, Mr David, but
what I am getting at is, how many different Indian agents are being
dealt with here by the Wet'suwet'en?
MR GRANT: I would object. I think that is a matter that is, probably, a
matter of historical record which is at least in the knowledge of the
defendant.
MR MILNE: True enough, but maybe I should phrase it this way. How
many Indian agents do you remember the Wet'suwet'en had dealt
with for the period say 1900 to 1930? You have already mentioned
some of them.
MR GRANT: Yes, answer that question but my objection still stands.
[MR MILNE:] You said the problem was brought up with the Indian
Agent. Who was the Indian agent that that problem was brought up
with, if you know?
*Mr Loring. He was the one that took the Indian people off their lands and put
them on the reserves.*

So that – was it discussed with any other Indian Agents as well?
*The Indian Agent would take the advice of the white people and that is how he
went about moving Indian people around.*

But did you discuss with the Indian Agents other than Mr Loring?
He was the only Indian agent.

OFF THE RECORD DISCUSSION IN WET'SUWET'EN

After Mr Loring there was Mr Hanz (?) who took his place.

There was some white people on your territory. You said that Mr Hall and others were actually on Smogelgem's territory, and that there was a Mr McGuinness, I think, as well in that territory. These are white men. There was an Izman in the Kilwoneetzen territory and a Gardner. Did you have trouble with these people?
MR GRANT: Izman, Gardner, McGuinnnes and?
MR MILNE: Hall.
THE INTERPRETER: Hall.
MR GRANT: Personally or the Wet'suwet'en?
MR MILNE: Personally.
No. McGuinness stay[ed] on the land, didn't trap. He didn't give me any trouble.

You said a long time ago that David Dennis used to let white people use the territory, the Kilwoneetzen territory. I think you said that he leased it to white people. Tell me about that. What was their arrangement if you know?
David Dennis leased some lands to some white people for so much a year. I don't know what the arrangements were. I was just told about it.

Was this land that David Dennis had obtained through pre-emption?
It was just a small piece of land that he had grew up on and that was the area that he leased to the white people.

Is this area close to the Copper River Range?
Yes. He was brought up on that land similar to the way I was brought up on the land that I am talking about, and this land was given to him by us after to work.

Do you know then if he ever got that land by pre-emption?
No.

Do you know if other Wet'suwet'en had agreements with white people for the use of their land?
Before, when there were very few laws, the Indian people were not afraid of the white people. They would take a stick after them and chase them off the land. But once the white laws became stronger the Indian people became afraid of the white man.

You said that before that white people had taken sticks and chased people off the land –

MR GRANT: I think he said that the Indian people. I'm sorry, I thought he said, before the laws weren't that strong that the Indian people threw the white people off. Possibly the answer should be re-read.

MR MILNE: Maybe. Would you re-read the answer to the last question please?

THE REPORTER: Answer: 'Before, when there were very few laws, the Indian people were not afraid of the white people. They would take a stick after them and chase them off the land. But once the white laws became stronger the Indian people became afraid of the white man.'

Do you know of any names of people who used their sticks to chase white people off the land?

I can't, I don't remember. I was quite young then.

Do you know if this has been when people were on your traplines?

Yes.

When you were on your traplines did you meet white people there?

MR GRANT: When?

I had got two young men, two white men on my territory, and I took them to the Indian agent's office and then they backed off.

Who backed off?

The two white people.

Did you ever have any other trouble with white people on your trap line?

MR GRANT: In what time period?

Oh, well, basically I am going from the general to the specific, so at any time. You mentioned two people. Did you have trouble with others?

No.

Do you remember when it was that you had trouble with these two white men?

I don't know exactly what year that was. These young white boys had, they knew me, they lived in the area and because of that they did not go into my territory again.

The territory that we are talking about is North Bulkley?

THE INTERPRETER: Yes.

No, Perow.

What about the other Indians in your territory, did you have trouble with them?

MR GRANT: Who are you referring to, the Wet'suwet'en or any Indian groups?

MR MILNE: Any Indian groups.

OFF THE RECORD DISCUSSION IN WET'SUWET'EN

No. There are some who said that trapline is theirs, but it is not true. It was my father's trapline.

Who are these people that say the trapline is theirs?
When my father was alive not too many of his relatives or House members looked after him, and before he died he told me no matter what happens that you stay on the land and work it, and that is exactly what I am doing today.

Are there other people that say that that trapline is theirs?
They're all dead now, no longer around.

Do their families still say that that trap line is theirs?
No, they don't.

OFF THE RECORD DISCUSSION IN WET'SUWET'EN

Leonard George wants to get this trapline and I am saying no. I want you to hear this. Right now, Peter David has got some papers with the game warden and he is looking after the trapline for me. If Leonard was talking about the trapline, tell him no, tell him to wait till all the business is done then we'll discuss it.

Why does Leonard George want that trapline, do you know?
Because he holds my dad's name and that is why he wants the trapline.

This is in the territory of Smogelgem?
Yes.

You are the caretaker of the territories of Smogelgem?
Yes, I'm looking after Smogelgem's territory as he asked me to do. I grew up on the territories as a young man. Now Peter David is looking after the trapline.

It's getting close to lunch time and I am wondering if Mr David would like to continue on and then quit early in the afternoon, or would he rather take a break and come back later in the afternoon?

OFF THE RECORD DISCUSSION IN WET'SUWET'EN

MR MILNE: Go off the record.

OFF THE RECORD DISCUSSION
ADJOURNED FOR LUNCH AT 12.20 P.M.

UPON RESUMING AT 2.10 P.M.

MR MILNE: Let's go on the record.

Mr David, we are going to try and do some more this afternoon, so if you get tired or have trouble remembering about some of the things you want to talk about, let me know and we'll stop. You stated earlier in the cross-examination you had been a surveyor but you couldn't remember whether you were working for a government or if you were for which level of government, federal or provincial. When you were paid was your cheque from a government, do you remember?

OFF THE RECORD DISCUSSION IN WET'SUWET'EN

I worked for the railroad for 50 cents a day, and the roadmaster delivered the cheques to us.

When you worked for the railroad were you surveying for the railroad?
Yes, I did work with the survey crew.

But this was the railway survey crew and not the government survey crew?
It was with the railroad.

Have you ever worked for the government?
MR GRANT: Which government?
MR MILNE: Any government.
MR GRANT: I object to the question.
Have you worked for the government of the province of British Columbia?

OFF THE RECORD DISCUSSION IN WET'SUWET'EN

I don't know which government it was but I did work for them when I surveyed. Jack Milligan is the person who looked after the survey. He was the person who worked for the government.

What I am wondering, if you actually worked for Jack Milligan or you worked for the government. Were you a public servant at any time? If he knows what that is, fine, if he doesn't I'll explain it.

MR GRANT: Which of those questions – you have asked him three. You asked him if he worked for Jack Milligan, or if he worked for the government, or if he was a public servant.
MR MILNE: Yes.
MR GRANT: I think you should ask him one at a time.
MR MILNE: It seems to me he has the ability to answer the question.
MR GRANT: He may have the ability to answer all three, I don't know. I just think you should ask him one at a time.

Did you work for the government?
Yes, I did, with the government survey.

Did your pay cheque come from the government?
We start in the spring and work till late fall.

Have you ever voted in any federal or provincial election?
Yes I do.

In both of those, federal and provincial or just one?
Yes, both. The only time I go there is when my name is written down and I'm asked to go.

Have you voted as a regular thing?
Yes, whenever my name is on the voters' list I vote.

Have you ever served in the military of Canada?

MR GRANT: I object. There is this whole area of questions that I object to, this particular area, on the basis of relevance.
MR MILNE: You raised the objection once before when I asked the same sort of questions about the work record of Mr David. It is relevant to Section 55 of the Statement of Claim. I understand your objection as being the same as the one you made at that time. My reply is basically the Statement of Claim alleges certain things were done by the Wet'suwet'en, and this man is Wet'suwet'en, and we are just asking about the sorts of things he might have done as well. I certainly note your objection on the reservation for trial.

Have you ever served in the Canadian military or in the militia of the province of British Columbia?
I haven't but during the last war I was just ready to go and the war ended. In 1914.

I want to talk with you again about your territories and, in particular,

I'm interested in how you describe where your territory may be. Are you able to draw a map of your territory?

MR GRANT: Which one are you referring to?

[MR MILNE:] The Kilwoneetz territory or any of them, for that matter. Can you draw a map of any of your territories?

MR GRANT: Just a moment. I am going to object to how the question is framed up. It may take a bit longer but if you want to ask him about each of them, that's fine, but when you say any of your territories I think that question is so vague and general that he may interpret that you're talking about what you talked about this morning, when you were talking about some land he bought or something. I would like you to be specific as to which territory you're asking about.

MR MILNE: Sure, it will take longer but – Can you draw a map of the Kilwoneetz territory? Do you have the ability to do that?

No, I can't, but I know where the territory is.

Can you tell me what landmarks constitute the border of the Kilwoneetz territory?

There are names for everything in the territory – creeks and so forth have names and that is what we use.

What kind of shape is the Kilwoneetz territory? Is it long and narrow or round?

OFF THE RECORD DISCUSSION IN WET'SUWET'EN

The Kilwoneetz area is between two mountain peaks, it's in a valley. McDonnel Lake, let's say this area, McDonnel Lake is in this area and there is a creek that runs through, and that is used as the boundary, and the area this side of the creek is Kilwoneetz area.

What is the name of that creek?

The creek doesn't have a name. Big John from Andymole owns the territory above the Kilwoneetz area.

What are the names of the two mountain peaks?

The Hudson Bay Mountain and Dennis Mountain. It is between two mountains where the Kilwoneetz area is.

And the area above you belongs to Big John?

Yes. Sandstone Mountain and the creek, that creek there comes from McDonnel Lake. They meet. The area past there belongs to Thomas Danes, who is Gitksan.

Is Big John Gitksan?
Yes, he was Gitksan. He was from the village [Tsaytseetsuk] that used to be near [Carnaby] – he was Chief over there.

Do the territories of Big John and the other fellow you mentioned, do they touch each other?
Yes, they're side by side.

And both those territories touch the Kilwoneetz territory?
Yes, south. West of the two territories.

If I could –
Now, Lead Canyon to Seven Sisters, that belongs to Malahan, also Gitksan, and that's as far as I know the territory.

What about the other end of your territory. Where is the boundary for it?
There's an area known as Four-Mile Hill. There's the creek that runs near there and that is the boundary.

Does that creek have a name?
No name for the creek. Past the boundary the area belongs to Big Seymour. Their names are used to name the lakes that are in the area, such as Seymour Lake, Dennis Lake.

Big Seymour was Wet'suwet'en?
Yes.

What House is he from?

OFF THE RECORD DISCUSSION IN WET'SUWET'EN

Big Seymour was Gitdumden, and he was from Hagwilget, and his Chief's name was Gyologet.

Other than Big Seymour's territory, was there any other territory touching yours on what I'll call the lower end of it?
The Telkwa River lake area and the Howson Lake area all belong to Kilwoneetz, and the last mountain belonged to the grandfather of Mabel Sam.

What is the name of that mountain?
Laganzo and there was lots of other names for the mountains. Near the mountain I just told you about.

Is there a white man's name for that mountain?
I don't know what the English name for it is. And the English names are derived from the first white people who settled in the area. Neldzildat, that was the orig-

inal name for Howson Lake. Neldzildat is the Wet'suwet'en name for Howson Lake. Howson Lake was named for Mr Howson who had a big house.

Howson Lake is in the Kilwoneetz area?
Yes.

OFF THE RECORD

I want to be sure I know where the Kilwoneetz territory is, so I just want to summarize that it's between – it's the valley between two mountain peaks of Hudson Bay Mountain and Dennis Mountain, and one end of it is marked by the creek that has no name but comes out of the Sandstone Mountain area –
MR GRANT: I just think that –
MR MILNE: – and that the other end of it is a creek that comes from the Four Mile Hill area. Have I correctly described your territory?
MR GRANT: I object because we have just spent almost half an hour in which the witness has described in detail the boundaries of the territory and I think they speak for themselves, and for you to summarize in one sentence and ask him if you have correctly described it, I think it is an unfair question.
MR MILNE: Come on, Mr Grant. Surely I can ask him. He's described numerous canyons, creeks, and hills; surely he can generally say whether that area accurately represents his territories.
MR GRANT: I think his evidence speaks for itself –
MR MILNE: I am asking him to –
MR GRANT: You have taken part of his evidence out and the only correct answer he can give you is to restate all his evidence, and I object because I think the question is unfair.
MR MILNE: If you can produce a map for me that I can put to this witness and ask him whether or not that's his territory, I would appreciate it. Otherwise what we are dealing with are descriptions of his territory and I want to be clear in my own mind and I want it to be clear for the record as to what the territory's bounded by.
MR GRANT: He has given that evidence in detail on direct, and he has given it again to you on cross. It's not fair to have him summarize in one sentence what he has spent 25 minutes giving to you. I object.
MR MILNE: Your objection's noted and I would like –
MR GRANT: I instruct the witness not to answer.

MR MILNE: I would like to have you summarize the area by the boundaries. Does that accurately set out the boundaries of the area?

MR GRANT: I instruct the witness not to answer the question.

Mr David, have you seen a map of this area? A map of your territory?
There is a map of the area. David Dennis has it, and it is a map of 1902 but they are unable to locate it. On this map it has all the names of the lakes and the creeks and the mountains.

Who made the map?
I don't know who made the map but on the map it had 1902 written on it.

Did you see that map?
Yes I did.

Was it a general topographical or government map or was it a particular map made by the Wet'suwet'en?
MR GRANT: He said he doesn't know who made the map.
MR MILNE: I'm asking whether or not the map he saw was a government map.
MR GRANT: He's answered you. He said he doesn't know who made the map.

Describe the map to me please.
The map is coloured red and on the map it had all the roads. If it was here in front of me I would show you the old territory. I don't know what they've done with the map.

When you were a surveyor for the government you saw maps, lots of maps, right?
Yes, I did see many maps. This map I'm talking about had all the lakes, Francis Lake, Owen Lake, Big Ootsa Lake. I don't know what they have done with the map.

When you were a surveyor, you saw government maps, is that right?
MR GRANT: He answered that, he said yes I did see many maps.
MR MILNE: He said he saw many maps, but I want to particularize it, a government map.
MR GRANT: I'm sorry.
Yes I did.

Did this map look like one of those?
Yes, it was probably government map. On the map it had the roads and all the foot trails and everything else on it.

When you looked at that map, was there any drawing on it outlining your territory or was it simply a map of the area?

It was a map of the whole territory, even had the foot trails that went through the Hudson Bay Mountain. If it was here I could give you more information.

When was the last time you saw the map?
It wasn't too long ago. I used the map when I spoke at a feast at the hall and I gave it back to David, and then I don't know what they did with it.

Was that speech you gave at the feast within the last year?
(In English) *Three years ago. Three or four years ago.*
THE INTERPRETER: *About three or four years ago.*

Was this a very old map?
Yes it was an old map, 1902.

Is David Dennis a plaintiff?
MR GRANT: Do you want me to answer that?
MR MILNE: Yes, please.
MR GRANT: No, he's not a named plaintiff.

You described one of the landmarks on your territory as being Dennis Mountain. Who had the territory on the other side of Dennis Mountain?
THE INTERPRETER: You're talking on this side of Dennis Mountain – Hudson Bay Mountain here and Dennis Mountain here?
Yes.
It was all Kilwoneetz territory. Mabel Sam.

Mabel Sam had the Telkwa River territory? That is Kela's territory?
Yes.

Who had the next territory?

OFF THE RECORD DISCUSSION IN WET'SUWET'EN.

Thomas Holland. Julian Holland.
MR GRANT: Can you describe the answer as he has given it?
THE INTERPRETER: I forgot the first name he gave me.

OFF THE RECORD

There's Dennis Mountain and this area belongs to Kela, and the area next to Kela belonged to Old Dennis first and then Thomas Holland and then Julian Holland.[19]

Is there a landmark that you can tell me about between Kela's territory and Holland's territory? Is there a mountain or something between them?

Howson Lake was one of the boundaries and three miles from Howson Lake, that area belongs to Mooseskin Johnny.

Which direction?
THE INTERPRETER: This direction – (Indicating)
So going across?
THE INTERPRETER: *Going from Dennis Mountain, Kela, the three people [I] mentioned, Howson Lake and three miles from there begins Mooseskin Johnny's territory.*

Then is there a landmark between Kela's territory and Holland's territory?
MR GRANT: He said that was Howson Lake.

So Kela, Howson Lake, Holland, Mooseskin Johnny?
THE INTERPRETER: Yes.

Holland's Wet'suwet'en?
Yes. They were Wet'suwet'en and the territory was passed on because people died and new people taking on names.

House? Their House?
Kilwoneetz.

Mooseskin Johnny Wet'suwet'en?
Yes.

Kilwoneetz House?
He came from the same House as my grandfathers, which is Tsayu [Beaver Clan].

Kela's territory, what is the boundary up here – (Indicating)?
Where the Telkwa River starts is the boundary of Kela's.

The headwaters of the Telkwa?
THE INTERPRETER: The headwaters of the Telkwa River.

Is Kela's territory in the Telkwa Valley then?
Yes, the mountain peak runs this way and the area this side of the mountain peak belongs to Mooseskin Johnny and the area this side belongs to Kela.

MR GRANT: How is Johnny doing?
THE INTERPRETER: His mind starts to get mixed up sometimes.

MR GRANT: Is that how he is feeling now?
THE INTERPRETER: He's saying that when he is thinking a lot his mind begins to wander because he is weak, and he said that he is tired now.

MR MILNE: All right. Could you tell him that we'll continue tomorrow?
THE INTERPRETER: He said: *That's fine.*

MR MILNE: Time?
THE INTERPRETER: Same time as this morning.
MR GRANT: Nine-thirty.

MR MILNE: Mr Grant, you will try to get that list of the Houses for me?
MR GRANT: I won't be able to do it by tomorrow. Go off the record.

OFF THE RECORD DISCUSSION
PROCEEDINGS ADJOURNED AT 2.55 P.M.[20]

VICTOR WILLIAM JIM, Wet'suwet'en interpreter, previously sworn.
JOHN DAVID, a witness called on behalf of the plaintiffs, previously sworn, testifies as follows:

UPON COMMENCING AT 9.30 A.M., 22 APRIL, 1986

MR MILNE: This is the continuation of the cross-examination of Johnny David. The witness and the interpreter are still sworn, and the same parties are present that have been present on previous occasions. Just before getting into the cross-examination, I have a comment about some of the proceedings that were taken yesterday. Mr Grant, yesterday you instructed the witness not to answer a question on territory and, as these proceedings are akin to proceedings at trial, at trial you certainly have no right to instruct a witness not to answer, I am going to ask you to reconsider your position on that. I take the position the proper procedure is to object and then reserve the right before the introduction of this evidence at trial to make submissions to the trial judge on its admissibility. I intend to have the question read back to the witness at the end of the day and if you maintain your instruction to the witness rather than maintaining the right to object, as I have described, then I will have to adjourn my cross-examination to seek instructions. The instructions I would seek from my principals would be to see if there is some way in which the witness's evidence on the matter of territory would be struck out in its entirety at trial. Or, alternatively, seek instructions to possibly bring a motion before a justice in chambers before a ruling on the procedure. There's two reasons I'm waiting until the end of the day to do this. Obviously I want to give you an opportunity to consider your position and, secondly, I don't want to inconvenience the reporter or the video man, who have travelled from Vancouver.

MR GRANT: I want to be clear right now on the record. The only reason I instructed the witness not to answer the question is because he's a 96-year-old man, he's speaking through an interpreter and, as I stated to you yesterday when you asked that question, the question was a question that was difficult if not impossible to answer as it was framed. I have no objection – if it is the question I recall – I have no objection to you asking questions about that area. It was the wording of the question, that is, how you framed up the question, which confused me and I was certain would confuse the witness. That's the only problem I had. If you wish to deal with that area I am not going to be objecting. I didn't object to the area. I do not want the witness – I do not want this elderly witness to be put in a situation where he is asked questions which are not comprehensible to me, as counsel who understands English, and to be put in a situation whatever he answers probably won't be too helpful to either side. That would be the sole basis for that. I thought I had made it clear to you if you framed up the question in any of many different alternatives, I didn't object to the question. Before considering it I want to know exactly the question you want to frame up. If you frame up that question in a different way I am not going to be objecting.

MR MILNE: I think the question was recorded previously and I will have it read back, as I say, at the end of the day and then you can consider your position on it, primarily in response to instructing the witness not to answer the questions.

MR GRANT: You have my position on the record.

CROSS-EXAMINATION BY MR MILNE (CONTINUED)

Now, Mr David, I want to ask you some questions about the territory of Smogelgem. Are you authorized to speak concerning that territory at the feasts?
Yes.

In your direct examination you mentioned a few of the landmarks of that territory but, as I reviewed the transcript, I think you mentioned only two of them, that being China Nose Mountain and Wilson Lake. Are there other landmarks on the borders of that territory that you can tell me about?
THE INTERPRETER: That is what he said: *Wilson Creek.*

MR MILNE: Wilson Creek, not Wilson Lake?
THE INTERPRETER: You said Wilson Creek, didn't you?

MR MILNE: I said Wilson Lake.

THE INTERPRETER: Oh.

OFF THE RECORD DISCUSSION IN WET'SUWET'EN

Tahdzingakwah, that is just Nakot.

What is that?
Tahdzingakwah is a creek.

Is there an English name for that?
It's a creek that flows from Summit Lake.
THE INTERPRETER: And he thinks its called Summit Creek.

Is that the boundary of Smogelgem's territory?
Yes.

Are there other creeks or lakes that are also on the boundary?

OFF THE RECORD DISCUSSION IN WET'SUWET'EN

*McGilligan Lake. From McGilligan Lake, goes up to China Nose Mountain.
In north direction.*

MR GRANT: Just to clarify something, he referred to a creek there from Summit Lake. Did he give a Wet'suwet'en name for that? I believe he did.
MR MILNE: Yes.
MR GRANT: What was that name?
MR MILNE: Ms Mills has given me a piece of paper with the name on it for the record.
MR GRANT: Tahdzingakwah.

OFF THE RECORD DISCUSSION IN WET'SUWET'EN

The boundary for the trapline, when they first did it, they did not do the creek boundary. They put the boundary too far down.

Who did?

OFF THE RECORD DISCUSSION IN WET'SUWET'EN

Andrew Bavin, somebody like that, worked for Fish and Wildlife.[21]

OFF THE RECORD DISCUSSION IN WET'SUWET'EN

I showed him the boundaries but he still set the boundaries incorrectly. I am talking now on the old traditional boundary, not the trapline boundary.

That's what I want to hear, about the traditional boundary. Are there

any other landmarks on the boundary that you can tell me about, other than the ones you have mentioned?
From China Nose to the height of land is used for boundary.

I don't understand what you mean by height of land. Is there something, a ridge or something, coming from China Nose?

OFF THE RECORD DISCUSSION IN WET'SUWET'EN

Yindayelgutz.

What does that refer to?
It's a flat field. On the flat field there's a land that's kind of a hill and that's the corner for Smogelgem's territory.

OFF THE RECORD DISCUSSION IN WET'SUWET'EN

THE INTERPRETER: He said it is very difficult.
MR MILNE: What is difficult? To describe it?
THE INTERPRETER: For him to describe.
Gaos taway bunee yis, and the white people call it Whiskers Mountain.
THE INTERPRETER: *The Wet'suwet'en name for that is Gaos taway bunee yis, and that is just directly behind here.*

Is China Nose Mountain east of Burns Lake or west of Burns Lake or some other direction?
West of Burns Lake.

Is it on the south side of the territory?
MR GRANT: Smogelgem's territory?
MR MILNE: Smogelgem's territory.

OFF THE RECORD DISCUSSION IN WET'SUWET'EN

Yes, from China Nose.
THE INTERPRETER: He said: *It is north of China Nose, Smogelgem's territory.*

Is Summit Creek the east or west boundary of the territory?
Western boundary.

Is the line from McGilligan Lake up China Nose Mountain on the East Side?
MR GRANT: Just a minute, I didn't understand the question.
MR MILNE: He said that McGilligan up to China Nose Mountain was one of the boundaries.

MR GRANT: Yes.

MR MILNE: I am just wondering whether that is on the east side of the territory?

MR GRANT: Okay.

THE INTERPRETER: McGilligan Lake?

[MR MILNE:] McGilligan Lake, up to China Nose Mountain, is that on the east side of the territory or is that the boundary of the territory?

THE INTERPRETER: The line between McGilligan and China Nose, you're asking if that is east or west boundary?

[MR MILNE:] Yes.

East side.

OFF THE RECORD DISCUSSION

MR GRANT: For the record, Ms Mills was just asking to clarify a word for her assistance to the court reporter. Whether that was the correct name.

What is the north boundary?

North of China Nose, the boundary.

Is there a landmark north of China Nose?

MR GRANT: Could I suggest something? I think I know what you're seeking. When you say north he's going to north of China Nose but if you want to say, is there a point where it turns from east to west at China Nose – that is, where does it stop. I think that might assist you in where you're going and clarify it for the witness.

MR MILNE: Let's try this. Where does the north boundary stop?

Yindayelgutz. It's in a flat area and there's a mountain there, Yindayelgutz.

THE INTERPRETER: And he is describing, it's up like this.

Is that what he was describing before, when he said flat field with the hill?

Yes.

THE INTERPRETER: And he is describing from China Nose to the north, and then west goes back this way to Wilson Lake, that is what he was describing here.

Wilson Lake is also a corner marker of the territory?

The line goes a little past the lake and the creek, and that's where the boundary is. Summit Lake isn't within the territory.

He gave a name for a mountain, does he – I forget what the Indian name was, it's the last one that he gave. I believe it's this one – (Indicating).

THE INTERPRETER: *Gaos taway bunee yis, Whiskers Mountain.*

That is the name that he gave, the white name is Whiskers?
THE INTERPRETER: Whiskers Mountain.

All right. Who holds the territory that touches the east boundary of Smogelgem's territory?
Casbeen from Babine side holds that territory. They don't cross over each other's side.

Casbeen Wet'suwet'en?
THE INTERPRETER: He's from Babine. Old Fort.

Who holds the territory that touches the north boundary of Smogelgem's territory?
North side is Casbeen.

That's what I thought. Who holds the territory touching –

OFF THE RECORD DISCUSSION IN WET'SUWET'EN

THE INTERPRETER: He is saying: *Casbeen is Old Fort Indian. From Babine.*

Who holds the territory then touching the east side of Smogelgem's territory?
THE INTERPRETER: *He is asking what Mabel Sam's name was.*
MR GRANT: The name was given in the record that Mabel Sam's name was Kela.
Kela?
THE INTERPRETER: He said: *The East Side is Kela's territory.*

And the name of Kela's territory?
Alxkat, or the English, Graveyard Lake.
MR GRANT: What's the word?
THE INTERPRETER: Alxkat.
MR MILNE: For the record, Mr Grant, Kela is a plaintiff?
MR GRANT: Kela is not a named plaintiff, no.

OFF THE RECORD DISCUSSION IN WET'SUWET'EN

At Graveyard Lake two of Kela's grandfathers are buried there. That is the name she is holding now.
MR MILNE: I think that was gone into in the direct examination, in that area.

Who holds the territory touching the west boundary of Smogelgem's territory?
The corner of Smogelgem's territory, the territory belonged to Tyee Lake David [Chief Woos], and Old Patrick, who didn't have a Chief's name. Old Patrick is Kela's grandfather.

Are there other people's territory also touching the western boundary of Smogelgem's territory?
No. That's all.

Who holds the territory that touches the south boundary of Smogelgem's territory?
Lame Arthur Michell. And his three brothers. Lame Arthur Michell and his three brothers. They were one company. That's it, everybody surrounding the territory. Everything squared up.[22]
Thank you.

Is Lame Arthur Michell Wet'suwet'en?
Wet'suwet'en from Moricetown. His son is the same. All his sons are still alive.

I take it that Tyee Lake David and Old Patrick are also Wet'suwet'en?
Yes, they're Wet'suwet'en.

Is the word Alkut and the word that has been used, Alxkat, was the territory called Graveyard Lake or is that Alxkat?
   Maybe just go off the record for a minute while I refer to some other transcripts.

OFF THE RECORD DISCUSSION

MR GRANT: Just for the record. We have not located it but apparently in Volume IV, the transcript of December 19 and 20, there was a reference to Kela's territory and to this location around Graveyard Lake, which is known as Alxkat. There is a spelling given to it that seems different to that but counsel agree that what Mr David is referring to now is the same.
MR MILNE: I agree.
MR GRANT: When we can determine it at our next sitting, we'll just correct it for the record and give both spellings. Do we have both spellings?
MR MILNE: We have both spellings now on the record.
MR GRANT: Those two spellings are with reference to the same name and the same place, and Mr. Milne agrees.

MR MILNE: That's correct.

Mr David, you mentioned in your direct examination that you had consulted with Richard Overstall concerning boundaries of your territory –
MR GRANT: Which territory?
MR MILNE: Smogelgem's territory, I'm sorry. First of all, do you remember consulting with Mr Overstall about Smogelgem's territory?
THE INTERPRETER: He asked me: *White man?*
[MR MILNE:] White man.
THE INTERPRETER: He can't remember who he is.
I grew up as a small boy on the territory. I know the territory and that is what I am telling you now.

MR MILNE: Mr Grant, I previously mentioned that because a map was referred to in the direct examination I was going to be asking for production of that map.
MR GRANT: Do you have a reference to that?
MR MILNE: In the direct examination?
MR GRANT: Yes.
MR MILNE: It is on Volume IV, page 44, question 29 [4: 211 above]. The defendant's position is that the map is part of another judicial proceeding and if it was privileged it's lost its privilege as a result and we're requesting production of that now.
MR GRANT: I was going to actually mention it when you started on the definition of the territory. I don't object to production of that map. It is a matter of obtaining the requisite order to release that exhibit from the court, and I'll endeavour to do so.
MR MILNE: Thank you.
MR GRANT: Whether the map was duplicated in its present form or not, I don't know, but I have no problem obtaining it since Mr David referred to it. Just for the record I must say I have made some efforts to obtain the map. I thought there was a copy that I could have obtained more easily since the adjournment of this case in February but I have been so far unsuccessful.

MR MILNE: Yesterday you said that you had to chase some people off your territory, two young men I think you said, and we were at that time talking of the Kilwoneetz territory. Did you have any trouble with white people on Smogelgem's territory?
No, it was just those two young white men. No other white person gave me a hard time in Smogelgem's territory.

In your direct examination you said that after you married you were entitled to use the Nanika territory. Are you authorized to speak at the feast concerning that territory?

MR GRANT: Today or when he was married?

MR MILNE: First let's deal with when you were married.

I did sometimes speak on the territory when I first married but the Head Man for that area was Francis Lake John and his brother, Louie. I am going to tell you about it. Francis Lake John had told me, since you married my sister's daughter.[23] *Jimmy Thomas, who was non-status, was like a white man, therefore could not talk about the territory so Francis Lake John asked me to speak on the territory. I looked after the territory through speaking for them.*

THE INTERPRETER: He is asking me who is Caspit. He said: *All this time the territory belonged to Jimmy Thomas and now [I can't] remember who it was.* And he asked me: *Who held Caspit?* I told him it was Stanley Morris and now the territory's in Stanley Morris' name. He is asking me if Stanley Morris is Caspit and I told him yes.

Are you entitled now to speak about that territory at a feast?

Just after I first got married when I spoke on the territory because Francis Lake John asked me to, but now these people have learned their territory and I have no business in that territory therefore I don't speak about the territory.

Is Stanley Morris Wet'suwet'en?

Yes, he is Wet'suwet'en. He is John's sister's grandson. Stanley Morris.

I'm concerned about these names and maybe it's because I am not hearing properly – [Is the name] Casbeen?

THE INTERPRETER: Caspit.

I thought it was the person whose territory is north of Smogelgem's. Who is Casbeen?

OFF THE RECORD DISCUSSION

MR MILNE: Stanley Morris and Caspit are not named plaintiffs?

MR GRANT: No.

Because you're not authorized to speak of this territory now at the feast, I am not going to ask you to describe the boundaries but could you, if I did?

THE INTERPRETER: He said *I could.*

MR GRANT: I appreciate Mr Milne's efforts to bring us into a level of trying to get this commission completed.

[MR MILNE:] I want to go back and ask you some more questions about the Kilwoneetzen territory. I looked through the transcripts to find out what people or Houses made up the Kilwoneetz but I was unable to find out. Can you tell me what people or Houses the phrase Kilwoneetz refers to?

MR GRANT: Given the efforts you made yesterday about the fact that there may be two different names, I think you should [know] that you're asking two questions at once and you may get double answers or you may get answers in alternate forms. I think if you want to know the names of the Houses, I think that's what you should ask; if you want the names of the Chiefs, you should ask; and if you want to ask both, that's fine but I don't think you should do it both at the same time.

[MR MILNE:] What are the Houses that compose Kilwoneetz?

THE INTERPRETER: He asked me if we are talking about the feast House and I told him yes. He said: *They're called Kilwoneetz House and we all use it together.*

When you say we, to whom are you referring?
The people in my Clan.

That is?
THE INTERPRETER: *Laxsilyu [Small Frog].*
MR MILNE: Laxsilyu Clan.
You will see at the hall the way the people are seated. They're seated according to the Clan; they're all as one company. They're all in the House during the feast.

So what Houses within the Laxsilyu Clan compose the Kilwoneetz House?
No. Separate. It's only when they come into the feast hall they come in as one company.

Well, you have got me a bit confused, Mr David.
MR GRANT: Maybe we can go off the record if you want?
MR MILNE: Please.

OFF THE RECORD DISCUSSION

It has now been explained to me there are, as I understand it, three Houses within the Laxsilyu Clan. Would you please give me the names of those three Houses just so I can get it straight?
Ginehklaiya, Kwan beah ya weten, Tse kal kai ya weten. And Peter Alfred's wife is from Tse kal kai ya weten, within [that] House. When there is a feast they are named as such and are given materials accordingly.

Do all three of those Houses that you have just named have the right to the Kilwoneetz territory?

The people from Laxsilyu, [and] their spouses are able to use the territory. That was how it was done in the past and things are getting a little mixed up today and I'm finding it difficult to talk about this.

MR MILNE: Ask him if he's getting tired.

THE INTERPRETER: *He's not getting tired, it's just trying to sort everything out [and] he's finding [it] difficult.*

I want you to make sure if you don't understand what I am asking that you let me know and I'll do my best to try and ask questions that are understandable. The next territory I want to talk about is the one that you referred to as the Telkwa River territory or Kela's territory. Yesterday I believe that we had the one boundary of it as the Dennis Mountain area, the south boundary. Is that right?

OFF THE RECORD DISCUSSION

Yes, it is and there's a small lake, Blue Lake it's called, that belongs to the Coast Indians.

OFF THE RECORD DISCUSSION IN WET'SUWET'EN

Two hundred years ago there was a lake, Blue Lake, in the area, in this direction there. Kitselas Indians' territory.

Does that touch Kela's territory?
Yes, it's connected.

On the south side?
West side.

Is that above the headwaters of the Telkwa?
THE INTERPRETER: *The Telkwa River?*
[MR MILNE:] Yes.
Tsa moot'tsa is the mountain that has the Tsimshiam name. Tsimshiam Indian name and we call that by the same name. It's a long time ago.
MR GRANT: What was the name of the mountain that he gave?
THE INTERPRETER: Tsa moot'tsa.

OFF THE RECORD

That's the west boundary?
Yes.

OFF THE RECORD DISCUSSION IN WET'SUWET'EN

Deh 'kleye yis is the Wet'suwet'en name for Tsa moot'tsa.

Is there an English name for it?
*I think they call it Blue Lake Mountain. It's a mine there. There's a lot of sil-
ver there. I was there for two years and then war broke out and everything just
shut down.*[24]

I think you told me yesterday that the north boundary of Kela's terri-
tory was a lake known as Howson Lake. Is that correct?
*Yes, Howson Lake. The area next to Howson Lake belongs to Mooseskin
Johnny.*

But yesterday we didn't talk about what the east boundary of Kela's
territory may be. Can you name some landmarks on the east boundary
of Kela's territory?
The east boundary is identified by a creek that comes from Howson Lake.

Do you know the name of the creek?
THE INTERPRETER: He knows the names of all the creeks and rivers but
[is] having a difficult time remembering it.
MR MILNE: If he remembers it he can tell me at any time.
MR GRANT: During the commission.
MR MILNE: During the commission.

Does that creek –
THE INTERPRETER: He's just –

OFF THE RECORD DISCUSSION IN WET'SUWET'EN

MR GRANT: If it is hard for him to remember, I don't think he has to.
THE INTERPRETER: I think that is what he is trying.
MR GRANT: I don't think he has to strain himself out.
THE INTERPRETER: He's having problems remembering names.

Ask him if he would like to take a short break.
*No, I want to get done today. After lunch I am going to Smithers, but I'll
make a quick trip and I'll be back in one hour and we can start again at two
o'clock.*[25]
[MR MILNE:] That's fine.

Does this creek that comes from Howson Lake flow into the Telkwa
River?
Yes.

Does the territory of Maxlaxlex – let me change that around a bit here – the east boundary of the territory of Maxlaxlex, in other words the Copper River area, touches Gyoluget's territory?

MR GRANT: That's not a question.

[MR MILNE:] Is that correct?

MR GRANT: You're referring to the Kilwoneetz territory?

[MR MILNE:] Yes.

Yes it does. The ski jump. The territories are side by side. Big Seymour owned it before Gyoluget did.

Is there a lake called Guxsam Lake that is on the border?

No. Guxsam Lake belongs to the people from Skeena Crossing. The Indians from Skeena Crossing.

MR GRANT: There's a plaintiff, a named plaintiff Guxsam, for the record.

What landmark touches the boundary of Gyoluget and Copper River area, the Kilwoneetz territory?

There's a creek near Four Mile Hill that's the boundary between Gyoluget and the Kilwoneetz territory.

THE INTERPRETER: He's asking me what the heart-shaped building is near Toboggan Lake. He is talking about Adam's Igloo.

OFF THE RECORD DISCUSSION IN WET'SUWET'EN

Gyoluget's territory goes from Tatlow Station to reach to – between two mountains near Adam's Igloo and the area east of Toboggan Lake belongs to Wah Tah Keght.[26]

OFF THE RECORD DISCUSSION IN WET'SUWET'EN

Near Tatlow Station there's a creek, Seymour Creek, that uses this boundary. That's it.

The creek that comes from Four Mile Hill flows into the Bulkley, is that right?

Yes. Then east of there the territory belongs to Woos.

Who owns the territory that touches the south boundary of the Kilwoneetzen?

Kela and then, that's across the creek and in this direction, that area belongs to Woos.[27]

I'm not sure if I have got my map up the right way here but I think I'll leave that for now, except to ask, does Kela own the territory on both sides, the north and south sides?

THE INTERPRETER: Of?

MR GRANT: Of?

[MR MILNE:] Of the, well, this Kilwoneetzen territory.

THE INTERPRETER: You're asking if it runs north and south?

[MR MILNE:] No, I am asking if she has territory on – if there is –

MR GRANT: Two separate territories?

[MR MILNE:] Two separate territories, one on the north side and one on the south side?

It is in between the two mountain ranges and the creek runs in the middle, and it's just one territory, not two.[28]

MR GRANT: That is which territory? Kela's?

THE INTERPRETER: *Kela.*

Kela's territory is next to – touches Dennis Mountain?

Dennis Mountain is here and there is another mountain range here, and Kela's territory is in between the two mountains.[29]

On this side of Dennis Mountain is the Copper River?

THE INTERPRETER: You're asking for this?

Yes.

Yes.

Who owns the territory on the other side of Copper River further south?

Gitksan.

OFF THE RECORD DISCUSSION IN WET'SUWET'EN

Seven Sisters, that area belongs to Malahan, who is Gitksan, and the area south of McDonnel Lake belongs to the Kitselas Indians.

Okay.

THE INTERPRETER: He gets up and don't feel right about it.

Do your best, Mr David. I think you are doing wonderfully well.

I am telling you about the areas that I know, what I am telling you, I am not making up.

MR MILNE: For the record, yesterday he referred to a map of David Dennis – that David Dennis had, a 1902 map, and apparently it is not in this witness's control and he says not in David Dennis's control either.

MR GRANT: What does he say about that? I think he said that he returned it to David Dennis, if I recall rightly?

MR MILNE: He did, and it couldn't be found.

MR GRANT: I see.

MR MILNE: That map seems to me to be a fairly important item and I would ask if it does come into the control of any of the plaintiffs that it be produced, and perhaps it would be noted on your list of documents as something if it was in the control of the plaintiffs, may not now be in their control. Or possession.

THE INTERPRETER: Can I say something?

MR GRANT: No.

MR MILNE: Do you have something to say about the map?

MR GRANT: I don't want the interpreter to say anything to you about the map. We'll speak about it and maybe I'll say something later. I have noted your request.

MR MILNE: In any event, if it shows up I would like it.

MR GRANT: No offence.

BY MR MILNE: I want to talk now about the territory to the far east, the Wet'suwet'en territory that borders and touches the Nutseni territory –

MR GRANT: Go off the record for a moment please.

OFF THE RECORD DISCUSSION
SHORT RECESS

You told your lawyer, Mr Grant, some time ago about the border of the Wet'suwet'en territory and the Nutseni territory, and you said that Sebola Mountain was one-half Nutseni and one-half Wet'suwet'en. I am now going to ask you more questions about that border.

THE INTERPRETER: He's asking me where Sebola Mountain is.
It runs along Ootsa Lake. Do you remember that now?
Yes.

You also talked about Caspit, who was Wet'suwet'en and held territory near Morice Lake?

MR GRANT: That isn't a question.

MR MILNE: Just tell him.

And you talked about Chief Louie who was in the Cheslatta area?
Chief Louie was from Cheslatta and he was a big Chief there.[30]

And I believe you said that Chief Louie and Caspit had some problems but that they discussed them and everything worked out all right?

MR GRANT: Could you refer me to what reference you have from his evidence before you ask that question?

MR MILNE: It is in Volume V, starting at page 23 and in particular on the bottom of page 25 [5: 239–42 above].

MR GRANT: Well, yes, that is what I recall. I think you're referring to the answer, line 39, Volume V, page 25 [5: 242 above].

MR MILNE: Yes.

MR GRANT: I just don't want the witness to be misled. I have no objection to you asking about this but I think you should put to him the answer that he gave about Chief Louie and Caspit, which on the one part suggests there was problems but the other part of the same answer suggests there was no problem.

MR MILNE: That's right, that's why I'm asking him about it.

MR GRANT: I ask anyway that, could it be put to the witness so he understands what you're referring to?

MR MILNE: Okay.

MR GRANT: I would like the interpreter to read the answer to him.

MR MILNE: I can't remember my last question that was interrupted, can you read that back?

THE REPORTER: Question: 'And I believe you said that Chief Louie and Caspit had some problems but they discussed them and everything worked out all right?'

MR MILNE: Translate this then to him in Volume V of the commission evidence transcript at page 25. There was an answer given by this witness and that answer is noted as number 39.

MR GRANT: Line 39.

MR MILNE: Line 39.

At that time, Mr David, you said – after having said that he was a Nutseni Chief whose territory bordered on the Wet'suwet'en territory, you said: *Yes, he was and on several occasions he just about had a few problems but, since they knew each other, they would talk it over and there were no problems.*

Do you remember giving that answer?
Yes, that's right.

I would like to have you tell me about what you know about the few problems.
It was just about the land.

About the boundary between the two lands?
The problem probably arose from one person crossing the boundary of another person's and when that happened, they usually talked about it and that was the end of the problem.

Does he know if there was any feasts held to settle the problem?
THE INTERPRETER: This particular problem?

MR MILNE: This particular problem.

MR GRANT: About the one person passing over the boundary of another?

MR MILNE: What I want to know, whether or not there were any feasts held at this time to his knowledge between the Wet'suwet'en and the Nutseni concerning that boundary?

MR GRANT: I just think you have to give him a time frame.

MR MILNE: Well, within his knowledge, does he know whether or not feasts were held between the Nutseni and Wet'suwet'en getting together and settling a problem over the boundary?

MR GRANT: Okay, I'll –

MR MILNE: That's pretty –

MR GRANT: He's answered the question about the person crossing over the boundary. I think you should be clear what you're asking about that. That is what his last answer was, or are you jumping into an area –

MR MILNE: Let's deal with that first.

First of all, does he know the people involved and, secondly, was there a feast held to settle that dispute?
Yes, I know them.

Was there a feast held to settle that problem?
No, they didn't. They talked it over amongst themselves and the problem was settled.

Has there to your knowledge ever been a feast between the Nutseni and the Wet'suwet'en to settle the problem with that boundary?

MR GRANT: Caspit and Chief Louie.

MR MILNE: The boundary between Nutseni and the Wet'suwet'en?
They sometimes did hold a feast to discuss the boundary when the problem was spoken to or spoken about but the thing was settled and that was that.

Does he know any details of those feasts? When the last one might have been held?
I haven't seen one personally. I've been told about it and they did probably sometimes hold feasts to straighten boundary problems.

Can you tell me what you were told about it?
They would invite each other to a feast and gifts would be distributed, and the person who crossed over a boundary would be spoken to by the chiefs and, after that happened, the problem was solved and it never occurred again.

In February, when I was asking you questions about the border between the Wet'suwet'en and the Nutseni –
MR GRANT: What page?
MR MILNE: At page 35 [6: 303 above].

You gave an answer: *When the Nutseni say their boundary goes from Houston east, that is not so, they will not take that land. From Burns Lake to Skin Dyee's territory, that is the boundary of the Wet'suwet'en people.*
    Ask him if he remembers saying that.
Yes. And this area does not belong to the Nutseni; it belongs to Skin Dyee, who is a man from Hagwilget.

You know that the Nutseni say that that territory does belong to them?

MR GRANT: I don' t know if that is true.
MR MILNE: That is what I am asking him, if that is true.
MR GRANT: You're asking him if he knows that's what they're saying. I don't know if he knows that's what they're saying. If you're asking him, is that what they're saying, I have no objection.
MR MILNE: Well, he has already said that the Nutseni say their boundary goes from Houston east, and that is not so. I don't see what your objection is.
MR GRANT: I don't know what the Nutseni say. I think if you want to suggest to him what they say, that's fine.

It's true that the Nutseni say part of that territory is theirs, correct?
It seems they have been talking that way. The people gathered and talked about it not too long ago and since that happened we haven't heard from them. We don't know what they'll say.

All this leads me to believe that the border between the Nutseni and the Wet'suwet'en from the Nutseni point of view is unsettled. Would you agree with that?
MR GRANT: Objection. I don't think he knows. I don't think he can know what the Nutseni perception of that is.
[MR MILNE:] Well, Mr David, there's still a dispute over that border, isn't there?
MR GRANT: Between whom?
[MR MILNE:] Nutseni and Wet'suwet'en.
There's, they're not arguing over the territory. I have told you already where the lands of the Wet'suwet'en are. You have got it on paper and that is what I told you and that is it.

But there has been feasts in the past about that border?

MR GRANT: Object. He has already answered the question.

[MR MILNE:] It is true there have been feasts in the past and it is true recently there have been discussions over that border?

MR GRANT: My objection stands. You can ask the question but I am recording my objection to repetition and reiteration of the answers he has already given to you.

[MR MILNE:] This man is under cross-examination and I would like you [the translator] to translate those questions.

MR GRANT: Just for the record, my objection is even under cross-examination you do not have unlimited latitude to repeat the same questions over and over again.

[MR MILNE:] Wait until you hear my questions. I am asking them one at a time, as you so often ask me to do.

Put the question to him please?

THE INTERPRETER: May I have the first question read back please?

THE REPORTER: Question: 'But there [have] been feasts in the past about that border?'

Question: 'It is true there have been feasts in the past and it is true recently there have been discussions over that border?'

MR GRANT: Which one do you want him to answer?

[MR MILNE:] Both of them.

Yes, there were feasts and whenever a person who did not like what was happening, this was the person who would do the dancing at the feast, and he was the person who gave money away at the feast.

But if you agree that there have been feasts in the past concerning that boundary and in fact there have been discussions recently, how can you say there's no dispute over that boundary?

THE INTERPRETER: He's asking me: *[Is it] the discussions you're talking about? Discussions between Nutseni and the Wet'suwet'en?*

Maybe we have a different opinion of what a dispute and discussion is, but the question is: Is that boundary between the Nutseni and the Wet'suwet'en still being discussed between the two of them?

Yes, they're discussing the boundary and I'll give you the analogy of two Houses where this person here does not have any food and this person does, so this person who has no food goes to the person that does. He gives him food and then he walks back to his territory and after that they go out hunting together and everything is resolved.

Do you know if the Wet'suwet'en have had feasts concerning their boundaries with – where's my map – what you called earlier the Coast Indians on the west?
Our people did feast with the Coast Indians and at the feast each Clan had three Head Chiefs –
THE INTERPRETER: – and he was pointing in the directions –
– One of the High Chiefs would speak for their Clan and he would get his directions from the other two Head Chiefs. Today same thing is happening. You see Roy Morris getting up and speaking. He is not speaking for himself. He gets his words from the other two Head Chiefs and those are the words that he uses when he speaks at the potlatches.

Do you know if these feasts have been about the border between the Coast Indians and the Wet'suwet'en?
MR GRANT: That's the feast with the Coast Indians?
MR MILNE: Yes.
No, it is not about boundary, it's just your regular feast and they don't give each other any trouble.

Do you know if feasts have been held between the Wet'suwet'en and Nishga concerning the boundary between the Nishga – concerning the boundary between the Nishga territory and Wet'suwet'en territory?
No, they haven't. The only feast that they've held together is your regular feast when there's dancing. There are some people who have been telling the histories of our people. Some of them have been making it up but I haven't. The things I'm telling you about I have heard them, I have lived it, and that is the information I am giving you.

Who are these people who are making up the history?
It's people who are telling legends. I have heard them. They've got it all wrong. These are the people that I am talking about.

Are these Wet'suwet'en people or white people?
Both Indians and non-Indians.

Do you know if any feasts have been held between the Wet'suwet'en and the Talhtans concerning border disputes?
No, they haven't. Only if somebody crosses into somebody else's boundary.

Do you know if that has happened?
This probably happened before I was born. I have just been told about it. But I have been told that they would discuss it amongst themselves and their problems would be solved and there were no more problems.

Without a feast?
No, they would talk it over amongst themselves.

In the old days did the Wet'suwet'en have warriors?
There were many people who fought amongst themselves.

OFF THE RECORD DISCUSSION IN WET'SUWET'EN

There were disputes between the Indian people and non-Indian people, and I can tell you about it but I'm getting tired.[31]

Would you like to take a break for lunch and then to come back after lunch to talk about that?
THE INTERPRETER: He is asking me what time it is. He is asking if you guys are going for lunch.

MR GRANT: We'll go for lunch if he wants to. We can go off the record at this stage, I think.
MR MILNE: If he would rather continue straight through?
MR GRANT: Maybe we should have this chat off the record?
MR MILNE: Off the record.

OFF THE RECORD DISCUSSION
RECESSED FOR LUNCH AT 12.00 O'CLOCK

UPON RESUMING AT 2.10 P.M.
CROSS-EXAMINATION BY MR MILNE, (CONTINUED)

Before we broke for lunch I was going to start asking you some questions about any disputes or wars that the Wet'suwet'en might have had with other Indian people. Do you know or have you heard of any wars between the Wet'suwet'en and Nutseni?
THE INTERPRETER: When they war, I told him that is what you're asking. He asked me, war between here and the Nutseni.
That is what I would like to know.
I'm finding it difficult but I'll still try.
MR GRANT: Sorry?
THE INTERPRETER: He's finding it difficult but he will still try.
MR GRANT: Can you ask him if he is just tired or would he rather not go on this afternoon, or is it the topic, the questions that he is finding difficult?
THE INTERPRETER: He's finding it difficult to talk about the topic.
MR MILNE: About the topic?
THE INTERPRETER: Yes.

MR GRANT: Possibly you should rephrase your question. Maybe he had a problem with some of your questions.

Did the Wet'suwet'en have a war with the Nutseni?
There were many stories told about the wars and I don't know which versions are correct, and that is why I am reluctant to talk about it.[32]

I appreciate your candidness and I appreciate what you tell me about there may be more than one version of it, but I would like to hear one of the versions. I also appreciate that this may have been something that was settled long ago and that there might have been a determination or decision not to talk about it any more, but I would still like to hear about the war with the Nutseni.
I remember one incident; the Indians from Fraser Lake had a war during the summer. Some time in August, during the bear season. It was warm. And they came on foot from the east, from Fraser Lake. There is one gentleman who knew the people from this area and he started out with the war party. One of the ladies from here was getting water down by the river and there's an eddy there, where driftwood was floating around, and she was looking at the driftwood very carefully to see if there were any signs of people. Canyon and Trout Creek, there's an eddy there –

OFF THE RECORD DISCUSSION IN WET'SUWET'EN

And she saw wood floating around in the eddy. The man that had relatives in this area, old Nutseni, saw nothing. He would throw the burnt embers from the logs into the fire as well as twist leaves into little piles, and he would throw them in the river. The lady who was down in the canyon saw the burnt embers from the logs floating in the eddy as well as the twisted leaves or grass, and that was an indication to her that there was a war party approaching. On the hillside close to the canyon our people had dug a trench about a foot wide, and the lady came up and told them about the burnt embers as well as the twisted leaves and all the war party got ready. The Wet'suwet'en were called baxnee. All the warriors got into trenches. Their bows and arrows ready. They were protecting the hillside here and down in the canyon. In about one or two hours the Nutseni came.
THE INTERPRETER: He is asking me: *What [do] we call the Elders of the war party?* And [I] think they call them sergeants.
There was a young man named the Llee jai, who was the sergeant of the warriors. The llee jai was the boss or the sergeant of the Nutseni war party, and one of the ladies from here hollered out 'Don't kill him.' They fought until they ran out of arrows, and the Nutseni left but our people shot one of the Nutsenis through the leg and he couldn't run away so he crawled up the creek

and one of our Elders found him and put some Indian medicine on him and told him he wasn't going to kill him.

He healed him and let him go, and the old man that found the Nutseni fed him and gave him medicine, and when he got better they let him go back to his territory. This was about 300 years ago. None of the Wet'suwet'en were hurt. The only casualty was that man that got shot through the leg. That is how the story was told to me.

Do you know the reason for the attack?
I don't know what they fought about.

Do you know of any other times when the Nutseni have attacked the Wet'suwet'en?
Yes, people from here did war with the Nutseni after that. It was during the winter and the people left here on snowshoes. Our people went through the woods, they didn't take the main roads because they were being watched, and when they got to Fraser Lake there was a village there.

The Nutsenis would pour water on the roofs of their Houses so the arrows would not go through the roof. It was like a shield. There was no one outside, everybody was inside the Houses, or lodges, because it was too cold, and five at a time they would sneak into the lodges and hit the Nutseni up with sticks. I don't know how many of them were killed but that's how the story goes, as I've been told. In the morning our people came back this way.

How many Wet'suwet'en warriors were involved, do you know?
I don't know.

Do you know of any other –

OFF THE RECORD DISCUSSION IN WET'SUWET'EN

THE INTERPRETER: He just repeated again: *I don't know how many there were.*

Do you know any other stories of when there was a war between the Nutseni and the Wet'suwet'en?
THE INTERPRETER: He said: *That's all. That's as far back as they've told me and that's as much as I know.*

Were the Wet'suwet'en ever attacked by the Nishga?
No.

Were the Wet'suwet'en ever attacked by the Coast Indians?
Just in the very early days. There's stories told about the wars and there are too many different versions and I am not willing to talk about it at this time.

Do those wars involve the Tsimshiam?
THE INTERPRETER: That is what he said. That is what he said, the Tsim-shiam.

Did the Wet'suwet'en have wars with the Kitwancool?
No.

With the Tahltans?
THE INTERPRETER: I was telling him those were the people from the Telegraph Creek area.
No. I heard some stories but I am not too sure about them. I am not willing to talk about things that I personally don't know about.

Did the Wet'suwet'en and the Gitksan ever fight?
No, they didn't. They considered each other friends and therefore they didn't war with each other.

You described to us, in response to questions from Mr Grant, an incident with the Nass people, the Nishga, and where a gravestone was knocked over and, as a result, someone was killed. Do you remember telling us that incident?
Yes I do.

Were there any other of those incidents with the Nutseni as opposed to a war?
No.
THE INTERPRETER: He was just going to start telling that story again, I told him that you already heard it.
Yes, that is already on the record.
The people from Hagwilget who were Wet'suwet'en were very good warriors. They were smart, therefore not too many other groups wanted to war with them.

During any of those stories of war that you know, in considering those stories, what was the reason, if any, for the war or wars?
No, I don't. I just know that they warred but I don't know what they were warring about.

The Statement of Claim in this action, in paragraph 55(g), says that you protected – the Wet'suwet'en people protected – the boundaries of the territory. How did the Wet'suwet'en protect the boundaries of the territory?

OFF THE RECORD DISCUSSION IN WET'SUWET'EN

THE INTERPRETER: *[I] didn't hear of any actual wars regarding boundaries but when there was a dispute the people would talk it over and that's how your problems were resolved.* Again he said that: *[I'm] finding it difficult to talk on this.*

I take it you find it difficult to talk about it because you don't want to talk about disputes that have already been settled, is that right?
Yes.

While I appreciate your position, the defendant has asked me to come and ask questions and some of them are difficult for you to answer and, as much as possible, I would ask you to answer those questions.

MR GRANT: I think, for the record, the witness is doing his best. He's described two major incidents with the Nutseni. I think he is doing his best but he has indicated he's having trouble. I don't think there's any suggestion he's doing anything but the best he can.
MR MILNE: I didn't intend that by my statement. I wasn't intimating that he wasn't doing his best but in spite of the fact it might be difficult for him to talk about it, those are the questions that he has to answer.
MR GRANT: If he can.

MR MILNE: If he can. Can you translate the gist of our exchange?
THE INTERPRETER: He said: *I've told you as much as I know and I've tried to answer the questions you're asking me to the best of my ability.*

How did the Wet'suwet'en protect the boundaries of the territory from the missionaries?
MR GRANT: Just a second.
MR MILNE: If in fact they did.
MR GRANT: I don't understand that question. Are you suggesting the missionaries made war on the Wet'suwet'en?
MR MILNE: No. First ask if he feels the missionaries were a threat to the Wet'suwet'en?
MR GRANT: I think you can ask that question.
They were not afraid of the missionaries. They basically did what they were told by the missionaries.

Why did the Wet'suwet'en do what they were told by the missionaries?
These people believed in prayers and they did not want to do anything contrary to the beliefs of the church and, therefore, they did not say anything against the church.

How did the Wet'suwet'en protect the boundaries of their territory as against white settlers?
The white settlers would threaten the Indian people with their laws and, if the Indian people did go against the white people, they were usually taken before the law and thrown in jail.

Did the Wet'suwet'en take any steps to protect themselves or to protect the boundaries of their territories from the white people?

MR GRANT: Again I think the question is confusing as you framed it up. I think you should lead up to it if you want to know what the white people did with respect to the boundaries. You are being very specific. I can understand your question if you are talking about territories or something else. If you are talking about boundaries I suggest you lead up to it.
MR MILNE: The boundaries of the territories.
MR GRANT: I don't know if he has said whether the white people have threatened the boundaries of the territory. Your question implies that is his evidence and I don't think it is.
MR MILNE: Well –
MR GRANT: It may be implied. I think if you want to lead to it, fine.

Have the Wet'suwet'en boundaries of the territory been threatened by the white people?
The white people had no respect for the Indian people. They came and just took the land and just literally threw them off.
THE INTERPRETER: And he indicated by picking up a pen and throwing it on the table.

Threw them off what?
They kicked them off their lands, their traplines. The area I showed you near Barrett Lake, areas like that, people were thrown off their lands.

Did the Wet'suwet'en take action to protect them against that?

OFF THE RECORD DISCUSSION IN WET'SUWET'EN

THE INTERPRETER: He said: *The people, the white people had no respect for the Indian people. The Indian people would chase them off their land, they would go and get their law and they would throw our people in jail.*

    Right now, pointing at you, he is saying: *It is just like you, you don't care about Indian people.*

How did the Indian people chase whites off the land?

OFF THE RECORD DISCUSSION IN WET'SUWET'EN

They would ask them to leave and when they leave they come back with their white law and our people would be thrown in jail.

You have told us one incident of when you found somebody on your traplines in the Kilwoneetzen territory and you asked them to leave, and you took them to the Indian agent. Do you remember any other incidents of when you asked white people to leave your land?
Yes I do. I neglected to tell you there was an Indian named Pat Brown who had to go home by railroad. He had no money. In order to get home he sold the trapline for $15 to some white people. That's what he used to go home by rail.

OFF THE RECORD DISCUSSION IN WET'SUWET'EN

There was two young men told me right away when I got back to North Bulkley. When they told me about it, I took the two young men as well as Pat Brown into the Indian agent's office and told Pat Brown to give him the money back to the two young men, which he did, and there were no more problems after that.

OFF THE RECORD DISCUSSION IN WET'SUWET'EN

Then there were no other problems regarding the trapline after that. There is other people who would like to trap on my territory. If I say no they respect that and that's as far as it goes.

What about all the white settlers that came into your territory, either in the North Bulkley or Kilwoneetzen area. Did you ask them to leave?
He told us and there were laws here and we respected that, and we didn't chase them off.

So what do you think, Mr David, do the white settlers have a right to be where they are now?

MR GRANT: I object to the question.
MR MILNE: I thought you might.
MR GRANT: The answer is probably as useless as the question. That is the very issue in the least in the litigation.
MR MILNE: That is why I asked the question.
MR GRANT: It's a question of law.
MR MILNE: The plaintiffs are continuing to own and exercise jurisdiction to the present time, according to the Statement of Claim, and I am just wondering, this man is Wet'suwet'en and I think he has a right to say what really he is seeking, in his own words.

MR GRANT: That is not what you asked. It is a question of law you asked. He may be a remarkable witness but –

MR MILNE: What relief are you seeking as a Wet'suwet'en, Mr David?

MR GRANT: With respect to what?
MR MILNE: With respect to this claim.
MR GRANT: Well, I think you should put – I think the Statement of Claim can be put to him so he can look at it.
MR MILNE: I want him to explain in his own words what he is seeking.

MR MILNE: Let me ask you this question, Mr. David: As a Chief, were you consulted about this land claim before the action was commenced?
MR GRANT: That's subject to solicitor-client privilege.

Did you discuss it with other Chiefs, not with your lawyer, but did you discuss it with other Chiefs? That's not privileged.
MR GRANT: No, that is not privileged. The first one is. Go ahead and ask him.
[MR MILNE:] Before this action was commenced, as the Chief did you consult with other Chiefs about starting this action?

OFF THE RECORD DISCUSSION IN WET'SUWET'EN

THE INTERPRETER: There was a little exchange we had before, and he was asking me whether it was about the old days and I told him it was about now.
Now, before this court case was launched the Chiefs and the elected Chiefs got together and they did talk about it, and now our people are getting more educated and they're saying no to a lot of things.

When the elected Chiefs talked about it, did they decide what they wanted?
MR GRANT: When the elected Chiefs talked about it?
MR MILNE: That is what he said, the elected –
MR GRANT: He said he talked with the Chiefs and the elected Chiefs.
[MR MILNE:] When the Chiefs and the elected Chiefs got together and talked about it, what did they decide they wanted?
MR GRANT: Referring to the Wet'suwet'en?
MR MILNE: I am trying to confine all of this to the Wet'suwet'en.

OFF THE RECORD DISCUSSION IN WET'SUWET'EN

The people of this village will get together and make their – make their words into one, and that's what they will go by.[33]

Maybe you didn't understand my question because I don't think that answers it. When the Chiefs and elected Chiefs got together to discuss their land and what the white people had done to their land, what was decided as to what the Wet'suwet'en wanted from the white people?

MR GRANT: Could you read that question back to me?

THE REPORTER: Question: 'Maybe you didn't understand my question because I don't think that answers it. When the Chiefs and elected Chiefs got together to discuss their land and what the white people had done to their land, what was decided as to what the Wet'suwet'en wanted from the white people?'

MR GRANT: That's a different question to what you asked earlier and it covers a much wider ambit.

MR MILNE: Let's see what –

MR GRANT: We have three minutes on the tape.

MR MILNE: There are lots of tapes. Let's see what the witness has to answer.

MR GRANT: I am just saying that question – I would like you to give the witness a time frame you're talking about before you intend tying it to the discussion of this litigation.

MR MILNE: I still intend on tying it to the discussion of this litigation. The whole thing is in the context of this litigation. I wouldn't be here but for this litigation.

MR GRANT: The last time you asked, when they met to discuss this case, and now you're saying when they met to discuss the land, what was being done on the land, and that's much broader.

MR MILNE: What was discussed, being done to the land and this case. In relation to this case.

MR GRANT: And you're referring [to] when they decided to take the case and discuss it in that manner.

MR MILNE: Yes. Now, maybe we could have a tape change. Maybe give him the question and let him think about it while the tape is being changed.

MR GRANT: Off the record.

THE INTERPRETER: Off the record?

MR GRANT: You can ask him the question.

MR MILNE: Yes.

OFF THE RECORD DISCUSSION

MR MILNE: On the record now.
You can see throughout our territory all the stumps and the white people have

pocketed millions and millions of dollars. All the money that has been taken off our territory, we want that back and we want our territory back to the way they were. Once we get back the money we would like to go back to our old Indian laws, to make life better for our people. The other Hereditary Chiefs as well as the other leaders are thinking about some way and it is with their words and my words that I am giving you today. It's the generation that will follow me that will use these resources. I will not be able to use it. I am ready to go. That's all.

All right. Those are my questions for today. Mr Grant has to catch an aeroplane so I think we'll call it a day at this point. There is only one issue, as to your instructions, Mr Grant, not to answer the question on the territory and I don't know if you have considered your position yet as to what you may take, either instructing the witness to answer that or objecting to that and retaining your right to objection at trial as to the admissibility of the evidence. What is your position?

OFF THE RECORD

MR MILNE: Back on the record. For the record I'll have the reporter read back the question that is in dispute.
THE REPORTER: Question: 'I want to be sure I know where the Kilwoneetzen territory is, so I just want to summarize that it's between – it's the valley between two mountain peaks of Hudson Bay Mountain and Dennis Mountain, and one end of it is marked by a creek that has no name but is – comes out of the Sandstone Mountain area –'
MR GRANT: I just think that –
THE REPORTER: Question: '– and at the other end of it is a creek that comes from the Four Mile Hill area? Have I correctly described your territory?'
MR MILNE: That is the question that is in issue.
MR GRANT: I objected yesterday to the question. My objection – and I objected this morning to the question – I requested that you rephrase the question so that it would be fair to the witness. You have taken the position you don't have to rephrase it to be fair to the witness. My objection is maintained. However, in the circumstances of the commission I believe the question can be put to the witness, but I also want translated to the witness that the question is unfair and if it does not accurately set out – your question does not accurately summarize or summarize [*sic*] the boundaries or it is difficult for him to answer, he should tell you that.
MR MILNE: That's fine with me. Thank you, Mr Grant. Let's continue on with this on Monday.

MR GRANT: Do you want him to answer that question or not?
MR MILNE: He can answer it on Monday.
THE INTERPRETER: That's it?
MR MILNE: That's it. Go off the record.

OFF THE RECORD DISCUSSION

PROCEEDINGS ADJOURNED AT 3.15 P.M.
TO BE RESUMED MONDAY, 29 APRIL, 1986[34]

VOLUME 8

Cross-Examination of Johnny David by John Milne,
28 April 1986

UPON COMMENCING AT 9:40 A.M., 28 APRIL, 1986

VICTOR WILLIAM JIM, Wet'suwet'en interpreter, previously sworn.
JOHN DAVID, witness called on behalf of the plaintiffs, previously sworn, testifies as follows:

MR MILNE: For the record, this is continuation of the cross-examination of John David. We had adjourned from the 22nd of April, 1986. All parties are present that were present at the last continuation, except for the reporter, who has changed and is now Bev Ferguson.

CROSS-EXAMINATION BY MR MILNE, CONTINUED:

Q   Mr David, you are still under oath. Do you understand that?
A   *Yes.*

Q   And Mr Interpreter, you are as well, you understand that?
A   THE INTERPRETER: Yes.

MR MILNE: Just as we broke last time, we were going to have a question put back to the witness. And that question is set out on page 107 of Volume VII of the transcript at line 32 [7: 374 above]. And I will now put that question to the witness and I understand that you, Mr Grant, may have something to say about it before the witness answers.

   The question is – in fact, would you just read the question to him, please, Mr Interpreter, rather than me repeating it at this time?

THE INTERPRETER: It's line 32?

MR MILNE: Starting at line 32. [Question shown to translator, not read aloud: 'I want to be sure I know where the Kilwoneetzen territory is, so I just want to summarize that it's between – it's the valley between two mountain peaks of Hudson Bay Mountain and Dennis Mountain, and one end of it is marked by a creek that has no name but is – comes out of Sandstone Mountain area, and at the other end of it is a creek that comes from the Four Mile Hill area. Have I correctly described your territory?']

THE INTERPRETER: You want me to translate it?

MR MILNE: Please.

MR GRANT: Tell him not to answer until I have commented on it. Did you translate the bottom part of it, line 442? [This is Mr Grant's objection in 7: 374 above]

THE INTERPRETER: Oh.

MR GRANT: I have objected to this question because I have suggested that it is an unfair question. If it does not accurately describe the boundaries of the Kilwoneetzen territory – you [Johnny David] should tell that to Mr Milne. Can you translate that and I'll continue.

You gave evidence for 20 minutes or more about those boundaries and I'm objecting because I think it's unfair to put all of that evidence in one question. So when you answer this question, if you agree with that summary, be certain that it is accurate or if you have problems with the question, tell Mr Milne.

THE INTERPRETER: He is describing the territory, wondering if I could just draw a rough map from the information here, which might –

MR GRANT: I think you should just give his answer as he is describing it.

THE INTERPRETER: He is saying: *From Four Mile Hill there is a creek that runs through there, and that is one of the boundaries. And territory near that belongs to Gyologet.* He is asking: *[Is] that all you want?*

MR MILNE: What I was asking was if I could just summarize your area as to be generally between Hudson's Bay Mountain, Dennis Mountain, the creek from Four Mile Hill, and on the other end of the territory, something, a creek that comes out of Sandstone Mountain area.

MR GRANT: My objection applies.

MR MILNE: Could you translate that, please?

THE INTERPRETER: He is saying: *What he [Mr Milne] is saying here is correct.*

Mr David, you speak on behalf of members of your House. Is that correct?
THE INTERPRETER: He asked me if you are referring to him. I told him yes and he said: *Yes, I do speak for the House members.*

And do you know how many members there are of your House?
THE INTERPRETER: You are asking for all the numbers, all the people in the House?
Yes, in the House.
There are three Main Chiefs from each House. And these three Chiefs are the ones that speak, and I am one of those speakers.

Do you know how many people, in terms of number, that those three Chiefs speak for?
There are many of us. In the feast hallway we sit in twos, and there are many of us, and I sit in the middle.

Are there 50 or more people for whom you speak and who are members of your House?
MR GRANT: I don' t want the witness to be guessing. So tell the witness if he doesn't know, he can say he doesn't know and not to guess.
There are many of us. We sit along the wall as well as in front, and I don't know the exact numbers.

I'm not talking only of the people who are sitting in the feast hall. I'm talking about all of the people for whom you speak in the House. Do you have any idea how many people there are in your House?
I don't know the numbers.

Are you aware that a land claim was submitted to the government of Canada in November of 1977 by your people?
MR GRANT: Object on the grounds of relevance, for the record.
MR MILNE: Thank you. Would you translate it?
Yes, I know about that.

Did you participate in the decision to advance that claim?
Yes, I was one of the participants.

And what was it that you decided you wanted from the government of Canada?
I have forgotten what we talked about. I only talk about what I know or remember. Things I don't remember, I don't talk about.

It's a good policy. Within the Wet'suwet'en territory, are there any areas that are what I call open areas? In other words, areas that are not claimed by any House or Chief?

MR GRANT: Within the Wet'suwet'en territory?

MR MILNE: Yes.

MR GRANT: So this would be the territory of all of the Houses of the Wet'suwet'en.

MR MILNE: Yes.

MR GRANT: I think that should be made clear.

THE WITNESS: *All our people know where their boundaries are and they stay within that. And there are none that are open.*

Mr David, you had previously said in your direct examination that no feasts were held in the Kilwoneetzen territory, or in the territory of Smogelgem. Why is it that no feasts are held in those territories?

THE INTERPRETER: We're getting a little confused about the questioning. He finally straightened it out, and he said: *All the feasts were held at Hagwilget and the animals that were hunted and trapped meat would first be distributed among the guests at the feasts, which were held in Hagwilget.*

MR MILNE: Any time.

MR GRANT: Are you talking about after Mr David was born or before? I think you should break it up somehow.

MR MILNE: Let's deal first, before you were born. Do you know if there were any poles in the territory of Kilwoneetzen or in Smogelgem's territory?

No.

And were there any poles in either of those two territories after he was born?

No. They were erected in the villages in Moricetown as well as in Hagwilget. And at Hagwilget it was down in the camp.

And do you know if before you were born, there were permanent buildings in the territory of the Kilwoneetzen or the territory of Smogelgem?

MR GRANT: What do you mean by permanent buildings?

MR MILNE: In the direct examination he was talking about some branch Houses. What I'm wondering, if there was any more permanent structures made of wood, or something that remains there all year around?

MR GRANT: So say a building that would last a whole year?

MR MILNE: Or longer, a building that would last indefinitely.

MR GRANT: I think the description of what is meant by permanent building should be put to the witness.

MR MILNE: Reasonable wear and tear excepted.

THE INTERPRETER: Before I asked him, I again had to clarify the question. And he said: *In Smogelgem's territory, there were cabins they used for hunting and trapping, and when those rotted down or were burnt down, they would build another one. And when the white people came, that's when the cabins started to be burnt to the ground. And then there was a big building, and that was again burnt by white people.*

I think you mentioned that once before in your direct examination. At that time I wanted to know how do you know it was burnt by white people?
I saw them and they're all dead now.

You saw the white people?
I was told by people. I knew their names and now they are all dead.

I just want to get this straight. You were told by somebody else that white people burned it down. Is that right?
Old David Dennis and my wife all grew up under the building that was burned down by the white people.

I don't think that quite answers my question. What I'm wondering is did you see white people burn the building down?
No, I didn't. My wife knew white people who were prospecting. In Kilwoneetz territory there is another building that was burnt down by white people.

Well, this one building you are talking about that Dennis lived in, is that at Six Mile Flats?
He lived at Six Mile Flats as well as Dennis did.

And the other building was at Dennis Lake?
Yes. There was a village site at Six Mile Flats.

Did you go to these buildings in your lifetime?
Yes, I did.

Are there buildings there now?
Where the Houses were, you could still tell where they were.

There is rubble or something left, is there?
You can see the outline of house still on the ground. The materials they used from the old days, they may be still buried under the ground.

Do you know how many cabins there were on Smogelgem's territory?
MR GRANT: When?
MR MILNE: I think he said there used to be cabins before he was born, trapping cabins.

MR GRANT: Are you talking about at one time or cumulatively, before he answers the question?
Well, at any particular one time, what was the most number of cabins that would have been on the territory?
At Kooty Creek (phonetic), where our main settlement was, there were two cabins there. At Midzi-ya, there was one. Kuskabaywonnee there was one. And white people really made us suffer by burning down our buildings.

Did you see the white people burn down buildings on Smogelgem's territory?
I have seen them, I knew them, but I didn't say anything.

Why didn't you say anything?
I was afraid of the law. As soon as we talk about something, they put us in court and jail us.

Which cabin did you see burned down by white people?
Kooty Creek, which is Neloo kwah in our language, that is where I saw white people burn a cabin down.

Do you know why the white people burned the cabin down?
The white people had no respect for us. In their eyes, we were poor for them. They just fooled around with us. Whenever we spoke against them, they would call the law and they would put us in jail.

Are these the white settlers that you are talking about?
Yes. Akai McGuinness and Tom Hagen.

This is the incident of where they burned down your father' s house?
Yes.

Mr Grant asked you some questions about your fishing sites in Moricetown and Hagwilget Canyon. Are the sites that are described in those – or are your fishing sites in those two canyons all on reserve lands?
MR GRANT: Objection, that's a question of law.
MR MILNE: Do you think it's on reserve land?
MR GRANT: Objection, his opinion about law is irrelevant.
MR MILNE: I'm not asking his opinion about law. I'm just wondering if they're on the reserve.
MR GRANT: Which is a question of law. Then you asked if he thought if they were on the reserve.
MR MILNE: Mr David, is your house on the reserve?
MR GRANT: Objection, that's a question of law.

MR MILNE: I think that's something which is in his knowledge, however. Just as I think it's within his knowledge whether the fishing sites may or may not be on the reserve. I'm not asking about a definitive reply of where they are, but what I want to know is whether he believes them to be on reserve land. I don't see anything objectionable about that. I note your objection.

MR GRANT: I think you should tell him what you mean by reserve so that he understands the question.

MR MILNE: Are there fishing sites in Moricetown and Hagwilget Canyon which you have described to Mr Grant on lands reserved for Indians?

MR GRANT: My objection stands, for the record.

THE WITNESS: *Yes, it's on reserve lands in Hagwilget.*

And what about Moricetown?
The same here in Moricetown.

Are there any major fishing sites of the Wet'suwet'en that are not in Moricetown Canyon or Hagwilget Canyon?

MR GRANT: I don't know what you mean by major. I think that's a very subjective word. And what you mean by major may be very different from what the witness means.

MR MILNE: Let's see what he gives [as] the answer, and if it's different from what I'm requesting, I'll clarify it.

MR GRANT: What do you mean by major? Would you describe that for him?

MR MILNE: Let's see if he knows what I mean by major site. If the witness has difficulty with that, I'll further particularize it.

MR GRANT: The problem is the witness may interpret major in a different way than what you mean. It's a very subjective word.

MR MILNE: It is, and I want to find out what he means. I'll know that by his answer.

MR GRANT: My objection is noted for the record. Tell the witness if he does not know what the lawyer means by major, he should say so after you ask the question.

THE INTERPRETER: Major –

MR GRANT: If he does not know what Mr Milne means by major fishing sites, he should tell Mr Milne that. You may want the reporter to read the question back to you.

THE INTERPRETER: No, I'm having trouble with the word 'major' in Wet'suwet'en.

THE WITNESS: *In Francis Lake there are reserves set up and that's where people have major fishing sites, but not between Hagwilget and Moricetown.*

What about between Moricetown and Francis Lake?
Between Moricetown and Francis Lake, our people know where good fishing spots are. And that's where they fish for salmon, using nets.
[THE INTERPRETER:] And he described one area at Morice Canyon near Morice Lake.

On what river?
The creek that comes from Morice Lake.

Do you know if that's called Morice River?
Yes, and in Wet'suwet'en it's called Wadzun Kwah. And Father Morice was the one who gave away most of our territory. He also put names to lakes using his name.

How do you mean Father Morice is the one that gave away your territories? Did he act for the Wet'suwet'en?
Our people acted as guides for Father Morice. They showed him the territory and throughout the territory, he gave out names. Sometimes using his own to lakes, creeks, and even Moricetown. And our people acted as guides for him for no money at all.

But you said that he gave away territory?
He did not give away territory. He just gave names, names to the territories.

Are there any other sites that you remember, other than the one at Morice Canyon?
MR GRANT: About what? He has described a number more than that.
MR MILNE: He described the ones at Francis Lake, and I had asked him about the sites between Moricetown and Francis Lake, and he said there was one at Morice Canyon.
     Do you remember any others?
MR GRANT: He said our people have good fishing spots and that's where they fish for salmon with nets and then he described one area, Morice Canyon near Morice Lake.
MR MILNE: Now I'm asking if he can describe any other areas.
MR GRANT: Between Moricetown and Francis Lake.
MR MILNE: Yes.
THE WITNESS: *Wherever people have territories near lakes people usually fish for salmon using nets – lakes which are on their territories.*

Have you ever seen a map of the fishing sites in Hagwilget Canyon?
I haven't seen maps of fishing sites in Hagwilget, but I know where all the platforms and fish traps were.

Have you seen a map of the sites in Moricetown Canyon?
No, I haven't seen maps of the Moricetown fishing sites in Moricetown.

I think that a long time ago, when we first started this and you were going through your direct examination, Mr Grant asked you if you had seen a map made by Alfred Joseph. It's been a long time, and I appreciate the amount of time that's gone by, but do you remember Alfred Joseph showing you a map of fishing sites in Moricetown or Hagwilget Canyon?
The map Alfred showed [me] are the maps from today, and they are done properly. There are no maps from the earlier times.

Did you give Alfred Joseph information to help him make those maps?
When the maps were first done, there were some mistakes on it. So he brought them here to me and I gave him the information, and from the information I gave him, that's what he put down on the maps.

MR MILNE: For the record, Mr Grant, I'm requesting production of those maps.
MR GRANT: They were prepared for litigation on solicitor-client privilege. However, I note your request. They will be in lists of the documents at least under privileged documents.

MR MILNE: Ask Mr David, if you would, whether he wants to take a short break or to continue on?
THE INTERPRETER: He says: *I'm fine, continue on.*

Do you know if there are fishing sites where only your people are allowed to fish?
MR GRANT: What do you mean by 'your people'?
MR MILNE: The Wet'suwet'en, such that other Indians or whites are not allowed to fish there.
MR GRANT: Under the traditional rules, or Fisheries Act?
MR MILNE: Let's go under the traditional rules first.
MR GRANT: So you are asking if he knows of sites where, under traditional Wet'suwet'en laws, only Wet'suwet'en are allowed to fish. Is that correct?
MR MILNE: That's right. And those are today's sites.
In the earlier days our people would give salmon to the white people for no charge. And once there became law by Fisheries, this was all outlawed.

Are there sites where your people only fish under white man's law?
MR GRANT: Before he answers, I want to object to that, for the record, because it's a question of law and irrelevant.
The only area I know of that only Indians are allowed to fish is in Moricetown Canyon, and I don't know about any other areas.

Mr David, you said in your direct examination that you were baptized by Father Morice, and that that took place I believe some time around 1896. Is that correct?
Yes, that's what I have been told.

Did you attend church as a child. Do you remember?
MR GRANT: Object on the grounds of relevance.
Yes, I did. I still go now.
In reply to the objection, it's directed towards section 55, subsection (e), Amended Statement of Claim, which deals with spiritual beliefs of the territory.
MR GRANT: My objection still stands.
MR MILNE: So you still attend church now?
Yes.

Do you know if your parents attended church?
Yes, they did. And we don't go to any other church except for the Catholic Church.

Where was the church that your parents attended?
Hagwilget, there was an old log building church.

Did you go to that church as well?
Yes.

What church do you go to now?
Church in Moricetown.

And you were married in a church as well?
Yes, the church in Hagwilget, at the new church.

And did you have your children baptized in the church?
Yes.

MR GRANT: My objection goes to all of these questions, for the record, rather than interrupting you for each question.
MR MILNE: Thank you, it's noted.

The Statement of Claim that has been filed by the Wet'suwet'en, in paragraph 55, says that the Wet'suwet'en or the plaintiffs conserve the resources within the territory, and that's within the Wet'suwet'en and Gitksan territory. What particular things did the Wet'suwet'en do to conserve the resources?

MR GRANT: I think you should specify the resources you want him to answer to.

MR MILNE: Let's deal first with the fish.

MR GRANT: So to clarify, your question is what did the Wet'suwet'en do to conserve the fish within the Wet'suwet'en territory. Is that correct?

MR MILNE: Yes.

The Wet'suwet'en would fish for salmon until the 15th of August. After that date, they ceased all fishing, and they would go to their mountains for mountain goat. And when they come back, the meat in the mountain goat and some of the smoked salmon would be used at feasts.

Did you stop fishing on that date because you had to go to the mountains, or because you thought it was good for the fishery resource to stop fishing then?

By that date, most everyone has enough supplies for the winter. So they quit fishing, and that's when they go up to the mountains for goat, and that meat is dried and used at feasts.

How do the Wet'suwet'en conserve the berries within the Wet'suwet'en territory?

The berries would be dried in the summer, and [in] the winter they were shared with people who came to feasts.

I think there is a distinction here between preserve and conserve. What did the Wet'suwet'en do, if anything, to make sure that the berries would always be available to them, they would always be grown?

In their territories, there are many berries and people only pick what they need.

Only need for personal eating, or only what they need for personal eating and other things like trade?

Berries are picked for their own use, as well as for feasting. And they quit picking berries when they get soft.

Do you know if the Wet'suwet'en managed the berry patches by doing things like cutting them back or burning the area or anything like that?

MR GRANT: You mean cutting back the bushes?

MR MILNE: The bushes, yes.

Our people protected the berry patches from forest fires. It was with the com-

ing of the white prospectors that they did not look after the fires and burnt all the berry patches, which ruined them.

How did you protect the berry patches from fires?
In the early days, our people did not want to burn berry patches, because there were animals that they trapped there and it was with the coming of the white prospectors who didn't look after their fires, that forest fires were started.

And is there anything in particular that the Wet'suwet'en did within their territory to conserve the trees and other plants, generally speaking?
MR GRANT: Other than berries?
MR MILNE: Other than berries.
The trees were protected from forest fires by protecting the roots. They didn't want the trees to die, so they would make sure the roots of the trees always received enough water. Because if they didn't, the trees would die and then the animals would die along with the dead trees.

How did you make sure that the trees got enough water?
My father, sometimes they would put snow around the trees so that they would get enough water. When my father died, I did the same. Those trees belonged to us. Now the government has come. They claim it as theirs and they are making a lot of money off the trees.

These trees that you put snow around and where your father put snow around, where were they? Were they in the forest, in your garden, what?
The campfires would be put out to make sure that they don't start a forest fire.

But you were telling me about your father and yourself at times putting snow around the trees to give them water. How many trees would you do this around? Did you go through the forest and put snow around the bottom of the trees?
MR GRANT: Which question do you want him to answer?
MR MILNE: Let's deal with the first one.
How many trees would you have done this for and, secondly, where were they? In the forest or somewhere else?
THE INTERPRETER: Okay, I misunderstood him. He said: *The snow was put around the campfire so that it doesn't spread, not around the trees.*

Thank you. And how did the Wet'suwet'en conserve the animals within the Wet'suwet'en territory?
For the beavers, they are similar to humans, they live in the house like this. And after you kill two or three, you stop. And they always quit before the 1st of May because they were ready to have their young.

Do you have any other examples of animals that were conserved by the Wet'suwet'en?

MR GRANT: Other animals?

MR MILNE: Other than the beaver.

It was the same for the other animals, similar to the beaver I just described. You kill few and you don't kill them all, and at certain times of the year you don't kill the female, and at certain times of the year you don't kill the male. So that they are able to reproduce.

You have described how the territory of the Wet'suwet'en is transferred from one person to another. And that transfer takes place along matrilineal lines. This is going to be a very broad question. Do you know of any exceptions where the territory was not transferred by matrilineal lines? And to limit the question, I'd like to deal, say, within the last 40 years, first of all, since the Second World War.

MR GRANT: Are you suggesting it was transferred father to son or –

MR MILNE: Other than matrilineally.

MR GRANT: Any other way?

MR MILNE: Other than caretaking as well.

MR GRANT: Could you read that question back, please? I'm not sure if I want to object to that.

THE REPORTER: Question: 'You have described how the territory of the Wet'suwet'en is transferred from one person to another. And that transfer takes place along matrilineal lines. This is going to be a very broad question. Do you know of any exceptions where the territory was not transferred by matrilineal lines? And to limit the question, I'd like to deal, say, within the last 40 years, first of all, since the Second World War.'

MR GRANT: I just wondered if I could, given the question has been reread, I wonder if you can phrase your questions within a limitation. I'm not objecting to the area you are focusing on as irrelevant. I think [the way] the question is framed, it's quite confusing.

MR MILNE: As I say, it's a very broad question.

MR GRANT: And what I'm wondering if you are trying to focus on the father-to-son inheritance as an example, or brother-to-sister, or any other?

MR MILNE: I hadn't actually sort of considered the specific examples, because for me to go through each one, I think, would be almost impossible, given the relationships between parties. But what I want to put to the witness is are there exceptions that he recalls to the tradi-

tional transfer of territories in exception to the matrilineal transfer of
territories?

MR GRANT: Can we go off the record for a moment, please?

OFF THE RECORD DISCUSSION

MR GRANT: For the record, I had asked for a break because the way the
last question was framed, I think it was confusing and potentially misleading, not only to the witness, but possibly to Mr Milne. And as
result of that, I have discussed with Mr. Milne what he is seeking and
he has framed the question more on the lines of what he is trying to
determine.

MR MILNE: Thank you for your assistance.

Mr David, the normal way for transfers of territory to take place is
matrilineally? In other words, transfers within the house, correct?
*Names and the lands are transferred through the mother's side, and this is
getting very difficult.*

Are you getting tired, Mr David?
Yes.

Maybe I can just –
I want you to finish once and for all.
I'm getting there, and I'll be done very shortly, probably before lunch.
If we continue until lunch, I believe I will be finished by then.

THE INTERPRETER: *And he said for you to finish.*

MR MILNE: I'll do my best.

Do you know of any transfers of territory within your house, well no,
from your house, that may have gone to someone outside of your
house?

MR GRANT: In his lifetime?

MR MILNE: In his lifetime, firstly. Secondly, anything he may have heard
of.
*That is not the way the business is done. It usually goes through the mother's
side. In some cases the spouses are allowed to go into other people's territories
with permission only for a year. After that it ceases.*

Have you ever heard of the territory not being transferred on the
mother's side?

MR GRANT: Within the mother's side?

MR MILNE: Within the mother's side?

*No, I haven't. I have heard of some instances before my time, and it's very dif-
ficult for me to speak about.*

Is it difficult to speak about because it's before your time?
*Yes, and the reason I'm reluctant to talk about this is because it was before my
time and I don't know whether I will be telling the correct version, a different
version. And I don't want to talk about anything that I'm unsure of.*

Was this territory from your house, the transfers that you have told us
about that may have occurred before your time, were those transfers of
territory from your house?
*It was people not from my house, and it happened before my time, and I didn't
see.*

Do you know from what house it happened?
*No, I don't know. The only thing I will tell you is about the things that I know
of.*
MR MILNE: We are very close to the end of the videotape and if [we]
want to break now for change of that tape, we'll break and I'll review
my notes and we may be able to end at that point.

SHORT RECESS

UPON RESUMING
MR MILNE: I have a piece of paper with some Indian names written on
it and it's divided into three columns. One is Clan, the other Head
Chief, and the other House. This document was given to me by Mr
Grant as a result of my request last time we were here, for relating the
names of the Clan to the Head Chief to the particular House. And this
is, as I understand it, the result of a great deal of time-saving from the
point of view of the defendant and the plaintiff. This is the result of an
interview with Mr David, and this is his information or his knowledge
of those three items. And in order to get it into evidence, I'm just going
to have the interpreter go through each area with Mr David, and then
we'll have the paper marked as an exhibit.
MR GRANT: Just for the record, you have given leave for him to be interviewed prior to the completion of the cross-examination, and I'll
arrange for that interview to take place. And this is what I understand
his evidence to be on those three factors.
MR MILNE: Thank you.

Mr Interpreter, would you put that information to him and make sure
his evidence coincides to what is on that paper?

THE WITNESS: *Yes, all this information is correct as I told you.*

MR MILNE: Thank you. We'll have that marked as Exhibit 21, I believe.

EXHIBIT NO. 21 – piece of paper listing Clans, Head Chiefs, and Houses.[1]

MR GRANT: For the record, that's my handwritten notes. I will endeavour to have a copy of this typed out to be attached to the back of the exhibit as well, and to be reviewed by Mr Milne.

MR MILNE: I think that's a good idea for the ease of reading. Well, Mr David, those are all of the questions I have of you on the cross-examination. I would like to thank you for putting up with me for so long. Perhaps you could translate that to him.

And, Mr Grant, just to review some of the items that I have requested production of, and I understand you may have some objection to some of them, one is the map of fish sites that was apparently in the control of Alfred Joseph.

The other is the map, which is referred to and was used in other judicial proceedings, of the trapline and which is referred to in Volume IV, page 44 at line 29 [4: 211 above].

And the other one is [if] you come across the map that was apparently in the possession of David Dennis, which the evidence I think shows that it was made around 1902.

MR GRANT: The map of the fish sites, which fish sites are you referring to?

MR MILNE: This witness only gave evidence of the ones in Moricetown, as I recall, on the cross-examination. In direct, I believe he did give some evidence and was shown photographs of fish sites in Hagwilget Canyon. So if there is a map of any of those sites, I would ask to have it produced. And other than that, I think we can adjourn for your re-direct.

MR GRANT: Yes, and your cross-examination is finished. You are just requesting production of these documents for the record.

MR MILNE: That's correct.

MR GRANT: I suggest then we adjourn until tomorrow morning at 9:30, 9:30 or 10:00 o'clock for re-direct. I don't believe re-direct will be that long.

MR MILNE: Okay.

PROCEEDINGS ADJOURNED AT 11.35 A.M.
TO BE RESUMED TUESDAY, 29 APRIL, 1986[2]

Redirect Examination of Johnny David by Peter Grant, 29 April 1986

VICTOR WILLIAM JIM, Wet'suwet'en interpreter, previously sworn.

JOHN DAVID, witness called on behalf of the plaintiffs, previously sworn, testifies as follows:

UPON COMMENCING AT 9.40 A.M., 29 APRIL, 1986

RE-DIRECT EXAMINATION BY MR GRANT:

Johnny, at the end of yesterday, just at the conclusion of your cross-examination, there was a list presented, which was Exhibit 21. I have taken the liberty of arranging for a typed copy of that list with the three columns not in exact order: The Head Chief, the Clan, and the House.

The only difference between that list and the handwritten list is the English names of the Chiefs and translation of the names of the Houses are included. I would like the interpreter to go through this list, which I have shown to Mr Milne, and to check with you as to whether or not that list, this additional list which is typed, is correct. You have read everything on the typed list I have given you to him?

THE INTERPRETER: Yes.

MR GRANT: I wonder if we could refer to the handwritten list as Exhibit 21A, and this Exhibit 21B.

MR MILNE: How about calling it Exhibit 22?

MR GRANT: So the typewritten list that's been read to Johnny David and he agrees with everything on that list –

THE INTERPRETER: Yes he does.

MR GRANT: – that will be marked Exhibit 22.

EXHIBIT NO. 22 – Typewritten list of Exhibit No. 21[3]

MR GRANT: Just the other continuing documentary for the record is that in Action No. 40/82 in the Smithers Registry, in the County Court of Prince Rupert, a map was tendered as an exhibit and I don't yet have the map, but I now understand that I will be able to get it and this was the map referred to by Johnny David.

MR MILNE: That was the one that was created for the trapline areas?

MR GRANT: Yes.

Exhibit 22

Johnny David: Houses of Head Chiefs Exhibit 74FF [retyped as submitted]

Head Chief	Clan	House
Hag Wil Negh Sylvester Williams	Laksilyu includes Kilwoneetz	Ginehklaiya House of Many Eyes
Wah Tah Keght Henry Alfred		Tsekalkaiya House on Top of a Flat Rock
Wah Tah Kwets John Namox		Kwan Beah ya House Beside the Fire
Goohlaht Lucy Namox	Gilserhyu	Yatsowitan Thin House
Knedebeas Sarah Layton		Yatsadkus Dark House
Samooh		Same house as Knedebeas
Gisdayway Alfred Joseph	Gitdumden	Kaiyawinits House in the Middle of Many
Madeek George Naziel		Kyas-ya Grizzly House
Woos Roy Morris		Kyas-Ya Grizzly House
Kweese Florence Hall	Tsayu	Tsayu Beaver House
Smogelgem Leonard George	Laksamshu	Saya Sun House
Kloumkhun Johnny Mack		Midzi-ya Owl House – also used for Smogelgem

Now, with respect to Exhibit 22, which we have just dealt with, did you describe that list of the names of Houses to Victor Jim on an earlier occasion? In other words, did you give him that list?
THE INTERPRETER: *Yes.*

And just to be clear, because you couldn't recall at an earlier stage, do you now remember who holds the name Goohlaht?
Pat Namox's wife.

Is her name Lucy?
Yes.

Mr Milne asked you a number of questions about lands that were pre-empted for you in 1920. Did the government, did anybody, ever tell you that those lands were as compensation for Smogelgem's territory or Kilwoneetz territory?
No.

You have described your role as a Chief with respect to Kilwoneetzen territory with Hag Wil Negh and also as caretaker of Smogelgem's territory. When you requested the pre-emption lands, did you request those lands on behalf of the Kilwoneetzen people?
I asked for the lands for myself.

Did you ever believe that in order to get that land, you had to give up your claim to Kilwoneetzen territory?
No.

Did you ever believe that to get that land, you had to give up your claim to be the caretaker of Smogelgem's territory?
No.

After you acquired this pre-emption, and I'm referring to Exhibit 'A' for identification, with reference to the block of Lot 3327, Range 5, Coast District, did you continue to use Smogelgem's territory and the Kilwoneetzen territory?
After I got the land, I still used the two territories and I didn't go trapping or in lieu of pre-emption.

I'm sorry, [re:] 'I didn't go trapping – in lieu of pre-emption.' Is it correct that you continued to trap as well as use this pre-empted land?
Yes.

Okay. You recall that at some time a government representative asked you about your trapping ground. Do you remember that? He asked you where it was, where you trapped?

I continued to trap and a game warden, Mr Muirhead, and a person who worked after him, I have forgotten his name, they all knew that I was trapping. I trapped on my own territory and the land is still ours.

You recall showing the boundaries of Smogelgem's territory to somebody from the government?

Yes.

Was that at the time that the government was registering traplines?

Yes, during the time they were registering traplines. When they were beginning to register traplines, I told them where the boundaries were and there was this one area that he didn't do correctly.

Did you show him the actual outer boundaries of Smogelgem's territory?

Yes.

Did you believe that by showing him those boundaries and the trapline being registered, that the government was recognizing Smogelgem's territory and your rights to it?

Yes.

Did anybody from the government tell you that they were not recognizing Smogelgem's territory at that time?

They would ask me questions and I answered for them concerning the boundaries.

Did anyone from the government tell you that they were not recognizing your rights to Smogelgem's territory at the time you showed them the boundary for the trapline purposes?

MR MILNE: I think he just answered that question.

MR GRANT: I don't think he answered it.

The game warden knew that it belonged to me. He also knew that it belonged to my father and that I took his place after he died.

You were asked by Mr Milne if the Wet'suwet'en people used to be called Gitksan-Carrier. Amongst yourselves, have your people, that is the people of Moricetown and Hagwilget, always been known as Wet'suwet'en?

The people from Hagwilget and Moricetown have always been called Wet'suwet'en, since they lived here all their lives.[4]

Were you ever, your people, ever called Carrier and, if so, who started to call your people Carrier?
I don't know who gave them the name. People's names are given to them according to the area they live and they can't be changed.

Can you explain what Wet'suwet'en means?
It's an old name that's been with our people from here and Hagwilget for a long time.

You were asked, and I think there was some confusion in the question, who was Gisdaywa before Alfred Joseph and your answer was Thomas George. I would like to clarify it. Do you know who held the name Gisdaywa before Alfred Joseph did? For the record, I'm referring to page 6–9, lines 14 to 17 [6: 278 above].
Thomas George.

You were asked how long it would take to get to the Kilwoneetzen territory and you said it takes two hours by car. Is that two hours from Moricetown?
Yes, from Moricetown. When we're trapping, we take our time.

You were asked on page 6–17, line 4 [6: 286 above], If there is any other territory of the Wet'suwet'en Chiefs you personally did not trap upon? Now, your answer was I think a triple negative. So I'd like to clarify it. Have you trapped on the territory of each and every Wet'suwet'en Chief some time in your life?
I know the territories of each of the Hereditary Chiefs. I know the names of their territories, and I have trapped with most of them. I go along with them and some have been my wife's relatives.

You indicated that your language has been written down. Was your language written down by Father Morice, that is the Wet'suwet'en language?
Yes, he did.

And before the white man came, was your tradition and your history all oral, that is, not in writing?
Yes, they did. Because not too many people knew how to read or write.

Mr Milne asked you a lot of questions about the kinds of work you did in your lifetime. I just want to follow up on that in this next series of questions. When you worked for the railroad, did you still hunt at the same time?
When we were laid off, I would trap. I worked all summer.

You said you trapped. Did you hunt and did you fish in those years that you worked for the railroad?
Yes, I continued to fish and trap. And what we fished and trapped is what we survived on during the winter months.

When you worked as a surveyor, did you continue to hunt, trap, and fish during those years that you were surveying?
When I was surveying, I would continue to hunt and trap [when] the job was done, or whenever I had time.

And did you fish at that time as well?
Yes.

When you worked at the Owen Lake Mine, did you continue to hunt, fish, and trap during the years you were at the Owen Lake Mine?
Whenever we had time, we would go hunting, fishing, trapping.

When you farmed that North Bulkley [area] and you had hay and cattle, did you still continue to hunt, fish, and trap?
When I was farming, in the evenings I would go hunting, trapping, or fishing for salmon and that's what we ate.

And when you worked at the sawmills, did you hunt, fish, and trap during that time?
Yes, I did.

When did you stop hunting, fishing, and trapping?
I quit when I began to get weak.

Was this when you became too old to do the work?
Yes, I quit hunting, fishing, and trapping when I got older and had trouble walking and when I got too old to hunt, fish, and trap, I got Moses, my son, to trap for me.

Based on what you have explained, would it be correct to say that the occupation you have spent most of your time in your life at, is the occupation of a trapper, a hunter, and a fisherman?
Yes.

And was all that hunting, fishing, and trapping done on your territory, that is, the Kilwoneetzen territory, or your father's, that is, the Smogelgem's territory, or was the majority of it done on those two territories?
The majority of my hunting, trapping, and fishing was done on Smogelgem's territory. He showed me the territory when I was a young man. When I

became too weak to hunt, trap, or fish, I showed my son Moses the territory
and he did the trapping and hunting for me.

You were asked about and described about things that were stolen
from your father by McGuinness. And you were asked why you didn't
tell persons in authority such as the Indian agent about what had happened. And you said 'The Indian agent didn't care about us.' When
you said that, were you referring to Mr Loring? Was he the Indian
agent that you remember as not helping you in those problems, or not
caring?
Yes, it was Mr Loring.

You were asked earlier if you ever had a fishing licence and you said
you didn't have a fishing licence. Then you said you only did when
you were down at the coast. Did Smogelgem or Maxlaxlex have any
Aboriginal rights or fishing rights at the coast?
MR MILNE: Objection. I think you are going to have to describe what
Aboriginal is. I don't know what it means. I'm not sure the witness
does.
MR GRANT: Ask him the question.
MR MILNE: Perhaps it could be phrased, 'Did the Wet'suwet'en have
any fishing sites on the coast'?
MR GRANT: Just put the question as I put it.
At that time many of our Indian people would go up there and they were given
licences and they would fish for salmon.

Did the Wet'suwet'en have rights under Wet'suwet'en tradition to fish
at the coast, and had the Wet'suwet'en actually fished at the coast before
the white man came?
Yes. Our people used to be invited to fish up there. They would go up by
steamboat. But now there are many Japanese and white people fishing and
they're slowly pushing the Indian people out.

Did you get fishing licences to fish in Smogelgem's territory or at Moricetown, or at Hagwilget?
No, we didn't require a licence. The land belonged to the Indian people and
they fished for salmon which belonged to them.

You referred to two relatives, Alex Long Charlie and another lady who
is partially blind and the wife of Francis Charlie, who were in the Nutseni territory. Are those two people or three people, are they Nutseni
or Wet'suwet'en people?
They're Wet'suwet'en.

You indicated earlier that your people let the missionaries enter your territory, or the missionaries came in. Were the Wet'suwet'en Chiefs aware when the first missionaries came that they would support the taking of Wet'suwet'en land by the white people?

MR MILNE: I have a problem with that question. I think you are asking him whether or not – it's implicit in the question whether or not the Wet'suwet'en Chiefs were aware that missionaries were going to support the white people, and it's certainly double hearsay for him to say what the Wet'suwet'en Chiefs may or may not have been aware of. So I object to the question.

MR GRANT: Okay, your objection is noted.

MR MILNE: I might also add, just before you give the answer to that question, I don't believe it's in evidence anywhere that the missionaries did support the white people in taking away the territory.

MR GRANT: He has given that evidence. He said that.

MR MILNE: Can you refer me to that?

MR GRANT: Not offhand. Go ahead with the answer.

We weren't aware that the missionaries were helping the white people take land. Many times they would tell our people to sign their names with an 'X' on a piece of paper. They didn't inform us what we were signing.

THE INTERPRETER: He is going to get paper.

MR GRANT: Off the record for moment.

OFF THE RECORD DISCUSSION

THE INTERPRETER: *He was asking if you want to hear about what happened.*

MR GRANT: Yes, go ahead.

In 1901, Father Morice and [the] bishop came from the east, and that is when the Wet'suwet'en quit potlatching because they were going to become Catholics. In the summer, in July, Father Morice and the bishop came to Moricetown. And at that time my father became church chief. He was first known as Chief David.

After he was baptized by the Catholic Church, he was given the name Chief Roosevelt. When he was baptized, I knelt beside him and the bishop baptized us all at once. And the bishop told me that the reason he had me kneeling beside my father is that I would speak after my father had died. And Father Morice was interpreting for the bishop and the bishop called all the Elders together and he had a document and he told all the Elders to come and sign with an 'X.'

Now, the Elders and the Hereditary Chiefs, as well as myself, all signed this document with an 'X.' And our people were not told why they were signing this document. And the priest covered the eyes of the Elders and Hereditary Chiefs while they were putting their 'X's' on the document.

After our people signed the document, the priest told them that they had become good people now and not to talk about anything. And shortly thereafter, about 1902, 1903, the white people began arriving in our territory. And there was at that time Mr Loring had begun working, and when our people would speak about their land they were put in jail, and it is these people who did that.

THE INTERPRETER: He said: *That's it.*

MR GRANT: Just for the record, the witness in the last part of his comment pointed to a book which he had in front of him which was opened to the front page, the title page, which was written in English on one side and French on the other, and entitled 'Carrier Prayer-Book Containing together with the usual Formularies, Hymns, Catechisms, Directions Relative to Various Points of Catholic Life by Rev. A.G. Morice, Stuarts Lake Mission, 1901.' He made no reference to anything inside it. It appears from examination inside that it's in Wet'suwet'en or another language and it's not with standard lettering. I'm just putting that on the record as it was in front of the witness and he pointed at the end to this book.

If my friend wishes a copy of the title page to go in, he is welcome. I will arrange for a photocopy. But I don't want to take this book away from the witness.

MR MILNE: I would be most interested to have copy of the entire book, if it could withstand photocopying.

MR GRANT: I don't think it can.

MR MILNE: If it can't stand photocopying, I think I would like to have the proceedings some other way, either as an exhibit or through some agreement.

MR GRANT: I have listed off the title page and that's the only page to which the witness has referred.

MR MILNE: Well, the entire book I think was refreshing the witness's memory and so I think that, for the record, I am going to ask for production of the entire book.

MR GRANT: The Witness opened it to one page only. He didn't make reference to any other pages.

MR MILNE: Anyways, my request, for the record, stands.

MR GRANT: And you would agree, Mr Milne, that you can't read anything inside the book beyond page 12 because it's in a formulation of language which neither you nor I are familiar with.

MR MILNE: That's correct. That's one of the reasons I want to have the book on the record so we can determine what the witness was refreshing his memory from.

MR GRANT: And you would agree for the record the witness had it only opened to one page?

MR MILNE: I don't know. I wasn't watching that closely.

MR GRANT: I was, and it's on the video.

When you were baptized at this service with the bishop, did you stop believing in the Wet'suwet'en's own spiritual beliefs at that time?
I did not give up my Wet'suwet'en spiritual beliefs.

MR GRANT: Just take a break for few moments.

SHORT RECESS

MR GRANT: You said that when the bishop and Father Morice came, the Wet'suwet'en quit potlatching. Did the bishop or Father Morice require you to burn the regalia at that time?
Yes, they did.

Before that time, was there a precedent within the Wet'suwet'en system for burning goods at potlatch?
Before my time, Andamanaak people who were dancing, they would throw the materials they had into the fire and I have just been told about this. It was way before my time. When they did this, they called it Stay ee deen lay – [that] was the name given for that.

Do your people potlatch today?
Yes.

And you potlatched at the time that you took the name Maxlaxlex that you have described to us in great detail?
Yes.

Have the Wet'suwet'en potlatched for most of your lifetime?
Yes, they did.

How long after the bishop and Father Morice were here did they start potlatching again?
It was about 1906 when they began potlatching again, where they start giving each other food and materials.

Johnny, Mr Milne and the government lawyers may want a copy of the book you have in front of you, and that book is open. Have you just

been using that book to refresh your memory as to the date of when
Father Morice came?
Yes, I did. And I considered [it] a Holy Bible.

Have you referred to the book for any other purpose today other than
that date?
Yes, just the date.

Would you mind having the interpreter hold the book up so that we
can put the cover page you have been looking at on the video? For the
record, I have requested the video operator to focus in on it so it's visible on the video. Now, could you please turn it to a few sample pages
throughout the book, part-way through.
MR MILNE: Now we're referring to the rest of the book, aren't we?
MR GRANT: I'm just having it on the video. And maybe three-quarters
of the way through. Thank you. You can close the book and give it
back to Mr David.

You were asked some questions about some of the other Chiefs, the
Wet'suwet'en, and one name which was mentioned was Bill Alec. Did
Bill Alec hold a Chief's name?
THE INTERPRETER: He asked me where he lived.
MR GRANT: If you can't recall, that's all right.
No, I don't know that. I know Peter Alec and Thomas Alec, but not Bill Alec.[5]

You were asked whether or not the Wet'suwet'en people took any
action as a result of the white man taking land. Have you heard of a
meeting which was held, or were you present at meeting which was
held in 1909 at Hagwilget with regard to the land problems of the
Wet'suwet'en? You indicated I think your father died around 1907, so
this would have been a couple of years after that, 1908. This would
have been one year after your father's death?
I was not there at the meeting, but I did hear about it.

Tell us what you heard about the meeting.
All I know is they talked about the land.

Did you know a man named Chief MacKenzie, who was alive at that
time?
My father's brother, he became Chief and he was probably at the meeting.

Did he become Chief when your father died?
Yes. Now he is a young man. Before they did not put me in.

Do you know a man who is called David Francis?
THE INTERPRETER: He is asking me: *[Is] that Tyee Lake David?*

Did you know Tyee Lake David to also have the name David Francis?
Yes.

Did you know a man named James Yami?
Yes, I knew Yami. It's an old name.[6]

Was he Wet'suwet'en?
Yes, he was Wet'suwet'en.

Did you know Francis Lake John?
Yes, I knew him.

And Bill Nye?
Yes.

Do you know an Indian named Losier?
Yes, I know Losier.[7]

Was he Wet'suwet'en?
Yes, he was Wet'suwet'en.

Do you know whether or not he was driven off his land?
Yes, he had land at Two Mile and he was put in jail for speaking up about the land. And it was MacKenzie who got the land.

Was this MacKenzie a white man?
Yes, a white man.

Do you know if he threatened MacKenzie, that is, if Losier threatened MacKenzie when MacKenzie tried to take his land?
No, he did not threaten him. They called the law on him and he was put in jail. Now we see how white people have been playing around with us.

Do you know if Yami had lost land or had his houses burned by white people?
I don't know.

Do you know a place that was named as Lyetate?
Lyetate is just above Buckley Ranch.

Does that mean a crossroads in Wet'suwet'en?
It means where the roads meet. The road comes from here and one from Francis Lake and they meet.

Did Lame [Arthur] Michell have any land at Lyetate?
Lame Michell did have a land area that is now known as Barrett Lake. They had built a home for Mr Thompson. Problems developed from that, and Lame Michell and his family were kicked off the land and put in jail.

Did you know a man, and I don't know his last name, but his first name was Patrick and he had a place on a lake called Beaver Dam Lake?
THE INTERPRETER: He is asking me: *[Is] that what's now referred to as Graveyard Lake, across Topley.*

Is what you are calling Graveyard Lake the same as Alcott?
Yes. There is two graveyards there and that's why our people gave it the name Alcott [Alxkat] and that is what is now referred to as Graveyard Lake.

Is that in Kela's territory?
Kela is buried there. Kela and his brother.

Do you know whether or not Isaac's place was burned by a white man?
No, I don't know.

Did you know of a man named Peter, an Indian person who had cabins burned by white people?
Peter lived at Hatt Lake, and they did burn his house down. White people had no respect for the Indians. They took everything that belonged to the Indians, and they did not look upon the Indians favourably.

Do you know of a man named Billy Clark, a white man? Did you ever hear of him having anything to do with Isaac, Patty Isaac's father?
Yes, I did.

What did you hear about what Billy Clark did?
Bulkley Lake Isaac came back to his land to do some haying. They found Billy Clark there. Billy Clark told them that he had bought the land off the government and he told Isaac to leave and chased him off his land.

Had Isaac had a house on that land that Billy Clark took?
Yes, he had a smokehouse and that was burnt down.

Do you know where Isaac moved to when he was thrown off the land?
For one year he lived here in Moricetown. After a year here he moved to Broman Lake.

Were his wife and children in the smokehouse when it was burned?
They burned the smokehouse while they were here in Moricetown.

Is Broman Lake what's also known as Old Woman's Lake?
Yes. It is referred to as Old Woman's Lake and Isaac had land below there in the field and that's where he was chased off.

Did you know of a man named Chief Tibbets?
Yes.

Was he a Wet'suwet'en Chief named Gitdumskaneese?
Yes, that was my father's father.

It was your father's father?
Yes, his sister's son.

Just to get this clear, was Chief Tibbets your father's father's sister's son?
Yes.

Did you know a man named Old Andrew?
Yes, I knew him.

Where did he live or where was his land that he lived on?
Ootsa Lake. He had a trapline and he also had a house in Hagwilget.

What Clan was he from?
Gilserhyu [Frog Clan].

Did you know a man named Little Isaac?
Yes, I knew him, and he was also Gilserhyu.

Where was his territory?
His father's territory [was] near Francis Lake.

OFF THE RECORD DISCUSSION

Now, I have just asked you about a number of people. The last one I believe was Chief Tibbets, and I'll refer to them. Chief Tibbets – I'm sorry, maybe the last one was Little Isaac. Little Isaac, Old Andrew, Chief Tibbets, Old Isaac, Old Patrick, David Francis, were all of these people alive in 1909? That is the year after your father's death, to your knowledge?
Yes, they were.

Do you know if they protested against the white man coming onto each of their lands?
Yes, they did.

Did you know a man named Yami Royce?
No.

Did you know a person whose name was Yami who was related to Caspit, Jimmy Michell's father?
Yes, I knew him.

And did he have land? Was his territory near Francis Lake?
Yes.

Was he alive in 1909?
Yes.

Do you know if he protested the white people coming onto his territory?
Yes.

Did you know a person who [lived] on a lake known then as Trout Lake near Francis Lake?
Yes. That area around Trout Lake, Trout Creek, Gisdaywa, his wife and family had lived in that area.

Was he alive in 1909?
Yes, he was alive.

And did he protest the white people coming onto the land?
Yes.

Do you know of a man whose name was Nachlach who had land near Owen Lake?[8]
Territory near Owen Lake belonged to his father – Gisdaywa [was his] father.

And what was his name?
I have forgotten his name. I can't remember the name.

Did you know, you have already referred, I believe, to Matthew Sam. Did he have territory? Was his territory about six miles this side of Aldermere? Was that within his territory?
Matthew Sam's father.

Was Matthew Sam or his father alive in 1909?
Yes, they were.

Do you know if he protested the white people coming onto his land?
Yes. He looked after the territory near Telkwa River.

Do you know of a place known as Bob Creek?
I don't know where Bob Creek is.

THE INTERPRETER: And then he is asking me: *Which territory [is] it in?*

Do you know of an area?
Above Houston.

Was this in, was this in Mooseskin Johnny's territory?
The only Bob Creek I know is above Houston.

Is that in Mooseskin Johnny's territory?
No, it isn't. It's in Bill Nye's territory.

Was this area – was this an area where Mooseskin Johnny's son farmed?
Yes, Jim Mooseskin farmed there. Bill Nye's sister's son was Deer Mooseskin.

Do you know if Jim Mooseskin or Mooseskin Johnny protested the white people coming onto their lands?
Yes, white people were afraid of Mooseskin Johnny. They were really afraid of him.

Do you know of lands claimed by Joe Nass at the head of the Telkwa River?
Old Sam's youngest son looked after the territory in Telkwa River.

Was that Joe Nass?
Yes.

And do you know the name of a person named Yesane?
No, I don't.

Do you know if Joe Nass or Old Sam were alive in 1909?
Yes, they were.

And did they protest the white people coming onto their lands at the head of the Telkwa River?
Yes, they did. They told them no –
THE INTERPRETER: I'm asking him what he said at the end. I didn't quite catch it.
– The prospectors went through the territory. They didn't bother the land.

Do you know if Old Dennis and his three sons requested the territory around Dennis Lake in the Kilwoneetzen? I'm sorry, wanted the white man to stay off the land around Dennis Lake?
Yes.

And was Old Dennis alive in 1909?
Yes, he was alive. Old Dennis just has one son, two daughters. Steve Dennis is alive now.

And David Dennis is older than yourself?
Yes, his youngest son is a little older than me. He is still alive today.

But he cannot talk very well?
He can speak, but his mind tends to wander and if he still had his mind, he would be sitting here working with you today.

Did Old Dennis have three sons in 1909?
Old Dennis in 1909 had two sons, one had died, and three sisters. And now David Dennis is left.

Do you remember these people talking with you or around 1909, or even with your father before then, before your father died, about their frustration or their feelings about the white man coming onto their land and taking their land?
Yes, the people did talk about it. Whenever they did, they were put in jail and that is how the white people looked upon the Indians.

Do you know or remember a meeting held with the Wet'suwet'en Chiefs and a man named MacDougall in 1910 in which this land problem with the white people was discussed?
I heard about it, but I wasn't there.

In your cross-examination, you were asked questions about any wars with the Coast Indians. Now, Mr Milne didn't describe to you what he meant by Coast Indians. Can you tell me what you meant by Coast Indians and where those people live? In other words, do they have another name that you know them by?
Tsimshian.

Do you have a name for the Indian people that live at what's now Kitimat?
They're referred to as Tsimshian.

You were asked about feasts with the Nishga, about boundaries. And I know this may not have been about the boundary, but is it correct from your earlier evidence that the feasts in which Samaxsam's name was given to a Wet'suwet'en, was that a feast with the Nishga?
No, they did not hold a feast.

In your cross-examination, one of the broader questions Mr Milne asked you was [about] any other Wet'suwet'en who pre-empted land in their traditional territories – do you know of any – and you indicated Matthew Sam, Thomas George, and Bill Alec. Maybe you could

translate that and I'll go on. Now, aside from those people, do you know if August Pete acquired land through pre-emption?
Yes.

Do you know if Patty Isaac got land, or Old Isaac?
Patty Isaac lived on his father's territory in the area of Old Woman's Lake.

Do you know if he got a pre-emption?
No.

MR MILNE: Is the answer no, he doesn't know, or no, he didn't get pre-emption?
THE INTERPRETER: He didn't get pre-emption. Then he said: *[I don't] know what took place regarding the lands they're living on now at Broman Lake.*

Do you know if Jack Joseph got a pre-emption?
Yes, he did, across Smithers.

When you say across Smithers, you mean the other side of Smithers from here, or the other side of the river?
In the Canyon Creek area, Canyon Creek area up on the hill.

And was he a Wet'suwet'en?
Yes.

Did Round Lake Tommy get a pre-emption, to your knowledge?
Round Lake Tommy was kicked off his land at Round Lake. After two years he was given a pre-emption.

Now, with respect to those people, as well as Thomas George and Bill Alec, do you know if any of them accepted the pre-emption on behalf of their tribe in return for giving up the rest of their territory?
MR MILNE: Just before he answers that, I'm going to register my objection, for the record. It's impossible for him to know whether or not what was in the minds of people at the time they got the pre-emption.
MR GRANT: There is an extensive system here that's been described in detail.
No, they didn't. They paid school taxes, just like everybody else.

If any of those Chiefs were to agree to give up their territory in return for land from the government, other lands from the government or something else, would they have had to announce that at a feast?
MR MILNE: Under Wet'suwet'en tradition?
MR GRANT: Under Wet'suwet'en tradition?

No, they don't.

I referred you to Bill Alec. Was he also known as Peter Alec?
All I know is that Peter Alec had some land.

You were asked some questions earlier at one point in cross-examination, you described Stanley Morris as a Wet'suwet'en who was your sister's grandson. Could you tell me who is your sister who is Stanley Morris' grandmother? In other words, what was her name?
THE INTERPRETER: Now he knows who Stanley Morris is. Can you repeat your question?

Okay. You said earlier that his grandmother was, I believe what we had was your sister. Just a moment. When Mr Milne was asking you questions. You said 'Stanley Morris is Wet'suwet'en. He is my sister's grandson.' Can you tell the name of your sister of whom he is the grandson?
It's my wife's nephew.

Who was his grandmother then? Was his grandmother your wife's sister?
Stanley Morris' grandmother is Big Joseph or in English, Elizabeth Joseph.

And was she your wife's sister?
Yes.

You were asked questions about a war with the Nutseni a long time ago and you described that your people dug a trench above a canyon. And this is when the warriors were getting ready. Was that above the canyon at Moricetown here, or was it above the canyon at Trout Creek?
Right here in Moricetown, right near where the store is.

That's the handicraft store down by the canyon?
THE INTERPRETER: Yes.

Later you described how one of the Wet'suwet'en helped a Nutseni who was injured in that fight and let him go back home. Was there a settlement at which a rock was put up near what's now known as Quick to settle this dispute between the Nutseni and the Wet'suwet'en?
No, no, they didn't.

Was a rock put up there or marked there at some time later to settle a difference between the Wet'suwet'en and Nutseni?
I haven't heard of the rock.

You were asked about disputes over boundaries and you said that you didn't want to answer about disputes that had been settled. Under Wet'suwet'en tradition, is it not proper to talk about disputes with other Indian groups once they have been settled?
After it's settled, that is it. It's not talked about again.

Okay. If we could just go off the record for a moment, please.

OFF THE RECORD DISCUSSION

Yesterday you were asked about the [conservation] of different resources by Mr Milne for the government. And one of the things was how you conserved fish. Did the Wet'suwet'en, right up to the time of Louie Tommy, use traps as one of the means of catching fish?
Yes, he did have fish traps in the canyon.

Did the Wet'suwet'en pull the traps to allow a certain number of fish through so that there would always be fish coming back?
Yes, they would pull it out so the fish would go upstream to spawn and this was done every Saturday.

Was this done at Hagwilget as well as Moricetown?
Yes.

And was the Chief, were the Chiefs of the Houses the ones who decided when the traps would be pulled in the old days?
Yes, as well as the other people who had fish traps knew when to pull the fish traps.

Now, Mr Milne also asked you about conserving berries. Did the Wet'suwet'en people harvest from different parts of their territory each year so that there would be some years for the berries to regenerate themselves before they returned to that area?
Yes, that is what they did.

He also asked you, Mr Milne also asked you, about conserving animals in your territory. Did you harvest beaver or catch beaver from different parts of your territory in different years so that the beaver could replenish their population in the years in between, rather than taking all of the beaver from one area until there were none left?
Yes, that is what they did. They were saving some.

How many years would you leave an area where there were beaver before you would return to it?

You would continue checking the place and to see how many were there. If there were many there, then you would go back.

And what about with the berry grounds, how many years would you leave a berry ground before you would return to it after you picked the berries for one year?
They go to areas where [there are] plentiful berries and they don't go to areas where there are no berries.

Could we just go off the record for a moment?

OFF THE RECORD DISCUSSION

You were asked a number of questions by Mr Milne with respect to what the Chiefs wanted out of this land claim. Johnny, have you, or did your father or the Kilwoneetzen people, ever have an opportunity before this lawsuit to fully present the Wet'suwet'en case and describe your territory and your relation to the territory to representatives of the government of British Columbia?
Yes, they did. But they did not listen to the people. Every time it was mentioned they would say oh, we'll take care of it next year and next year never came.

Thank you, Johnny. Those are all the questions I have for you. Mr Milne may have a couple of minutes of questions.

Cross-Examination of Johnny David by John Milne, 29 April 1986

CROSS-EXAMINATION BY MR MILNE, CONTINUED:

Mr David, just for a qualification, when you mentioned or talked of potlatches, do you mean the same thing as feasts?
Yes.

Mr Grant asked you a question about Aboriginal rights on the coast for fishing. Do you know what the word 'Aboriginal' means?
MR GRANT: Which you objected to.
MR MILNE: Which I objected to. Do you know what the word aboriginal means? Well, maybe my question won't need answering if, Mr Interpreter, you tell me how you translated the word 'Aboriginal' to him first?
THE INTERPRETER: I explained to him that the white man [uses] the

word 'aboriginal,' and then I told him that when we say Aboriginal [Rights], we are referring to the land, the ownership of the land, and its resources.

Then, Mr David, When the word 'Aboriginal' is used by the white man, do you take that to mean by Wet'suwet'en tradition when it's in relation to your people?
MR GRANT: To mean what?
MR MILNE: By Wet'suwet'en tradition.
MR GRANT: I'm going to object to the question, for the record.
Yes.

The other thing that we talked about, or that Mr Grant asked you about, was the baptismal process of some of the Elders by Father Morice and the bishop. You said that people signed the document because the priest told them and that they had then become good people. Do you know what document it was that was signed?
They did not tell the people what they were signing. They just told them to come up and sign.

But do you know now what was signed?
We don't know what we signed.

Have you seen that document since the time of signing?
I haven't. No, I haven't seen it since we signed it. They had it in a book form and they took it with them when they left. The Natives didn't know what they were signing.

Do you recall if anybody asked what the document was about?
My father asked them what they were signing. They just told him to sign their names and they kept it a secret from them what they were signing.

Did your father ever tell you what he may have suspected he may have signed?
No, he didn't.

The book that you have referred to which you have called your Bible, who gave you that book?
Father Morice. My father bought it for me.

How old were you when you got that book?
I think I was about 10 years old. I was getting pretty strong then. Father Morice told me to hang onto the book throughout my life, and that's what I'm doing.

Mr Grant asked you questions about a large number of people who protested, in his words, the taking of their land, and some people who you described the white people as having burned their smokehouses or houses.

MR GRANT: I object to recross on this because it's been raised on cross.

MR MILNE: What I am going to ask him, if all of these people you have described, there are about 20 of them or so that have never been dealt with in cross-examination that is totally new that could have been examined on in direct, I might add. All I want to know is on some of those places you said that white people burned down the houses or the smokehouses. Did you see that happen, or is it from what people have told you?

People told me about it.

Those are all of my questions, Mr David. Thank you very much.

THE INTERPRETER: He closed by saying: *If you hang on to these words that I have told you, everything will be fine.*

MR GRANT: We'll complete this examination.

PROCEEDINGS CONCLUDED AT 12.10 P.M.[9]

Notes

Introduction

1 Of course Johnny David's commission evidence was not continuous from September 1985 to April 1986. In fact, he gave evidence on 17 separate days over this period: 20 September 1985 (vol. 1); 26–7 September 1985 (vol. 2); 17–19 October 1985 (vol. 3); 19–20 December 1985 (vol. 4); 29–31 January 1986 (vol. 5); 24–5 February 1986 (vol. 6); 21–2 April 1986 (vol. 7); and 28–9 April 1986 (vol. 8).

2 Several linguists had been hired by the Witsuwit'en and Gitxsan. Dr James Kari assisted the Witsuwit'en in preparing for *Delgamuukw*, gave testimony therein, and provided the spellings of place names in the *Gazeteer of the Gitxsan and Witsuwit'en Atlas* (1987). I use his spelling of Witsuwit'en. Dr Sharon Hargus, an Athapaskan linguist, has been working with the Witsuwit'en since 1988. Dr Bruce Rigsby is a linguist who worked with the Gitxsan over many years. Dr Hargus provided the correct spellings for the Witsuwit'en words and Dr Rigsby provided correct spellings for the Gitxsan words in the glossary. See the glossary for further information about their assistance in unlocking the meaning of words.

3 As I write, the problems within the Western/Anglo-Saxon/Celtic countries of Ireland and Northern Ireland remain unsolved; the Palestinian-Israeli conflict remains intense; genocide of peoples not considered fully human continues in Indonesia. We have reached a time when there is an International Declaration of Human Rights, which is an important achievement, but the level of mistrust and devaluation of the rights of 'the other' remains very strong (Said 1978). It is in the interests of all human beings for different interest groups and/or cultures to learn to communicate with, and listen compassionately to, one another. All peoples have the right to exist.

4 With 39 Gitxsan and 12 Witsuwit'en head chiefs as plaintiffs, the name for the case was shortened to *Delgamuukw*, the name of the first head chief listed, who is Gitxsan. The *Delgamuukw* website (*http://www.delgamuukw.org*) refers to the case as the Delgamuukw / Gisday Wa National Process, adding the name of the first Witsuwit'en head chief listed. The Witsuwit'en often refer to it as the *Gisdaywa-Delgamuukw* case.

5 Later, Michael Asch (1999: 445) was to write that '*Delgamuukw v. Regina*, from the trial to the Supreme Court judgment, represents a defining moment in Canadian law respecting Aboriginal peoples.'

6 I am using the terms *Indian, Native, indigenous, Aboriginal*, and *First Nations* interchangeably, as do scholars both Native (Alfred 1998, Monture-Angus 1995) and non-Native (Asch et al. 1997, Culhane 1998). The term *First Nations*, has found growing use, as in the Assembly of First Nations; it obviously has the purpose of pointing out the priority of the Native population on the North American continent. In volume 8 the lawyer for the government sought clarification of the meaning of these terms as well as Johnny David's understanding of his Aboriginal rights. Thus, *Delgamuukw* was not only about Aboriginal rights, but also about Aboriginal title.

7 These population figures are for the Crown colonies of Vancouver Island and British Columbia ca 1866 (McDonald and Joseph 2000: 198). McDonald and Joseph add, 'the estimate for the Aboriginal population is likely low, but it is clear that the political power of the colonial regime was clearly invested in a minority sector' (ibid). See Cole Harris (1997) for a discussion of the decline of First Nations populations in British Columbia, Georges Sioui (1992) for a discussion of the effect of population decimation among the Six Nations of eastern Canada, and Ward Churchill (1998) for a discussion of genocide in the Americas.

8 See Cole Harris (2002) for an excellent summary of the process British Columbia followed in creating reserves and restricting First Nations to them.

9 The potlatch varies considerably, as do the forms of kinship succession, on the Northwest Coast. The Kwakwakawak potlatch has been described by Boas (1920), Boas and Hunt (1921), and others. See the video *Potlatch: A Strict Law Bids Us Dance* for a dramatic portrayal of the impact of the outlawing of the Kwakiutl potlatch, and the resurgence and repatriation of potlatch regalia since that prohibition was lifted.

10 The Gitxsan people of the village of Kitwancool have remained vocal up to the present. They opted to make a separate land claim from the Gitxsan and Witsuwit'en, and have found themselves in particular conflict with the Nisga'a, who signed a treaty in 1999 with the federal and provincial governments claiming an area that the Kitwancool, or Gitanyow village, claims

as theirs. The *Luxhaans* court case launched by Gitanyow established that the 8 per cent of 'Nisga'a territory' earmarked by the province included territory claimed by the Gitanyow or Kitwancool Gitxsan people and that the government did not have the right to extinguish the Gitanyow claim to the territory without hearing the Gitanyow case. See Duff (1959) for the Kitwancool articulation of their rights to their territories, as recorded in their oral traditions, Sterritt et al. (1998) for a detailed depiction of contemporary territorial disputes, Mills (2000) for a brief description of the recent Gitanyow legal action in this regard, and Roth (2001) for a summary of the interplay of the Nisga'a and Kitwancool rights.

11 As Barbara Lane (1987) notes, surveyors of such lands were instructed to note when there were Indian dwellings on the land, but typically they did not do so. Lane notes further that Boer War scrip was often purchased by land speculators and changed hands several times before veterans arrived to take up occupancy, only then finding and displacing the Witsuwit'en residents.

12 Lane's *Land Transfers and Indian Preemptions in the Bulkley Valley: Summary of Opinion* details the tensions between the provincial and federal governments over land matters and preemptions. Preemptions, or the right to buy (what was considered) public land by settling on it, were in general denied to First Nations people. Lane notes that officials of the British Columbia Land Department were also reluctant to make preemptions for Indians dispossessed by Boer War scrip: 'Fulton to Ellison, 3 November 1909 – My personal opinion about these applications of Indians for preemption records is that in view of the present situation with regard to Indian reserves generally it might be unwise to grant them preemption records. The Province claims more land is held as reserves than is necessary for the Indians' requirements and it seems to me it would be rather stultifying this claim to allow them to take up preemptions as it would be somewhat in the nature of an admission that they had not sufficient lands in their reserves' (Lane 1987: 8). These tensions continued, as noted in the following letter from the province to the federal Department of Indian Affairs: 'Response from Renwick to Green, 22 November 1911: – "as the Department of Indian Affairs at Ottawa has already been advised, until some steps are taken by the Dominion Government with a view to securing the necessary re-adjustment of Indian Affairs generally throughout this Province it is not the intention of the Minister of Lands to consent to the creation of any more Indian Reserves nor to make any further withdrawal of lands from the settlement by Whites at the request of the Department of Indian Affairs"' (Lane 1987: 7).

13 See Henderson (2000c) for a trenchant explication of the continued colonial practices of Canada and other United Nations member states towards indigenous peoples in the United Nations. Leroy Little Bear's chapter 'Jagged Worldviews Colliding' (2000) gives further insight into the difficulties of getting the United Nations member states to endorse the rights of indigenous peoples.

14 I had been hired because the Gitxsan and Witsuwit'en appreciated the importance of having an anthropologist work as a cultural translator to try to make the meaning of the Witsuwit'en system of governance of their land comprehensible to a court that was not used to thinking outside its usual cultural parameters. The Gitxsan speak a language in a language group entirely unrelated to that of the Witsuwit'en, yet the two nations have maintained a close connection and intermarried over thousands of years. I was hired partly on the basis that the Witsuwit'en are Athapaskan speakers, and I had worked with the Beaver, or Dunneza, another Athapaskan First Nation in British Columbia, for many years.

15 Dara Culhane (1998: 29) comments on this ruling: 'In his 400 page Reasons for Judgment, the Chief Justice analyzed the testimony, reviewed the relevant points of law, and then dismissed the Gitksan and Witsuwit'en claim. No Aboriginal title or rights had pre-existed European settlement, he ruled; and even if they had, they had been extinguished by the simple fact of Britain asserting sovereignty. Treaties had not been made, nor compensation paid, nor Aboriginal consent acquired. Nor were they required, he ruled.' The colonial desire for land and resources meant the First Nations simply did not count. This is the essence of colonialism and Eurocentrism. Henderson has defined Eurocentrism thus: 'Among colonized peoples, the cognitive legacy of colonization is labeled "Eurocentrism" ... Eurocentrism is a dominant intellectual and educational movement that postulates the superiority of Europeans over non-Europeans. Modernists tend to think of Eurocentrism as a prejudice that can be eliminated in the same way that attempts have been made to eliminate racism, sexism, and religious bigotry. However Eurocentrism is not a matter of attitudes in the sense of values and prejudices. It has been the dominant artificial context for the last five centuries and it is an integral part of all scholarship, opinion, and law. As an institutional and imaginative context, it includes a set of institutions and beliefs about empirical reality. Habitually educated and usually unprejudiced Europeans accept these assumptions and beliefs as true, as supported by "the facts"' (Henderson 2000b: 58). The Witsuwit'en and Gitxsan know from experience that Eurocentrism is related to the concept of *terra nullius* (cf. Culhane 1998), which embraces the concept of diffusionism:

Classic diffusion asserts an emptiness of basic cultural institutions and people in much of the non-European world. This is known as the diffusionist myth of emptiness. This idea plays a role in the physical movement of Europeans into non-European regions, displacing or eliminating the native inhabitants. The propositions of emptiness make a series of claims, each layered upon the other: A non-European region is empty or nearly empty of people (so settlement by Europeans does not displace any Native people).

The region is empty of settled population: the inhabitants are mobile, nomadic wanderers (European settlement violates no political sovereignty since wanderers make no claim to territory).

The cultures of this region do not possess an understanding of private property, so the region is empty of property rights and claims (colonial occupiers can freely give land to settlers since no one owns it).

The final layer, applied to all the 'outside,' is an emptiness of intellectual creativity and spiritual values, sometimes described by Europeans as an absence of 'rationality.' (Henderson 2000b: 61)

16 The Gitxsan and Witsuwit'en often refer to the BC Supreme Court decision as *Delgamuukw I*, the BC Court of Appeal decision as *Delgamuukw II*, and the Supreme Court of Canada decision as *Delgamuukw III*. Although, strictly speaking, this does not follow accepted legal systems of citation, I have adopted their usage in the introduction because of its clarity.

17 The Liberal government of Gordon Campbell, elected in May 2001, cut funding to the BC Forest Renewal program, as well as to many other programs, with the result that such archaeological assessment is at this time seriously curtailed.

18 The Chiefs present at the meeting with the Dalai Lama were Antillibix / Mary Johnson, Hannamukw / Joan Ryan, Maas Gaak / Don Ryan, Satsan / Herb George, and Yagalahl / Dora Wilson.

19 Since 11 September 2001 the challenge to and the need for the Dalai Lama's message of compassionate non-violent dialogue as the appropriate response to terrorism and takeover of land has become greater. The Dalai Lama emphasized this again when he returned to Vancouver in April 2004. When asked how the conflict between Tibetans and the majority immigrant Chinese population in Tibet should be solved, the Dalai Lama said 'By talk' (www.DalaiLamainVancouver).

20 Much has been written about Chief Justice McEachern's decision (see, e.g., Asch 1992, 1997, 2001; Cassidy 1992; Cruikshank 1992; Culhane 1992, 1998; Daly & Mills 1993; Fisher 1992b; Mills 1995b, 1996, 2000, 2001; Miller 1992a, 1992b; Monet and Skanu'u 1992b; Ridington 1992; Roth 2002; Satsan / Herb

George 1992; Wilson-Kenni 1992). Chief Justice McEachern dismissed the evidence of the anthropologists who testified on behalf of the Gitxsan and the Witsuwit'en (myself, Richard Daly, and Hugh Brody) on the basis that we 'were too closely associated with the plaintiffs after the commencement of litigation' (McEachern 1991: 50). He was equally dismissive of my reincarnation research in his 1991 reasons for judgment, where he said that I was 'more interested in reincarnation than Wet'suwet'en culture' (ibid). While working for the Gitxsan-Witsuwit'en Tribal Council, I held a two-year Social Sciences and Humanities Research Council of Canada postdoctoral fellowship to study Witsuwit'en and Gitxsan reincarnation belief. A stack of my research papers were disclosed to the court in my testimony (see Mills 1998a, 1988b, 1994b, 1995a, Mills and Champion 1996, Mills and Slobodin 1994 for reports of some of the reincarnation research). I appreciate that this research challenges Eurocentrism. My opinion report *Eagle Down Is Our Law: Witsuwit'en Law, Feasts, and Land Claims* (Mills 1994a) addresses these issues.

21 *Once Upon an Elephant* by Ashok Mathur (1998) provides a wonderfully sardonic fictional depiction of Justice McEachern deciding a case in which the Hindu 'myth' of Ganesha comes alive in modern British Columbia, thus portraying of the vagaries of deciding the truth of oral (and written) traditions that play a huge part in the lives of many people.

22 Elsewhere (Mills 2000, 2001), I have expressed dismay at how the federal government has acted as if the *Delgamuukw* and *Marshall* decisions have no bearing on the legally sanctioned but emotionally charged issue of Mi'kmaq rights to sell fish.

23 Head chiefs are typically elders in Witsuwit'en society. Elders are very important at any time in Gitxsan and Witsuwit'en history; to a certain extent their government is a gerontocracy, where the elders are the high and head chiefs who have the responsibility of overseeing house territories and affairs. In addition the chiefs were particularly cherished as givers of evidence in *Delgamuukw*. They can speak eloquently about the importance of the land and why the Witsuwit'en and Gitxsan were seeking title; that generation had spent their lives traditionally, moving to their territories annually from the permanent village sites, using the trails, rivers, and creeks and the wildlife resources that abounded on the territories; they had also encountered some of the most difficult diminishment of their rights to their traditional territories. The resources are used extensively by the younger generations as well, who have the benefit of vehicles and circumstances. Like the generations before them, they continue to feel the impact of prejudicial policies and attitudes. See Wii Mukwillixw (1996) for a poi-

gnant portrayal by a Gitxsan wing chief of some of the difficult encounters regarding the rights to use his territory and its resources.

24 When the holder of such a title passes away, the title is passed on to the person he or she has designated, with the assistance of the clan. See Mills 1994a for a fuller depiction of this system, which includes pretenders to titles and the creation of new titles, as Johnny David describes in his testimony.

25 Besides reading the anthropological literature on the Witsuwit'en, my duties included reading the transcripts of tapes that the Witsuwit'en had made of chiefs talking about their territories. Witsuwit'en Gisdaywa / Alfred Joseph and Smogelgem / Leonard George had worked with Johnny David, making audio records of what he said about the territories, territorial sites, and boundaries and their Witsuwit'en names, and about the system of matrilineal hereditary chiefs who act as stewards for these territories. Alfred Joseph and Leonard George were selected to do this research with all the elderly chiefs to make sure that their treasure house of knowledge was recorded before they died. Alfred Joseph and Leonard George are head chiefs of their respective matrilineal houses, and both are fluent in Witsuwit'en, so they were appropriate people to do this research. They travelled to the traditional territories, where chiefs like Johnny David could point out territorial boundaries and place names. Some of these tapes were made years before the court case opened, in readiness to confirm that the Witsuwit'en, like the Gitxsan, had an ongoing system in which their watersheds belonged to different matrilineal houses for the use of house members and their spouses. They recorded information from a number of such chiefs, including Leonard George's mother, Mary George, who died before the commission evidence began. The Witsuwit'en chiefs who gave commission evidence after Johnny David were Huttakumay / Bazil Michell and Kweese / Florence Hall. The Witsuwit'en chiefs who gave testimony in court were Gisdaywa / Alfred Joseph, Dzee / Madeline Alfred, Wah tah keg'ht / Henry Aldred, Txemsim / Alfred Mitchell, Wigetimstochol / Dan Michell, Knedebeas / Sarah Layton, and Yaga'lahl / Dora Wilson (Monet and Skanu'u 1992: 66, 72, 172–3).

26 Linda Malinowski was the court reporter for volumes 1 and 4; Veronica Harper for volumes 2, 3, 5, 6, and 7; and Beverly Ferguson for volume 8. Veronica Harper transcribed the interpreter's voice more often than did the other court reporters. See the section on editing (pp. 3K–49) to understand how I have moved some of the interpreter's comments to the notes, to highlight that it was Johnny David who was giving the answers. In the notes to the commission evidence I have preserved how the court reporter transcribed the passages.

27 Strong words characterize both First Nations formal proceedings such as potlatches and court proceedings in the Western tradition. The drama of Western courts is popular in television and films. For examples of potlatch strong words see Anderson and Halpin's rendition of William Beynon's 1945 field notes of Gitxsan feasts (2002, especially 129).

28 See Monet and Skanu'u (1992) for poignant depictions of the difficulty plaintiff Mary Johnson had in singing her song in court. Justice McEachern noted that it could not be recorded by the court stenographer and that, in any case, he had a 'tin ear.' That has occasioned naxnox comic portrayals of the judge with a metal horn in his ear for hearing at some subsequent Gitxsan events, such as a pole raising in Kitsegukla.

29 See Katherine Buhler's MA thesis, 'Come Hell or High Water: The Relocation of the Cheslatta,' for a thorough depiction of how the Department of Indian Affairs backed the building of the Kenny Dam, which was promoted by Alcan against the wishes of the Cheslatta Carrier and Witsuwit'en people.

30 This was an interesting account of a case where the Natives, along with the white man they engaged, did make money from the mine. By contrast, Johnny spoke a number of times in his testimony about how the Witsuwit'en would find and report their discovery of minerals, only to be told they were no good. Then the settler society would move in and mine them, oblivious to the fact that they were necessarily on some chief's traditional territory, and that by Witsuwit'en law, his or her permission should have been sought, and he or she should have been given some of the proceeds.

31 In Witsuwit'en, the term 'grandfather' may refer to either the generation of one's parents' parents or one's great-grandparents, and is used by extension to refer to one who is related to through marriage. Most probably the person to whom Johnny was referring to here as his grandfather is Alfred Namox, who held the chief's name Namox and was renowned as an eloquent teller of the story of the Kweese War on the Kitimat (Mills and Naziel, forthcoming). Alfred Namox was Johnny David's classificatory grandfather in the sense of being married to a Laksilyu woman related to Johnny. Elsewhere, (in volume 8, the re-direct), Johnny uses 'grandfather' and 'grandmother' in their usual extended Witsuwit'en sense, saying that the current Caspit, Stanley Morris, was his grandson. When asked, Johnny explains that Stanley Morris is his wife's sister's grandson. He does not elaborate, but since his wife would correctly call him grandson, it is correct for Johnny to also call him grandson. What Johnny is saying in the statement that he had a Tsayu grandfather is essentially that he had heard and learned to tell the story of the Kweese War on the Kitimat from someone

authorized to tell it, and that he considered it part of his grandchildren's education to tell them the story.

32 The story of the Kweese War on the Kitimat as told by Kweese / Florence Hall will be published as 'Kweese War on the Kitimat: An Oral Tradition of the Cordilleran Witsuwit'en' by Antonia Mills and Warner Naziel (forthcoming).

33 See Mills 1994a: 149–52 for Jenness's depiction of the Mooseskin Johnny incident, which he dates as occurring in 1885 (Jenness 1943: 565) and for the account of Chief Lilloos / Emma Michell given in 1982.

34 See Fiske and Patrick (2000) for a description of the use of eagle down in the Lake Babine culture, which is closely related to that of the Witsuwit'en.

35 To get to the point more directly, I have edited out from this point, the following:

MR GRANT: Within the mother's side?

MR MILNE: Within the mother's side? See 8:862 for the full text.

36 See Cole Harris (1997) for a discussion of the population decline of First Nations peoples in British Columbia.

37 In Eagle Down Is Our Law (Mills 1994a) I explain the Witsuwit'en pattern of rotating from the houses at Tse Kya / Hagwilget and Moricetown / Kya Wiget in summertime to the houses out on the territories in the wintertime.

38 Leroy Little Bear discusses the difficulties of having indigenous rights reconized by the countries that form the United Nations. The challenges are identical at both the intranational and the international level: issues of power and the endorsement of the over-riding right of capitalism to make profits keep nation states from acting on the principles they know are correct. The absence of corporate conscience and the complicity of governments in endorsing endeavours that are carried out in ecologically unsound ways affect not only First Nationals but everyone.

39 Winona LaDuke, in her preface to Struggle for the Land, says, 'The native struggle in North America today can only be properly understood as the recovery of land rights which are guaranteed by treaties. What Indians ask – what we really expect – from those who claim to be our friends and allies is respect and support for those treaty rights' (1999:12). In British Columbia, this issue has been even the right to make treaties. Since British Columbia has endorsed the Treaty process in 1993, the question has been, on whose terms? See Henderson (1985) and Churchill (1999) for pieces that address the land rights issues on a broader basis, noting the absence of friendship in these relations.

40 Chief Hattakumex / Bazil Michell, mentioned other dramatic instances of eviction from Witsuwit'en homes in his commission evidence.

41 It is quite possible that the Babine were unaware that they no longer had jurisdiction over their traditional territories in the eyes of the government. Harris states that Peter O'Reilly, the reserve land commissioner, 'arrived in 1891 to allot reserves, and set aside 4,348 acres of land for the Babine' (D. Harris, 2001: 89). The Babine did not recognize this as giving up rights to their territories, just as the Witsuwit'en did and do not recognize the granting of reserves as the extinguishment of their rights to their traditional territories.

42 The rocks at Hagwilget were blasted by the Department of Fisheries in 1958–9, permanently destroying both Gitxsan and Witsuwit'en fishing sites at this location. The Hugh Brody video *On Indian Land* (1986) contains a poignant depiction of this incident by a chief who is now deceased. She relates how she had to be talked out of shooting the men doing the blasting, which would have escalated this event into confrontation unmatched by the Babine Barricade War.

43 As Johnny explains in volume 3, he had an arranged marriage to his maternal uncle's daughter, Miriam Dennis, the daughter of Old Dennis. Marriages between cousins were often arranged by the Witsuwit'en, as they reconfirmed the rights of the husband to his uncle's territory. By Witsuwit'en law, one has rights to use one's father's and one's father-in-law's territory, with their permission, while they are alive. One has rights to one's maternal uncle's territory in perpetuity. When a Witsuwti'en has been raised largely on his father's territory, his maternal uncle is all the more concerned to teach him to know the uncle's territory, as the nephew will use the land to support his wife, the daughter of the uncle. Johnny David's father also married someone who was a classificatory cross-cousin; but instead of it being his mother's brother's daughter, it was someone in the same house as his father's sister's daughter. We can deduce this from the fact that Johnny identifies his father's father as Gitdumskanees, one of the high chiefs of Ginehklaiya (House of Many Eyes).

44 Johnnyt David's uncle, Old Dennis, is undoubtedly the 'blind old man tottering toward his grave' Jenness (1943: 479) refers to as the teller of the story, in 1924, of how the Witsuwit'en chief Gyedamskanish was killed by the Nisga'a. Jenness, without naming the narrator, says he was 'one of the last survivors' of 'an episode that occurred around 1864' (478). Johnny David says Old Dennis 'went blind, was blind for 35 years' (2: 102). In volume 2 Johnny relates the story of this incident, which he had undoubtedly heard from Old Dennis. See volume 2, note 8 for Jenness's (1943: 478–9) version of this incident. The two accounts complement each other. In Johnny's account he names the name that was given to the Witsuwit'en in

compensation for the death of Gyedamskanish and his brother. He explains that the name Samaxsam was given to Old Tiljoe, the brother of the murdered Gyedamskanish, and was later passed on to Jimmy Michell at the time that Johnny David was given the name Maxlaxlex, upon the death of Old Dennis's brother Old Sam). Indeed in his commission evidence Johnny sings the song that was gifted with the name. In Jenness's account of the event, the giving of the feast name is not mentioned, nor does Jenness list Samaxsam among the Laksilyu feast names. Johnny David explains that the name was gifted by the Nisga'a after the event to prevent retaliation. Both intertribal marriages and feast names meshed the Witsuwit'en to their neighboring tribes.

45 Johnny identifies Jimmy Michell as the person who spoke about the territory at the feast where Johnny received the name Maxlaxlex when Old Sam died. Had Johnny's mother's brother, Old Dennis, who was also his father-in-law, been attending feasts, it would have been he who would have spoken about the territory that went with the name.

46 In defence of this procedure, I had initially made some temporary choices about how to shorten it from the copious and sometimes tedious court format into a format that preserves Johnny's statements and position – what in these postmodern times is called His Voice. Of course the closest to Johnny David's voice would be to hand the reader the ability to comprehend his original Witsuwit'en utterances. That unfortunately is a daunting task completely beyond my ability. The next best thing seemed to be to present the translation of his answers, but including often the leading question when necessary to comprehend the sense of his answer. Because the information initially came from Johnny David, it seemed appropriate to transform the transcripts of the commission evidence from the tedious court question/answer format into a simpler version that I hoped would capture the voice of Johnny David.

47 That way the reader can see the question that prompted the reply and read Johnny's reply, but is spared the length of reading the whole evidence in the longer question-answer format. That version is used in the text of Johnny David's commission evidence.'

48 Here is an example from volume 4. The transcript says: *When his father was alive he was the one that gave permission for other people to use the territory. Now that his father is gone it is Johnny himself who would give other people permission to use the territory.* This has been changed to: *When [my] father was alive he was the one that gave permission for other people to use the territory. Now that [my] father is gone it is [I] myself who would give other people permission to use the territory.* It is obvious that the latter reflects how Johnny said it: he did

not put himself into the third person. Nonetheless, the reading is different enough that I felt it useful to use square brackets and the notes to alert the reader to these changes.

49 My thanks to research assistant Norman Skelton for reinserting the 'okays.'

Volume 1

1 The reference was to a book of prayers in the Witsuwit'en language written by Father Morice.

2 Peter Grant is referring to the Statement of Claim, which listed the head chiefs of the Witsuwit'en and Gitxsan houses who launched the *Delgamuukw* court case in the name of the members of their houses. Johnny David (Chief Maxlaxlex) and Willy Simms (Chief Gitdumskanees) are high chiefs in the House Ginehklaiya (House of Many Eyes), with Sylvester Williams (Hag Wil Negh) as the head chief of that house.

3 In his preparation for his testimony Johnny David had previously explained that he was given the name Yaybestee at birth because he was recognized as the reincarnation of the former Yaybestee.

4 Pat Namox in fact took the name Wah Tah Kwets held by his brother John Namox – after his brother's death. Wah Tah Kwets is the head chief of another Laksilyu House – Kwanbeahya House Beside the Fire.

5 'D-S-E-E-'H' has been removed from this point as spelling is obvious.

6 The following redundant passage was omitted just before Grant's rephrasing:

> MR GRANT: Okay, I will just interrupt here. For the record, I've requested after the lunch break for the video operator to have his camera set up outside so that Johnny can point to that pole and then when we come in and go back on and to describe the crests on that pole. You can translate that to him but it's not a question.
>
> THE INTERPRETER: Want to say that again

7 The 'pardon me' was interjected by the interpreter, who had not included 'Mrs' before 'Mathew Sam' in the initial response. Johnny David is emphasizing the connection to Mrs Mathew Sam because her daughter is in the same house as she, rather than in the house and clan of her father, Mr Mathew Sam.

8 '(PROCEEDINGS ADJOURNED SINE DIE)
'I hereby certify the foregoing is a true and accurate transcript of the proceedings herein, to the best of my skill and ability: Linda Malinowski Offical Court Reporter' has been omitted for reasons explained in the introduction.

Volume 2

1 I have removed the following from the opening of volume 2:
   TRIAL EXHIBIT 74B – 24 & 27 SEPTEMBER, 1986
   Extracts from COMMISSION EVIDENCE OF JOHN DAVID, Volume II
   INDEX TO EXHIBITS 1 Photograph of Totem Pole dated October 25, 1976 by
   National Museum of Canada Stamp, negative No. 59526, Page 22.
   REPORTER'S NOTE: Wherever Laksilyn appears in this transcript it should
   be spelled LAKSILYU.'
   All references to *Laksilyn*, a typographical error, have been changed to
   Laksilyu.

2 Original text had 'THE INTERPRETER: And he said,' which has been removed
   from the beginning of this sentence.

3 'THE INTERPRETER: He said ... Okay he said that ...' has been omitted from
   the beginning of this sentence.

4 'THE INTERPRETER: Then he described' has been omitted from the beginning
   of this sentence. 'He said' has been taken out of the next sentence.

5 'THE INTERPRETER: Then he described a pole that is in Hagwilget' has been
   changed to 'There is a pole that is in Hagwilget'

6 'THE INTERPRETER: He said it was' has been omitted from the beginning of
   this sentence.

7 'THE INTERPRETER: Then Johnny said' has been omitted from the beginning
   of this sentence. 'And his children's blankets ...' has been changed to 'And
   her children's blankets ...' This is the only instance where the interpreter
   followed the Athapaskan and Witsuwit'en format of not marking gender in
   pronouns by using a masculine pronoun when a woman was referred to. In
   all other instances the interpreter, who is more than fluent in English, followed the English usage of making the gender agree with the person
   referred to. The next two references to 'THE INTERPRETER' in the original
   transcript have been taken out, as it is clear whose children Johnny David is
   talking about, and it is he who is saying that the display of the crest is similar to his blanket on the wall.

8 Diamond Jenness (1943: 478–9) records this incident, saying, 'they ... still
   remember with bitterness an episode that occurred about 1864. The story,
   as related by one of the last survivors, who in 1924 was a blind old man tottering toward his grave, throws an interesting light on the customs of the
   Indians at that time.' The blind old man who told of this event was
   undoubtedly Johnny David's maternal uncle, Old Dennis, who, as Johnny
   said in his commission evidence, 'went blind, and was blind for 35 years.'
   Jenness' account is as follows:

One winter when our people were starving, my family, together with my uncle Gyedamskanish [a Chief referred to by Johnny David, and also the name held by Johnny David's father's father], Bini, the Chief of the Beaver phratry [what Johnny calls Clan] and many others traveled overland to Gitlaxdamks village [New Aiyansh] on the Nass River to buy oolakan grease. Soon after our arrival my father discovered that one of the inhabitants bore the same title and crest as himself, and, claiming kinship, ordered me to lodge for the night with his namesake while he and the rest of the family lodged elsewhere. [Old Dennis's father was presumably Johnny's mother's father, namely Chief Spookx of the Gitxsan.] He came to the door early next morning and said to me, 'We have bought all that we want and will leave the village before noon.' So a number of us started back for Hagwilgate, and after traveling a few miles camped near a stump that supported a huge stone. I and some other youths tried in turn to push this stone over, and when it crashed to the ground under our united efforts we raised a shout of victory and returned to our camp.

Now some Gitwinlkul [Kitwankool] men who were passing heard our shouts and came to see what was happening. My father said to them, 'Our lads were merely pushing a stone off a stump.' But they answered, 'That was the gravestone of the late Chief of the village.' Greatly alarmed, my father begged them to keep the deed secret, but they immediately went to the village and spread the news everywhere. Then a woman rushed weeping into a house where some of our people were eating and cried, 'Why do we feast these wretches? They have disturbed the grave of our Chief.' About half our people, led by Bini, retreated inside another house; the rest hastened after us and told us to flee, because Nass, Kispiox, and Gitwinlkul Indians were all mustering in pursuit. We did flee, but the Nass natives overtook and captured those who were in the rear. One captive, a noblewoman named Anklo', they proposed to enslave, but she said to them, 'You cannot make me a slave, for I am the daughter of a Chief. If you carry me off as a captive, you must take also two slave girls for me to lean upon. Besides, why do you want to make me a prisoner? Neither I nor my family touched the grave, but Gyedamskanish yonder and his family.' They led her away nevertheless, and with her two slave girls to attend to her wants. A Kispiox Indian then disarmed Gyedamskanish, who said to them, 'Remember that I am a Chief. What are you going to do to me?' 'You must return with us,' they answered, 'to pay for the insult you offered the grave.' 'Take my brother also,' he said, 'We will die together'; and when they paid no attention to his words he turned and said, 'Come. Let us go together.'

The two men were led out onto the ice of the river and ordered to run up and down while their enemies mocked them and shot at them with guns. Gyedamskanish's brother dropped dead at the first shot, but Gyedamskanish himself, though frequently wounded, ran up and down for nearly half an hour before he fell with a bullet in his thigh. The Nass Indians then burned their corpses and returned to Gitlaxdamks [New Aiyansh].

Meanwhile an influential Indian had concealed another of my uncles inside a large chest, and when the villagers searched the house sat on top of it and refused to move away; his countrymen dared not disturb him on account of his high rank. My uncle's wife stood near him, grasping a large knife in readiness to stab the first man who molested her husband or herself, but no one laid a hand on her. Bini and the rest of our people barricaded themselves inside another house throughout the night, while their enemies threatened them from outside and occasionally fired off their guns.

Early the following morning the principal Chief of the village sent round word to all the Houses that the fighting should cease and that our people should move over to his house along a path strewn with the white eagle-down that symbolizes peace. Preceded by a messenger carrying a white feather, he then conducted them to our camp, a day's journey away, and we returned home without further mishap.

Some time afterward a party of Nass Indians came to Hazelton to conclude a peace with us. They assembled within the potlatch House beside a huge pile of blankets, and we went down from Hagwilgate and stood outside, myself and another youth, the nearest relatives of Gyedamskanish, in the forefront. After our enemies had presented us with a number of blankets, we followed them inside the house and ranged ourselves along one wall while they lined up against the other. Every man was dressed in his finest clothes and carried a gun and a knife, but, to prevent trouble, I and my companions sat in front of the Nass River Chief. As soon as we were thus seated, the two ringleaders in the murder approached us and placed a red-tipped feather on each of our heads to indicate that they intended to pay full compensation. Then one of them delivered a speech declaring that they wanted to make peace, and, shaking a rattle, danced and sang a sonel. The sonel that he sang is a special chant used by the Carrier, Tsimshian, Haida, Kitimat, Bella Coola, and other tribes whenever they make peace with each other. Though I know the words, I cannot understand their meaning, because they are neither in the Tsimshian nor the Carrier tongue.

As the man repeated the song, both his Nass companions and my own people joined in. I, for my part, rose to my feet and, to show that he was smoothing out the issue, held flat on my outstretched palm a tail feather from an eagle. But before the singing ended I thought to myself, 'They haven't paid us enough,' and I turned the feather on its edge. Immediately the man broke off his chant, and he added more blankets to those they had surrendered to us already. He then began his song anew, and this time I held the feather flat on my hand until he ended. Since we all felt too sad to hold a feast in common, my kinsmen, without further delay, gathered up the blankets and returned to Hagwilgate, while I and my companion, to cement the peace, stayed 4 days in Hazelton with the Nass Indians and danced with them each evening.

Two years after my uncles were murdered some of us went over to the Nass River, collected their bones, and deposited them on top of the pole at Hagwilgate. At the same time we brought back Gyedamskanish' widow, whom the Nass Indians had detained after her husband's death. (Jenness 1943: 478–80)

Jenness does not describe the title Samaxsam in his monograph *The Carrier Indians of the Bulkley River: Their Social and Religious Life*, from which this account is taken. Johnny David clearly names the title. (Jenness does give Maxlaxlex, and the other titles that Johnny David, Chief Maxlaxlex, describes.) Jenness's monograph was based on fieldwork from 1924 but was not published until 1943, when it came out as part of the Anthropological Papers series (No. 25) of the Bureau of American Ethnology, Smithsonian Institution. Johnny David would have heard of this event from his uncle Old Dennis. As his heir, he is entitled to tell the story.

9 'THE INTERPRETER:' has been omitted from the beginning of the sentence.

10 'THE INTERPRETER: He said' has been omitted from the beginning of the response.

11 'THE INTERPRETER: His father' has been changed to '*My father.*' 'He had told Johnny, that is what he is telling us now' has been changed to '*He had told me, that is what I am telling you now.*'

12 The following has been omitted, for reasons given in the introduction: '– EXAMINATION ADJOURNED AT 10.25 a.m. UNTIL TOMORROW. I hereby certify the foregoing to be a true and accurate transcript of the proceedings herein, to the best of my skill and ability. Veronica Harper (Ms.) Official Court Reporter: VH-Oct.12/85 B.C.S.R.A. #263.'

13 'THE INTERPRETER' They did call his name' has been changed to '*They did call my name.*'

14 'THE INTERPRETER: He is describing the name' has been omitted from the beginning of this sentence. Diamond Jenness (1943: 493) gives the meaning of Dikyannualat as 'Grizzly that Bites and Scratches Trees.' He goes on to

say: 'The present holder of the title, since becoming a Christian, does not attend potlatches, and his seat has been taken by Gwinu', a Tsimshian Indian from Gitwinlklul, for whom there was really no seat.'

15 The following has been omitted: 'SINE DIE I hereby certify the foregoing to be a true and accurate transcript of the proceedings herein, to the best of my skill and ability. Veronica Harper (Ms.) Official Court Reporter: VH-Oct.14/85+B.C.S.R.A. #263'

Volume 3

1 Before this question, the following exchange has been omitted:
Was there anything wrong in the Wet'suwet'en tradition for people to pay – what's the name here, Louie Tommy for the fish that he gave them?
THE INTERPRETER: Would you repeat that?
In the extant question, I changed 'wrong for' to 'wrong with.'

2 The following has been omitted after this sentence:
MR GRANT: I'm asking the Interpreter, did he give the names of those people before Mabel Sam and if so could you –
THE INTERPRETER: Yes he did. I've got –
MR GRANT: You ask him again
THE INTERPRETER: I've got it.
MR. GRANT: Go ahead.
THE INTERPRETER: *The five people previous to Mable Sam were –*
MR GRANT: This is the first one?
THE INTERPRETER:

3 Literally, as noted in the glossary, Kilwoneetz means 'in the middle of spawning salmon,' and does not refer to the copper in the river.

4 Peter Grant is asking whether the suffix – 'bun' in the word 'Tsilgutznaytie-bun' signifies a lake, in this case Dennis Lake.

5 The following has been omitted after this sentence: 'MR GRANT: For the record, just to be clear, there was a reference to this village earlier today and the spelling would be T-S-A-Y-T-S-E-E-T-S-U-K and that was referred to this morning. For the record, I would like to make the correction. That is the way it should be spelled.'

6 The following exchange has been omitted after this sentence:
THE INTERPRETER: I'm lost here.
MR GRANT: Can you read that question back?
THE REPORTER: Question: 'Now, has the Kilwoneetzen territory always belonged to the House which Maxlaxlex is in?'
THE WITNESS:

7 The following exchange has been omitted prior to Johnny David's
response: 'This morning you told us that an ancestor of Kela is buried at
this lake. Before that person was alive was there a Kela? Before the Kela
who is buried?

THE INTERPRETER: Before the Kela was buried. Let me re-ask that. I got
mixed up here.

MR GRANT: Let me just – I'll re-phrase the question for you.'

8 The following exchange has been omitted prior to Johnny David's response:

MR GRANT: You want her to re-read it?

THE INTERPRETER: Yes.

THE REPORTER: Question: 'Was any part of Kilwoneetz territory or the
Alkut territory given as compensation by some other House or Clan to
Maxlaxlex and Kela?'

THE WITNESS:

9 'THE INTERPRETER: Old Sam looked after the territory near Telkwa River
area' has been omitted following this sentence.

10 The following exchange has been omitted following Johnny David's
response:

MR GRANT: He's finished?

THE INTERPRETER: Yes.

BY MR GRANT:

11 The following exchange has been omitted after the question:

THE INTERPRETER: Marten, you've got me!

OFF THE RECORD

THE INTERPRETER: Oh yes.

THE WITNESS:

12 'THE WITNESS' has been omitted before the Wit'suwit'en names, and 'THE
INTERPRETER' from before the English names for the animals, here and in
the exchanges that follow.

13 The following has been omitted from the end of this response: 'THE INTER-
PRETER: – I believe was – the marten.'

14 'THE INTERPRETER: – testlee is another word for steelhead – THE WITNESS' has
been omitted in the middle of Johnny David's response.

15 'THE INTERPRETER' has been omitted prior to the English names of the fish.

16 'THE INTERPRETER: And he mentioned that' has been omitted frolm the
beginning of the last sentence.

17 'THE INTERPRETER: – which is the' has been omitted before the word 'huckleberries.

18 The following exchange has been omitted following Johnny David's
response: 'THE INTERPRETER: Stuck for the words for other plants.

MR GRANT: Maybe go off the record for moment?
OFF THE RECORD DISCUSSION
MR GRANT: Go back on the record.'

19 The original had said:
... was *nawus*
THE INTERPRETER: – which is the soapberries –
THE WITNESS: some of the other –
THE INTERPRETER: – and blueberries, the Wet'suwet'en word for that is
yinloewee.

20 The following exchange has been omitted following Peter Grant's question:
THE INTERPRETER: What was your question?
THE REPORTER: Question: 'Are they still used at the feast today?'
THE INTERPRETER: He said.

21 'THE INTERPRETER: I just can't remember the English name for that plant'
has been omitted after 'konyay.'

22 The following exchange has been omitted following Peter Grant's question:
THE INTERPRETER: *Yes.*
MR GRANT: Is he finished?
THE INTERPRETER: Yes. He said he will remember some more as we go on.
MR GRANT: You indicated in your answer Devil's Club, and the answer
was Devil's Club which you described earlier – is this the plant you
didn't translate earlier?
THE INTERPRETER: Yes, it was.
MR GRANT: What was the Wet'suwet'en word for that?
THE INTERPRETER: Konyay.
I have also removed several instances of 'THE INTERPRETER: He said' from
this section.

23 'THE INTERPRETER: He said' has been omitted from the beginning of this
response.

24 The following has been omitted following Peter Grant's question:
Go off the record for a moment please.
OFF THE RECORD DISCUSSION
MR GRANT: Go back on the record.
THE INTERPRETER: Can you repeat the question please?
THE REPORTER: Question: 'Did your people use particular rocks to make
arrowheads in the old days?'

25 In fact, the examination was not reconvened until 19 December. 'I hereby
certify the foregoing to be a true and accurate transcript of the proceedings
herein, to the best of my skill and ability. Veronica Harper (Ms) Official
Court Reporter VH/lre-Oct. 22/85 B.C.S.R.A. #263' has been omitted.

Volume 4

1 In the original, the translator said, 'When his father was alive,' which has been changed to 'When my father was alive.' The next sentence began 'Now that his father is gone it is Johnny himself.'
2 In the original, the translator began this sentence with 'Okay. He said that.' The sentence finished with 'He said yes his house.'
3 Tsaykya is not Old Muldoe's chief's name; it was where he had a fishing spot.
4 Johnny's father has been changed to 'my father.'
5 In the original the translator said, 'And he would listen and Johnny would ask his father what they are saying and his father would tell Johnny ...' The final sentence in this response was originally 'And that is how he is telling us this information.'
6 In the original the response began with the translator saying 'His uncle – okay, his uncle.'
7 The photograph that constituted Exhibit 5 canot be reproduced because its access has been restricted by the British Columbia Provincial Archives.
8 'And he's saying that' has been omitted from the beginning of this response.
9 'He said' has been omitted from the beginning of the last sentence.
10 In the original transcript, the response was: '... the smokehouse in the photograph belonged to Wah Tah Keght and he said there was another one behind this one which belonged to Wah Tah Kwets and then he said that this is where the dried salmon was stored.'
11 'Okay, he told me that' has been omitted from the beginning of this response.
12 The original read, 'Yes. Yes, it was okay with McKenzie and his father or my father.'
13 The following has been omitted: 'I hereby certify the foregoing is a true and accurate transcript of the proceedings herein, to the best of my skill and ability: Linda Malinowski Official Court Reporter.'

Volume 5

1 'THE INTERPRETER: He is saying that –' has been eliminated.
2 'THE INTERPRETER: – he mentioned the white people' has been eliminated.
3 The following has been omitted after Johnny David's response:
  MR GRANT: With the?
  THE INTERPRETER: Salmon.

4 'THE INTERPRETER: He also said that' has been eliminated from the begin-
    ning of the last sentence.
5 The following has been eliminated prior to the last sentence:
    MR MILNE: Can I have the spelling of that?
    MR GRANT: For the record, it is X-E-L-X-T-U-K.'
6 The following has been eliminated after the second sentence:
    THE INTERPRETER: *Then he gave an example of myself and my family.*
    THE WITNESS:
7 The original answer is as follows:
    That's poison.
    OFF THE RECORD
    THE INTERPRETER: He said Oxyenikyo is poison. It is used –
    THE WITNESS: *If horses or cattle who eat it they would die ...*
8 The following has been eliminated following Johnny David's response:
    MR GRANT: For my father?
    THE INTERPRETER: *For my father.*
9 MR. GRANT'S query,
    'Okay. Who –' has been eliminated prior to the last sentence in Johnny
    David's response.
10 THE INTERPRETER: He doesn't. He said that has been omitted following
    'No.'
11 Exhibit 12 is not available, as it was destroyed during the 1998 fire at the
    Moricetown / Kya Wiget Office of the Wet'suwet'en.
12 The response is incorrect. The pole belongs to Chief Satsan / David Dennis,
    of Kaiya (Birchbark) House of the Gilseehyu (Frog) Clan. This pole is down
    the street from Johnny David's home and poles.
13 Johnny David's eyesight was not good; hence the error.
14 The statement of the count reporter has been omitted: 'PROCEEDINGS
    ADJOURNED AT 1.20 P.M. I hereby certify the foregoing to be a true and accu-
    rate transcript of the proceedings herein to the best of my skill and ability.
    Veronica Harper (Ms.) Official Court Reporter VH/lre-Feb. 8/86 B.C.S.R.A.
    #263 Transcript continues on page 5–22 which follows.'
15 The following has been omitted from the day's opening statement because
    the errata Peter Grant refers to have been corrected:
    Before proceeding further I have spoken with the Court Reporter, and
    also with Ms Mills, who is doing the word spelling, and with Mr Milne,
    counsel for the Defendant in this case. It appears that there are some
    errors in volume III of the commission evidence which are some misun-
    derstandings and may not be able to be corrected. First of all at page 30 of
    volume III, at line 41, the answer is given as Gitdumskaneese. That

answer should read Gitdumden. At page 34 of the same volume, lines 7, 8, 13 and 14, all refer to Gitdumskaneese and again that was a misunderstanding as it should be Gitdumden. Finally, Mr Milne has been courteous enough to look at his notes with respect to page 37, the answer at line 37 reads: 'Yes, I did and the crests are on my blanket and my jug.' The 'jug' should be 'drum' and that is consistent with Ms Mills's notes, Mr Milne's notes, and with my own notes. I would like to make those corrections on the record at this time so that confusion will be economized. I understand Mr Milne doesn't mind the corrections being put in in this manner.

MR MILNE: No objection to that.

There are also to be errata in that Volume and the Reporter has indicated she will be putting a supplemental sheet in that Volume or the next Volume with respect to the errata.

OFF THE RECORD DISCUSSION.'

16 In fact, it was the water behind the dam that flooded the area.
17 Literally, Nutseni means 'people who live upriver.'
18 'THE INTERPRETER: He says' has been eliminated from the beginning of this response.
19 The following exchange has been omitted here:
MR GRANT: Just to clarify with the Interpreter, are you translating Ma'dzee Bun into English to mean Caribou Lake?
THE INTERPRETER: Yes.
MR GRANT: Go ahead.
20 'THE INTERPRETER: He thinks it's –' has been eliminated from the beginning of this sentence.
21 'THE INTERPRETER: He thinks' has been eliminated from the beginning of this sentence.
22 The following has been omitted prior to this question:
Would you read the last answer please:
THE REPORTER: Question: 'Did your son Moses know where the rock was?' Answer: 'Yes, he knew where the place was, I told him and that's all I'm going to tell you. One time David Dennis and myself had gone to the location. We parked close by to where the rocks would be found and it started to thunder and we just left.'
23 Johnny David knew the story of Kweese's War on Kitimat and told it many times to his granddaughter Jennifer David. That story also features the distribution of mocassins to many people in a potlatch to help prepare them for going on a war party with Kweese against Kitimat. Kweese / Florence Hall told the story of Kweese's War on the Kitimat in her commission evidence, which was taken after Johnny David's.

24 'THE INTERPRETER: He said' has been eliminated from the beginning of this
    sentence. Doubtless part of the reason that Johnny did not want to tell the
    story is that, particularly in official circumstances, the story should be told
    by the head chief of the house whose story it is.
25 The following has been omitted from the end of volume 5: 'I hereby certify
    the foregoing to be a true and accurate transcript of the proceedings herein
    to the best of my skill and ability. Veronica Harper (Ms) Official Court
    Reporter VH/lre-Feb. 10/86 B.C.S.R.A. #263.'

Volume 6

1 'TRIAL EXHIBIT 74F – 24 & 25 February, 1986
   Extracts from COMMISSION EVIDENCE of JOHN DAVID, Volume VI 6–2' has
   been omitted here.
2 The original was: 'THE INTERPRETER: He said that whatever he's been telling us he would like to have it written down properly and the way he tells
   it is the way it happened.'
3 To clarify, it is likely here that Johnny David, in using the term 'potlatch
   houses,' is actually referring to Clans, who each had a smokehouse for potlatch, as opposed to the 'Houses' within each Clan. When he says, using the
   past tense, 'there were four potlatch Houses,' he is referring to the time
   when, because of depopulation, the Tsayu (Beaver) and Laksamshu
   (Fireweed) Clans, shown as separate clans in Figure X, amalgamated.
4 The following has been omitted after the notice of adjournment: 'I hereby
   certify the foregoing to be a true and accurate transcript of the proceedings
   herein, to the best of my skill and ability. Veronica Harper (Ms) Official
   Court ReporterVH:1 Mar/86 B.C.S.R.A. #263 TRANSCRIPT CONTINUES ON
   NEXT PAGE 6-30.'
5 There is no record in the transcripts of this question having been answered.
6 The original says, 'THE INTERPRETER: He said' before the response.
7 The following has been omitted from the end of the volume: 'I hereby certify the foregoing to be a true and accurate transcript of the proceedings
   herein, to the best of my skill and ability. Veronica Harper (Ms) Official
   Court Reporter VH:2 Mar/86 B.C.S.R.A. #263 wp/bd102.'

Volume 7

1 In the original transcripts, the response was: 'THE INTERPRETER: He said he
   has seen this. He got a similar one when he got the land.'
2 The original says, 'THE INTERPRETER: He said he got it first through pre-
   emption. After three years on it then he got it through Crown Grant.'

3 The original says, 'THE INTERPRETER: Roy McDonald, he used to look after the Fisheries throughout the whole area and talked to Johnny about this and they got into a disagreement and they had a little argument. Roy McDonald never came back again to bother Johnny about this area.'

4 In the original transcripts, the response began: 'THE INTERPRETER: He said that the people didn't bother him initially. It was after the coming of the white man that he started being hassled and before there were no white people there were many salmon in the area that you are describing.'

5 In the original transcripts, this paragraph began 'THE WITNESS.'

6 In the original transcript, the response began 'THE INTERPRETER: He said....

7 In the original transcripts, the response began: 'THE INTERPRETER: He said he.'

8 The original transcripts, the responses was: 'THE INTERPRETER: He said he saw that paper as well. After he sold the land.'

9 In the original transcript, the response began: 'THE INTERPRETER: He said.'

10 In the original transcript, the response began: 'THE INTERPRETER: He said.'

11 In the original transcript, the response began: 'THE INTERPRETER: He said.'

12 In the original transcript, the response began: 'THE INTERPRETER:'

13 In the original transcripts, the response was: 'THE INTERPRETER: Mr Hart was the person who did up all the documents for the land office and he was the one who told him he had 160 acres. Johnny said that he was the person in charge of giving out the land.'

14 In the original transcript, the response was: 'THE INTERPRETER: He said that he sold them the area that was fenced off, the river property, and he still has the documents where he paid school and land tax.'

15 In fact, Woos in the Head Chief of the Grizzly House; Gyologet in another chief of the Grizzly house; Madeek is the Head Chief of another House of the Wolf Clan. called Anskaski (Where It Lies Blocking the Trail) House.

16 The name of the major House is often used for the whole Wolf Clan.

17 In fact, the territory Madeek owns is distinct from the territory of Gisdaywa. See map 2 in the Introduction.

18 In the original transcripts, the response begins: 'THE INTERPRETER: He said.'

19 In the original transcripts, the response begins: 'THE INTERPRETER:'.

20 The following has been omitted from the end of the day's evidence: 'I hereby certify the foregoing to be a true and accurate transcript of the proceedings herein, to the best of my skill and ability. VH/jg-Apr. 25/86 Veronica Harper (Ms) Official Court Reporter B.C.S.R.A. #263 TRANSCRIPT CONTINUES ON NEXT PAGE 7–75.'

21 In the original transcripts, the rsponse begins: 'THE INTERPRETER.'

22 In the original transcripts, the last sentence begins: 'THE INTERPRETER: He said.'

23 In the original transcript, this sentence began, 'THE INTERPRETER: Francis Lake John had told Johnny, since you married my sister's daughter.'

24 In the original transcripts, the last two sentences of this response are as follows: 'THE INTERPRETER: He said there's a lot of silver there. He was there for two years and then war broke out and everything just shut down.'

25 In the original transcripts, this response began as follows: 'THE INTERPRETER: He says, no, I want to get done today. He says after lunch I am going ...'

26 In the original transcript, this response began: 'THE INTERPRETER: He is saying that.'

27 In the original transcript, this response began: 'THE INTERPRETER: He's saying that.'

28 In the original transcript, this response began: 'THE INTERPRETER: He's saying.'

29 In the original transcript, this response began: 'THE INTERPRETER: He's saying.'

30 In the original transcript, this response began: 'THE INTERPRETER: He's saying that.'

31 In the original transcript, this response began: 'THE INTERPRETER: He said.'

32 In the original transcript, this response began: 'THE INTERPRETER: He said.'

33 In the original transcript, this response began: 'THE INTERPRETER: He said.'

34 The following has been omitted from the end of volume 7: 'I hereby certify the foregoing to be a true and accurate transcript of the proceedings herein, to the best of my skill and ability. VH/jg-Apr. 25/86 Veronica Harper (Ms) Official Court Reporter B.C.S.R.A. #263.'

Volume 8

1 A legible copy of Exhibit 21 is unavailable. The information was reproduced in typewritten form in Exhibit 22. Because Exhibit 22 is also unavailable it has been retyped. Figure 4 in the introduction also presents Witsuwit'en clans, houses, and head chiefs with both the old spellings as in Exhibit 22, and the DWV or Distinctly Witsuwit'en Version of spellings. See the glossary for an explanation of the variations in spelling.

2 The following has been omitted from the end of the cross-examination. 'I hereby certify the foregoing to be true and accurate transcript of the proceedings herein, to the best of my skill and ability. Beverly Ferguson (Ms) Official Court Reporter BF/jg-May 8/86 B.C.S.R.A. #259.'

3 A typed copy of Exhibit 21 was provided as more legible than the original, Exhibit 21 which is not available. It is the same as Exhibit 22. The information also appears, in slightly modified form, in Figure 4, page 21.

4 In the original transcripts, the responses began: 'THE INTERPRETER: His people ...'

5 In the originial this sentence begins, 'He said he doesn't know ...'

6 Barbara Lane reports: 'The following statement was made by James Yami to Special Commissioner S. Stewart, at a conference in Hazelton, July 19, 1909 ... [It] is taken from the formal minutes of the conference recorded by the Department of Indian Affairs and retained in its files:

James Yami says: – The Bulkley River is our river and we get our living therefrom. On the lakes are located some of our houses. They are small and crude of pattern, but we cannot do without them. In those houses we have many articles such as hunting, trapping and fishing implements. A white man comes along and sets fire to the houses, and on remonstration we are told by the settler: – 'You get away from here, I bought this land and if I catch you here again I will have you jailed.' (Lane 1987: 5).

See also p. 895 for another mention of Yami.

7 Losier is an alternate spelling of Looseeya. In volume 7, Johnny David talked about how Looseeya was jailed and fined for protesting when his land at Two Mile near Moricetown was taken by Pete Van Happy (see 7: 331).

8 In the original transcript the sentence ended: 'spelled N-A-C-H-L-A-C-H.'

9 The following has been omitted from the end of volume 8: 'I hereby certify the foregoing to be a true and accurate transcript of the proceedings herein, to the best of my skill and ability. Beverly Ferguson Official Court Reporter B.C.S.R.A. #259.'

Glossary

The glossary presents the Witsuwit'en and Gitxsan words in the transcripts of Johnny David's commission evidence. Each word appears in italics followed by variations in spellings that occur in the commission evidence. Following this, where available, is the abbreviation for the origin of the word (W for Witsuwit'en, G for Gitxsan, Ch for the Chinook trade language that derived from Nuu Chal Nuth and which became a part of a few terms that Johnny David used, etc.). The abbreviations on page 442 list the languages in question. Next, in square brackets, the word is given in the current Witsuwit'en or Gitxsan linguistic orthography, rather than in phonetic script. The current Witsuwit'en spellings are called the distinctly Witsuwit'en version (DWV). Also where available, a literal translation of the word from the original Native language to English is given in double quotation marks. Finally, a definition of the meaning of the term is provided.

The spellings in square brackets and translations in quotation marks have been provided by trained linguists: Dr Sharon Hargus provided the current orthography of Witsuwit'en words and Dr Bruce Rigsby provided the spelling and meaning of words of Gitxsan origin. Some of his explanations indicate that the Witsuwit'en have taken and transformed Gitxsan words in a way that is non-Gitxsan. This is the nature of cross-linguistic borrowings. *LM* refers to Lillian Morris, a Witsuwit'en speaker trained in the current orthography, who provided spellings of words Dr Hargus did not recognize. I am not a trained linguist, so for the commission evidence I had often supplied the spellings used by Jenness (1929, 1934, 1943), who likewise was not trained in linguistics. Sometimes his portrayals are strikingly different from the linguistically correct forms. Moreover some words were new to me, or I heard them as new and unfamiliar. Sometimes I made a stab at portraying what I had heard so that the court reporters would not have to arrest the flow of testimony to record what was said in a language very foreign to English ears.

When there is no indication of the language the word comes from, the linguists did not recognize the word as derived from the Witsuwit'en or Gitxsan language. This may be because I provided a spelling that does not capture the actual sound accurately enough for it to be discernable.

The two different kinds of spellings represent more differences than going from Old English to Shakespearean English to modern standardized forms. The Witsuwit'en old spellings are retained in the testimony both because they were the ones used in the *Delgamuukw* case and because they had become familiar to the Witsuwit'en. The new DWV spellings are important because they represent the correct sounds and they are being used currently by many Witsuwit'en as well as by Witsuwit'en children, but not by all chiefs. Just as phonetic spellings are not commonly used in English, they are not universally used by the Witsuwit'en. The glossary provides the DWV version of words but does not list the word under that spelling.

The glossary and figure 4 in the introduction (p. 21) represent the ongoing effort to evolve correct and standardized spellings that correct misspellings made by foreigners unused to the different phonemes in Witsuwit'en. The process of implementing a standardized spelling is complex in any language, but all the more so for a First Nation and Athapaskan language with sounds not found in the English alphabet. Recording Witsuwit'en words correctly is but one of the problems of cross-cultural communication.

Abbreviations

Language of Origin

Ch	Chinook
E	English
E+Ch	English with Chinook jargon
E>W	From English to Witsuwit'en
G	Gitxsan
G>W	Gitxsan to Witsuwit'en
N	Nisga'a
W	Witsuwit'en

Other

lit.	literally
LM	Lillian Morris
pl.	plural
sing.	singular

Alusinuk. G: The name of a Gitxsan man who fell on the *konyay* or devil's club

alxbainy. W ['il bin yikh] "brush lean-to": A shelter made of branches whose ends are buried or stuck in the ground

Alcott, Alkut, Alxka, Alxkat. W ['Ilh K'it] "on boughs": The name for the northern territory of Kela, where a Chief Kela was buried

Alxkatbun. W ['Ilh K'it Bin] "on boughs lake": Sunset Lake or Graveyard Lake

amakloo, ammeelow'k. G>W ['imïluc] "mask": A headdress worn as part of regalia

Anabel's. W: Feast name in the Gilserhyu (Frog) Clan, held by Alex Michell and by his mother's brother before him

anaydoskee. W [Neggizgï]: Black fox

andamanaak, andamanuk. G>W [W: 'indimenik; G: ant'imhanak̲' (sing.) ant'imhaanak̲' (pl.)] "spouse of host," "spouse's donation": The spouses of the members of the clan that is giving a feast

Anklo'. W: The feast name of a woman, a daughter of a chief taken prisoner by the Nisga'a

Anskaski. W ['Insggisgï] "where it lies blocking the trail": Name of the house of the Witsuwit'en chief Madeek of the Gitdumden (Wolf) Clan

Babine. French? W [U'in Wit'en] "people way over": Refers to the First Nations people living to the east of the mountains at the northeast part of Witsuwit'en territory in Lake Babine watershed

Bagee. W: The brother of Chief Louie from Cheslatta, member of Tsayu (Beaver) Clan

Baine, Bain. W [Ben] "mother of"

Balna. E>W: A Witsuwit'en, also known as Bilna and Bill Nye, who held the name Madeek; involved in *Gojiget* incident; member of Kyas ya (Grizzly) House and Gitdumden (Wolf) Clan

basalkanutzlee, bezageelzutgitnee. W [bits'ac'elts'itnï] "those whom compact object fell off from": The group of (adult) children using their father's territory; pl. of *basalkelzut*

basalkelzut. W [bits'ac'elts'it] "his father clan"; lit. "that which compact object fell off from": A man's child or offspring, who belong to his or her mother's house and clan

baxkay. W [bikh kë] "war moccasin": Moccasins called 'brothers' moccasins,' used as gifts to warriors in a war party

baxnee. W [bikhnï] "warriors"

beez. W [bïs] "flint": Rock used for arrowheads

bezageelzutgitnee. See *basalkanutzlee*

Bini. W [bïnï] "his mind": Name of the Witsuwit'en prophet who was also Head Chief Kweese, of the Tsayu (Beaver) Clan

Bisgeebul. [Bisgï bul (LM)]: A creek that flows in the Old Hazelton area where the Tsimshian would come ashore to trade

buguy. W [dik'ay] "cutthroat trout, lake trout"

bun. W [bin] "lake"

Buningasxkas. W [Binin C'itcis] "May–June"/August; lit. "month of moulting": Refers to young birds who are not yet able to fly

Casbeen, Kas baine, Kasbaine. W [Cas Ben] "grizzly mother": The name of a Babine or Old Fort Indian whose territory is to the north of Smogelgem's

Caspit. W [Cas Bit] chief name, lit. "grizzly abdomen": Feast name in Gilserhyu (Frog) Clan; held by Jimmy Thomas and now by Stanley Morris

Cheslatta. W [Nyen Wit'en] "people across": François Lake, Carrier/Witsuwit'en community

dagee, tahkee. W [digï] "huckleberry"

datnee. W [ditnï] "groundhog": Marmot

dayweetz. W [dewïts] "spout": Wedge; rock shaped into a wedge, used for splitting wood; also used for making arrowheads

deesgut', deesgut'k'aas, disklas. W [dïstggis] "twisted cedar-bark neck ring": Headband or neck ring made of red cedar worn by the healing society or *kaxluhxhkm* or *Ggilulhëm*

Deh 'Kleye yis, Tsa moot'tsa. W [Dekh Tl'ëyiyis] "tears it [brush] away from legs": Blue Lake Mountain

Delgamuukw. G [G: Delg_am Uuk_] "talking copper or speaking copper": One of the 45 Gitxsan head chiefs who, with the 12 Witsuwit'en head chiefs, brought the Gitxsan-Witsuwit'en land claims court case that became known as *Delgamuukw.* The Witsuwit'en refer to the court case as the *Gisday Wa–Delgamuukw* case to emphasize that the Witsuwit'en are equal participants.

Dicanyu. W [dicin yu] "used for bush medicine": Wild plant used for medicine

dikanteztsias. W [dicin + ?] "tree falling over": The name for the ceremony of cutting down the tree to be carved into a totem pole

Dikyannualat, Dikyan nualat. W [dicin ultlat] "he's jumping towards the tree"; chief name of Ginehklaiya (House of Many Eyes), Laksilyu (Small Frog) Clan, or in Johnny David's words, "A grizzly bear that grabs a piece of wood and pulls it off": Chief name held by David Dennis's father, Old Dennis

disgus. W: Plant that grows along the Skeena River

disklas. See *deesgut'*

diyenee. W [diyinï] "medicine men"

Djankanya. W [C'ikën Yikh] Beaver House of Tsayu (Beaver) Clan whose head chief is Kweese

Dsee'h, Dzee, Dzee'h. [dzïh]: Feast name in Wah Tah Keght's Tse kal kai ya House (House or Top of a Flat Rock) of the Laksilyu (Small Frog) Clan; held by Madeline Alfred (Mrs Peter Alfred) and then by her daughter, Mrs Amos Brown

Dyee, Tyee, dyeez. From Ch [W: dayi, G: Tayi] "chief": A name used to designate a chief, often used by the early Catholic missionaries to create church chiefs who they hoped would leave the potlatch system; *Tayi* is from Chinook jargon, and ultimately from the Nootka or Nuu-chah-Nulth language. *Dyee* is masculine; *dyeez* is feminine. See also *Skin Dyee; Tyee Lake David*

Dzee, Dzee'h. See *Dsee'h*

Dzï bin. W [Dzï bin] "heart lake": Coffin Lake

Dzibun. W: Alexander Dzibun, the second husband of Johnny David's mother, Suwitsbain; perhaps from English name Stephens

Dzikens. E>G>W [Dziknis; dziginis (LM): G. Tsigins; G loanword from E]: Johnny David gave William Dzikens as the name of the owner of a fishing site at Hagwilget.

Dzilh K'inetiy Bin. W [dzilh k'inetiy]: Dennis Lake

Gaos taway bunee yis, Gisdewe bin yis. W [gisdewe bin yis]: lit. Whiskers Mountain. Gisdaywa Lake Ridge

gaxlowk. [galhok]: A dangerous plant that grows in the swamp behind Kya Wiget / Moricetown and that brings great luck; used for luck when hunting

ggikh. W [ggikh]: rabbit, rabbits

gibsco. W [dicin c'ists'o'] "black birch burl, cinder conk (fungus)" (botanical name *Inonotus obliquus*): A tree with fungus that feels like rubber; the fungus, once pounded into powder and mixed with water is used for painting *amakloo* (mask or head dress)

Gibukun. G: Feast name held by the Witsuwit'en Skin Dyee, brother of Samooh, of Ya'tsalkas (Dark) House of the Gilserhyu (Frog) Clan

Gidumden, Gitdumden. G>W [Gidimt'en] (from Gitxsan *gidim*, a phonetically reduced form of /kat-im/ 'man,' and Witsuwit'en *t'en*) "person who resides" or "owners of an area": Wolf Clan

giitsugun, Gitsugun. W [c'idzuk'in]: A kind of wood or tree that is used for making the arrow shaft and bow

Gilloo kluk. W [dik tiltlic] "It jumps up," "where the fish jump up": Smogelgem's fishing site on the other side of the Bulkley Canyon from Highway 16 at Kya Wiget / Moricetown

gilluy'. W [c'ile'] "bark" (especially cedar or spruce): Bark from trees used for the roof of smokehouses

Gilseehyu, Gilserhyu. GW [C'ilhts'ëkhyu; G: Gelts'eexyu] (the -*yu* suffix is Witsuwit'en; the first part, while not analysable, is of Gitxsan phonological pattern; second spelling is from Jenness 1943): Frog Clan

Ginehklaiya, Gineeklaiya, Ginerklaiya. W [C'inegh Lhay Yikh] "House of Many Eyes" in Laksilyu (Small Frog) Clan

Gisdaywa, Gisday Wa, Gisdayway. [Gisdewe]: Head chief of the Kaiyawinits House (House in the Middle of Many) of the Gitdumden (Wolf) Clan; held by Alfred Joseph at the time of Johnny David's evidence; held earlier by Thomas George

Gisdewe bin yis. See *Gaos taway bunee yis*

Gitanmaax. G [G: Git-an'maaks]: Name for the Gitxsan village called Old Hazelton in English

Gitdumskaneese, Gut-dum-ska-neese, Gyedamskanish. G>W [W: C'idimsggin'ïs; G: Gedim Ska'nist] "Man Mountain": One of the Head Chiefs of Ginehklaiya (the House of Many Eyes) of the Laksilyu (Small Frog) Clan. The feast name was held by Willy Simms at the time of Johnny David's evidence, and previously by Chief Charles; by Chief Tibbets, Johnny David's father's father's sister's son; and by Johnny David's father's father. Also name of Witsuwit'en chief killed in the Samaxsam incident

Gitdumden. See *Gidumden*

Gitksan, Gitxsan. G [Eastern spelling: Gitxsan; Western spelling: Gitksen] W [C'itne] "people of the Skeena": People to the west of the Witsuwit'en with an unrelated language, called Gitnay (Gitneys) by the Wit'suwit'en. The Gitksan language is related to Nisga'a and Tsimshian.

Gitlaxdamks. N [G: Gitlaxt'aamiks]: Nisga'a village also called New Aiyansh

Gitsugun. See *Giitsugun*

Gitwinlkul, Gitwinlklul, Kitwankool. G [Gitwinhlguu'l]: A Gitxsan village north of Kitsegukla in the northwest portion of Gitxsan territory, which borders on Nisga'a territory, also known as Gitanyow. This village is making a separate land claim from the Gitxsan.

Goes we bay winee, Kuskabaywonne. W [Ggusgï Be Winï] "Sucker Lake" lit. "it is there for sucker": The Witsuwit'en name for the North Bulkley territory of Smogelgem; place where a cabin was burned down on Witsuwit'en territory

Gojiget, Gwatsikyet, Kosteeget. G>W [K'ots'igit; G from: *kots* "cut" and *get* "man," "person" in Gitxsan but not in Gitxsan grammatical construction]: Feast name meaning 'he that cuts off the head with a knife' (or saw), held by Francis Lake Johnny, a Nutseni of the Yatsowitan (Thin House) of the Gilserhyu (Frog) Clan; now held by Virginia Pierre

gonzay. W? [k'undzee] "inner basket of fish weir": Fish trap

gonzayeegutz. W [k'undze k'ët: fish basket] "fish basket" + "hole": Place where the fish basket is at Kya Wiget / Moricetown

Goohheak. G [gguhe']: Feast name in the Laksilyu (Small Frog) Clan, held by
Lucy Basil

Goohlaht. G/W [W: Gguhlat, G: Guu Let'] G: "has diarrhea": Head chief of
Ya'tsowitan (Thin) House, of the Gilseehyu (Frog) Clan; name held by Lucy
Namox

Guksan, Guxsam. G>W [W: Ggucsan (LM); G: Guxwsen] Gitksan plaintiff in the
Delgamuukw court case, from Skeena Crossing

Gut-dum-ska-neese. See *Gitdumskaneese*

Guxsam Lake: A Lake in Guxsam territory, to the west of Kilwoneetz

Gwatsikyet. See *Gojiget*

Gyoluget. G>W [G: Ky'ooluu Get] "One Man Alone": Feast name in the Git-
dumden (Wolf) Clan, held by the warrior in the story of Tas Dleese, later by
Big Seymour, then by Mathew Sam, then by Dennis Hall; currently held by
Darlene Glaim. Gyoluget's territory is in the area near Smithers and the
Hudson Bay Mountain ski area.

Hagwilgate, Hagwilget. W "below the rock": Village near the confluence of the
Wadzun Kwah or Bulkley River and the Skeena River; also called Tse Kya

Hag Wil Neg, Hagwilnegh, Hag Wil Negh. G [W: Hagwilnekhlh; G: Hagwilne-
exhl; G: *hagwil* or /*hakw Be l*/ "slowly" + *neexhl* 'killer whale'; grammatical
form is not Gitxsan; the Witsuwit'en name may be an interlanguage attempt
to say slow killer whale, it is not proper Gitxsan]: Chief name, head chief of
the House of Ginehklaiya (House of Many Eyes) in the Laksilyu (Small
Frog) Clan; held by Sylvester Williams at the time of Johnny David's evidence; currently held by Ronald Mitchell

Hakasbaine. W [Hakas? + ben] "mother of hakas": Woman whose father was
given rights to use Klayslahtl's territory for one year in return for the oolichan grease and berries given Klaylahtl when he was without food

H'Kahk. W [khikh] "goose": Feast name in Tse kal kai ya (House on Top of a
Flat Rock) in the Laksilyu (Small Frog) Clan, held by George Holland

H'laughkhak. G?>W [wikaklh]: Feast name in the House of Ginehklaiya (House
of Many Eyes) of the Laksilyu (Small Frog) Clan; held by Lizette Naziel

Hohn. N?>W [lhum] "salmon": Formerly the feast name of Dick Alec from the
Laksilyu (Small Frog) Clan of Topley Landing and Burns Lake; the name
was previously held by Alec Joseph

Hottamaneh'k, Huttakumay. G: Feast name in the House of Ginehklaiya (House
of Many Eyes), in the Laksilyu (Small Frog) Clan; held by Bazil Michell

Joenassbain, Joenassbaine. E + W [Joenass Ben] "Joe Nass Ben" (mother of Joe
Nass): Johnny David's mother's mother. See also *baine*

k'aas. W [ggïs] "spring salmon"

Kaiget. G [K'ëgit]: Name of Kela's totem pole, the first that was erected in the Hagwilget Canyon

Kai ya. W [këyikh, K'iy Yikh] "village" Birch House of the Gilserhyu (Frog) Clan

Kaiyawinits, Kaiyexweniits, Yahoneetz. W [Këyikh Winïts] "in the middle of the village": House in the Middle of Many, also called House in the Middle of the Village, Gitdumden (Wolf) Clan, whose head chief is Gisdaywa

Kal: Second leading chief from Laksilyu (Small Frog) Clan, in dispute over Klayslahtl's territory

kandew. W [cindu] "jack pine"

ka nee yet li. W [kaneyedl'i'] "he held a shame feast" (on account of being shamed by an accident)

Kas baine, Kasbaine. See *Casbeen*

Kasya, Kyas ya. W [Cas Yikh] "Grizzly House": One of three houses of the Gitdumden (Wolf) Clan; house of Balna, Mathew Sam, Peter Alfred, George Naziel, and of Chief Madeek

Kaxluhxhkm. G>W [Ggilulhëm]: Proper name of the Witsuwit'en healing society, or secret society similar to the Gitxsan healers known as *halait*

Kela. G>W [K'ëlikh]: Feast name in the House of Ginehklaiya (House of Many Eyes); held by Kela, then by Big Thomas Nikal, then by Thomas Holland, then by Jim Holland, then by Mabel Sam Crich's mother, Rose Sam; currently held by Mabel Sam Crich

Kelzil, KeLHil. W [cel dzil of *cel*, "salmon in spawning colours" + *dzilh*, "mountain"]: Dennis Mountain, a mountain near Sagwendax (McDonnell Lake)

Kengitlow't, Kengitlowt. W [kën git] "old beaver lodge": Mountain near Hudson Bay Mountain, near the town of Dowdy about five or six miles from Kya Wiget/Moricetown

Ken' oo ee Kwah, Ken'ooeekwah. W [c'inu'iy kwah] lit. "creek upriver": Canyon Creek

ketneeayelgee. W [c'ik'ët nïyilye] "they were traded, trade": Trade goods

Khenegasxgunxgut, Khenegashgun hat. W [kwineggis kun k'ët] "fire poker camp": Camp near Wilssa Creek on Cut Box or Cutoff Box Mountain, a small mountain on the west side of Hudson Bay Mountain; the boundary between Kilwoneetz and Gyoluget territory

Kilwinits Tlocit, Kilwoneetz Kloohkut. W [Cel winïts tl'o kit] (from cel winits, "meadow," "area or marsh on north side of Copper River"): Six Mile Flat

Kilwoneetsweten, Kitwoneetzen. W [Cel winïts wit'en] "people of Copper River": People of the Kilwoneetz territory

Kilwoneetz. W [Cel winïts] lit. "in middle of spawning salmon": Area of the Copper River and the Telkwa River; territory of Johnny David, Kela, Old Dennis, Old Sam, Joe Nass, and Joenassbaine. Referred to as a house by Johnny David

Kilwoneetz kloohkut. See *Kilwinits Tlocit*

Kisgegas. G [G: Gisgaga'as]: The name of a Gitxsan village

Kispiox. G [G: Gisbayakws]: Gitxsan village north of Gitaanmax on the Kispiox River

Kitsegukla. G [G: Gijigyukwhla]: Gitxsan village downstream from Hagwilget on the Skeena River

Kitselas. G [G: Gits'ilaasxw]: A village of the Tsimshian whose territory includes Tsamoot tsa

Kitwancool. See *Gitwinlkul*

Klatden. W [Lht'at'en] "bear lake people": Chief name of Sekani and Tahltan; chief name of Tom Alex's wife

Klayslahtl. A man from Cheslatta given berries and oolichan grease by Hakasbaine's father; Klayslahtl gave in return rights to Hakasbaine's father to use Klayslahtl's territory around Ootsa Lake, for one year

Kloktuktulgwes. W, "fish jump up (or falls)": A creek within Johnny David's territory near the road to McDonnell Lake; also a fishing site in Moricetown Canyon

Kloncheetoygikwuh, Kloncheetaygikwuh. W [Tl'o tsët to yïkwah] "water drains from the meadow": Name of the creek called Willow Creek by the white people; coming out of Sagwendax (McDonnell Lake) near the grassy area.

Kloohkut. W [tl'o k'it]: Meadow

Kloooguseye. W [Ts'ighen]: A mountain near Sagwendax (McDonnell Lake)

Kloumkhun. G>W [Lho'imggin]: Head chief of Midzi-ya (Owl) House, of the Laksamshu (Fireweed) Clan; the name was held by Johnny Mack at the time of Johnny David's testimony; now held by Alphonse Gagnon

kloxnayklus. "straighten out one's ways": Improving one's behaviour so as to have the right to use territory and go in the feast hall

Knedebeas. G>W [Nedïbïs G Neediibiis] lit. "common nighthawk": Head chief of Yatsadkus (Dark) House, of the Gilserhyu (Frog) Clan, held by Sarah Layton at the time of Johnny David's evidence (once held by Tommy Layton)

Knhuux Noo. G>W [Kwinu]: Chief name of Stanley Nikal Sr, feast name in the Laksilyu (Small Frog) Clan

konyay. W? [kunye]: Indian hellebore, root of mountain lady slipper or devil's club (botanical name *Veratrum viride*). The roots are used for medicinal purposes and for cleaning or purifying a rifle.

Kosteeget. See *Gojiget*

Ksan, 'Ksan G: Gitxsan Heritage Centre in Gitanmaax, or Old Hazelton, site of old village and trading centre

Kuminyay. Feast name of Satsan's brother, who received Mooseskin Johnny's sister's daughter as compensation for a killing by Mooseskin Johnny

kungalx. W [c'inkalh, c'inkatl] "chocolate lily root," "wild rice root" (botanical name *Fritillaria camschatcensis*): Wild rice

Kuskabaywonnee. See *Goes we bay winee*

Kwan beah ya. W [Kwin Begh Yikh] "house beside the fire": Name of House Beside the Fire (Laksilyu [Small Frog] Clan), whose head chief is Wah Tah Kwets

Kwan beah ya weten. W [Kwin Begh Yikh Wit'en] "people of Kwan beah ya"

Kweese. G?>W [W: Kw'is G: Cn'iis]: Head chief of the Tsayu (Beaver) Clan, held by Florence Hall, Mrs Gordon Hall, nee Beaulah Dennis. The house is sometimes referred to as Tsayu and somestimes as Djankanya.

Kyas hya. See *Kasya*

Kya Wiget. W [Këyikh Wigit] "old village": Name for the village at the falls on the Wadzun Kwah or Bulkley River, named Moricetown by Father Morice

Laganzo. Mountain in the Telkwa River Kilwoneetz territory

Laksamshu. G>W [Likhts'amisyu]: Killerwhale or Fireweed Clan

Laksilyu, Laxsilyu. G>W [G: Lax See'l; W: Likhsilyu; loan word from Gitxsan Lax See'l, Frog Raven Clan] "small frog clan": The Small Frog Clan, which contains three houses: Ginehklaiya (House of Many Eyes), Kwan beah ya (House beside the Fire), and Tse kal kai ya (House on Top of a Flat Rock)

latlad: deer

Lawelxges. Paul Lawelxges, given as name of fish site owner at Hagwilget

lexalzut, logalgut. Person of the father's clan (e.g., Thomas George *logalgut* Rose Sam means Rose Sam is related on her father's side to Thomas George. Her father was in the same Gilseehyu (Frog) Clan as Thomas George's father, who was Goohlaht.

Lhak'its, Llee jai. G?>W [lhak'its] "seaweed": Name of sergeant or boss of Nutseni war party

Lleejai. See *Lhak'its*

Looseeya, Losier. G>W [Losya]: Gilseehyu (Frog Clan) chief name, held by Sylvester Williams's grandfather, who was put in jail and fined for speaking up against white people taking land at Two Mile

Lyetate. W [Lhetet] "cross-roads," "where the roads meet": Called Hungry Hill in English

Madeek. G [W: Midïc] from Gitxsan *Sim Midiik,* "Real, True Grizzly Bear": Head
chief of Anskaski House (Gitdumden [Wolf] Clan), held by Peter Alfred at
the time of Johnny David's testimony, passed on to James Brown at Mr.
Alfred's death, previously held by Bill Nye (Balna) and George Naziel
Note: Johnny David did not give the Anskaski House of Madeek in his
testimony.

Ma'dzee Bun, Me'dzee Bun. W [Midzïh Bin] "caribou lake": The boundary of the
Nutseni land to the east of Skin Dyee's territory

Malahan. G [mila han] "button +?": Name of a Gitksan whose territory is from
Lead Canyon to the Seven Sisters mountains

mansilh, mansilx. W [mintsetl] "red-breasted sapsucker," "common flicker":
The figure of a bird at the top of the totem pole of Agnes Dennis, Chief
Samooh, of Gilseehyu Clan, at Kya Wiget/Moricetown

Maxlaxlex. G>W [W: Mikhlikhlekh; G: Maxhlalaxleeks]: In Gitxsan it means
'Go Barefoot around (Something)' and was held by Jonathan Johnson of the
Wolf Clan in Kispiox. Johnny David's feast name, which means 'a person
jumping over something,' held by Johnny David's mother's brother, Old
Sam, before Johnny, and by Old Sam's mother's brother before Old Sam

me'dzee. W [midzïh, widzïh] "caribou." See also *Ma'dzee Bun*

Misdziah, Misdzi ya, Midzi-ya. W [Misdzï Yikh] "owl house": Owl House of the
Laksamshu (Fireweed) Clan at Hagwilget; the head chief is Kloumkhun

moo'tie.? [mudïh] "manager," "boss": A person who oversees the affairs of the
village

Nabistes. [Nabistes]: John Nabistes, a fish-site owner at Hagwilget

Nachlach. [Nachlach]: Last name of Joseph Nachlach

Nadina. W [Nedïn'a]: Nadina River, Lake, and Mountain; called Nadina in
English also

Namox. G?>W [Namoks]: Feast name in the Tsayu (Beaver) Clan; also used as a
last name by the relatives of Chief Namox

Nanika. W [Nenikëkh] "mountain at inlet to Tëzdlï Dzil body of water": Refers
to the mountain as well as the lake and river territory of Francis Lake John
and of Miriam Dennis, Johnny David's wife

Nanika Lake. W [C'iniggit Nenikëkh] 'upper' + nenikekh: Nanika Lake above
Kid Price Lake

Nanika River. W [Nenikëkh Kwah]: Nanika River

nanilate nee. W [ninil'iy'nï] "those who sneak around": People who sneak
around on territory they have no right to use

Nass River. from Southern Tlingit [naas]: A large river whose watershed is in
the Tsimshian, Nisga'a, and Gitxsan territories

nastl, noostel. W [nustël] "wolverine" also chief name in Gilseehyu (Frog) Clan

nawus. W [niwis] "soapberry" (botanical name *shepherdia canadensis*)

Naxnox. G [naxnox] "spirit being," as intransitive verb or adjective "to be knowledgeable or skilled": used for enactment of a crest

Nayistendie. W [niyisdiye] "he's walking in snow": Mountain in Skin Dyee's territory, Gilseehyu (Frog Clan)

Neldildat, Neldzildat. W [Nelgï T'at Ts'anlï]: Howson Creek, Howson Lake, in the Kilwoneetz area

Neloo kwah. W [Neluh kwah] "eyebrow creek": In English, Kooty Creek

Netanlii. W [Netanlï Bin]: Wit'suwit'en name for Skin Lake

netseyeee. W [nitsiy] "crest, crests"

Niggiyotsi. W [nec'odzï] "it (name) was taken back": The custom of the high chief's calling out the name of someone taking a new chief's name, and saying something about the crest

Nilchick. W? [nelhdzï, nïlhdzïkw] "otter" (note: both words are less common than *ts'ant'iy* for 'otter'): Crest of Ginehklaiya (House of Many Eyes) and of Maxlaxlex

Nisga'a, Nisga, Nishga. G>W [W: nisgga']: Nisga'a, people of the Nass River.

Noostel. *W* [nustël] "wolverine": Chief's name in Gilseehyu (Frog) Clan, held by Stephens Alexander, who was Johnny David's mother's second husband; currently held by Warner William

nulwass. W [nilhwis] "rattle"

Nutseni, Nnutsenee. W [Nu'ts'inï] lit. "people who live upriver": Carrier people to east of the Witsuwit'en

oolichan, oolakan. G? [sac]: Eulachon, a fish commonly found in the Nass River whose oil is made into oolichan grease

Ootsa Bin. W [Utsewh Bin] lit. "lake downhill in general area": Territory of Miriam Dennis, Johnny David's wife of Gilseehyu Clan

oxyenikyo. W [wighen co, honghenï co] lit. "big killer": Douglas water-hemlock, water-parsnip (botanical name *Cicuta douglasii*) – a poisonous plant that grows around the edges of the lakes. If horses or cattle eat it, they die.

potlatch. Feast; the government and ceremonial system of the Northwest Coast First Nations and the Witsuwit'en

sabay. W [sabe] "Dolly Varden trout"

Sagwendax, Tsaywints, Tsayxingls. [Sikwendih (LM)]: The name for McDonnell Lake and the area in Kilwooneetz territory near the lake of the Laksilyu (Small Frog) Clan

Samaxsam. [Simikhsam]: Feast name in Ginehklaiya (House of Many Eyes) of Laksilyu (Small Frog) Clan. The name was held by Billy Mitchel, Jimmy Michell, and Old Sam, and before that by Old Sam's uncle Old Tiljoe; given by Nisga'a Samaxsam to make peace after he killed a Wit'suwit'en for inadvertently disturbing a Nisga'a grave marker

Samooh. G?>W [W: Simuyh; G: Semuuyk]: Feast name in the Ya'tsalkas (Dark House) of Gilseehyu (Frog) Clan; the name was held by Johnny David's wife's mother, Agnes Dennis, by Agnes's brother Skin Dyee, by Johnny David's wife Miriam Dennis, and later by their son Moses David; currently held by Herb Naziel

sas. W [sis]: "black bear," "bear"

Satsan. W? [Sa ts'an] lit. "sun totem pole" (if this is Witsuwit'en): Feast name in Kai ya (Birch) House (Gilserhyu [Frog] Clan); held by Old Bill, later by David Dennis, when Johnny David testified; currently by Herb George

Saya. W [Sa Yikh] "sun house": Sun House of the Laksamshu (Fireweed) Clan; head chief is Smogelgem

Sebola. W [Nde' Ditëst'ay Bighikh] "beside [mountain ridge] heading north": Mountain near Ootsa Lake

Sekanne. Language spoken by Sekani Indians and Tom Alex; Sekani are to the northeast of the Witsuwit'en

Skallithx, Skaxllee. [Sggile]: Chief's name of Jean Baptiste, brother of Tyee Lake David, who was Chief Woos of Kyas ya (Grizzly) House, Gitdumden (Wolf) Clan. Jean Baptiste alone was able to keep his land at Burnt Cabin Road, now known as Jean Baptiste Indian Reserve. The chief name is now held by Madeleine Dennis of the Babine Gitdumden (Wolf) Clan, passed on at a Babine Burns Lake potlatch in 1985.

Skeena. G [Ksen; Xsan] "river of mists": River with its headwaters in Gitxsan territory, which flows then through Tsimshian territory to the Pacific Ocean

Skin Dyee. E+Ch: Skin + [dayï], name, "skin + chief" Chinook: Originally name of a François Lake trapper, hence "skin"; a Witsuwit'en chief who lived in Hagwilget, brother of Samooh, with the feast name Gibukan and Samooh, of the Yatsadkus (Dark) House of the Gilserhyu (Frog) Clan. His land was flooded by the Alcan dam. Johnny refers to him as his half-brother: he was the son of Johnny's mother's brother, Old Dennis (Chief Dikyannualat), and Johnny's mother-in-law Agnes Dennis (Chief Samooh).

Skitkanu. Child feast name of David McKenzie, the older brother of Chief Roosevelt, Johnny David's father; Chief Roosevelt and then David McKenzie held the head chief name Smogelgem

Skokumlesas. G>W [Sk'okimisas]: Feast name in the Laksilyu (Small Frog) Clan; held by Little Jimmy Michell at the time of Johnny David's evidence; now held by Nora Van Tunen

Skokumwaha. G [Xsgooqam Lax̱ Ha]: "First in the sky": Feast name of Mary
   Joseph of the Saya (Sun House) of the Laksamshu (Fireweed) Clan

Smogelgem. Coast Tsimshian / G?>W [Smogilhgim] (Note: Form of the Coast
   Tsimshian attributive phrase Sim'oogidim Gamk 'Chief Sun,' perhaps bor-
   rowed through western Gitksan): Head chief of the Laksamshu (Fireweed)
   Clan; feast name held by Johnny David's father, Chief Roosevelt, then by
   Johnny David's father's brother David McKenzie, then by Abraham Nikal;
   currently held by Leonard George

sonanadeenlate li. W [so' nineyinilhtiy] "he laid him in a better place": Said of
   someone who improves a situation; also to sit down properly in the feast
   hall; the ceremony to accept the criticism of the chiefs and come back into
   the feast hall and the Witsuwit'en system

sonel. W? [sinelh] "lament": Song sung when shaking a rattle and dancing; the
   sonel sung by the Nisga'a in making peace with the Witsuwit'en 'is a special
   chant used by the Carrier, Tsimshian, Haida, Kitimat, Bella Coola, and other
   tribes whenever they make peace with each other' (Jenness 1943: 480)

Spookx, Spoaks. G>W [W: Sboks, G: Sbookxw]: Chief name, a Gitxsan head chief
   and plaintiff; the name was also formerly held by Johnny David's mother's
   father; also by Johnson Alexander of Kispiox

Stay ee deen lay. W "he/she put them in fire": Practice, of *andamanaak* people, who
   danced and threw materials into the fire long before Johnny David's time

stelkay. W [ts'ëlkiy'] "eel"

Suwitsbaine, Su witsbain. (Siwïts)? + W (ben), [Siwïts Ben] "mother of Siwïts":
   Chief name, formerly held by Adeline Holland, and by Agnes Dennis,
   mother of Johnny David

s'wah'. W [tsiyh] "ochre": Dye used to paint cedar bark headdress red colour

swinak. G? [swïnik from x̱s'wing]: Herring eggs on seaweed (traded for from
   the coast Indians)

Tahal Zinga Kwah, Tahdzingakwah. W [Talhdzen Kwah] "blue water + edge of
   river + tears it [brush] away from legs": Summit Creek, which flows from
   Summit Lake

Tah Galain. G>W [K'ilisët]: Feast name in the Laksilyu (Small Frog) Clan, held
   currently by Violet Gellenbeck

tahkee. See *dagee*

Tas Dleese. W [Tasdlïz] "boiled in water": Boiling Rock, the Witsuwit'en name
   for Lake Kathlyn, near Smithers

tegul. W [dighil] "drum": A drum used when a song is sung

Telkwa, Del kwah. W [Nde' ïlkwah] "it flows west": The Telkwa River, in Kilwoneetz territory

testlee. W [tësdli̇] "steelhead trout"

Teytalwus. W [Teetalwis] "they will run outside": Name mistakenly given for Chief Charles, who was Chief Gitdumskaneese of Ginehklaiya (House of Laksilyu (Small Frog) Clan

Tsadzalh. Chief who gave permission for Tom Alex's wife, Klatden, to use his territory for a year

tsa kan. W [tsacin, tsëcin] "pole cache": Cache built on stilts for storing dried salmon

tsamon. G>W [sdimon]: Pink, humpback salmon

Tsa moot'tsa. Tsimshian name for Deh' kleye yis (Blue Lake Mountain), the mountain to the west of Kela's territory

Tsantat'lay. W [Tsan Tatl'et] "he/she is throwing excrement into the water," "shit falling in the water": The name of a fishing area in the Bulkley Canyon at Kya Wiget / Moricetown

tsaste'l. W [tsalhts'ëgh]: Blue clay used as paint

tsate'l. W [Tsa tël] "blanket beaver": An especially large beaver

Tsaykya, Tse Kya. W [tsa k'ayh] "dried beaver meat": The Witsuwit'en village of Hagwilget

Tsaytseetsuk, Tsay Tsee Tsik, Tsi'tse'gut, Tseetsaytuk. W [tsëk +] "open fire" +?: A Gitxsan village near Carnaby village; Big John of Kitsegukla was the hereditary chief in this village

Tsayu. W [Tsayu]. "beaver people" house: Beaver Clan, whose head chief Kweese was, at the time of Johnny David's evidence, Florence Hall

tsayx. W [ts'ëkh] "sinew": Sinew, often made from caribou, used to tie an arrowhead to the shaft of an arrow

Tsayxingls, Tsaywingts. See *Sagwendax*

Tsee tsaytuk. See *Tsaytseetsuk*

Tse hangel. W [tsë hanc'il] "rock torn off": A split rock at Hagwilget that went clear across the river

ts'e'in dini hinli. W [ts'e'in dini̇ hinli̇] "he's an honest man"

ts'e'in holh'iy. W [ts'e'in holh'ay] "he's honest"

Tse kal kai ya, Tsekalkaiya, Tsee K'al K'e yex. W [Tsë Kal K'iyikh] "house on the flat rock": House of the Laksilyu (Small Frog) Clan; the head chief is Wah Tah Keght

Tse kal kai ya weten. W [Tsë Kal K'iyikh Wit'en]: People of Tse kal kai ya (House on the Flat Rock) of Laksilyu (Small Frog) Clan

Tse Kya. See *Tsaykya*

tsel'ste. W [tsalhtsë]: High-bush cranberries (botanical name *Viburnum edule*).

tsel 'ste. W [tse tselh? tselh tse?] "clay or stone"

Tsez zul. W [Tsë Zul] "shale": China Nose Mountain, southeast corner marker of Smogelgem's territory

Tsilgutznaytie. W [Dzilh K'inetiy] "trail over the mountain": The road leading to Dennis Mountain

Tsilgutznaytiebun. W [Dzilh k'inetiy bin]: The Witsuwit'en name of Dennis Lake [*Bun* means lake].

Tsimshian. G?>W [Lhts'imsanï]: People who live downstream from the Gitxsan on the Skeena River, related in language to the Gitxsan and Nisga'a; also people to the west of the territory of Kela

Tsi'tse'gut. See *Tsaytseetsuk*

Tso'o tay, Tso'O tay. W [Ts'ot'iy] "Skins Dome": A mountain near Skin Lake in the territory of Skin Dyee; Skin Dyee's grandson Francis Skin is now looking after the territory

Tutdeenah. W? [Tudïn'ay]: Bluff or hill five miles east of Telkwa, behind the Georges' house; Wah Tah Kwets' territory; called Pencil Mountain in English

Tyee Lake, tyee. (Ch) + *bin* (W) [Tyee Bin] "Tyee Lake": Lake near the Telkwa Highroad in the territory of Tyee Lake David

Tyee Lake David: Had the head chief name Woos of Kyas ya (Grizzly) House and Gitdumden (Wolf) Clan; brother of Jean Baptiste and Peter Pierre. See also *Dyee*.

tylook. W [talok] "sockeye salmon"

Wadzun Kwah. W [Widzin Kwah] "below Morice–Bulkley confluence": The Witsuwit'en name for downstream from the Morice River and its confluence with the Bulkley River; often used for Bulkey River

Waganadeex. W [wighinhidïlh] "they're going around inviting (people)": The tradition of inviting chiefs from another village to a feast by going to their home in regalia and making a formal invitation often with song and dance.

Wagtahdeexx. Chief from Burns Lake Bear Clan

Wah Tah Keght, Wah Tah Keg'ht, Wahtah-keg'ht. G>W [W: Ut'akhgit; loan word from western Gitksan: Wit'ax̱ Get, "Old Man"]: Head chief of the Laksilyu (Small Frog) Clan, Tse kal kai ya (House on Top of a Flat Rock); name held by Henry Alfred now and at time of Johnny David's testimony; previously held by his mother's grandfather

Wah Tah Kwets. G>W [W: Ut'akhgwits; loan word from western G: Wit'ax̱ Kw'ets] "big shits": Head chief of the Laksilyu (Small Frog) Clan, Kwan beah ya (House Beside the Fire); name held by Louie Tommy, then by John Namox, later by Pat Namox. The Babine Wah Tah' Kwets at the time of Johnny David's testimony is Frank Patrick.

wah tie ee kie.? W [kë tiy] "foot trail": Bulkley Valley Road

waneeyeh. W [wighiniye] "s/he is going around inviting (people)": The person who goes around to invite other people to feasts for his/her clan

wastyelgilsut. W: The responsibility of the father's relations to carve the crest or totem pole. See *basalkelzut*.

wa'tsoo. W [ts'o] "spruce": Spruce tree; the bark was used for medicine

wa'tso'tee. W: Wooden structure or bridge made over the Wadzun Kwah at Kya Wiget/Moricetown

wee. W: Salmon trap at Hagwilget

Weehalite. G>W [G: Wii Halayt] "Great Shaman": Feast name in the Laksilyu (Small Frog) Clan, held by Sarah Tait at the time of Johnny David's testimony, then by Theresa Tait Day. The name refers to a *halait*, or Indian doctor, blowing eagle feathers on the patient.

Welxges, Lawelxges. G [welxges] "carry a head": The chief name of Paul

Wet'en. W [wit'en] "person of an area" (from "s/he inhabits"): People of a particular area or drainage

Wet'suwet'en, Wetsuwet'en, Witsuwit'en. [Witsuwit'en] Carrier *witsu + W wit'en* "people downhill in general area": People of the lower drainage, or Bulkley River area

Whom duk Bun, Who n duk Bun. W [Hondik Bin] "way up lake": The lake that is on the boundary of Skin Dyee's territory

Wigetimschol. G>W W [Wigidimsts'ol] G [WiiGedim Sts'ol] "Great Man-Beaver": Chief of Tsayu (Beaver) Clan who represented Tsayu House of Namox in statement of claim

wilgus. W [ggus] "wild rhubarb, cow parsnip" (botanical name *Heracleum Lanatum*)

Wistace. G?>W "big hand": Feast name in Ginehklaiya (House of Many Eyes) Laksilyu (Small Frog) Clan; held at the time of Johnny David's by Lawrence Michell

Wonsamoos. G [Wonsamoos]: The Seven Sisters mountains, which can be seen from Kitsegukla

Woos. G>W [W: Wos; G: 'Woos (/'wos/), a kind of monster, some people say it's a bear]: Chief name, head chief of the Kyas ya (Grizzly) House of the Gitdumden (Wolf) Clan; held by Tyee Lake David; currently and at the time of Johnny David's testimony held by Roy Morris

wucannityut. W [wic'anïtyut] "he was denied access"

Wuyaniyay. W [Uyeni] François Lake people (way across people): Inviting people to a feast by going to their home in regalia and making a formal invitation, often with song and dance

xelxtuk. W [khëlh t'ic] "backpack rope": A plant that grows by rivers, lakes, or swamps; it is called bad medicine because 'people who don't know how to use it pick it and they would get sick'

xha. W [khë] "grease, ooligan grease": Oolikan grease traded by the people from the Nass River area

Yahoneetz. W [yikhwinïts] "in the middle of the House." See *Kaiyawinits*

Yatsadkus, Ya'tsalkas, Yatsalkus. W [Yikh tsawilhggis] "dark house": Dark House of the Gilserhyu (Frog) Clan, whose head chief is Knedebeas

Yatsowitan, Ya'tsowitan. W [Yikh ts'iwit'a'n] "thin house": Thin House of the Gilseehyu (Frog) Clan; Goohlaht is head chief and Gojiget a member

Yaybestee.? [Yebesdï]: Chief name, the childhood name of Johnny David, formerly held by his maternal grandmother's brother

Yesane.?

yinanlay, yingxunlee. W [yighinlï] "he takes care of him": Caretaker

Yindayelgutz.? [Yin diyil k'its]: A hill that's the boundary corner for Smogelgem's territory

yinsaylx. W: Fungus from this plant is dried and made into powder; when mixed, it is used for paint

yintoewee'. W (yin "land" + tah (ti) "among") + G>W mï', "berry") [yintimï'] "low-bush blueberry, dwarf blueberry" (botanical name *Vaccinium caespitosum*)

yis. W [yis] "wolf, timber wolf"

References

Alfred, Taiaiake. 1998. *Peace, Power, Righteousness: An Indigenous Manifesto*. Don Mills, ON: Oxford University Press.

Anderson, Margaret, and Marjorie Halpin, eds. 2000. *Potlatch at Gitsegukla: William Beynon's 1945 Field Notebooks*. Vancouver: UBC Press.

Asch, Michael. 1992. 'Errors in *Delgamuukw*: An Aboriginal Perspective.' In *Aboriginal Title in British Columbia: Delgamuukw v. the Queen*, edited by Frank Cassidy, 221–43. Lantzville, BC, and Montreal: Oolichan Books and the Institute for Research on Public Policy.

– 1999. Review of *The Pleasure of the Crown: Anthropology, Law, and First Nations*, by Dara Culhane. *Canadian Review of Sociology and Anthropology* 36 (3): 445–6.

– 2001. 'Indigenous Self-Determination and Applied Anthropology in Canada: Finding a Place to Stand.' *Anthropologica* 43: 201–7.

Asch, Michael, ed. 1997. *Aboriginal and Treaty Rights in Canada: Essays on Law, Equality, and Respect for Difference*. Vancouver: UBC Press.

Assembly of First Nations. 2004.'The Delgamuuk / Gisday'wa National Process.' Hartley Media Ltd. April 2003:Sept. 10, 2004. http://www.delgamuukw.org/

Battiste, Marie, ed. 2000. *Reclaiming Indigenous Voice and Vision*. Vancouver: UBC Press.

Berger, Thomas. June 13, 1990. Legal Opinion: Babine Barricades 1906–1907.

Boas, Franz. 1920. 'The Social Organization of the Kwakiutl.' *American Anthropologist* (n.s.) 22: 111–26.

Boas, Franz, and George Hunt. 1921. 'Ethnology of the Kwakiutl, Based on Data Collected by George Hunt.' In *Thirty-fifth Annual Report of the American Bureau of Ethnology, 1913–14*. Washington: Government Publications Office, 43–1481.

Brody, Hugh. 1986. *On Indian Land*. Hazelton, BC: Gitxsan Witsuwit'en Hereditary Chiefs. Video.

Buhler, Katherine. 1998. 'Come Hell or High Water: The Relocation of the Cheslatta.' MA thesis, University of Northern British Columbia.

Cassidy, Frank, ed. 1992. *Aboriginal Title in British Columbia: Delgamuukw v. The Queen*. Lantzville, BC, and Montreal: Oolichan Books and the Institute for Research on Public Policy.

Cassidy, Maureen, and Frank Cassidy. 1980. *Proud Past: A History of the Wet'suwet'en of Moricetown, B.C.* Moricetown, BC: Moricetown Band.

Churchill, Ward. 1998. *A Little Matter of Genocide*. Winnipeg: Arbeiter Ring Publishing.

– 1999. *Struggle for the Land: Native North American Resistance to Genocide, Ecocide, and Colonization*. Winnipeg: Arbeiter Ring Publishing.

Cruikshank, Julie. 1992. 'Invention of Anthropology in British Columbia's Supreme Court: Oral Tradition as Evidence in *Delgamuukw v. BC*.' *BC Studies* 95: 25–42.

– 1998. *The Social Life of Stories: Narrative and Knowledge in the Yukon Territory*. Vancouver: UBC Press.

Cruikshank, Julie, in collaboration with Angela Sidney, Kitty Smith, and Annie Ned. 1990. *Life Lived Like a Story: Life Stories of Three Yukon Native Elders*. Lincoln: University of Nebraska Press.

Culhane, Dara. 1992. 'Adding Insult to Injury: Her Majesty's Loyal Anthropologist.' *BC Studies* 95: 66–92.

– 1998. *The Pleasure of the Crown: Anthropology, Law and First Nations*. Burnaby, BC: Talon Books.

Daly, Richard, and Antonia Mills. 1993. 'Ethics and Objectivity: AAA Principles of Responsibility Used to Discredit Anthropological Testimony." *Anthropology Newsletter* 34(8): 1, 6.

Delgamuukw v. British Columbia. 1991. Reasons for Judgment No. 0843 Smithers Registry [Reasons for Judgment of The Honourable Chief Justice Allan McEachern].

Delgamuukw v. A.G. B.C. 1993. Reasons for Judgment CA 013770 Vancouver Registry [Reasons for Judgment of the British Columbia Court of Appeal].

Delgamuukw v. British Columbia. 1997. File No. 23799 [Reasons for judgment of the Supreme Court of Canada [also known as *Delgamuukw III*].

Drucker, Philip. 1958. *The Native Brotherhoods: Modern Intertribal Organizations on the Northwest Coast*. Bureau of American Ethnology, Bulletin 168. Washington: Smithsonian Institution.

Duff, Wilson, ed. 1959. *Histories, Territories and Laws of the Kitwancool*. Anthro-

pology in British Columbia, Victoria: Royal British Provincial Museum. Rep., Columbia, NC: Columbia Museum, 1989.

Fisher, Robin. 1992a *Contact and Conflict: Indian-European Relations in British Columbia 1774–1890*. 2nd ed. Vancouver: UBC Press.

– 1992b. 'Judging History: Reflections on the Reasons for Judgment in *Delgamuukw v. BC.' BC Studies* 95: 43–54.

Fiske, Jo-Anne, and Betty Patrick. 2000. *Cis dideen kat (When the Plumes Rise): The Way of the Lake Babine Nation*. Vancouver: UBC Press.

Frideres, James. 1998. *Aboriginal Peoples in Canada: Contemporary Conflicts*. Scarborough, ON: Prentice-Hall.

Gisday Wa and Delgam Uuk. 1989. *The Spirit in the Land: The Opening Statement of the Gitksan and Wet'suwet'en Hereditary Chiefs in the Supreme Court of British Columbia*. Gabriola, BC: Reflections.

Gitxsan and Witsuwit'en Atlas. 1987. New Westminster, BC: Cartographics.

Hargus, Sharon. Forthcoming. *Witsuwit'en Grammar: Phonology and Morphology*. Vancouver: UBC Press.

Harris, Cole. 1997. *The Resettlement of British Columbia: Essays on Colonialism and Geographic Change*. Vancouver: UBC Press.

– 2002. *Making Native Space: Colonialism, Resistance, and Reserves in British Columbia*. Vancouver: UBC Press.

Harris, Douglas. 1997. 'Babine Fish Weirs and the Canadian Law in Twentieth-Century British Columbia.' Paper presented at the Canadian Law and Society Association Conference, St John's. available at http://www.acds-clsa.org/en/acas/harris.php.

– 2001. *Fish, Law, and Colonialism: The Legal Capture of Salmon in British Columbia*. Toronto: University of Toronto Press.

Henderson, James (Sakej) Youngblood. 1985. 'The Doctrine of Aboriginal Rights in Western Legal Tradition.' In *The Quest for Justice: Aboriginal Peoples and Aboriginal Rights*, edited by M. Boldt and J.A. Long, 185–220. Toronto: University of Toronto Press.

– 2000a. 'Indigenous Peoples and Postcolonial Colonialism.' In *Reclaiming Indigenous Voice and Vision*, edited by Marie Battiste, 11–38. Vancouver: UBC Press.

– 2000b. 'Postcolonial Ghostdancing: Diagnosing European Colonialism.' In *Reclaiming Indigenous Voice and Vision*, edited by Marie Battiste, 57–76. Vancouver: UBC Press.

– 2000c. 'Postcolonial Ledger Drawing: Legal Reform.' In *Reclaiming Indigenous Voice and Vision*, edited by Marie Battiste, 161–71. Vancouver: UBC Press.

Hymes, Dell. 1996. *Ethnography, Linguistics, Narrative Inequality: Toward an Understanding of Voice*. London: Taylor and Francis.
– 2000a. 'Poetry.' *Journal of Linguistic Anthropology* 9 (1–2): 191–3.
– 2000b. 'Survivors and Renewers.' *Folklore Forum* 31 (1): 3–16.
– 2000c. 'Variation and Narrative Competence.' In *Organic Variation and Textuality in Oral Traditions*, edited by L. Honko, 77–92. Studia Fennica, Folkloristica 7. Helsinki: Finnish Literature Society.
Jenness, Diamond. 1929. 'The Ancient Education of a Carrier Indian.' *Bulletin of the National Museum of Canada* 62: 22–7.
– 1934. 'Myths of the Carrier Indians of British Columbia, Canada.' *Journal of American Folklore* 47 (184–5): 97–257.
– 1943. *The Carrier Indians of the Bulkley River: Their Social and Religious Life*. Special issue, Bureau of American Ethnology, 133 (25): 469–586.
LaDuke, Winona. 1999. Preface to *Struggle for the Land*, by Ward Churchill, 11–14. Winnipeg: Arbeiter Ring Publishing.
Lane, Barbara. 1987. *Land Transfers and Indian Preemptions in the Bulkley Valley: Summary of Opinion*. Hazelton, BC: Gitksan-Witsuwit'en Tribal Council.
Leeder, Jessica. 2002. 'B.C. Set to Release Land Vote Results.' *National Post*, 3 July. A1, A6
Little Bear, Leroy. 2000. 'Jagged Worldviews Colliding.' In *Reclaiming Indigenous Voice and Vision*, edited by Marie Battiste, 77–85. Vancouver: UBC Press.
Lyons, Oren. 1985. 'Traditional Native Philosophies Relating to Aboriginal Rights.' In *The Quest for Justice: Aboriginal Peoples and Aboriginal Rights*, edited by Menno Boldt and J. Anthony Long, 19–23. Toronto: University of Toronto Press.
Mathur, Ashok. 1998. *Once Upon an Elephant*. Vancouver: Talon Books.
McDonald, James A., and Jennifer Joseph. 2000. 'Key Events in the Gitksan Encounter with the Colonial World.' In *Potlatch at Gitsegukla: William Beynon's 1945 Field Notebooks*, edited by Margaret Anderson and Marjorie Halpin, 193–214. Vancouver: UBC Press.
McEachern, Allen. 1991. *Reasons for Judgment of the Honourable Chief Justice Allan McEachern*. Smithers, BC: Smithers Registry No. 0843, Supreme Court of B.C.
McKee, Christopher. 1997. *Treaty Talks in British Columbia: Negotiating a Mutually Beneficial Future*. Vancouver: UBC Press.
Miller, Bruce G., ed. 1992a. 'Anthropology and History in the Courts.' *BC Studies* 95: 3–112.
– 1992b. 'Common Sense and Plain Language.' *BC Studies* 95: 55–65.

Mills, Antonia. 1988a. 'A Preliminary Investigation of Reincarnation among Beaver and Gitksan Indians.' *Anthropologica* 30 (1): 23–59.

– 1988b. 'A Comparison of Witsuwit'en Cases of the Reincarnation Type with Gitksan and Beaver.' *Journal of Anthropological Research* 44 (4): 385–415.

– 1994a. *Eagle Down Is Our Law: Witsuwit'en Laws, Feasts, and Land Claims*. Vancouver: UBC Press.

– 1994b. 'Making a Scientific Investigation of Ethnographic Cases Suggestive of Reincarnation.' In *Being Changed: The Anthropological Experience*, edited by David Young and Jean-Guy Goulet, 237–69. Peterborough, ON: Broadview Press.

– 1995a. 'Cultural Contrast: The British Columbia Court's Evaluation of the Gitksan and Witsuwit'en and Their Own Sense of Self and Self-Worth as Revealed in Cases of Reported Reincarnation.' *BC Studies* 104: 149–72.

– 1995b. 'First Nations Help Create a Viable Human Future.' *Anthropology Newsletter* 36 (5): 7, 36.

– 1996. 'Problems of Establishing Authority in Testifying on Behalf of the Witsuwit'en.' *Political and Legal Anthropology Review* 19(2): 39–51.

– 2000. 'Three Years after *Delgamuukw*: The Continuing Battle over Respect for First Nations Interests to and Rights to Work in Their Territories.' *Anthropology of Work Review* 21(2): 22–9.

– 2001. 'The Gitxsan and Witsuwit'en Challenge: The Long Road to Establishing Ownership and Jurisdiction of Traditional Territories.' In *Endangered Peoples of North America: Struggles to Survive and Thrive*, edited by Tom Greaves, 58–78. Westport, CT: Greenwood Press.

– Forthcoming. 'Johnny David on the Babine Barricade War/Treaty: Who Has Rights to the Fish?' Paper presented at the annual meeting of the Canadian Indigenous and Native Study Association, 2002, University of Toronto.

Mills, Antonia, and Linda Champion. 1996. 'Reincarnation as Integration, Adoption Out as Dissociation: Examples from First Nations of Northwest BC.' *Journal of the Anthropology of Consciousness* 7(3): 30–43.

Mills, Antonia, and Warner Naziel. Forthcoming. 'Kweese War on the Kitimat: An Oral Tradition of the Cordilleran Witsuwit'en.' In *Anthropology of the Northern Cordillera: Essays to Honour the Memory of Arne and Leslie Carlson*, edited by Catherine Carlson. Vancouver: UBC Press.

Mills, Antonia, and Richard Slobodin, eds. 1994. *Amerindian Rebirth: Reincarnation Belief among North American Indians and Inuit*. Toronto: University of Toronto Press.

Monet, Don, and Skanu'u (Ardyth Wilson). 1992. *Colonialism on Trial: Indige-*

nous Land Rights and the Gitksan and Wet'suwet'en Sovereignty Case. Gabriola Island, BC: New Society Publishers.

Monture-Angus, Patricia. 1995. *Thunder Knows My Soul: A Mohawk Woman Speaks*. Halifax: Fernwood Publishing.

Morice, Adrian G. 1930. *Fifty Years in Western Canada, being the Abridged Memoirs of Rev. A.G. Morice, O.M.I.* Toronto: Ryerson Press.

Peters, Sheila. 1998. *Canyon Creek: A Script*. Smithers, BC: Creekstone Press.

Potlatch: A Strict Law Bids Us Dance. VHS. 1975. Vancouver: Pacific Cinematheque.

Ridington, Robin. 1992. 'Fieldwork in Courtroom 53: A Witness to *Delgamuukw.*' *BC Studies* 95: 12–24. Reprinted in *Aboriginal Title in British Columbia: Delgamuukw v. The Queen*, edited by Frank Cassidy, 206–20. Lantzville, BC, and Montreal: Oolichan Books and the Institute for Research on Public Policy.

R. v. Marshall. [1999] 3 SCR 456. [17 September].

R. v. Marshall. 1999. 3. SCR 523. [17 November Motion dismissed for Rehearing and Stay].

Roth, Christopher. 2000. '*The Social Life of Names*.' PhD diss., University of Chicago.

– 2002. 'Without Treaty, Without Conquest: Indigenous Sovereignty in Post-*Delgamuukw* British Columbia.' *Wicazo Sa Review* 17(2): 143–65.

Royal Commission on Aboriginal Affairs. 1995. *Public Hearings and Round Table*, Ottawa. http://www.indigenous.bc.ca/rcap/rcapeng1.html

Ryan, Don / Masgaak. 1997. 'Indigenous Perspectives on Race, Class, Gender and Power.' Guest Lecture to First Nations Studies 607, University of Northern British Columbia.

Said, Edward. 1978. *Orientalism*. New York: Pantheon.

– 1993. *Culture and Imperialism*. New York: Vintage Books.

Satsan / Herb George. 1992. 'The Fire within Us.' In *Aboriginal Title in British Columbia: Delgamuukw v. The Queen* edited by Frank Cassidy, 53–7. Lantzville, BC, and Montreal: Oolichan Books and the Institute for Research on Public Policy.

Sherry, Erin. 2002. 'Constructing Partnership' A Delphi Study of Shared Resource Management in the North Yukon,' PhD thesis, University of Northern British Columbia.

Sioui, Georges. 1992. *For an Amerindian Autohistory: An Essay on the Foundations of a Social Ethic*. Montreal: McGill-Queen's University Press.

Sterritt, Neil J., Peter Grant, Susan Marsden, and Richard Overstall. 1998. *Tribal Boundaries in the Nass Watershed*. Vancouver: UBC Press.

Suzuki, David, and Peter Knudtson. 1992. *Wisdom of the Elders: Honoring Sacred Native Visions of Nature.* New York: Bantam Books.

Tennant, Paul. 1990. *Aboriginal Peoples and Politics: The Land Question in British Columbia, 1849–1989.* Vancouver: UBC Press.

University of British Columbia. 2004. 'Official Site, Dalai Lama Vancouver Visit 2004.' ReVibe Marketing Inc. April. Available at http://events. onlinebroadcasting.com/dalailama/042004/index2.php?page=launch

Wii Mukwillixw / Art Wilson. 1996. *Heartbeat of the Earth.* Gabriola Island, BC: New Society Publishers.

Wild, Nettie. 1993. *Blockade: It's about the Land and Who Controls It.* National Film Board of Canada. Video.

Wilson-Kenni, Dora / Yagalahl. 1992. 'Time of Trial: The Gitksan and Wet'suwet'en in Court.' *BC Studies* 95: 7–11.

Credits and Sources

Exhibit 1. Totem poles at Hagwilget, 1976. Canadian Museum of Civilization, negative #59526 (Exhibit 74 I). In commission evidence this is listed as National Museum of Canada stamp #59526.

Exhibit 3. Fishing stations at Hagwilget. Canadian Museum of Civilization, negative #34615 (Exhibit 74 K). In commission evidence this is listed as National Museum of Canada stamp #34615.

Exhibit 4. Indian salmon trap, Hazelton. Provincial Archives of British Columbia catalogue #28541, negative #B-705 (Exhibit 74 L).

Exhibit 6. Houses and smokehouses at Moricetown / Kya Wiget. Provincial Archives of British Columbia, catalogue #88705, negative #E-8399 (Exhibit 74 N).

Exhibit 7. Buildings and bridge at Moricetown / Kya Wiget. National Archives of Canada, #PA 21434 (Exhibit 74 O)

Exhibit 8. Bridge over river at Moricetown / Kya Wiget. National Archives of Canada, #PA 82992 (Exhibit 74 P).

Exhibit 9. Fish trap at canyon at Moricetown / Kya Wiget. National Archives of Canada, catalogue #30393, negative #B-1717 (Exhibit 74 Q).

Exhibit 10. Fishing stations and fish traps at Hagwilget. Provincial Archives of British Columbia, catalogue #15534, negative #A-6063 (Exhibit 74 R).

Exhibit 11. Cache and smokehouse at Moricetown / Kya Wiget. Provincial Archives of British Columbia, catalogue #88690, negative #E-8384 (Exhibit 74 S).

Exhibit 13. Johnny David totem pole at Moricetown. BC Provincial Museum, negative #PN3233 (Exhibit 74 U).

Exhibit 14. Hagwilget Canyon. BC Provincial Museum, negative #PN3918 (Exhibit 73 I).

Exhibit 15. Moricetown / Kya Wiget chiefs. National Museum of Canada, negative #59520 (Exhibit 74 V).

Exhibit 16. Totem pole at Moricetown / Kya Wiget. BC Provincial Museum, negative #PN10233, Exhibit 74 W).

Index